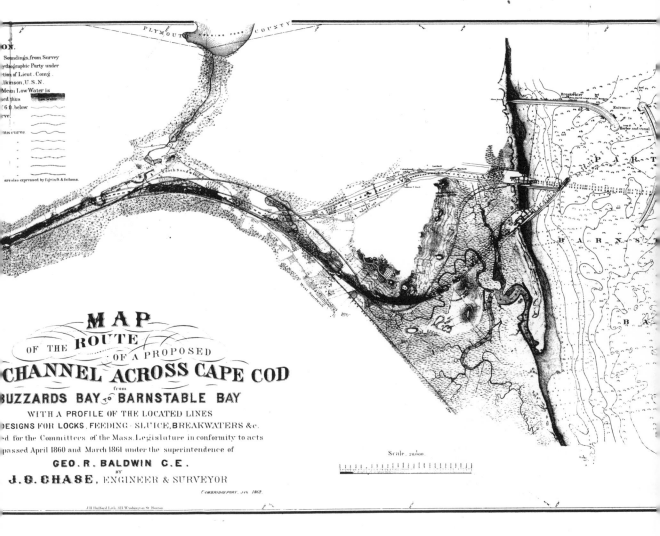

UNFINISHED VOYAGES

A Chronology of Shipwrecks in the Northeastern United States

By: John Perry Fish

Library of Congress Catalog Card Number 88-84151

Manufactured in the United States of America

ISBN 0-936972-10-6

First Edition

Lower Cape Publishing
Orleans, Massachusetts
1989

This book is dedicated to
the memory of my father, Robert S. Fish, Sr.
and to Madelyn and Colby.

Although the wreck of the *Vincenzo Bonanno* was refloated after going ashore at Fire Island, NY (the top of the wrecking tug can be seen beyond the wave crest to the left of the stranded ship), these life savers found it a picturesque background for their photograph in June 1906. *Photo from the collection of William P. Quinn, Orleans MA*

Contents

In this 1880 engraving of New York waterways, Hell Gate is shown in the upper right near Ward's Island. From the time of the earliest explorers, Hell Gate's swift and deceptive currents have been the cause of over one hundred shipwrecks.

Foreword

In this book, John Fish has given us accounts of some noteworthy shipwrecks and a list of over 6000 shipwrecks which span a period of 350 years. If we were to look for them, would they be easy to find? Not true, as the wrecks are obscured by the oceans and distributed over a large underwater surface, and many areas have no wrecks at all.

At the moment, the wrecks in this list are simply listed by name, date and place of loss. Eventually, as techniques improve and wrecks are found, a complete description of these wrecks including latitude and longitude may become available. In this book the author tells us of the *Titanic* which went down after colliding with an iceberg. When found, the known latitude and longitude were incorrect. Dr. Robert Ballard and his French/American crews were lucky to have completed the job. Persistence had a lot to do with it!

In the last chapter, John explains what I have always felt is very important; technical aids do a great deal for the researcher. Sonar, in particular, is a necessary exploratory tool as it can reveal many underwater factors which often lead to the discovery of a shipwreck.

I will never forget the 1963 search for the *Vineyard* Lightship (briefly related in this book) since it was among my first shipwreck search experiences. Bradford Luther, Jr. told me about the history of this 1944 hurricane wreck. He appealed to me to help him. After considerable discussions and thought, our team decided to use a conventional sonar-with the transmitter rotated 90 degrees. We tested this new theory on known wrecks which we could "see" on the bottom, enabling us to guide the divers to the scene.

As explained in the following pages, almost everyone who makes an underwater search starts with a grid plan. If all goes according to plan, every wreck or target can be located with accuracy. However, there are many obstacles; anyone who has attempted to make a systematic shipwreck survey search will agree that wind and waves often interfere with success.

Some advice to the shipwreck researcher: be sure to get some technical help, such as sonar or a magnetic device, as the unaided eye is usually of no use.

It is my hope that the readers of this book will be encouraged to get off the shore, and do some underwater exploration.

Harold E. Edgerton
M.I.T., January 1989

Preface

Studying our maritime heritage through the many ships lost beneath the sea can be very rewarding and informative. Of the estimated nine to ten thousand shipwrecks in the northeastern United States only one tenth have been located and identified. The rest remain where they sank as time capsules holding the secrets of our maritime history. These secrets will remain locked away until either time takes it's toll as these wrecks disintegrate or, before that time, they are discovered and studied. The process of discovering these wrecks is complex and usually very difficult. Even though sophisticated technology is making undersea search easier, prior research and organized survey plans are as important as the instrumentation used in the search. The first step in this process is a thorough study to determine the construction of the sunken vessel, the cause and the location of it's sinking.

In researching the location and causes of shipwrecks in the northeastern United States, I have found that there exists a large amount of information in a great variety of sources. However, there are few concise sources that bring this information together for the researcher in a comprehensive listing of shipwrecks for the area. The key information needed to thoroughly research any shipwreck includes the name and type of the vessel, the date of the sinking and the area where it was lost. Armed with this information, the researcher can go to further specialized resources in order to determine the precise location of the sinking. Only after this kind of research is performed, is it advisable to perform underwater surveys using sophisticated equipment.

Computers are playing a more and more important role in research and they have been key in processing the information in this book. In the late 1970's associates and I began compiling a computerized data base of shipwrecks in the northeastern United States. Each record in the database originally contained twelve fields for the parameters of each shipwreck. However, since that time, the scope of the shipwreck list has grown to include twenty-two fields for each shipwreck. A database of this sort is very helpful to anyone who is either studying shipwreck incidents or searching for specific sites. When the database is complete, the computer can arrange the information in any number of ways. More important, as the computerized database of shipwrecks gets large, duplicate entries from different sources can be rapidly identified and consolidated.

Many people have contributed to the results published in this book. Publishing would have been far more difficult without the tireless help and numerous contributions of William P. Quinn. Dr. Harold "Doc" Edgerton's ingenuity and generous help with our early exploratory efforts was a continual inspiration. Captain Bradford Luther Jr.'s early research provided the root structure for continuing research on Massachusetts and Rhode Island Shipwrecks. William McElroy conceived the original shipwreck database and brought it to fruition. H. Arnold Carr's unselfish sharing of his decades of shipwreck survey experience has been a tremendous help as has maritime author Paul Morris' generous contribution of many photographs included in this book. I would also like to acknowledge the assistance of the following people for their help in providing their knowledge of the sea and maritime history: Peter L. Sachs, Captain Robert Ryder, Story Fish, William Carter, Captain Frank Mirachi, Richard Limeburner, Captain Joseph Amaral, Richard Weckler, Thomas O'Brien, Captain James Hardy and Captain Matthew Stommel. The support of the following people has helped to bring this book to publication: Jean Mooney, Ruth and Dave Shepard, Laurel Moore and Joan Southworth. I would like to thank my wife, Marjorie, who contributed many hours of editorial and design consultation.

It is my hope that this book will assist researchers and undersea explorers with the difficult task of research on any of the thousands of shipwrecks that lay under the coastal waters of the northeastern United States.

John Fish
Cataumet, MA January 1989

1 Early Shipwrecks

THE REGION

The heritage of many people living in the northeastern United States is closely tied to the sea. From the early settlers, who made the treacherous Atlantic crossing, to present day fishermen and ship pilots who use the sea for their livelihood, the people of the northeast have always relied on this vast resource for survival, but living on the northeast coast has required adapting to a great variety in shoreline types including sheer ragged rock cliffs, miles of shallow shoaling sands and bays of miring mud.

This entire coast stretches over 400 miles of latitude; however, if one were to follow the shoreline, where the tide flows and ebbs, he would follow a path more than two thousand miles long from New York Harbor to the Canadian border at Calais, Maine. These ragged coastal indentations have provided a haven for many sailors who have had to flee a fierce storm or an even fiercer enemy during war time.

Since the types of coastline that occur here are often directly responsible for the cause and condition of northeastern shipwrecks, the topography bears some examination. As we move south from the Maine-Canada border we find first the rugged rock-strewn coast of Maine. This shore, formed during the ice age, was gouged from sheer bedrock by glaciers moving toward the sea. It can be more hostile in a bad gale than one can imagine. The sea will pound a ship to pieces on this shore, regardless of its size or construction, taking all life on board with it. On the other hand, one of the beauties of the Maine coast is that it also has many harbors and bays that provide a particularly safe haven against an angry sea. Farther south, the similarly rocky shore of Cape Ann offers the same insult and blessing as shores to the north.

One of the largest harbors on this rocky coast is Boston's, a few miles south of Cape Ann. It is a large natural harbor that became a successful trading port early in the colonial period. More than a few vessels were lost on her shores throughout the 16 and 1700's.

It seems remarkable that Boston became a major port so early. There are many more protective harbors and coves dotting the coast of Maine to the north, and to the south below Cape Cod is the great inland waterway of Long Island Sound. The rich fishing grounds of the Grand Banks are closer to bays on Newfoundland and Cape Breton. Bays to the south, such as the Chesapeake and Delaware are larger and closer to east coast agriculture centers. Nevertheless, the port of Boston survived and prospered, and the rocky islands around the harbor entrance claimed many ships and crews.

Although Boston Harbor freezes only about once in a century, the bottom of Massachusetts Bay has large irregularities, which made positioning difficult for the early sea captains. When headed for Boston in thick weather, a bad compass bearing could cost a captain his reputation either on the rocks at Cohassett or in the Graves. Many Boston bound east India merchants and China traders approached the port from the Long Island side, and worked their vessels up through Block Island Sound, Nantucket Sound, and Pollock Rip. Weather detained many vessels for weeks at Holme's Hole on Martha's Vineyard, waiting to round Cape Cod. Even with these delays, this was better than approaching Boston directly from the sea, but it resulted in shipwrecks over a much wider area than the harbor entrance alone.

In the middle of the region, Cape Cod and the Islands extend out to sea over 45 miles, surrounded by dangerous, sandy shoals. When a ship stranded there, the creeping action of the sand would often trap and bury its hull in a surprisingly short time, entombing it. Some of these shoals shift constantly, making it impossible to chart certain areas. At times, the mariner of the past could only consult the "locals" to determine areas of safe passage.

South of Cape Cod and off the Rhode Island Coast is Block Island. Located directly in the older trade shipping lanes between Boston and New York, has caused many shipwrecks in the past three hundred years.

Toward the southern portion of the area is the huge 80 mile length of Long Island guarding the entire Connecticut shore from the fiercest of ocean storms and protecting much of the shipping in Long Island Sound. For this reason we see very few storm-driven wrecks in this sound. In contrast, the great outer beach of Long Island is as much a threat to the mariner as the Sound is a haven. Much of New York's shipwreck history lies beneath the shifting sands of Long Island's outer beach.

At the southern edge of the region is the largest, and by far the busiest, port. New York became a serious shipping competitor to Boston during the late 1700s, and in the early 1800s surpassed other ports in both imports and exports by sea. The shoals of Sandy Hook, Lower New York Bay and Rockaway resulted in many strandings. However, wrecking companies were often able to pull many of these vessels off, because of the sandy seabed which is less fluid than that to the north. This resulted in a lower loss per incident than an area surrounded by rock ledge such as Boston.

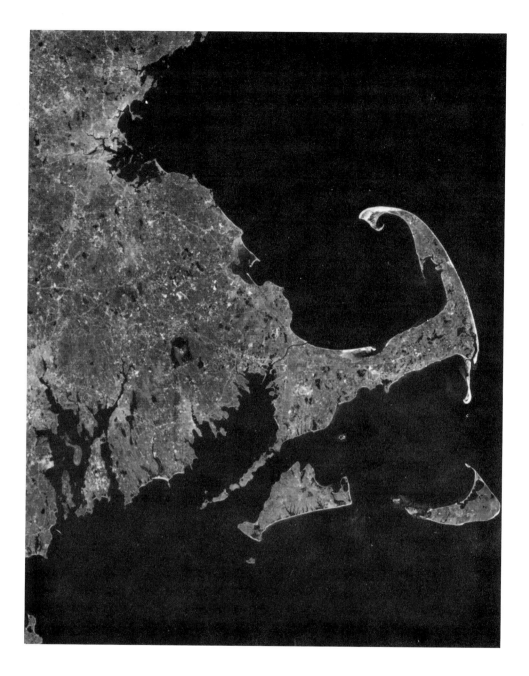

Cape Cod extends over 40 miles out to sea. This satellite view shows the hook-like obstruction that presented to coastal shipping prior to the opening of the Cape Cod Canal in 1914. Along with the Great South Beach of Long Island, Cape Cod's "backside" was an unforgiving lee shore for the hundreds of ships that found their graves on it's outer bars. *Photo courtesy NASA*

More recently though, New York has played a larger shipwreck role than other large ports of the region, since shipping there remained strong after the turn of the century and through both world wars.

During the precolonial years, when a large ship wrecked on the coast, it was generally a well known occurrence and records of these wrecks are often found in European archives. However, during that period smaller shipwrecks often occurred without notice, and it is difficult to find records of these incidents. Another reason there are few records of wrecks during the early 1600's is that maritime activity was relatively sparse except for some exploration by the Europeans. Also, if a vessel went ashore and was badly damaged, it was often salvaged and repaired. During the exploration era, most shipwrecks of which we have a record were the result of either storms or fires. Collisions were rare with so few vessels on the waterways.

In the early 1600's, New York was attractive to the settlers because of its protection and river access. New Amsterdam, as New York was known under the Dutch, exported large quantities of beaver pelts to Europe. At its peak this export exceeded 85,000 skins per year. Traders from the territories to the west and north brought their bounty to the port on a regular basis. This commerce, as well the region's topographical layout, made New York an attractive territorial target.

On a summer day in 1664, during a century when England easily expressed its might around the world, four English frigates sailed into New Amsterdam Harbor, quietly but firmly proclaimed it to be British territory, and, forthwith, named the area New York. The English knew that the area's main export, whether trapped or traded, was one of the few from the New World that did not threaten commerce at home and "Mother England" was quite happy with its new acquisition.

More settlers moved into the new territory in the next few decades. Many of these new arrivals began to clear and till the land, and gradually flour made from wheat they grew began to replace skins as an export commodity. The flour was brought to New York over the network of tributaries that flowed into the harbor. Flour became an important political issue, and in 1678 the colony passed an act requiring the sifting of export flour only at the port. This act almost assured the success of New York as a center for export to the overseas market.

In spite of this increase in maritime activity in New York, for most of the late 1600's and early 1700's, the port was commercially overshadowed by Boston. Many of its goods arrived by way of Boston which seemed to have a lock on British imports. To curb this trend, New York imposed a stiff tax on any imports it received via Boston, and by 1742 had taken a considerable amount of British

Even with the advent of sophisticated electronics for depth finding, navigation and weather forecasting, ships still wreck in the more treacherous waterways of the northeastern United States. Shown above is the *Argo Merchant* lost on Nantucket Shoals. When the big tanker broke in half, seven and one half million gallons of oil spilled into the Atlantic. Within 45 days, the remains of the ship succumbed to the force of the sea and slipped below the surface. *Photo from the collection of William P. Quinn, Orleans MA*

trade from the city to the north. By the mid 1700's more and more shipwrecks were occurring around the port of New York.

As decades passed, shipwrecks occurred all along the northeast coast, but more occurred at the mouths of the large ports of New York and Boston simply because of the high level of traffic. The shipping records of both cities provide us with an indication of the levels of activity of these ports. In only three years, from 1715-1718, the average vessel traffic out of New York reported as: 112 to the West Indies, 71 in the coasting trade, 21 to the United Kingdom, 11 to other ports in Europe, and the average vessel was only 35 tons. Boston was even more active in the same three years, sending out twice as many vessels at an average of 50 tons each.

Throughout the maritime development of the region there were spurts and recessions in growth. On the whole, however, as the population increased, so did trade, shipping and shipwrecks. The Revolutionary War and War of 1812 caused many wrecks but there were few losses within the region from later wars. Storms took their toll on men and ships from time to time, but most notably in 1635, 1839, 1841, 1898 and 1914. Throughout the three century period there were frequent disasters from fire and fog, but the loss from collisions became greater as the waterways became more crowded, particularly in the last quarter of the 19th century before the advent of marine electronics.

During the second quarter of the 20th century, ship positioning and collision avoidance technology advanced so rapidly that the number of large shipwrecks dwindled to almost nothing in a few decades. Now in the last quarter of the 20th century, most vessel losses are from the men who work the sea on a daily basis. Small fishing craft, often less than 10 tons, sink at a rate of ten to twenty per year. Although there is an occasional large vessel loss in the area, such as the *Argo Merchant* lost off Nantucket in the 1970's, most ship captains are able to navigate very accurately, using radar at night or in fog, and receiving highly accurate satellite maps in order to avoid severe weather. The technology that has allowed this precision developed very rapidly near the time of World War II and increases with each passing year.

The same technology that allows captains to position accurately and avoid running aground also provides us with the tools that we need to locate those ships lost in the past. But, in order to locate vessels using this new technology, we must first know their approximate location and understand the facts surrounding their demise. This requires thorough research and patience. The following pages discuss only a few of the wrecks in the northeast but provides the researcher with basic chronological information on some of the thousands of wrecks in the area. For many researchers, this information can be an important start in locating and identifying some of our lost maritime heritage in the northeastern United States.

PORT FORTUNE

The desire to explore is born in the curious nature of man. It was this desire that drove the Europeans to investigate the northeastern coast of the United States over 350 years ago. Some of the Northeast's early shipwrecks occurred as a result of those early exploratory efforts.

In the early 1600's, the French established an exploration base-camp named Port Royal near the mouth of the St. Croix River, near what is now the Maine-New Brunswick border. However, they found the winters very harsh, and they sent exploration parties to find suitable sites farther south.

On September fifth, 1606, one of these expeditions, led by a man named Jean de Poutrincourt, sailed from Port Royal aboard an 18 ton bark. Among the crew was explorer Samuel de Champlain, and an Indian chief, who was brought along to help in dealing with any natives the party might encounter. They had in tow a shallop or small sailboat which they used to scout shallow waters. For several days they followed the rugged coastline towards what is now Cape Cod. They put into the lee of that peninsula for three days during bad weather and then continued their voyage to the south. On October third, while traversing the treacherous shoals northeast of Nantucket Island, the bark ran hard aground. Before the men could work her off, the force of the tides snapped her rudder and left the vessel almost totally at the mercy of the wind and tide.

Champlain wrote of the incident that the depth suddenly diminished to a fathom and a half, they saw the sea breaking all around, but there was no passage to retrace their course. With a makeshift steering oar, they immediately sought a safe harbor to repair their rudder. They headed toward a landfall to the north, and anchored the bark while a few of them went ashore in the shallop. They met an Indian, who directed them to anchor the large vessel farther to the east. They did this and found it to be a safe anchorage on the northern side of Nantucket Sound. The crew came ashore, and in the following days, set about mending the rudder, and baking bread for the return trip. They named this anchorage Port Fortune.

Close to 500 Indians of the Monomoyick Tribe lived in the area of Port Fortune, or traveled there to see and trade with the white men. These Indians brought necklaces, shells, tobacco, corn, beans, and arrows to trade. However, on October fourteenth friendly relations ended while Poutrincourt and some of the crew were investigating the country farther inland. The records suggest that the men left at the camp found a hatchet missing during a visit from some Indians. As a result they fired their guns at the Indians, who ran off. The Indians felt the whites were too hostile. Poutrincourt, upon returning to the camp, saw groups of Indians moving their belongings away from Port Fortune. He became worried when he noticed that the Indians hid among the trees upon seeing him and his men. Poutrincourt ordered most of the crew and supplies to be put aboard the bark. The following morning the Indians took revenge.

Champlain wrote that "the savages did not fail to come and see in what condition our men were, whom they found asleep, except one who was near the fire. When they saw them in this condition, they came to the number of 400, softly over the hill, and sent them such a volley of arrows that to rise up was death."

With this attack the Indians killed two of the French immediately and wounded two others. Some of the French crew still on board left their ship to help fight off the attack, but the Indians fled before they could reach the beach. The explorers buried their two dead companions at the foot of a cross. During the funeral service, the Indians made mocking displays at a safe distance away with considerable yelling and jumping on the beach. When the explorers returned to their ship, the Indians dug up the corpses, stripped them of their clothing and dragged the bodies up and down the shore. The men on the ship returned to the beach, drove the Indians off and reburied the bodies.

With their rudder repaired, the French, their shallop in tow, sailed westward. However, they shortly ran into bad weather with the wind against them. So they returned to the anchorage where they decided to capture some Indians and force them to return to Port Royal, where they could be put to work grinding corn. Their plan failed. The Indians were wary of the ruse to entice them aboard the shallop. The French, instead of enslaving some Indians, killed six or seven in a number of skirmishes over several days. The weather worsened before they left and a strong wind began to blow out of the southeast. The French managed to leave the shore without losing a man, but as they boarded the bark, they lost the heavily constructed shallop. It drifted rapidly on the windblown sea, was swept onto the shore and quickly smashed to pieces by the pounding waves near the site of the settlement.

The French were concerned over the loss of their shallop but, having had their fill of the Indian skirmishes, headed back to northern Maine carrying little good news of places to settle. The shallop, age unknown, was one of the earliest small wrecks in the northeastern United States. Even if the hostile natives collected the floor and ceiling planks, the vessel's ribs are probably still buried on the Cape Cod beach, not far from the bones of the two unfortunate explorers.

ADRIAN BLOCK'S *TIGER*

While the French were exploring northern regions of the new continent's coast, others were charting the coast to the south. Seven years after the Monomoyick Indian attack in Massachusetts, the Dutch were exploring the area now known as New York. The protection of Long Island and the potential for trading on the Hudson River made the area attractive for colonization. Here another early explorer's ship was lost.

Captain Adrian Block commanded a Dutch ship called the *Tiger*. Block was an accomplished mariner and a strong leader. He had made many trips to the New World across the Atlantic and had become an accomplished trader. He left Amsterdam on a fur trading voyage in early October of 1613. A good navigator, he had made his own charts on earlier voyages and was a consultant to cartographers in his homeland.

Many of this new world's harbors, shoals and reefs, were not charted, and made dangerous sailing during bad weather. Block, on this trip, was in command of his own ship and another called the *Fortune*. Upon arriving in what was to become known as New Amsterdam, the two vessels separated. The *Fortune* continued up the river to trade with the Indians and attempt to establish a post there. The *Tiger* anchored at the mouth of the river, Block engaged in charting the surrounding lands.

The days grew shorter. Winter weather brought frigid temperatures to the area. For these early explorers the ship was a reliable and safe home, and although it was sometimes cramped, sailors preferred the "house afloat" in unknown territories. Block's men were living on board their ship anchored near the protection of the shore.

On a winter day in early 1614, the ships stove overheated. It ignited the timbers surrounding the gally and the ship became engulfed in a sheet of flame within minutes. The tar and pitch used to waterproof the seams in the oceangoing vessel added fuel to the flames. This made the fire virtually impossible to extinguish. Block and his men were able to escape with a few provisions and materials in the ship's boat. The raging fire gained on the wooden hull and the ship's upper structure was rapidly consumed. The *Tiger* sank near what is now called Manhattan.

In the following months Block built a small vessel to replace his lost *Tiger*. He used the oak and pine that was so prevalent in the area. He called his new vessel the *Onrust*. She was not a large vessel, measuring 45 feet in length and 12 feet in beam, but she was sturdily built.

Over the next few months both the *Fortune* and the *Onrust* explored and mapped large areas of the northeastern United States including the Connecticut River, Rhode Island Sound, Block Island (which the Dutch explorer named), and the entire Massachusetts coast. Block even mapped out the ferocious channel at Hell Gate between New York and Long Island.

He eventually sailed back to Amsterdam, Holland in the *Fortune* but he continued his explorations for many years and significantly increased Europe's knowledge of the "New World."

Although records show that the first large vessel constructed by Europeans in the New World was the pinnace *Virginia*, built on the Kennebec River in 1607, the *Onrust* was the first built in the New York region. The early explorers were probably unaware that it was to be the first of many.

As for the fate of the unusual shipwreck of the *Tiger*, a subway excavation uncovered the remains of a very old vessel in the early 1900's in New York. After carefully examining its construction, historians believed it to be the remains of the *Tiger*.

AN EXPLORER'S FATE

Another one of the earliest recorded shipwrecks occurred in 1616 on the outer beach at Cape Cod about 20 miles north of the landing in 1606. This craft, name unknown, wrecked with about two dozen sailors on the beach at what is now Chatham, Massachusetts. The area was then a wild wooded peninsula inhabited only by natives.

The vessel struck in a storm and pounded to pieces on the outer bar of Cape Cod; the massive storm breakers pushed the survivors up on the beach. They pulled themselves together on the beach and assessed their situation. Not knowing exactly where they were or what resources existed, they did know that unless they gathered whatever they could from the wreckage, they might not survive for long. The remains of their ship could be seen off shore. Flotsam was washing in and out in the surf. They gathered what they could including spars, planking, rope and casks of meat and preserves.

The wretched sailors did not know it, but a group of natives had seen the wreck from the distance and had assembled in the protection of the dunes. They had heard stories of ruthless white explorers, some of these natives may have been in the skirmish 10 years earlier. They prepared to attack the foreigners.

The sailors buried their provisions on the beach thinking that the goods were protected from animals. They could be re-trieved when needed. They moved out into the dunes to look for better shelter. The hoard of natives suddenly set upon and attacked them ferociously.

Though weakened, the shipwrecked sailors fought back with tenacity. But the natives fought with the advantage of skill, numbers

The longshore currents move thousands of tons of sand along the coast every year. Like this wooden schooner, most of the vessels wrecked on Long Island and Cape Cod outer beaches were buried within a few years. *Photo courtesy William P. Quinn, Orleans MA*

and strength. In the end, they killed all but five of the sailors. The Indians forced the men they had spared to disclose the place where they had buried their salvaged goods. Horrified over the brutal killing of their mates, the sailors realized that they had little choice. They dug up the hidden stores and turned them over to their captors.

Little is known about the fate of those poor souls but we do know that their immediate future was gruesome as described in *The History Of Chatham* by William Smith:

"...their captors distributed them about in captivity. Sent up and down the Cape from sachem to sachem to be made sport of, they were fed with the food of dogs while as hewers of wood and drawers of water they experienced a fate worse than that of slaves."

Many of the shipwreck stories that were popular in the 17th and 18th centuries telling of cannibalism and horrors inflicted upon poor sea-ravaged sailors, were born from areas like Australia and New Zealand. Although some explorers found cannibalism in the Caribbean Islands, it was rare in North America. To the contrary, the natives of the northeast coast were more often benevolent than not when a vessel wrecked and they found survivors on the beach.

This empathy for the sailor was continued into following years by both the old and new inhabitants of North America with the establishment of lighthouses, the Humane Society life saving huts and life saving services on the American coastline.

Poor record-keeping leaves very little for us in the way of news accounts to tell of the vessels shipwrecked during the early years. It is certain, though, that for every one of which we have a record, there were many others that went down on the rocky islands of Maine and sandy shoals on Georges Bank and Nantucket. Wreckage from these ships probably dissipated at sea or was strewn along distant shorelines to the south. This leaves us with no record of their demise. Nor does it leave a record of the suffering endured by those on board during their last hours.

The northeast was sparsely populated then and most of the inland territory was a wilderness until 1730. For over a century after the Mayflower's voyage, few farms in the area were more than 30 miles from the sea or one of its tributaries. All the inhabitants of the New World felt the influence of the sea in one way or another. Shipping brought the farmer needed goods and supported his livelihood through the maritime distribution of his produce. Ships that came to the New World from Europe carried back products ranging from barreled pork to axe handles and shake shingles.

THE *ANGEL GABRIEL*

As the 17th century progressed, transatlantic passage became more and more frequent, primarily with immigrant ships from Europe and the British Isles. More often than thought, these immigrant ships were wrecked on the New World's coastline.

One such ship was the *Angel Gabriel* which wrecked at Pemiquid Harbor, Maine, on August fifteenth, 1635. The difference between many of the sunken immigrant ships and the *Gabriel* is that she had completed her voyage and was at anchor in the harbor when a violent August storm hit the region. For this reason the loss of life was not as severe as with the wrecking of later immigrant ships like the *Mexico* wrecked on New York shores on January second, 1837, and the *St. John* wrecked at Cohassett, Massachusetts, October seventh, 1849.

The story of the loss of the *Angel Gabriel* began one month earlier when she set sail for the Maine coast with immigrants and supplies. Even though settlements were already established in the New World, the settlers still relied on England to ease survival. They needed these supplies.

The *Angel Gabriel* departed in mid June with a group of vessels bound for the east coast of North America. Because of the good sailing weather during the summer months in the North Atlantic the crossing was uneventful. The captain was an experienced sailor and he was carrying more than the usual waterfront rabble that might make up a freight carrying crew. He attempted to see to the needs of his often seasick passengers.

The 250 ton *Angel Gabriel* made the voyage in about one month and arrived at Pemiquid Harbor, Maine in mid August 1635. The cable and anchor were set in the peaceful Maine cove. Two things pleased the passengers who were unaccustomed to sea travel. First, they were thankful to have solid ground under their feet and second, they were awed by the beauty of this new world, where they expected a new start. The immigrants gave thanks for their deliverance across the Atlantic.

During the 17th century many vessels left England and the continent, headed for North America, and were never heard from again. Mariners presumed that either the hand of God sank these vessels or one of the many "sea monsters" that were known to await ships in the North Atlantic attacked them. Whether these disappearances involved a mightier hand or not, vessels often succumbed to relentless storms in the North Atlantic. As we now know, others were too old to make the journey, and sank in the mid Atlantic simply because of age.

In Pemiquid Harbor Maine, the settlers began the lengthy process of unloading the *Angel Gabriel*. This was not an easy task since the *Gabriel* probably had livestock and large casks of provisions on board. Each load had to be transferred to a smaller boat, rowed to shore and then unloaded onto dry ground.

The settlers were taken by surprise, while the vessel was still only half unloaded, by a ferocious hurricane hitting the little settlement at Pemiquid in the early morning of August fifteenth. Several crew members or passengers may have been aboard the ship overnight, but it would have been usual procedure for the majority to be on shore.

One can only imagine the horror of anyone on board, with the livestock in terror, while the ship tossed on the waves, even in the assumed protection of the harbor. At some point the *Gabriel* failed to withstand the force of the wind and waves which buffeted her. We do not know exactly how she sank, but her sinking was a serious blow to the settlers. Since the ship was not fully unloaded, much of their foodstuffs and supplies were lost. Undoubtedly the resourceful settlers salvaged many things from the wreck. Still, they would not have replacement for lost provisions until the next supply ship arrived from home, which may have been months. Records show that the *Angel Gabriel* went entirely to pieces while at anchor in the harbor. It is more likely that she either snapped her cables or dragged her ground tackle into shallow water where her hull smashed to pieces.

This 1635 storm ravaged the entire northeast, and although the *Angel Gabriel* may have been the largest ship sunk in the storm, other vessels were lost as well. Records state that many houses were blown down and numerous vessels were sunk at sea from New York to northern Maine. Farther south on the northeast coast, an even sadder tragedy took place: the sudden loss of all the children of one family.

THE *WATCH AND WAIT*

Earlier in 1635, Anthony Thatcher, his wife, and family came to North America by ship and settled on the north shore of what is now Boston. Mr. Thatcher was a family man and he considered his wife and their children his greatest treasures. The Thatchers were slowly getting to know this new territory and the coast that surrounded it.

Several months after their arrival, Anthony decided to take his family with him to Marblehead from Ipswich, Massachusetts. They left on a warm, beautiful August day in a pinnace called the *Watch and Wait*. In the boat were his wife, four children and fourteen other passengers.

During the trip to Boston, the wind began to blow and on August fourteenth it blew hard enough to completely impede the boat's progress. After dropping anchor, the skipper secured the anchor line to hold the vessel in the strong wind. The passengers were nervous, huddled in the bilge of the vessel. They suspected the worst, and it began to unfold. The pinnace slowly began to drag her anchor. It was dark enough by now that the captain and crew did not realize their danger until the hull came down hard on what is known as Crackwood's Ledge. This ledge is a small rock outcrop a few hundred yards from a large island just off Cape Ann.

Several passengers were immediately thrown into the sea by the poding of the vessel on the rocks. This was the beginning of the end for the boat and many of the passengers. The sea quickly decimated the pinnace and threw the remaining passengers including the Thatcher family into the water.

The confusing sea separated most of the human flotsam. Anthony heard the cries of his children but was helpless to save them. Soon, Anthony was washed up on the nearby island. As he climbed to safety, he saw his wife clinging to a piece of wreckage as the waves pushed her to him. He staggered into the water to pull her to safety. They lay at the water's edge for several hours, unable to move. No other signs of life could be seen or heard above the din of the ocean waves and wind.

They had little clothing left after the angry seas had repeatedly dashed them about. If the wreck had taken place at any colder time of year, they would not have survived more than a few hours.

They had landed on an island from which they could see the mainland, but it was too far to swim to in their condition. Anthony and his wife were almost insane with the thought that their children

In the early years of colonization, coastal transportation was often faster and more direct than overland travel. As in this early engraving, it was not uncommon to see families on board small vessels like the ill-fated *Watch and Wait* lost off Cape Ann in August 1635. *From* Harper's Weekly

had died within earshot and that they had been powerless to help them. They huddled on the island for two days and nights until rescued by a passing vessel.

For months afterwards the Thatchers asked if any vessel had picked up other survivors. None had. Of all those on board the *Watch and Wait* only Anthony and his wife survived. The New World settlers were accustomed to hardship, but the loss of all their children in a single stroke was a shattering blow to the Thatchers.

Anthony Thatcher eventually settled in Yarmouth, Massachusetts on Cape Cod, but he left something that can be seen on today's charts of the northeast coast. Anthony named that island, situated just off Cape Ann, "Thatchers Woe." In the centuries since, history has changed the name to "Thatchers Island." It stands today, as it has for a millennium, facing the murderous storms that roar out of the northeast.

2 The Colonies and Mother England

HMS *ASTREA*

During the 17th century Europeans began to emigrate from their native homelands to the New World at a greater rate. The number of vessel losses in northern New England were increasing in similar proportions. Many ships wrecked on the New England coast due to storms and poor navigation. Among them were ships like the Dutch vessel *Exploration*, wrecked at Nantucket, Massachusetts during July 1673, the *Dolphin* caught in the dangerous shoals that extend south of Cape Cod, in May of 1691, and the *Prins Maurits* lost May eighth, 1657 on the Great Beach at Fire Island in New York.

British vessels arrived in the new colonies more and more often as better designed ships were built to take the rigors of oceanic travel. Shipwrecks continued toward the turn of the century, like the loss of the valued *Adventure* from London carrying gold specie and twenty-two guns, which sank northeast of Long Island in 1699.

The population of the New World grew steadily until the middle of the 18th century. Early census data shows that Boston increased in population from 7,000 in 1690 to over 17,000 in 1740. It remained the largest town in the new world until surpassed by Philadelphia in 1755. After the 1750's, there was a slump in this trend until the years following the Revolutionary War. This was apparently due to several epidemics and a slowing of immigration due to the heavy tax burden that was placed on the colonists. During this period of lessened immigration there was also a drop in the number of recorded, non-weather-related shipwreck incidents. But from a seafaring standpoint, this period of slower growth was significant in that it provided an opportunity for the smaller seaports such as Gloucester, New York and Portsmouth, New Hampshire to gain a foothold in the maritime trades. Nevertheless, the European empires continued their concerted effort to take advantage of the resources in the new world. In order to protect these interests, the British sent many armed warships to the colonies. As the 1700's wore on, this British presence became even stronger.

One of these armed ships, the HMS *Astrea*, was at anchor in January 1744, in a small bay near Goat Island about one mile from

Portsmouth, New Hampshire. She had arrived a few weeks earlier and had orders to remain there for the winter. Her powder and guns had been brought ashore along with her sails and sea gear. It was not uncommon for the crews of these big ships to live on board when their vessels were in colonial ports and the *Astrea's* crew was no exception. The captain anchored her with another craft which was loading long trees to be transported to England for ship's masts. Both vessels had their anchors set deep in the harbor's mud.

The temperature during January of 1744 was well below zero, colder than it had been for many years. On January sixteenth a northeast wind forced all off duty crew members on the *Astrea* into the protection of the ship's lower decks. The crew huddled around the ship's stove while the cook prepared the evening meal.

In this bitter New England winter, it was difficult to adequately heat any part of a ship's interior, and the cook's stove was about the only place to drive the chill out of one's bones. The cook had stoked a particularly hot fire in order to heat the ship's interior. The men ate the standard fare of hot stew with baked bread for dinner, while talking of warm July days when bare backed men could sleep on the upper deck out of the fetid air of the 'tween decks.

At eight bells the commanding officer made the rounds and told the cook to secure the stove for the night. He was unaware that the coals blazing in the cookstove for the past four hours had heated the firebrick enough to scorch the timbers behind them. Except for the watch, most turned in for the night. The men were out of the wind but a deep chill penetrated the ship's hull. In order to keep warm, the sailors wrapped themselves in as much bedclothing as they could secure. While they slept in spite of the sub zero temperatures, the timbers around the stove smoldered.

At three o'clock on the morning of January seventeenth the charred timbers under the ship's stove burst into flames. Not unlike a blacksmith's bellows, the northwest wind spread the fire rapidly. The forward part of the ship was ablaze in minutes. The watch on deck called alarm. The crew tumbled out of their bedclothes.

The men moved sluggishly at first. They pulled on their stiff boots and made their way to the upper deck. Groggy eyes and foggy brains snapped to crisp consciousness as the men became fully aware of the emergency. They began to move quickly in response to orders shouted by the officers on deck. This excitement was seen on shore and soon the fire was seen as well. On shore people gathered together and started rowing to the *Astrea*.

The men on board began to gather water in buckets from the wind whipped waves and pass it, man to man, over the deck to the fire. The night had brought even colder temperatures, however, and the water froze in the buckets before it reached the last man. By the time the bucket was across the deck less than a quart was left unfrozen. As they tried to battle the fire, which encroached on the rest of the vessel, the crew's fingers and toes began to freeze, making their frantic task even more difficult. Panic began to break out on deck and like an epidemic, infected more men with the passing minutes; the blaze was rapidly becoming worse. The men from shore pulled alongside and began to help the crew.

It quickly became apparent to the men fighting the fire that the mast vessel alongside the *Astrea* was in serious danger of catching fire. The crew of the masting vessel knew that it would be foolhardy to pull up the anchor or let the cable slip in this wind so they pulled in on the mooring cable as far as they could. The vessel inched away from the *Astrea*, which was now almost fully ablaze. Only this timely act saved the second vessel from sure immolation.

The crew of the *Astrea*, even with help from those from shore, now realized the hopelessness of trying to save her. The order was given to retrieve as much of the small arms from the *Astrea* as possible and abandon ship. The crew did as ordered, carrying the rescued goods across the deck to the waiting long boats.

As the men abandoned the blazing *Astrea*, she lost her mooring and drifted across the little harbor grounding near Goat Island. There she burned to the water line until the sea extinguished the flames. Then, urged by the currents of the Piscatequa River, the charred hull slipped into deeper water and settled to the bottom. The following morning the only evidence of the disaster was the scorched side of the masting vessel as it lay in the harbor, stark and alone.

Over 200 years later, during the 1960's, warmly dressed divers slipped into the swift currents of a small tributary of the Piscatequa River in search of the *Astrea*'s remains. After searching hundreds of yards of river bottom, the divers came upon parts of old bottles lying near a small bridge that connected the mainland with Goat Island. Initial inspection of these pieces suggested that they were of an early design. They had been blown perhaps 200-250 years earlier. Realizing that these artifacts could have been thrown into the water by decades of passers-by, the divers continued searching in their quest for the colonial ship. Further searching brought more bottle parts and even a few whole bottles! Carefully covering areas adjacent to where they found these bottles, the divers came upon the warship's timbers. The century-old planks and frames lay in the last place the searchers expected - directly under the bridge in only 30 feet of water. The scouring action of the currents in the area helped to expose portions of the ship's hull. The divers recovered bottles, musket shot and leather shoes from the wreck which provided a glimpse into the precolonial way of life.

In the mid 1800s the local inhabitants constructed the bridge between two islands in the area. The divers discovered that the bridge pilings had been driven, unknowingly, through the middle of the wrecksite, destroying much of the vessel, but the artifacts recovered by the divers were saved from further destruction by bridge rebuilding that occurred in 1986.

THE PENOBSCOT DISASTER

It can be seen in a chronological outline of shipwrecks that there were few major incidents that caused maritime disasters in the region until the revolutionary war. When the war broke out there were many memorable battles and numerous vessel losses, not only in the northeast but up and down the entire coast. There was actually very little military action in New York that caused shipwrecks because the British occupied the entire area after 1776.

During that summer, Sir William Howe arrived in New York to negotiate peace with the revolting colonies. Over 100 British ships arrived with him. These forces landed at Staten Island, encountered little resistance, and made encampment there. They transmitted word to the King of the revolutionary army's strength and in August 104 more ships sailed into New York's Lower Bay. They contained thousands of troops, many of whom were Hessians.

In late August they crossed the channel from Staten Island to Gravesend Bay and started what became known as the Battle of Long Island. They had one immediate target in Brooklyn. The Revolutionaries were holding Brooklyn Heights which was then a wooded area studded with fields and pastures. The British used chain shot fired from cannon to destroy hundreds of Revolutionary troops during their approach to the Heights. Once there, even though the patriots fought with the guerrilla tactics they had learned from the native Indians, the British took Brooklyn Heights through sheer numbers.

Earlier, Washington had withdrawn from Governor's Island, and within 20 days of winning Brooklyn, the British took the town of New York. With it they won the whole of Long Island, where they remained for the duration of the war. Most of the Revolutionaries fled to Connecticut and New Jersey. From there, they harassed the British using small boats which they rowed or sailed into "enemy territory" at New York. The British set up a naval base in Gardiner's Bay, at the tip of Long Island, and occasionally engaged the troops from Connecticut or the French fleets that were friendly to the patriotic cause. However, there were few major conflicts that stood out as responsible for shipwrecks in the New York area.

To the North, however, there were many sea battles that affected the number of shipwrecks during this era. The Penobscot Expedition or the "Bagaduce Blunder" was one such battle. This battle reduced the Colonial Navy to its lowest terms. Not since the Penobscot Expedition has the American Navy lost such a large percentage of its fleet at one time.

In early July 1779 General Washington planned an attack on the British. This plan was known as the "Penobscot Expedition." It called for a group of forty-one revolutionary vessels, many of which were privateers, to sail from Boston. Their mission was to rout the British from Fort George at Majabagaduce, Maine. Once they departed, it took several days for the convoy to reach the Penobscot. Commodore Dudley Saltonstall led the expedition and he had Brigadier General Peleg Wadsworth, grandfather of poet Henry Wadsworth Longfellow, and Lieutenant Colonel Paul Revere as his immediate subordinates. The convoy consisted of 24 transports and 17 ships of force. Together they carried hundreds of foot soldiers to be landed at Fort George.

Meanwhile, the British, under Brigadier Francis Mclean, were completing the final construction of the Fort in Maine. This was to be the establishment of a major British base north of New York. He had far fewer men than the approaching revolutionary forces, and only three ships carrying a total of 56 cannons. He was not at all prepared to defend the only partially completed British installment.

When Saltonstall's forces arrived off the Majabagaduce River, the commander had his ships stand off in order to carefully assess the fort's defenses. At this point, he did not want to get close enough to risk taking any hostile fire. But he did not wait long before he sent the foot soldiers ashore under General Solomon Lovell in an effort to take the fort. Light fire from the fort repeatedly repelled them. Saltonstall continued to send in the men with hopes that they they could accomplish the task without any Naval engagements.

For several weeks the American forces assaulted the fort with the marines attempting to scale the cliffs near the fort. These actions sent the British back behind the fort walls. However, the Naval Group did not attack with supporting cannon fire because of the threat of retaliation from the three little British sloops in the harbor. There was also a lack of intelligence concerning the amount of fire power contained within the fort. Even after all this time, Saltonstall wanted to continue the attack using only the land troops.

By now, so much time had passed that British headquarters in New York learned that their installment at the Penobscot was under attack. Headquarters dispatched six large ships to defend the northern outpost with the 64 gun Man of War *Raisonable* commanded by Admiral George Collier heading the squadron. The British worried because they knew that the reinforcements might not be enough to save the installation from the tough Revolutionary Naval group. They knew from intelligence reports that even with the six ship reinforcements they were seriously out-manned and out-gunned.

On August thirteenth the British reinforcements arrived at the north end of Penobscot Bay and came within sight of the Revolutionary Naval Forces. The sight of the menacing British vessels sailing in to save the fort, stunned Saltonstall. He had hoped that the taking of the Fort would not have lasted so long and never considered that the British would send reinforcements. What followed is an event that has overshadowed much of the heroism performed during the Revolutionary War.

Saltonstall, upon seeing the approaching British warships, ordered his entire fleet to retreat up the Penobscot River. His men followed their Commander's orders, scrambling to make up sail, weigh anchor and head into the protection of the River.

Unfortunately, the transports were unable to make rapid way and were left behind by the war vessels as they ran. During the retreat, Wadsworth called on Colonel Revere to help in assisting a supply ship but Revere refused and continued his retreat. Feeling abandoned, the commanders of the transports headed for the nearest shore. As these heavy vessels lurched to a halt in shallow water, their crews jumped off and hastily sloshed ashore. They disappeared into the dense Maine woods and, with little other choice, headed for Boston, many miles distant.

The next 24 hours was a free-for-all for the British. They were able to capture three of the fleeing ships immediately. Then, as they looked on with awe, the remaining 38 were set on fire or blown up by the Revolutionary commanders and crew.

One site of these sinkings is in Stockton Harbor just outside the mouth of the river. Commander John Edmonds captained the 16 gun American brig *Defense*. Edmonds thought he might be able to escape and evasively slipped the brig into the little harbor just west of the river mouth. Hoping that the British would not spot the hidden brig, he was prepared to run for open water when the enemy sailed farther up the river.

Unfortunately, Captain Collins of the HMS *Camilla* saw Edmonds sail into Stockton and he positioned his ship off the mouth of the harbor and lay in wait. Edmonds spotted the topsails of the *Camilla* over the trees and realized he was in a hopeless position. He decided to abandon ship and quickly had the *Defense*'s longboats lowered. He set a slow fuse to her powder room. Rowing away from the vessel, the crew heard the explosion of the ship's munitions. They shuddered from the blast as pieces of the *Defense* showered down around them. The resulting explosion and fire ball sank the ship almost instantly.

Many other vessels joined the *Defense* that day with explosions, scuttlings and simple groundings. Most of the expedition fled into the small, upper reaches of the Penobscot River. A little farther up the Penobscot, the *Springbird*, carrying 12 guns, was burned by her crew. She sank on the spot. At Oak Point Cove, the expedition Commander destroyed the 32 gun ship *Warren*, the fiercest of the American vessels. It is not surprising that the rest of the expedition members did the same. A short distance farther north, the 18 gun *Vengeance* and the 20 gun *General Putnam* met the same fate.

The final blows to the expedition came as their own crews destroyed the largest portion of the fleet at the joining of the Kenduskeag and Penobscot rivers. Here, the *Charming Sally*, the *Hector*, the *Monmouth*, the *Black Prince*, the *Hazard*, the *Tyrannicide*, the *Diligence*, and *Providence* all slipped below the cold Maine waters. In total these vessels carried 140 cannon that were as important to the revolutionary war effort as the vessels themselves. Their hulls and guns rest there today. The ships *Revenge*, *Sky Rocket*, *Defiance* and the Brig *Active* were also scuttled by their Officers during the expedition. Most of these vessel's crewmembers successfully travelled back to Boston after abandoning their vessels under orders. The British losses for the entire Battle were about 70 men, while the revolutionary force lost over 450.

The news of this humiliating defeat suffered by his forces in Maine shocked General Washington. For months later he wondered if the Revolutionary Navy would ever recover from this loss. Although there were still some vessels left in the fleet, he refused to let another expedition try to dislodge the enemy from the Penobscot. Because of the "Penobscot Disaster," military authorities removed Commodore Saltonstall from the Navy, severely reprimanded Wadsworth and court-martialed but acquitted Revere. Even with this severe defeat, the revolutionary forces, with their constant help from privateers, continued to harass the enemy until they gained independence.

Of all the vessels lost in the Penobscot disaster, only the *Warren* and the *Defense* have been positively identified. A bridge construction in the 1950's uncovered the *Warren*'s cannons. The remains of the *Defense* were the site of an archaeological project in the 1970's and 1980's.

One of the ironies of history is that Revere, who had such disagreements with Wadsworth, would eventually be immortalized by Wadsworth's grandson in a still famous poem, *The Midnight Ride of Paul Revere*.

From the time the China trade was opened to America by New York interests in the 1790s, Chinese pirates were a constant threat to traders in the Pacific. Ship owners and captains learned to arm their ships with sufficient firepower like the trader depicted in this engraving. Even today piracy is not uncommon in the straights of Southeast Asia.

3 The Growth of American Shipping

After the revolutionary war, the colonies had the difficult task of adjusting to a peacetime economy while coping with the new experience of independence. This transition was difficult for the infant nation. A severe depression occurred in the post war years. While other areas on the east coast were able to regain economic stability within a few years, the northeast, so heavily dependent on maritime trade, took much longer to stabilize. The fishing fleet, idle for over five years, needed extensive repairs. Most of the ships used in the war were captured or burned. Even the powerful whaling fleets had suffered this fate.

After the Revolution shipbuilding dwindled to almost nothing, and with it the frequency of coastal shipping and local shipwrecks. But slowly, over the next two decades, the shipping industry came alive in the Northeast. For daring entrepreneurs, the world market was very competitive. New York and Boston ports competed heavily in the maritime trades during the reconstruction.

In one incident in 1783 the little fifty-five ton sloop *Harriet* of Hingham, Massachusetts left Boston with cargo for Canton, China. She was to be the first American vessel to enter the Far East trade. However, upon arriving at the Cape of Good Hope, a group of British traders, concerned about competition, bought the cargo at twice its value. It was a mixed blessing for the Captain. He made a good profit but was unable to claim credit for opening the trade to China.

Meanwhile, New York interests organized a similar effort. The ship *Empress of China* sailed out of New York backed by wealthy merchants. In 1784 she arrived in Macao and became the first to hoist the American flag there, signaling the beginning of fifty years of increasing far eastern trade. This increased trans-Pacific trade also would affect the number of shipwrecks on the northeastern coast. Many vessels returning from Cape Horn ended their days on this coast. One of these vessels, out of Salem, Massachusetts, was the *Grand Turk*, wrecked on the rugged coast of Maine in the 1790's.

Unfortunately, after the Revolution the British would accept no trade from the colonies, leaving the West Indies as the only real export target for the colonies' immediate future. As a result, some vessels began trade with the Caribbean, but until the early 1800s the local coasting trade was the area's major maritime activity other than fishing. The Northerners plied their goods with the more prosperous middle Atlantic states along the Chesapeake and farther south.

When England joined the French revolutionary struggle in 1793, exports from America began to rise, especially out of New York. This is evident in the value of all exported goods during the 1790s. Historical records show that these were as follows: 2.5 million dollars in 1792, 5.4 million in 1794, 13.3 million in 1797, with a peak of 26.3 million in 1807. The tonnage of exported goods doubled in 5 years and had tripled in 15. This increased maritime activity is evident in the increase in shipwrecks in the early 1800s.

To some extent the ships out of the northeast engaged in the slave trade, even though the General Court banned it in 1788. Providence and Salem ships had regular trade with Africa by the first few years of the 1790s. They exported rum and fish in trade for gold dust, and ivory. But from the early colonial court records of Boston and New York, there is some evidence that the slave trade was far too tempting to resist.

As an economic measure in 1807, the Government enacted the Jefferson Embargo. It barred American vessels from foreign trade and closed virtually all shipping out of northeastern ports. In 1807 there were over four-hundred and fifty idle vessels in New York Harbor. The embargo had a long lasting effect. Even though the government repealed the act and the ports of the region were on their way to a rapid recovery, the war of 1812 was quickly upon them.

WAR OF 1812

Before the war, the maritime heart of the young country was the northeast. Trade tonnage by sea out of Massachusetts was 30% of the country's total and her fishing fleet tonnage was better than 80% of the total. For this reason, when the American government declared war against England some of the populace in the northeast protested. They knew it would have a severe effect on the maritime trades. There was a deep division in the United States among the citizens. The democratic towns were in favor of the conflict, while the Federalists were sympathetic with the British. As a result of Federalist activities a considerable amount of trade with the British flourished during the first year of the war.

Also during that year, the United States had again put together fighting forces made up from vessels of opportunity. As rag-tag as these privateers seemed, they actually did capture some British vessels during the first year of the war.

But in 1813 even the activity of the Federalist trading began to change. Congress passed a new embargo act that was devastating to American seaborne commerce. As a result, in September of 1813, 91 ships, 111 barks and brigs and 45 schooners were reported laying idle in Boston Harbor. This, of course, had a similar effect on the number of wrecks occurring at the time because virtually all shipping had been shut down. Congress repealed the act in the spring of 1814 but this did not increase shipping. British ships, cruising off the coast had begun a blockade from New York to the Penobscot. During the blockade the British would occasionally come ashore for food and provisions but they usually kept their vessels just off the coast.

The British headquartered two frigates at Provincetown, Massachusetts. There was another British base at Castine near the site of the Penobscot disaster 33 years earlier and the *HMS Nimrod* cruised the waters south of Cape Cod. By the summer of 1813 the British had a blockading squadron off Sandy Hook, New Jersey halting commerce out of New York. By winter of that year they were sailing Long Island Sound as well. A few vessels were able to occasionally slip into New York from the sound, but not many were able to get by the blockade. During this time commodity prices around the port of New York more than doubled.

The war, which at first was rather ineffectual and caused little grievance to either side now became a serious affair. Napoleon, who previously had kept the Empire occupied, was no longer a problem, and the British began to concentrate on their bothersome little neighbor to the west. There were few aggressive landings by the British, but they occasionally landed in Federalist towns where they were given water and provisions. In the democratic towns a good showing of the local militia usually drove off any landing parties. Wareham, in southern Massachusetts, and Falmouth, on Cape Cod were attacked during the summer of 1814 but most of the action consisted of a few cannon shot lobbed at the shore.

Many of the shipwrecks we see from this period were a result of the burning and sinking of American vessels by the British. In June of 1814 they took their toll on American shipping and even the small coastal vessels were not out of danger from British ships cruising the New England coast. On the fourteenth of that month the British burned four schooners and two sloops near Boston. The schooners *Lucy*, *James Bayard*, *James*, and *Independence* were all set on fire at Scituate. The sloop *Diligence* was tied up with another sloop in Gloucester, Massachusetts when several British ships sailed into the harbor and set both on fire. The *Diligence*'s homeport was Gloucester and she had a cargo of lime aboard.

The British were active in other areas on the same day as evidenced by reports from Saco, Maine where the 74-gun British ship *Bulwark* burned three more American vessels. Two Cape Cod schooners with loads of wood bound south were burned to the water line and sunk at Winter Harbor by the big ship. A brig owned by Thomas Cutts of Saco met the same fate. In New York, the blockading vessel *Nimrod* burned the sloop *Woodcock* owned by a U.S. Senator. She sank at Fire Island.

On June twenty-fifth, a Swedish schooner, the *Nordkoping* approached the coast of New England and sighted a large British ship. Having heard of the harassment the British were inflicting on vessels near New York, the Captain wanted to avoid any contact with the Empire's Navy. He changed his course to the south and watched carefully as the British ship did the same. The warship bore down on the smaller schooner. The captain knew that the British were likely to burn his vessel if they captured him. It was a bright day with a strong wind but the *Nordkoping* was losing ground as the distance between the two vessels lessened. The captain made a decision that most mariners never have to make. He saw the coast of Nantucket in the distance and thought the British would never risk following him into shoal water. As he headed for the dangerous shallows around Nantucket, he watched with surprise as the British ship followed. He wondered if he should attempt to run his own vessel onto the beach at Nantucket. Looking over his shoulder at the rapidly approaching British, he soon found himself in transition from indecision to commitment. The schooner lurched up solidly onto the sands at Wauwinet, Nantucket under full sail. Records show that she was hard enough aground that she was never pulled off. Even though his little ship was a total loss, the captain had the satisfaction of keeping his vessel from the torches of the British.

In John's Bay, off the coast of Maine, a similar chase took place between a local centerboard schooner and a British Corvette. Although a shipwreck did not result from this chase, British cannons still lie on the ocean floor as a result of some skillful Yankee sailing. To this day, grandfathers tell the story to children around January fireplaces in Maine.

According to the story, a local Yankee captain could see that he was not going to be able to outrun a British Corvette who had been trailing him for the better part of the day. Now the aggressor had bent on all sail and was vigorously trying to catch up to the little schooner. The Yank headed into one of the local bays. There, he knew there was a shallow rock ledge. He eased sail a little bit to allow the chasing corvette to close distance. Then he sailed directly over the small ledge while his crew winched up the centerboard. Now drawing the minimum of water, the schooner glided over the ledge without even scratching the bottom paint. The Captain was a brave mariner; if the tide had been a foot or two lower he would have fetched up hard and been completely at the mercy of the enemy.

Although her keel was laid in 1806, the *Alabama*'s construction was halted after the imposition of the Jefferson Embargo in 1807. She lay on the ways in Bath, Maine until the Civil War when she was completed and renamed *Granite State*. Later, she was a receiving ship for the Navy until she caught fire in New York on May 23, 1921. Over a year after the fire, the ship was towed north to be scrapped. She broke from her tow after clearing Boston and drifted ashore in Manchester, MA. Now known as the *New Hampshire*, she lays in 25 feet of water. *Photo courtesy Paul Morris, Nantucket MA*

As the warship followed, her hull struck the ledge with a crunch. The granite outcrop stopped the Corvette in her bow wake. Cursing, the British Commander of the little warship watched helplessly as the schooner's skipper sailed his vessel lazily away with a slight smile on his face. The British had to abandon most of her cannon overboard to lighten the vessel. She finally floated off the ledge many hours later. Ever since 1814 this ledge near Pemiquid Point, Maine has been known as Corvette Ledge.

Since the British had established a base at Castine, Maine there was considerable activity in Penobscot Bay during the fall of 1814. On September third the British blew up the 113 foot armed American sloop *Adams* at Hampden. Before they destroyed her, the British sailors boarded the sloop and removed her armament. It was a valuable prize consisting of 26, 18 pound columbards and one long 12 pounder.

In retrospect, it almost seems that the British re-enacted the Penobscot Expedition during the fall of 1814. On November first of that year the Empire's Navy burned the American vessels *Decateur* and *Kutsoff* along with thirteen other vessels at Hampden, Maine making a total of fifteen ships sunk in one day. Historians refer to this period as "very colorful" on the Northeastern waterfront because there were few losses of life during these attacks. However, as can be seen when examining a chronological listing of northeastern shipwrecks, the vessels losses were high with the burning of so many vessels during the summer and fall of 1814.

At year's end, 1814, two emotional incidents occurred in the New York region. First, the popular New York frigate *President* tried to run the blockade and ran aground on the bar at Sandy Hook. Stranded like a whale and pounding her bottom out on the shoal, she was in clear sight of the New York citizens while the enemy captured her. Second, the British blockade vessel *Sylph* ran ashore on Long Island in a gale and the people of Southhampton watched with mixed feelings as most of her crew drowned within their sight.

THE *SYLPH*

The British Sloop-of-War *Sylph* had been patrolling the waters of Long Island Sound during the blockade. This blockade was a serious problem to the people of New York and Long Island since it kept necessary foreign goods and commerce out of their reach. After the December truce was signed, it took almost three months for the word of peace to reach the Americans and the British patrolling there. On January sixteenth, 1815 there was a fierce snowstorm. Due to the British blockade there were hardly any American sailors out of port. However, the *Sylph* was just off the south shore of Long Island when the storm hit. Captain Henry Dickens of the big sloop first became concerned when snow began to fall heavily. He knew this coast well from many months of patrolling but limited visibility could keep him from seeing the shore. Soundings were difficult in the big swells driven by winds that gusted up to forty knots.

He had 133 men on board and put several of them up forward when visibility dropped to 100 yards. It was becoming dark and he wanted to stay clear of shore as he steered the *Sylph* to the eastern end of Long Island. Soon, the snow thickened until he could not see the bow of his vessel. He knew approximately where he was and he hoped to get out to Montauk before daybreak.

Suddenly the bow watch shouted "Breakers!" The captain heard the crash of the waves as well but simultaneously realized that it was too late to avoid them. The helmsman spun the wheel to starboard out of reflex. The sloop hit the bar hard and threw most of the men to the deck.

The wind howled and the seas crashed into the side of the stranded vessel. Dickens had the awful feeling that they would tear his grounded ship apart in minutes, giving him and his men no chance for survival. Mercifully, or unmercifully, they didn't.

At daybreak a local Long Island resident, Nathan White, spotted the wreck. He called a group of volunteers together to aid the stricken men however possible. They recognized her as a blockading vessel but at the moment, their only concern was for the fragile lives that were clinging to her shrouds.

Throughout the morning the wind remained at gale force and this prevented the men on the beach from launching a lifeboat. Wave after wave hit the *Sylph*, each one knocking one or two of the crew into the boiling surf, never to be seen alive again.

At midday, in a few consecutive moments, a series of heavy seas struck the *Sylph*, knocking most of the remaining men overboard. Although the New Yorkers knew that the British blockading vessels had caused many of their hardships for months, the sight of these dying men was too much to bear. Shortly after this the vessel turned on her side. A few hours later, after repeated tries, the men on the beach managed to launch a dory and fight the heavy surf in an effort to reach the shattered sloop. When they finally pulled up to the Sylph, only six men remained clinging to the wreckage. With some difficulty these men were rescued although several had to have the frozen rigging cut away from their arms and legs.

The gallant rescuers landed the dory through the surf and the inhabitants of Southhampton, Long Island cared for the rescued. During and after the storm, bodies washed up repeatedly on Great South Beach. Many of them are buried in the cliffs of the beach, overlooking one of the worst disasters of the War.

THE ZOO SHIP

On the rocky bottom of Penobscot Bay lie the ribs of a century old steamboat. Within these decaying timbers are the bones of an odd assortment of animals. If a zoologist were to examine this site he might be able to identify the remains of chimpanzees, leopards, lions and tigers. Close by, one could find the bones of three purebred Arabian horses, exotic reptiles and even camels.

The story of the northeast's first "zoo ship" tragedy started over 150 years ago on a cool fall morning in 1836. The steamer *Royal Tar* was preparing to carry passengers and cargo from St. John, New Brunswick to Portland, Maine. On that clear day, the 19th century weather predictions were for good weather that would hold for at least a few days. The hurricane season was just about past, and there was no expectation of sudden storm activity.

The *Royal Tar* was a wooden paddlewheel steamer built in Canada in 1836. This type of steamship, although used for some years on inland lakes and rivers, was somewhat of a new sight on the ocean waterways. The early steamers had a long way to go before they would resemble the later designs that were to carry thousands along the coast over a half century later.

The *Royal Tar* made her maiden voyage in May of 1836 on this very same run. She was a smart looking vessel with one square rigged mast between two smokestacks on her bow. With the strong tidal currents encountered down east, canvas would often help the steam power. Not a large ship, she was 160 feet in length with a 24 foot beam and of 400 tons displacement. Her skipper was Captain Thomas Reed, a good master with whom most anyone should have been comfortable sailing.

On Friday, October twenty-first, 1836 he took on board the strangest cargo he had ever carried. When the dock lines slipped and the *Royal Tar* drifted from the pier, she had both the brass band of "Dexter's Locomotive Museum" on board and "Burgess' World Famed Circus," along with her many passengers. The animals on board included six arabian horses, lions, a leopard, a Bengal tiger, two camels, an elephant, monkeys, pythons, cobras and other reptiles held in cages below decks. The huge lumbering elephant named Mogul was much too big to get below decks and so was chained to the upper deck. Mogul was so heavy that the crew had to put wooden wedges between the upper deck and the steam boiler so the deck could support him. Although this action was to be the steamer's undoing during the voyage, at the time, only with these wedges did the decking seem to hold satisfactorily.

The passenger list numbered eighty-five and the crew compliment was twenty-one making 106 persons on board. The little *Royal Tar* was overloaded but more room was made for the comfort of the passengers by leaving three of the five lifeboats ashore in St. John. The brass band played a concert for all aboard as the preparations for setting sail were made. There were brightly colored caravans and wagons on deck. All this made for a very colorful scene as she fell away from St. John's Harbor headed west for the big city of Portland.

The voyage proceeded smoothly for the first day or so, but the wind whipped up and the sky became overcast on Sunday the twenty-third. The animals on board were getting restless and although "Mogul" had become accustomed to the swaying of the ship as he stood chained to one spot he, too, did not like the look of the weather and often trumpeted his uneasiness. The passengers were not becoming accustomed to the smell of the animals and the buffeting that the ship was taking caused many to feel queasy. Captain Reed put into Eastport giving the animals and passengers a chance to exercise. Of course, excitement ran high amongst the people of Eastport when the ship made its unscheduled stop there. The *Royal Tar* remained in port until Tuesday, when Captain Reed judged that although the weather had not improved, he could not delay the voyage much longer. They set sail and headed west through the Grand Manan Channel and off the islands of Maine. With Frenchman's Bay passing off to starboard and then Mount

Desert, the little steamer headed for the channels at Deer Isle. The circus was to unload at Thomaston before the *Royal Tar* would continue her coastal passage.

The weather was now getting worse and the wind was gaining in strength from the northwest. By the time he reached Crotch Island on the western side of the Thorofare, Captain Reed could see that the north west wind had developed gale force. He put all the steam on and headed across the East Bay in order to get inside the lee of the Islands. There, he would be able to minimize seasickness of the passengers and keep the animals quiet.

Unbeknownst to Captain Reed and the assistant engineer in the boiler room, the water level in the boilers had dropped dangerously low. When about two miles from the entrance to Fox Island Thorofare, the white faced assistant alerted the Captain of the danger. The Captain was aghast. "How could this situation have occurred?" he asked himself. It was true that the Chief Engineer had worked into the early morning on a leak in the boilers and then had gone to get some sleep, leaving his assistant in charge. Not pondering on the causes of the emergency any longer, Captain Reed immediately anchored the ship to fill the boilers. However, this act was too late to prevent the overheated boilers from igniting the little wooden ship. The crew attempted to battle the small fire in the area of the coal room. Later, inquests revealed that the wooden wedges used to support the elephants weight on the upper deck had first ignited and the rest of the wooden structure had followed suit. To avoid panic the crew did not alert the passengers to the fire when it first broke out. Ironically, the crew alone were unable to extinguish or even contain the blaze. Without the knowledge of the captain, while most of the crew battled the blaze, the engineer and several other crew members lowered one of the only two lifeboats and rowed towards shore.

The passengers prepared to sit down to a late luncheon when the crew finally announced that the ship was on fire. The captain had raised the distress signal to the masthead. Soon the mid section of the *Royal Tar* was fully ablaze. With no hope of stopping the conflagration, Captain Reed attempted to get the ship underway towards the nearest shore. He raised the canvas sails and slipped the anchor cable. The wind was strong and fanned the flames, spreading the fire. There was now mass confusion among those aboard the steamer. The wind blew sparks up into the sails and they were rapidly consumed by the fire. The tiller ropes burned and the *Royal Tar*, unanchored, began to drift off towards the open sea. The scene on board was now horrific. The blaze had a firm hold on the ship from the forward quarter to the stern.

Captain Reed, realizing that this might be the only way to save any of the passengers, secured the only remaining boat. He stayed off to windward and picked up the passengers who jumped

In a tragic accident, the "Zoo Ship" *Royal Tar* caught fire and burned in Penobscot Bay, Maine. She was one of the early steamers to ply the "down-east" routes and, when she was lost, many exotic animals and a number of wealthy passengers lost their lives. *Photo from the collection of William P. Quinn, Orleans MA*

from the burning deck of the ship. The roar of the fire and screams of the men, women and children were almost overshadowed by the trumpeting of Mogul and the roars of the lions and tigers as they realized the hopelessness of their position. Mothers threw their children overboard and jumped into the icy sea after them. Passengers who were unable to swim clung to ropes they had hung over the ship's rail. These ropes soon burned and dropped helpless passengers into the sea.

There was a small section of the foredeck that had not yet started to burn. Captain Reed could see animals and men alike huddled there. One passenger who had removed dozens of silver dollars from his stateroom and filled his pockets with them was waiting on this small section of deck. After some time, he carefully lowered himself by a rope to the water. He saw a spar nearby and, releasing his hold on the rope, tried to swim towards it. As soon as he let go of the rope, the weight of his silver pulled him beneath the waves. He never regained the surface.

In an effort to save some of the animals, those who realized any left on board had no chance in the fire, pushed many overboard. The six arabians were backed over the rail because they would not leap forwards. Instinctually, three of them immediately headed for shore, miles distant. The other three swam continuously around the burning ship until they sank from exhaustion. The more ferocious animals such as the lions and tigers were not set loose and succumbed to the fire in their cages.

Most of the remaining people on the ship had left the deck and clung to the overboard sides in an effort to escape the heat and flames. Mogul the elephant had broken his chains and stood, poised, with his two front legs on the ship's rail with the fire raging behind him. He stayed there for a long time occasionally trumpeting his indecision.

The wind was blowing a full gale now and the waves rocked and lashed at the rolling, drifting ship of flames. Several people drowned after falling from the ropes to which they had clung. Someone spotted a sail on the horizon and passed the word to the survivors. Soon the shape of the United States Revenue Cutter from Castine came into view. Captain Reed pulled his longboat up wind to the cutter and unloaded his precious cargo of lives. In a quick discussion with the captain of the cutter, Reed learned that the cutter could not stand to get near the fire as it was carrying an appreciable load of gunpowder. Captain Reed made many trips back to the burning *Royal Tar* rescuing all those on board. Mogul finally jumped into the sea and struck out for the nearest shore. Although he made a gallant effort, he did not make it alive. His body washed up on Brimstone Island several days later.

The last rescue trip left the *Royal Tar* just before sunset with all the remaining passengers save one. A frantic woman whose sister and child burned before her eyes would not leave the drifting hulk. As the steamer drifted out to sea, it could be seen by those on shore until nine p.m. when her sinking extinguished the conflagration off Widows Island. The seventy four survivors landed that night at Isle au Haut. They had high praise for Captain Reed's action and credited him with the saving of all the survivors. Thirty-two of the passengers and crew were lost in the disaster. This was far short of the worst case of lives lost by shipwreck in the northeast, but for years afterward the survivors would recall the trumpeting of Mogul and the screeches of the animals on the night the zoo ship burned.

TRIPLE HURRICANES OF 1839

There was more than one severe storm that took its toll on shipping during the 1800s. Some were offshore such as the 1842 storm that hit the Grand Banks and devastated the fishing fleet at Portland and Gloucester. Other storms hit the northeast coastline directly. Their ferocity has been sometimes measured by the number of lives lost and vessels sunk. Although not the worst storm to occur on this coastline, there is little question that The Triple Hurricanes of 1839 took a heavy toll on the maritime communities of the northeast, particularly in northern New England.

Henry Wadsworth Longfellow, the grandson of Peleg Wadsworth who fought in the Penobscot Expedition, immortalized himself by writing of Paul Revere's ride through the Boston countryside to warn its citizens of the enemy's arrival. Longfellow was 32 years old when the triple hurricanes hit the New England waterfront and he witnessed the fury of the blow first hand. It was this storm that inspired him to write his immortal poem *The Wreck Of The HESPERUS*, which describes the wreck of a schooner on Norman's Woe Reef in Gloucester Harbor, Massachusetts. The author took considerable poetic license but effectively conveyed the tragedy of the storm. The poet's diary contains a description of his desire to write a ballad about the "shipwrecks horrible on the coast" in the gale of 1839. His tale is that of the death of a small girl and her father who were on a ship during the storm.

The rugged, rocky reef of Norman's Woe was the scene of several ships' sinkings and one woman's body did wash ashore lashed to a piece of wreckage, further inspiring the poet. But no vessel named *Hesperus* was sunk in Gloucester in the storm. A schooner of that name was, however, torn from her moorings in Boston Harbor and badly damaged in a collision with a wharf in this terrible series of storms.

> *It was the schooner Hesperus,*
> *That sailed the wintry sea;*
> *And the skipper had taken his little daughter,*
> *To bear him company.*

On December sixteenth, 1839, eighteen corpses lay on the beach in the harbor at Gloucester, Massachusetts. Wreckage of sailing vessels could be seen on shore while the cargo from other vessels could be seen floating in the bay. Six days later the schooner *Charlotte* and several other large sailing vessels became shattered hulks on the Massachusetts coast between Cape Cod and Boston. Off the coast several vessels were to be seen floating bottom up with no sign of their crews. Five days after that the old Charleston Bridge was devastated in Boston. With her supports crushed and a gaping slice through her middle, the bridge barely stood. A tall building nearby was entirely demolished. This destruction might have been the result of a battle in one of the early wars in American history. In reality, it was the result of a series of New England's worst storms which became known as The Triple Hurricanes of 1839.

The skipper he stood beside the helm,
His pipe was in his mouth,
And he watched how the veering flaw did blow
The smoke now West, now South.

The first of the storms came on December fifteenth, 1839. The weather did not deteriorate very rapidly. This gave experienced skippers who were near shore time to put into a nearby port for protection. The weather had worsened during Saturday night, December fourteenth.

Then up and spake an old Sailor,
Had sailed to the Spanish Main,
'I pray thee put into yonder port,
For I fear a hurricane.

On Sunday the sky was thick with clouds. The rain and snow began early in the morning. The wind whipped the ocean, bays, and inlets into a froth. In Gloucester Harbor over fifty sailing vessels, crowded on their moorings, sought protection before the Sunday gale struck. The weather glass showed the pressure falling and the older sea captains sensed a storm brewing. It would not be a light one.

'Last night the moon had a golden ring,
And tonight no moon we see!'
The skipper he blew a whiff from his pipe,
And a scornful laugh laughed he.

On the waterfront the wind was up early on the morning of Sunday, December fifteenth, and brought snow after dawn. The wind shifted to the northeast at noon. Many vessels strained at their moorings but so far they held.

Colder and louder blew the wind,
A gale from the northeast,
The snow fell hissing in the brine,
And the billows frothed like yeast.

In the early afternoon the snow stopped, but as if to compensate, the wind velocity increased. Now some vessels were dragging their anchors and crews began to fear for their safety. The schooner *Antioch* from Ellsworth, Maine, snapped both anchor lines while pitching in the angry sea. The crew immediately cut away her masts and set two more anchors. With less windage she now held for a time. When one of these anchor chains parted, the crew managed to launch a small boat and leave her. An hour later another anchor let go and she was swept out to sea, a bobbing derelict. Days later Cohassett inhabitants found her shattered on their shore with her cargo washing in and out amongst the breakers.

The schooner *Brilliant*, of Mt. Desert, Maine had sought protection at Gloucester Harbor loaded with stone for a southern port. She was heavily loaded and pulled hard at her anchor chains.

> *'Come hither! come hither! my little daughter,*
> *And do not tremble so;*
> *For I can weather the roughest gale*
> *That ever the wind did blow.'*

In the afternoon the *Brilliant* began to drag her anchors towards the shore. The master, Amos Eaton, and his crew realized that the heavy vessel was going ashore. Hoping to save their lives, they let go both anchor chains and managed to turn the vessel and bring her onshore bow first. But when she grounded there was still boiling surf between the ship and solid ground. With the sea breaking over the hull, the crew climbed into the forward rigging. After an hour the repeated pounding of the waves on her hull brought her stern around so the vessel was lying parallel to the shore. Those watching this horrifying scene from shore saw the vessel break in half with the men still in the rigging. Their condition seemed hopeless.

One observer was quoted as saying, "Were I in their situation, I should want a very clear hope of heaven, and a very strong faith." The crew of the *Brilliant* must have been terrified.

Suddenly a wave larger than those preceding it shattered both masts and they fell into the sea away from shore. The crew's death was certain. After a few minutes the onlookers heard a piercing cry of "a rope...a rope!" from within the mass of wreckage. All attempts to get a line to the nameless soul were fruitless. They heard the cry again and again but could do nothing to save the sailor. After watching the seething wreckage for a quarter of an hour or more and hearing nothing, many left the beach. Three quarters of an hour after the masts fell a man was finally seen in the surf and rescued barely alive. Eventually the bodies of two crew were found amongst the twisted wreckage. No trace of the others was ever found.

Of the townspeople of Gloucester watched ship after ship crash onto the beach. Onboard one vessel, stranded a mere 10 yards off the beach, they watched as a man and a woman remained on their ship until the last fragments broke up and they perished in the foaming sea.

> *Then the maiden clasped her hands and prayed*
> *That saved she might be;*
> *And she thought of Christ who stilled the wave,*
> *On the lake of Galilee.*

On yet another ship, the crewmembers threw a rope to rescuers on shore and lashed themselves to it. The rescuers started to pull the men towards the beach. The rope fouled on some wreckage between the ship and the beach and the struggling crew drowned in the surf.

Of the fifty or more ships that had put into Gloucester Harbor, only eighteen remained afloat on Monday morning. Not one had any masts or rigging left standing and the shoreline at Gloucester was littered with wrecks. This devastation was not isolated to the famous fishing port. On the shores of Cape Cod there were many wrecked ships, and Boston Harbor had scores of ships either sunk or damaged.

> *Down came the storm and smote amain*
> *The vessel in its strength;*
> *She shuddered and paused,*
> *like a frightened steed,*
> *Then leaped her cables length.*

In Provincetown, Massachusetts, the scene was not unlike that at Gloucester. The storm had reached this fishing port earlier and during his Sunday sermon an Alderman told the Reverend John Dods that the sloop *Independence* was sinking in the harbor. He suspended his service and joined other townspeople to rescue the crewmembers of the *Independence*. They launched a boat and attempted to reach the stricken craft. The winter gale overcame their efforts. Turning back for more men, they double manned the lifeboat. Only then, successfully pulling the small boat out to the sloop, did they rescue the crewmembers and bring them safely ashore.

Shortly afterwards, east of Provincetown, at Peaked Hill
Bars the brig *Rideout* wrecked. Newly built, the *Rideout* was on her
maiden voyage. Captain Purrington saw the offshore breakers from
the *Rideout's* helm. Under the influence of hurricane force winds,
he was unable to steer clear of the bars and she struck in the early
afternoon of December fifteenth.

> *He wrapped her warm in his seaman's coat*
> *Against the stinging blast;*
> *He cut a rope from a broken spar,*
> *And bound her to the mast.*

The force of the storm drove the brig upon the Peaked Hill
Bars with such force that both masts snapped off and she capsized.
The vessel rolled in the furious surf like a log for hours. The
watchers on shore realized that no one could survive such a furious
shipwreck. Salvage teams floated the *Rideout* days later from the
bar, a complete derelict. The captain and all crewmembers had
perished.

Gloucester, Massachusetts lost many vessels during the maelstrom which was the first of three gales
that struck in December of 1839. It was these storms that caused Longfellow to pen his famous
poem *The Wreck of the Hesperus*. Although no vessel of that name was lost in the storms, the poet
effectively described the disasters on the coast. *From the author's collection*

ABOVE: When a ship stranded near shore during the early 1800's, it was immediately stripped by local residents. In this picture of an unknown vessel, the wrecker's work is nearly complete. *Photo courtesy Paul C. Morris, Nantucket MA.* **BELOW:** The bones of many shipwrecks in the northeast lay hidden in the sands. At times, shifting sediments will expose them, allowing us to identify and study them briefly. The wreck of the *Mondego* was uncovered for a time in the 1980's on Cape Cod's outer beach. *Photo from the collection of William P. Quinn, Orleans MA.*

The brig *Pocahontas* was one of the more tragic shipwrecks in the second of the "Triple Hurricanes". The townspeople on shore watched helplessly as the brig's crew were washed off the wrecked vessel one by one. *From the author's collection.*

Before the end of this first storm no fewer than 21 vessels would wreck on the outlying towns of Cape Cod. Meeting a similar fate to the *Rideout* and the *Independence* was the brig *Austin*, which struck Peaked Hill Bars, pounded over the outlying bar, and was almost driven onshore. She was close enough to the beach for the townspeople to rescue all the men by rope through the raging surf. One man, too sick to come ashore by himself, was aided by a small Provincetown boy who went aboard and helped him off the ship.

> *'Oh father, I hear the church bells ring,*
> *Oh say, what may it be?'*
> *'Tis a fog bell on a rock bound coast!'*
> *And he steered for the open sea.*

The brig *Carrabassett* was sailing from Havana, Cuba to Boston carrying sugar and molasses when the gale struck. It came ashore near Truro, Massachusetts. The waves pounded her on the bar until her keel snapped, but the lifesavers were unable to rescue the crew in the raging storm. The *Carrabassett* broke in half. One of the crew members, John Locke, launched a small boat and attempted to row to shore. When the boat overturned in the surf, he sank to his death. A second crew member, Walter White, was a powerful swimmer and he felt that his only chance of survival would be to attempt a swim to shore. Stripping off his clothing which would only encumber his efforts, he plunged into the icy December waters and swam with powerful strokes towards the beach.

Two features of the local waters of which White was unaware became well known to the lifesavers of Cape Cod during the latter part of the 19th century. One is that the undertow from storm waves washing back off the beach will prevent even the strongest swimmer from gaining the shore without assistance. The other is that north and east storm generated waves create a very strong long shore current on the outer beach of Cape Cod.

The men onshore watched Walter White and prayed for his success. As White approached the surf line the undertow pushed him back out and the longshore current drove him parallel to the beach. He swam high out of the water for a quarter of a mile along the beach. The men on shore followed his progress anxiously until he sank exhausted beneath the waves.

During this first of three storms, the wind wildly whipped the waters of the New England coast. At Ipswich the schooner *Deposit* was driven ashore with seven passengers. As the sky lightened on Monday, the ship was seen to be intact but slowly being broken up by the raging surf. Many of the towns people had rushed to the scene, where the lighthouse keeper, Mr. Greenwood, and others were making efforts to rescue the crew. People on shore could see that the passengers were in a perilous position and in fear for their lives. Mr. Greenwood and a fellow samaritan pulled themselves in the lifeboat to the side of the ship. Climbing on board they could see the body of a boy, and others, dead or dying, lying in the scuppers. They realized that the survivors could not live on board much longer.

The rescuers decided that the captain, almost senseless with exhaustion, would be lowered to the waiting lifeboat first. His wife would go next. The captain and one rescuer were lowered but the boat was upset in the waves. The rescuer was able to grab a line but the captain could not help himself and drowned. The lighthouse keeper later reported that "The horrors of the storm, the sight of the dead around him and the cries of the dying for succor, were nothing to the terrific shrieks of the captain's wife as she saw her husband buried beneath the waters."

Two of the three remaining survivors got ashore on a spar and the lifesavers managed to get the grief stricken wife ashore. The victims were immediately taken to the town doctors and cared for. The December Atlantic slammed the hull of the *Deposit* to pieces later that day.

> 'Oh father, I hear the sound of guns,
> Oh say, what may it be?'
> 'Some ship in distress, that cannot live
> In such an angry sea!'

The shoreline communities of New England were attempting to locate their mariners who were offshore during the storm and just beginning to clear their beaches of wreckage when, one week later, another storm hit on December twenty-two. Tides again rose high, driven by the fierce winds. Many ships had survived the first blow only to succumb to the second storm.

While walking on the beach, a local sea captain on Plum Island, a few miles north of Boston, saw some signs of fresh wreckage. Walking farther east he came upon more wreckage and he knew that a ship and the men who crewed her were in trouble off the beach. He then spotted the Boston bound brig *Pocahontas* on the outlying bar about 150 yards from the beach.

He could tell that she was in a bad spot. She was dismasted by the grounding and the sea was making a repeated breach over her. The bar upon which she stranded was far enough off shore that there was deep water between it and the beach. Had she sailed a thousand feet either side of the reef, she would have been saved. She probably had anchored offshore and dragged in during the night. Now the sea was pounding her with such ferocity that she would soon be a mere skeleton of a ship.

> *She struck where the white and fleecy waves*
> *Looked soft as carded wool,*
> *But the cruel rocks, they gored her side*
> *Like the horns of an angry bull.*

Of greater concern were the three men that could be seen still on board the vessel. One man was naked and lashed to the ships taffrail. He was repeatedly washed by the cold winter sea and it was apparent that he must either be already dead or soon die of exposure. There were two more men who could be seen clinging to the bowsprit. The ship was breaking up under the pounding she was receiving. The crew must have felt that this was as safe a place as any. The men that had gathered on the beach knew that, with this wild sea running, there was no way to rescue the men on board the *Pocahontas*. A large wave, roaring down on the hull of the ship, swept both men from their hold on the bowsprit.

> *The Breakers were right beneath her bows,*
> *She drifted a dreary wreck,*
> *And a whooping billow swept the crew*
> *Like icicles from her deck.*

As the townspeople held their breath, only one man was able to climb back on. This lone survivor must have been strong to have lasted so long with wave after wave washing over him. But he became drained of all his strength and after several hours washed out of the bow rigging, lost in the surf in sight of those on the beach. One local was quoted as saying, "It is a true tragedy for a mariner who struggles in the battle for survival at sea to lose his life within sight of his home."

Farther south on the beach at Nantasket, Massachusetts, a schooner and a bark were also driven ashore. The bark *Lloyd* wrecked and immediately began to break up. In command of the *Lloyd* was Captain Mountfort of Portland, Maine. He was the oldest ship captain out of Portland and was highly respected in shipping circles. He had a wife and three daughters who waited at home as this winter storm raged outside. His wife had hoped this would be his last voyage and now, as she looked toward the sea from their home in Portland, she feared that it might be.

Onboard the *Lloyd*, the captain ordered the lifeboat launched and six of his crew started through the surf for shore. The small boat capsized, however, and five of the six quickly drowned. One of the crew surfaced and struck out for shore. He was almost overwhelmed by the surf but several of those on shore rushed into the water and pulled the half frozen, exhausted man out.

With the sea pounding the hull of the bark, the fore and main masts came crashing to the deck.

> *Her rattling shrouds, all sheathed in ice,*
> *With the masts went by the board;*
> *Like a vessel of glass, she stove and sank,*
> *Ho! Ho! the breakers roared.*

The impact of the wreck when it went aground had broken the top of the mizzen mast but her lower half was still standing. Captain Mountfort and the only two remaining crew tied themselves to the mast stub.

The schooner *Charlotte* had been driven ashore earlier near the *Lloyd* and she was in such a position as the crew was able to launch a longboat and row to shore. After landing safely, the *Charlotte*'s boat turned seaward again in an attempt to rescue those on the *Lloyd*.

The sea washed the captain and other men in the rigging over and over. On two occasions they were washed from their holdings only to climb back, with frozen arms and legs, to resecure themselves.

When the *Charlotte*'s boat arrived alongside the *Lloyd*, the captain had once again been washed out of the rigging and he was insensible. The rescuers managed to get him and the only other survivor, Mr. George Scott, aboard the lifeboat and bring them ashore. Captain Mountfort was rushed to the lifesaving hut of the Humane Society and all care was taken to bring his vital signs back to normal. All efforts were in vain, however, as he died from his awful ordeal shortly thereafter.

> 'Oh father! I see a gleaming light,
> Oh say, what may it be?'
> But the father never answered a word,
> A frozen Corpse was he.

The next day the vessel was so destroyed that her keel came ashore. The cargo, which had been so carefully laid in her holds, was strewn over the beach for miles, grim evidence of one of the tragedies left in the wake of this second storm of the triple hurricane of 1839.

The third and worst storm arrived on the twenty-seventh of that fateful month and blew out of the south and southeast. Rain started on Friday night and by ten o'clock in the evening the wind was howling in yet another full hurricane.

After the Triple Hurricanes, many shattered derelicts drifted without helmsmen off the northeast coast. As the industrial revolution brought more and more seaborne traffic, derelicts were responsible for many accidents. In the late 1800's there were extensive government efforts to sink or otherwise eliminate them. *From* Harper's Weekly

The destruction of property on the New England coast was as great during this storm as during the other two. The loss of life on the coast was not as high though for several reasons. Primarily, the maritime industries were at a virtual standstill from the damage wreaked upon it by the previous storms. Many vessels were up on the ways under repair and the people were more prepared after enduring the previous blows.

In Boston Harbor the 600 ton ship *Columbiana* was tied up at Swett's wharf loaded with block ice for a southern port. At five in the morning, her hull rose so high on the tide that her mooring lines slipped off the pilings. She was then driven into the harbor by the southeast wind. She came full force into the Old Charleston Bridge and cut it cleanly through. With the wind pushing her free of the Charleston Bridge, the big wooden hull collided with the wharf at the Warren Draw Bridge. The collision completely demolished the bridge-tender's house. The tender, Mr. Dix, and his family of eight were asleep at the time. In the following days the newspapers reported that moments after the collision took place "...no two parts of it are left together but all presents a scene of chaos which cannot be imagined. One large fragment of the chimney stands poised many feet from its original position, and directly beneath it is the family bureau, bedding and chairs. Part of the roof was thrown overboard and another part projected on the bridge."

The draw bridge wharf was also demolished in the collision. The howling wind slammed the ship against it repeatedly. Upon finding the ship adrift, several townspeople managed to get it under control after the collision with the wharf.

Again, the water front scenes up and down the New England coast were that of disaster. The storm-ravaged coast had been battered for a third time in two weeks. More ships that had put to sea were never heard from again. Ships in harbors wrecked against the shoreline and more men died. The force of the storm was felt most in the shipping centers like the harbors of Boston and Portland. Vessels at anchor tore from their moorings and shattered wharfs and shoreline buildings indiscriminately. The storm abated the next morning after dawn. Although few citizens of New England slept that night, when the sun rose they saw the damage that had been wreaked upon them.

At daybreak, on the bleak sea-beach
A fisherman stood aghast,
To see the form of a maiden fair,
Lashed close to a drifting mast.

The salt sea was frozen on her breast
The salt tears in her eyes;
And he saw her hair, like the brown sea-weed,
On the billows fall and rise.

When the first days of 1840 arrived, the coastal towns of New England began the task of putting their seafaring communities back together. They cleared their harbors of shipwreck debris and rebuilt damaged piers. The sea reluctantly gave up its dead. An occasional body would come ashore during the spring and summer of 1840, released from its temporary tomb beneath the sea. A few of the fishing vessels missing during the storms limped back to port. Many more were never heard from again.

The toll that the Triple Hurricanes took was staggering. One hundred and twenty one vessels were totally lost. Many of these carried their crews to their deaths. Another two hundred and eighteen vessels were damaged by dismasting, collision, or by being driven ashore. More than one hundred sixty people lost their lives in the three storms. In the following decades any given storm would be compared in strength to "December '39" by coast men. It was not until the great Portland Gale of 1898 that the Triple Hurricanes began to fade from the memory of the New England coastal community.

There were other severe winter storms during the lifetime of Henry Wadsworth Longfellow, but his experience of the December 1839 storms moved him to pen his famous poem. Even though he experienced the storm itself, many of his ideas for the literary work were derived from newspaper reports. However, the schooner *Hesperus* is symbolic in the poem and it is meant to represent all the vessels wrecked in the storms. His description of the death and tragedy was accurate, and to this day it brings to mind the devastating effect of a storm such as the Triple Hurricanes of 1839.

Such was the wreck of the Hesperus,
In the midnight and the snow!
Christ save us all from a death like this,
On the reef of Norman's Woe!

4 Saving Shipwrecked Lives

On January sixteenth, 1884, the dark shadow of a steamship loomed through the light snowfall just offshore from Great South Beach, Long Island, New York. It was just dusk and the captain of the ship was not exactly sure of his position. Towards shore few lights were visible and from the bridge of the ship, the dunes of Long Island melded with the horizon in the spitting snow. The captain unknowingly had the vessel on a course that would soon bring him hard on the beach.

A lone man walking on the wave battered shore, as he would be for a good part of the night, squinted into the sea mist. His job was to keep a close lookout for vessels offshore and suddenly he saw the ship. He hurriedly unslung an odd looking brass and wood object. Working with experienced hands, he pushed a pin at one end and the other end kindled in a bright red glare. He held it high over his head and waved it back and forth.

The bright Coston Signal meant only one thing to the ship's captain. "Hard to starboard!," the captain on the steamer called as he saw the red flare appear where he thought there was only open ocean. Slowly the big ship turned away from its deadly course and headed back to sea.

The man on the beach watched as the dark shape of the steamer turned and disappeared into the snowfall. He continued his trek down the beach to his station where he entered a small notation in the log that this evening he signaled a vessel off the beach. He knew he would never learn the identity of the ship or how many people were on board.

This lone figure was a life saving service patrolman. He and hundreds like him worked long lonely hours, and saved countless lives during the late 1800s and early 1900s. They thought nothing of repeatedly risking their lives to save others.

This account is one of thousands noted only briefly in the annual report of the United States Life Saving Service every year since 1875 when the record keeping began. These reports detail many rescue efforts from the seemingly innocuous signaling of a vessel in danger to the exhausting and life threatening rescue of mariners from the surf, ice and snow.

EARLY LIFE SAVING EFFORTS

Formal life saving efforts began in the northeastern United States in 1785 with the founding of the Humane Society of Massachusetts. With collected funds, the Society built huts for castaways on the coast. The Government began the Revenue Cutter Service and the Revenue Marine in 1790 but their principle charter was defense. They were America's only armed force until the government organized the Navy in 1794.

By 1802 the Humane Society had built six shelters at Cape Cod, Massachusetts between Race Point and Chatham. Eventually, by getting more contributions they built boathouses with life boats which they manned by volunteers. The state also helped out by paying for some of the lifesaving boats. In these early days, everyone who lived by the sea kept a telescope handy and more than a few residents spent many hours studying the coast during storms. When someone sighted a vessel offshore, townsfolk passed the word from house to house. The men assembled to rescue the crew of the vessel while the women built fires, made coffee, and prepared linens and blankets for the rescued, who were sometimes brought in near death.

The success of the northeastern United States lifesavers was well respected in marine circles. Two of the lifeboat designs used on Cape Cod, called the "Monomoy" and the "Race Point," were eventually used in life saving stations at other locations around the country. Many of today's residents of the northeast have ancestors who, acting as volunteers, would haul these boats to the water's edge and launch them into the dangerous surf. Then, jumping aboard, they would pull hard on oars in an effort to rescue unfortunate, shipwrecked souls.

It was not unusual for these volunteers to lose their lives in these efforts. In places where there was not a boat or the seas were too rough, they lent whatever help they could to save lives.

On March twenty-second, 1847 a fierce gale raged over the northeast bringing heavy ocean waves that threw flotsam from distant shores high onto the beaches. A Wellfleet, Massachusetts citizen, Lemuel Pierce, along with two boys, Groves Lumford and Benjamin Higgins, were walking along the backside of the Cape to see what the storm might cast up.

Just before they reached the Humane Society hut, they saw a square rigger wrecked very close to the beach. She was the brig *Baltic* of Bath, Maine which had struck the outer bar, and been

Although not a formal service in mid-century, community lifesaving efforts were responsible for saving many lives of wrecked sailors. These informal lifesavers often passed the time playing cards or board games in the Life Saving huts during periods when there were no wrecks. As the service became more formalized, the stations were kept "shipshape" with a polish and shine that became one of their trademarks. But at any time the men knew that one of their patrolmen might burst in the door with the news of "Ship ashore!" *From Harper's Weekly*

pushed over by the storm waves. The Life Saving Service was not yet established and the locals did not have line guns and breeches buoys which later came into use.

However, the wreck was so close that Pierce found he could wade into the surf, and shout to the men aboard the wreck. He yelled for them to throw a line. The men on deck of the wreck assembled a length of rope and heaved it to Pierce. Making suitable arrangements with the line, Pierce and the two boys managed to pull all the men safely off the wreck one by one. The captain of the ship was ill and suffering from the cold. He was the last man pulled ashore and as he neared the edge of the sand, a receding wave started to pull him back out. He was courageously saved by Pierce who ran into the surf and pulled him to safety. The rescuers built a fire in the protection of the Humane Society Hut and all the men from the wreck of the *Baltic* survived.

Ironically, another ship, the *Cactus*, wrecked on almost the same spot that night. The *Cactus* was out of Boston and bound for Ireland with grain for the victims of the Irish famine. It was not long before she broke up in the mountainous seas. There was no one on the beach to help the mariners as the ship pounded to pieces. All ten men of the *Cactus* perished in the icy water that night.

A strange twist of fate occurred when the crew of the *Cactus*'s bodies washed ashore. Two of the seamen whose bodies washed up after the wreck were identified by the papers in their pockets. One was Charles Nye of Barnstable, Massachusetts and the other was F.W. Crocker of nearby Falmouth. The family of Mr. Crocker sent a friend to identify the body. When he arrived at the scene, he was puzzled. This was not Crocker's body. It was not until sometime later that the family realized that Crocker had exchanged papers with another seaman who had made that fatal voyage in Crocker's place.

In 1848 Congress enacted a bill allowing for "...the provision for surfboats, rockets and other apparatus for the better preservation of life and property from shipwreck." There were many life saving huts built in the New York area as a direct result of this bill. In 1849 a group of New York men created the Life Saving Benevolent Association which worked with the U.S. Government in improving the areas life saving capabilities. Although there was still no provision for salaried men at these "stations" by 1850 there were a total of twenty-two huts along the Long Island and New Jersey coasts.

On April twentieth, 1852, the British bark *Josephus* was driven onto the bar near Cape Cod Light, Massachusetts. The vessel had been sailing from England to Boston with a cargo of iron. As soon as she hit the outer bar, the sea began to break over her. This destructive action forced her 18 man crew into the rigging where they became covered with freezing spray. The townspeople had gathered on shore but all they could do was pray since the sea was running too high to safely launch a boat.

One by one the trapped mariners began to fall from the rigging and drown in the wild sea. Two of the spectators, Jon Collins and Daniel Cassidy could not watch this scene any longer. They launched a boat in an attempt to rescue the remaining sailors in the rigging. Pulling hard on the oars, they masterfully worked the lifeboat towards the wreck.

At one point, about midway between the wreck and shore, a huge comber hit the little boat and tumbled it over in the surf. Thrown clear of their lifeboat, the two men started to swim but the sea pulled them under and they perished in the April waters. Slowly, the men in the rigging of the *Josephus* joined the two volunteer life savers as they fell into the sea while their ship pounded to splinters.

In 1854 a huge ship ran ashore at Westhampton Beach on Long Island, New York. She was the paddle wheel steamer *Franklin*, captained by James Wooten. Inward bound from France, the *Franklin* was heavily loaded with passengers and imported cargo. There were only a few people walking the beach on that July seventeenth, as it was very foggy and overcast with gale winds blowing out of the northeast. A heavy sea accompanied the wind and fog which obscured the outer bar. Captain Wooten did not realize that he was so far off his course to New York until the lookout shouted "Bar ahead!."

The big iron paddle wheel steamers were not very responsive. Coupled with the difficulty in getting the "full astern" command to the engineer and the delay in response of the hull to drive speed changes, the lookouts warning was almost useless as the *Franklin* slid onto the outer bar and held firm a quarter mile off the beach.

With the sea running, Wooten realized that the waves may well push his ship farther towards shore and he had both anchors put out in an attempt to hold her off the beach. With the constant pounding from the waves, however, both chains parted and the

Franklin was driven over the outer bar and pushed almost to the waiting shore line.

The captain of the *Franklin* had the crew assure the passengers that all would be well and ordered everyone to don their lifejackets. Meanwhile he had the first mate begin firing the signal gun towards the beach in order to alert the local citizens of their predicament.

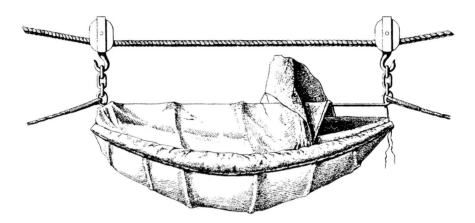

The "Life-Car" was an enclosed capsule designed for the rescue of sailors from wrecked ships. In the middle of the 19th century, it met with some success. **ABOVE**: One of the later designs with a canvas covering as drawn for a patent application. **BELOW**: Lifesavers successfully using the life-car during a rescue. However, the life-car had a tendency to fill with water in rough seas. After a number of sailors drowned inside the life-car on their way to shore, it's use was abandoned in favor of the "Breeches Buoy". *Illustration courtesy Richard Boonisar*

The townspeople heard the signals well across Moriches Bay and they assembled their boats and began to row across to the outer beach. Upon their arrival these brave volunteers carried their wooden dories across the sand and launched them into the foamy Atlantic. Some life boats had already been launched from the steamer and a few of them became unmanageable and overturned, dumping their human cargo. By this time there were many spectators on the beach and they, along with the rescuers, were able to pull the *Franklin's* passengers from the surf. The rescuers and citizens of the area saved the passengers and crew without losing a man.

The *Franklin* was a pretty vessel. She displaced 2195 tons and was 263 feet in length. Launched in 1850, she was 41 feet in beam and drew 26 feet. The following day the winds had subsided and wrecking vessels made their way to the site. Over the next few weeks the wreckers offloaded most of the cargo and, along with the passengers' baggage, brought it ashore. But the ship had become entombed in the sands of Long Island Beaches. She remains there to this day surrounded by the bass and lobster that dwell on Long Island's Coast.

With wrecks such as these occurring year after year on the shores of the United States and with brave rescues by volunteers such as those at Moriches in New York, the government became aware of the need for an organized Life Saving Service. In 1854 Congress passed a bill that allowed a salary of 200 dollars for the keeper at the stations on the coast.

The government realized over the next two decades that saving the lives on the many wrecks that occurred on our coast required a more formal service. In 1871, a man named Sumner Increase Kimball became the superintendent of life saving stations in Washington, DC. Born in Lebanon, Maine, Kimball had attended Bowdoin College and studied Law before working for the treasury department. In just a few short years Kimball became the driving force behind life saving practices in the United States. In 1871 this service was under the jurisdiction of the Revenue Cutter Service but it grew from a few stations scattered along the coast into a national institution over just a few years and Kimball was primarily responsible for this growth along with the complete organization of life saving practices along the coast.

Among other procedures outlined, each official boathouse was to have a keeper and seven surfmen during the stormy months of the year. Each crew was to have weekly drills including resuscitation techniques. They were to learn standard flag and light

As steam powered vessels became accepted as a reliable and consistent method of transoceanic travel, increasing numbers of people chose the steamer to travel to and from Europe. Entitled *First Sight of New York Bay*, this engraving depicts the arrival of a European steamer. Many of the shipwrecks on Long Island's shore, like the *Franklin*, carried transatlantic passengers. *From* Harper's Weekly

signals and conduct standardized beach patrols. In 1875 Congress passed an act requiring written records of the station's activities to be kept. These documented each activity of the patrols and rescues. They are very accurate and can supply the modern researcher with a wealth of information about certain shipwreck sites.

In 1878 Congress rewarded Kimball for his efforts by creating the Life Saving Service into a separate bureau and he was nominated as its first chief by President Hayes. After 1875 the equipment used by the Life Saving Service became more refined as its use dictated. Many experimental appliances were tested including line throwing devices, lifeboat delivery systems and even inventions designed to apply oil to the rough seas around shipwrecks. The USLSS, however, adopted a few reliable pieces of equipment and used them for many years.

Each patrolman carried a red flare known as the Coston Signal. He used it to signal ships. If vessels approached the coast, the signal meant to steer off. If ships were wrecked, it meant that help was on the way. Another important tool of the service was the life boat which, at the time, was an oar powered, double ended dory. The design of this vessel was under continual review and designers tried self-righting versions on many occasions. While they were manpowered, the boats remained non-self-righting as these were much more manageable for the lifesavers. These boats were brought to the beach and launched from horse drawn carts in the early days and by diesel powered tractors in the later years.

If the sea was too rough to launch a small boat, as was often the case when shipwrecks occurred, it was necessary to get a line to the stranded vessel in order to bring the crew of the ship to shore. Many early European line throwing devices incorporated a rocket but the more accurate and reliable units adopted by New England life savers used a mortar-like device called a Lyle Gun. It fired a projectile which carried a small line out to the ship. The crew of the vessel would then pull out a larger line. The end of this line had instructions on it in both French and English which read as follows:

Make the tail of the block fast to the lower mast, well up. If the masts are gone, then to the best place you can find. Cast off shot line, see that the rope in the block runs free, and show signal to the shore. When a second hawser is sent from shore, make it fast about two feet above the tail block...and show signal to the shore.

These instructions, if followed, resulted in a pulley assembly which allowed those on shore to slide a buoy with pant legs or "breeches" attached to it out to the stricken sailors. In this buoy, they were then hauled ashore. All these tools, and the men who used them, saved thousands of lives in the late 1800s.

Although the men who saved lives from shipwrecks worked selflessly and hard to accomplish their task, their efforts would have been only half as effective if it were not for the Lyle Gun.

THE *CIRCASSIAN*

On November twenty-fifth, 1876, the Scottish Bark *Heath Park* left the busy port of Perth Amboy, New Jersey bound for London, England. She had 160 tons of slate quarried in the hills of Pennsylvania on board. It had been carefully loaded in her hold to prevent any shifting of the cargo during the transatlantic voyage.

Winter is rough in the north Atlantic and the skipper had seen to the extra care taken in the loading process.

Almost as soon as the *Heath Park* left the protection of the eastern seaboard the weather turned sour. Although Captain Smith had twelve good men accustomed to the rigors of rough seas, he expected that the weather would moderate within a day or so.

On the second day out, the heavy seas began to work the vessel enough to cause serious leaking. The first mate reported to Captain Smith that there was two feet of water in the hold. Smith became concerned because this much water in the bilge was unusual at the start of an oceanic voyage. He knew that she must have a bad seam or two. The mate could see the concern in his eyes. Smith had several men start working the hand pumps. But after an hour the captain realized that this only stemmed the flow of water flowing

With minimum visibility, the *Gate City*, sister ship to the *City of Columbus*, ran aground at Moriches, Long Island on February 8, 1900. Lifesavers successfully delivered a line to the wreck using a Lyle gun. The crew on the wreck secured the line and pulled out the breeches buoy. Through these efforts, all those on board the wreck were saved. *Photo courtesy Paul Morris, Nantucket MA*

into the bilge and he ordered the men to man the pumps constantly, even through the night.

The next two days brought no relief for the men working on the deck pumps, and when they were three days out they could not stay ahead of the incoming water. Captain Smith replotted the course to head the ship for the nearest land which appeared to be Nantucket. The thought of crossing the poorly charted Nantucket Shoals was not a comforting one, particularly in this weather, so Captain Smith made the wise decision to put her a few points to the south and navigate the vessel for Long Island, New York.

With the water gaining in the hold, as a last resort, Smith instructed the few men he could spare from the pumps to get some of the cargo of slate out of the hold and jettison it.

The weather showed no sign of letting up now and the seas were running very high. The Bark was laboring heavily in the seas and little headway was being made. The men, using the ship's cargo rigging, struggled on the rolling deck in an effort to get the slate out of the hold. This was not an easy task in the stormy seas. If one piece of slate came loose from the blocks, it would smash the deck to splinters.

On the sixth day, with most of the men completely fatigued at the pumps, the remainder still struggling with the cargo and no land in sight, Smith became mindful that they might not make it to shore. Suddenly the mate shouted "...A ship!" and Smith looked over the foaming billow and spotted the gray shape of a vessel through the mist. He immediately ordered the distress flag raised. The men at the pumps paused to look at the big ship as it kept on its course to the west and Captain Smith wondered for a moment whether this chance to save his crew would be lost. Then the ship started towards them. Her captain had seen the Bark and her flag atop her mast. Her name was the *Circassian* and she was out of Liverpool for New York with thirty-five men in the crew and a 1,500 ton cargo of soda ash, lime, brick and hides.

Captain Richard Williams of the *Circassian* had seen the Bark laboring in the seas before its crew had seen him. He wondered if they would be seeking help. Surely the way the wooden vessel was handling in the storm the crew would need help soon. Then he saw the flag go up in the rigging and he felt momentary satisfaction at having foreseen the event. He ordered the crew to ease sail and told the mate to change course to 210 degrees. After coming around to the lee of the *Heath Park*, the mate at the helm of the *Circassian* headed her into the wind and, oblivious to the snapping canvas over his head, held position. Captain Williams stood at the rail as the *Circassian's* crew signaled the men of the *Heath Park* to board their long boat and row to the side of the big New York bound steel ship.

Captain Smith, with the knowledge that he was leaving his vessel for the last time, ordered the men to launch and man the longboat. He lashed the helm of the *Heath Park* to hold the vessel into the sea. She was very low in the water now and with the men away from the pumps, the sea was filling her fast. Smith knew she would not last long. The longboat was crashing into the side of the *Heath Park* as the crew tried to keep the little dory and the enormous Bark together in the 18 foot waves. They shouted for Smith, who was still on the quarter-deck, to get aboard the dory. Reluctantly, with a last look over the deck of his ship, Smith climbed down the ropes to the longboat. The men cast off in a hurried effort to get over to the blessed ship that had come to their rescue.

Williams watched with apprehension as the *Heath Park's* crew rowed over the waves to reach his ship. He had seen Smith hesitate before leaving his ship. As a fellow captain, he easily identified with a man who would resist the clear common sense to abandon his vessel. The longboat disappeared behind a huge wave and then reappeared again as it neared the *Circassian*. Its crew was strong but fatigued. Minutes passed like hours with the heavy canvas of the *Circassian's* sails rattling in the wind as the longboat came towards the ship. Upon reaching her side the rescued men grabbed the lines thrown to them and climbed from the wild hell of the sea to the soothing heaven of the *Circassian's* cabins, blankets and mugs of hot coffee. But Captain Smith remained outside for a few moments. He watched his ship, restrained by its fettered helm as it fell to the mercy of this angry sea. The *Heath Park* drifted rapidly to leeward.

As the *Circassian's* crew received the signal from the captain to wear about and bring her back on course for New York, Smith watched as the *Heath Park* sank, pulled down by her stone cargo. The Bark took a sea by the bow, plunged into a wave and never emerged from the other side. She left the surface and drifted into the depths. Peacefully, with no waves, wind or turbulence, the wooden ship slowly descended into four thousand feet of water. It was thirty minutes and the *Circassian* was miles away before the *Heath Park* settled gently into the radiolarian ooze of the Atlantic ocean floor. All her crew survived the sinking.

For another two days the *Circassian* battled the same sea that had robbed life from the wrecked Bark. Captain Williams had not had a good celestial sighting in almost a week but he was an experienced captain and was sure he was within one half day of New York. He ordered the second mate to confirm the depth with the lead line.

In the late 1800s this practice was commonplace when navigating coastal waters. The line thrower would pack the hollowed base of the lead with lard or soap, and after the helmsman slowed the ship, he threw the lead well ahead of the vessel. The line would pay out until the lead hit bottom. When it did, he would pick it up and drop it a few more times to assure it hit right side up and then retrieve it reading off the depth. If present, sand or mud would stick to the soap and the Captain could identify it by its color and grain size. This would show an approximate position to the experienced navigator. Today, nautical charts continue to indicate the bottom type in various areas even though this type of bathymetry is no longer used.

On board the *Circassian*, just as the lead was to be thrown, a sudden thump and shudder was felt by all the crew including the rescued men of the *Heath Park*. Captain Williams knew instantly what had happened. The *Circassian* had gone aground in a fierce snowstorm somewhere on the coast of the eastern United States. He had the sudden fear that he may have struck on the dreaded Nantucket Shoals, scores of miles from land. In actuality, he had struck the shore of Long Island, New York, only one quarter of a mile from a Life Saving Station.

Captain Williams knew that his ship could not survive the pounding of the seas on her stern and she would soon turn her beam to the sea. This would put her in a very dangerous position. Williams had the crew attempt to wear the ship around by maneuvering the sails and yards, but the ship was unmanageable in these seas, and the *Circassian* was repeatedly lifted and pushed harder aground on the bars.

The big iron ship had driven herself on the sands of Long Island opposite Bridgehampton. The crew of the Life Saving Station directly in front of the cite saw the dark hull of the *Circassian* almost immediately and they ran to the station to get the keeper. Upon viewing the wreck the keeper knew that to launch a boat in these seas would have been foolhardy and it would have been equally impossible at the time to reach the ship with the shot line. Her distance from shore and the resistance of the gale on the line surely would have prevented success. The darkness would have prevented the men firing the mortar and rockets from seeing, by the bowing of the line, what allowance in aiming to make for the force of the wind would have prevented the men on the ship from seeing the line if it fell into the rigging. The keeper could see that the ship had an iron hull and it seemed that she would hold together in her present position on the bar - at least for the night.

The captain and crew of the ship could occasionally see through the snow but still did not know exactly where they were. They could see some activity to the lee on what must be the shore and they had seen a red flare in that direction. With the knowledge that they had been seen, Williams turned his attention to assessing the damage to his ship. Reports slowly came in from the crew but it appeared that even though she was taking a terrific pounding from the sea, she ought to hold together for the time being. He knew it was futile to launch a life boat.

There was a heavy reliance on steam transportation during the last 60 years of the 1800s. Near the middle of the century the steamer became the transportation of choice for most transatlantic travelers. When one of these vessels wrecked, it often had prominent people on board and the incident was well publicized. *From* Harper's Weekly

Captain Williams kept a constant watch throughout the night. Little did he know that the Life Saving Station crew was watching him as well.

The morning brought no less tumultuous seas than the night before, but with the lengthening of the day the men on the beach saw the weather moderate. By noon the keeper of the Life Saving Station prepared to bring the crew of the stricken ship ashore.

In these early days of the Life Saving Service, the Lyle Gun per se did not exist and lifesavers tried different types of line throwing equipment at various places along the coast. At Bridgehampton they had used both rockets and mortars to get lifelines to ships with some success.

However, on this day Life Savers fired five separate rockets before getting a line over the stranded *Circassian*. The crew of the ship made the line fast to a lower mast and the life savers commenced the tasks for which they were so well trained. Using the line to the ship as a guideline, they pushed the little boat into the surf. They were continually thrown back, however, and only through sheer perseverance did they finally manage to get out to the *Circassian* and begin rescuing the frightened sailors.

For a time, the twelve men rescued from the sinking *Heath Park* thought that they would not be fortunate enough to survive two shipwrecks. But the life savers, aided by adjoining Stations, continued their trips out to the *Circassian* until all forty-seven of the men were safe on the shore.

If this were like other shipwrecks on the shores of the northeast, the tale would end here. But the real tragedy of the wreck of the *Circassian* was yet to be played out.

Originally a steamer built in Belfast, Ireland in 1856, the *Circassian's* length was 242 feet and she registered 1,558 tons in displacement. Shortly after she was built, during a transatlantic run, she had run ashore at Sable Island, but a professional wrecker named Captain John Lewis pulled her off. Later, she again went ashore at Squan, New Jersey, in 1869. However, she was refitted at Liverpool in 1874 as a sailing ship, bringing her tonnage up to 1900, and this was her first voyage under canvas. In spite of the ship's past navigational problems, the Liverpool Maritime Exchange rated the *Circassian* as a class A-1 vessel for twenty years.

After the Lifesavers of Bridgehampton rescued the crew of the *Circassian*, the weather further moderated as the storm center passed out to sea. During the following day the residual surf had pivoted the ship so that her head was to the sea and she lay obliquely to the bar.

On December twelfth, three days after the stranding, the Coast Wrecking Company began the work of salvaging the *Circassian*. Using thirty men along with the Tugs *Cyclops* and *Relief*, Captain John Lewis, the same man who rescued the *Circassian* once before, headed the effort this time.

They began the process of relieving the ship of her cargo in an effort to lighten her before pulling her off the bar. The weather, although moderated, was still bad and the men were not able to work full days at a time. They worked at lightening the vessel for two full weeks. On Thursday, December twenty-eighth, with about one third of her cargo discharged, Lewis had a strain put on the ship's huge anchors set off shore while, simultaneously, the two tow-boats tugged at their hawsers to pull the vessel towards the open sea. The *Circassian*'s hull complained. The tugs churned the water as their propellers bit into each wave. Suddenly Lewis felt the *Circassian* move. Slowly at first, then more steadily she moved over the sand. Lewis and the wreckers on board held their breath. Suddenly she stopped; the *Circassian* had run into a shallower area of bar just as she was freed. The towboats pulled. The steam winches complained as the cable's tension increased but the iron ship refused to move any farther.

Lewis and his associate, C.A. Pierson, called a halt to the operation. They realized that the tide was ebbing and further efforts would be futile until the next high tide on Friday.

On Friday morning, however, the wind sprang up, rapidly worsened and began to blow a gale out of the east. When the weather became too bad to continue work, eleven men of the wrecking company went ashore and left thirty-one men on board, under the command of John Lewis, to watch the vessel. Ten of the men on board were Indians from the Shinnecock Tribe of Southampton and Shinnecock Neck, Long Island. The rest of the men, including Captain Williams, were either from the wrecking company or the original crew of the ship.

At three p.m. the gale increased in strength. Those on board began to get concerned for their safety. The ship was taking a powerful sea on her quarter and it was decided to let the main anchors cables slip a bit to ease the ship towards the beach where the sea would be less intense. As the men on board eased the cable out, they found that the powerful longshore current, increased in force with the gale winds, would not allow her to come in as desired.

Lewis had the crew tighten up again on the cable and hoped that the wind would get no worse. He could feel the ship, now with much less cargo than when she struck, lifted by the gale sea and pounded back onto the bar hundreds of yards from where she first struck.

This position put the heavy iron ship athwart the outer bar, putting an excessive force on the vessel's midship. Her bow and stern were both suspended over slightly deeper water.

The people on the beach were keeping a careful eye on the wreck and she seemed to be "laying easy" until at seven that night when her keel suddenly broke in half. She immediately filled with water up to her upper decks. Within minutes the men on the beach saw the mainmast snap at its base and fall into the sea with a horrible crash. The remaining men on the *Circassian* climbed into the rigging of the masts that were still standing since the sea was making a terrific breach over the now flooded hull. The waves sent icy spray over eighty feet into the air.

The rocket was often the tool of preference for rescue line delivery during the first half of the 19th Century. This engraving depicts a rescue of the crew of a Spanish ship at Portland, England after a rocket delivered a line to the wreck. Although the first American lifesavers frequently used the rocket delivery system, in the latter part of the century, through the dedicated work of an American named Lyle, the mortar became the most accepted line throwing tool. *From* Harper's Weekly

The Lifesavers burned Coston signal flares to let the wreckers know that someone understood their plight. The men on shore built a bonfire on the beach under the sand hills as well. They knew that it would help to keep the stranded men's spirits up during the long rescue procedure. This time they used the mortar rather than the rockets due to the strong onshore wind blowing. But the conditions on the beach hampered preparations of the gun. They needed to get the gun as close to the wreck as possible to insure the line would reach, but the high seas running kept them well up on the shore. Cold wind driven rain hampered the effort. It was necessary to keep the shot line itself dry, free and unsnarled for it to fly efficiently and true on its course. Here, on the storm ravaged beach at Bridgehampton, the lines were now soaked by the rain and spray, clogged with drifting sand and frozen. But the Lifesavers had to try to get the line out to the ship.

The Lifesavers on the Beach managed to set up the linethrowing equipment a second time in a month to rescue men from the stricken *Circassian*. They fired the mortar repeatedly over the next four hours towards the hulk without one shot landing over the wreck.

On board the *Circassian*, the men in the rigging began to lose any hope of rescue as the freezing water coated the rigging and their limbs with ice. The shuddering of the ship with each wave frightened even the bravest of these men who had lived by the sea all their lives. They could see throughout the evening the attempts to get a line from the beach out to the wreck. They watched shot after shot either fall short or blown wide by the wind. The Indians loudly sang the hymns and prayers they had learned from their fathers and tried to keep each other in good spirits in spite of the apparent doom.

Three men had carried a cork buoyancy float from a life raft into the rigging with them and lashed themselves to it. They thought that if the sea carried them out of the rigging, or the ship rolled, they might be kept afloat by the little buoy.

The district captain of the Life Saving Service, H.E. Huntting, arrived during the evening and redoubled the Lifesavers efforts to get a line to the wreck without success.

In the early morning a series of waves struck the hull of the *Circassian* and pounded her against the bar. The riveted hull plates began to tear away from the ships iron keel. The black iron plates would have survived any one of these waves by itself but three of them hit one after another, with the final wave dealing a death blow to the ship and several men. The men clinging to the ship suddenly looked at each other in shock as they felt the ship vibrate with the impact of this series of waves. They could feel the difference between these seas and the previous ones. Suddenly it seemed to the men that the world turned upside down. Rigging pulled apart and the sea separated men from one another. Some were swung through the air like dolls.

The ship groaned and screeched as the hull split cleanly in two. As she broke, several men were pulled from the rigging and washed overboard. Two others survived the ships shattering and held on to a piece of railing. They were unable to regain their footing, however, and after a few minutes they could not withstand the seas repeated washing over them. They were torn from the railing and disappeared into the foamy seas. The remaining men on board climbed into the mizzen which was the last mast standing.

The men on shore were terribly agitated seeing the men washed from the wreck within their sight and unable to do anything about it. It was bad enough to watch the lives of unknown sailors lost in a tragic wreck, but these were neighbors and friends, family men whose children played with their children. They could hear the half frozen men on the wreck who began to scream their prayers for salvation and shout for rescue after seeing half of their number washed overboard when the ship broke in half.

As the eastern horizon became a visible line in the early dawn of Saturday morning the end came. At four a.m. the Lifesavers, using a telescope, watched the iron mizzen mast begin to careen to port. For one half an hour they watched helplessly as it dipped towards the sea with its living load. At four-thirty it reached the monstrous water into which it settled. All the men were plucked from the mast by the icy fingers of the sea. The only part of the wreck visible afterwards was a small portion of the iron bow and a confused sea where the ship lay beneath the waves.

Although they did not see the tangled mass of three men and a small float rise up from the ships grave to be cast along the wave tops, the lifesavers ran along the beach towards the east, where the breakers might carry a victim in the unlikely event anyone were to survive the entanglement at the wreck. Just a short distance down the beach, surfman E. Forest Stephens of the Mecox Life Saving Station pulled the three men and another who managed to cling to the float from the boiling surf. They had somehow managed to get free of the wreck and survive the punishing cold sea as it swept them to shore. Part of the *Circassian's* crew and the wrecking company,

ABOVE: When the five lasted schooner *William C. Carnegie* went ashore at Moriches Long Island, her decks were soon awash. On a wreck where the masts remained standing, climbing into the rigging of the vessel meant safety from the vast seas. The high masts with their complexes of rigging also provided the best opportunity for the lifesavers to get a line shot caught in the wreck. *Photo courtesy Paul Morris, Nantucket MA* **BELOW:** Even the standing rigging of the *Lizzie Carr*, wrecked in 1905 on the New Hampshire Coast, was destroyed in the disaster. The lack of masts and rigging left standing on a wreck usually prevented any rescue with a line throwing device. In this case, the Life Saving Service crew rescued the sailors by lifeboat. *Photo courtesy William P. Quinn, Orleans MA*

they were barely alive. These men were taken to the Life Saving stations where the Life Savers warmed and resuscitated them.

The tragedy of the *Circassian* struck the Indian population of the Shinnecock Village particularly hard. For days and weeks they combed the beach in search of the bodies of their fathers, sons, husbands and brothers. In all thirty-two people were directly dependent upon the labors of the ten Indians who died in the wreck. They were about the only able men in a community of over two hundred.

THE GUN THAT SAVED LIVES

Some years ago, a group of men found a small patina-covered cannon half buried in the sands of the outer beach of Long Island. With thoughts of Buccaneer treasure in their minds they convinced themselves that they had found the spot where a ship loaded with booty had wrecked centuries ago.

The cannon turned out to be a "Lyle Gun" which had probably been pulled into the surf by a wave that fell higher than those before it during a rescue attempt near the turn of the last century. Even though these modern beachcombers finally realized that there was no "treasure" nearby, their find was still important. These guns were not manufactured after the 1950s .

The success of the Lyle Gun in saving lives was significant along the northeastern coastline. Its development, however, did not occur overnight and is worthy of brief examination.

Early efforts in designing line throwing devices were made by the British in the 1790s. The particularly devastating wrecking of the ship *Adventure* on the English coast in 1789 prompted a movement to establish coastal lifesaving facilities. In 1791, Sergeant John Bell of the British Royal Artillery, demonstrated a method of firing a cannon shot which carried a line almost 400 yards. The idea did not immediately take hold, however, due to the 600 pound weight of the cannon.

But in 1807 a man named Captain G.W. Manby saved the crew of the brig *Nancy* at Yarmouth, England by firing a mortar with a hooked shot and line out to the wreck. The device was a five and one half inch mortar with very little capacity for accurate aiming. After the success of the *Nancy* rescue, Manby continued to perfect his linethrowing device. He developed a leather braid to connect the line to the shot thus preventing the line from being burnt from the muzzle blast. He also put bright burning fuses in the shot in order that stranded sailors could spot the projectile in it's long arc from the beach to the ship.

The results of Manby's experiments saved hundreds of lives in the following decades. But for all his work, Manby died in poverty with a mortgage even on his gravestone. However, the techniques which he developed were the basis of a linethrowing standardization adopted decades later.

Coincident with Manby's work, others were experimenting with rockets to deliver lines to wrecked ships. The early rockets were short ranged compared with the mortar but later designs could deliver a line up to 375 yards which was adequate for most purposes. Although the rocket afforded considerably greater portability than Manby's mortar, it had its drawbacks. Rockets were difficult to keep dry in storage. They were by nature a fire hazard and less stable in flight. Single tube rockets sometimes exploded on the launching stand and since they did not have the mass and inertia of the heavy mortar shot they were often adversely affected by the wind. Double tube rockets were a little more stable in flight, but if one tube "flamed out" prematurely, the rocket had the tendency to turn and fly back to the launching stand, certainly a frightening experience for the potential life savers. Since rockets were very portable and self illuminating, rescuers made many rescues using them.

In the 1860s, Englishman Colonel R.A. Boxer developed a true two stage rocket which gained wide acceptance in the United States. But work continued in the development of the mortar through the 1860s because of its predictability, accuracy and power. One of the biggest obstacles to its success was line breakage due to the high muzzle velocity of the shot during departure. Many inventions were applied to solve this and other problems in order to perfect the line throwing gun.

In the United States during the year 1875, the Secretary of War directed the Board of Experimental Guns to further investigate the problems associated with the lifesaving mortar. Engineers studied some of these problems over the next two years but major contributions to the project did not occur until after 1877. That year, a thirty-two year old Lieutenant named David Lyle was "specially assigned to this duty in addition to his regular duties" at the Springfield Armory in Springfield, Massachusetts.

David A. Lyle was born in Fairfield, Ohio on January twelfth, 1845. He attended West Point and graduated in 1869. He had worked at various posts, including San Francisco and Alaska, and taught philosophy at West Point from 1872 to 1875.

Taking on his new duties in 1877, Lyle tested many variations of Manby's original idea. He experimented with different bores, weights of powder, and many types of projectiles including one which contained the line rather than pulling it from a faked pile. Lyle made many of his experiments at the seaside on Sandy Hook, New Jersey. His first experiments were with an old bronze, rifled, 3 inch Howitzer which he cut down to about 5 inches ahead of the trunions. But after only a few tests he discounted further experiments with a rifled gun. He tested many patents and designs over the next two years but Lyle finally settled on his own variations of Manby's original design. These variations were the key to the success of his final product.

Traditional mortar design held that there should be a good clearance between the bore and the projectile to prevent the projectile from lodging in the barrel during firing. Unfortunately, this allowed hot gasses to "blow by" the projectile burning the line to be thrown. Using a smooth bore mortar Lyle reduced the blow by of hot gasses by creating a piston-like fit with very little clearance between the bore and projectile. By the 1870s machining tolerances had become consistent enough to eliminate any possibility of a projectile becoming lodged in the gun. To further lessen the risk of the line igniting, Lyle used an eye bolt on a long shaft to increase the distance between the attachment point and the muzzle. This arrangement had an additional advantage in that the projectile would turn end for end after leaving the gun and thus momentarily relieve strain on the line, reducing the risk of breakage.

For the actual gun construction Lyle realized that both lightweight and corrosion resistance was important. For this reason he chose bronze. The metal erosion that occurred in repeatedly fired bronze gunnery would not be a concern because Lifesavers would not normally fire the gun in such a manner.

The most efficient method of faking, or laying out, of the line was accomplished with the use of a box with pegs in it. The line faked in the box and around the pegs for storage. When needed, the crew could invert the box, remove the pegs and the line would be ready for the shot, tangle free.

Lyle's experiments with his designs showed that the maximum distance for throwing line was about four hundred yards. A hawser used for greater distances developed a self defeating

Line throwing gun designs were tested over many decades in the 1800's. A reliable and efficient design evolved through the efforts of David Lyle and, in the 1880's, the "Lyle Gun" came into use.

catenary that could not be pulled out of the line. With this catenary, the line would droop into the sea and be useless for saving lives. Lyle eventually recommended quantities of powder for the load and oversaw the inspection of the first guns produced. The final design was of a gun with a 2.5 inch bore, 5.5 inch breech and a 24.25 inch overall length.

Lyle completed his *Report On Life-Saving Apparatus* in 1878. He said at the time that he made "no claims of great originality" and that his system "is a direct evolution from the system of Captain Manby".

At the age of ninety-two, David Lyle died at St. David's, Pennsylvania but his contribution to lifesaving was a lasting one. Lyle's recommendation became the standard for the thousands of lifesaving guns used first in the United States and eventually around the world for over seventy years. The gun remained in production until 1952 and some are still in use to this day.

Of necessity, Lyle's gun had to be lightweight, but there were those that contended it was too light. The tight fitting projectile caused excessively high breech pressures in the gun but Lyle had to compromise between weight and maximum range in order to get the most favorable mix in his life saving gun. These high breech pressures would plague the Lyle gun for decades as those who fired it became acutely aware of the disastrous effect of charging it with excessive amounts of powder. However, there is no doubt that the work done by Lyle in the 1870s made a difference in the number of lives saved from shipwrecks. In 1908, Sumner Kimball said that the Lyle Guns were instrumental in the saving of over four thousand lives from shipwrecks to that date worldwide.

THE TRAGEDY OF THE *CALVIN ORCUTT*

The Life Saving stations that were built in the northeast spread along the Maine, New Hampshire, Massachusetts, Rhode Island and New York coasts wherever there was a serious danger to shipping. In the ensuing years, although these stations changed, the type of men who manned them, their purpose and their skill never did. Stations burned down, fell into the sea or were abandoned for better vantage points. Some stations came later as the need arose. One station, The Old Harbor Station in Massachusetts, was constructed as a result of a particularly bad shipwreck, the *Calvin B Orcutt*.

The *Calvin B. Orcutt* was a four masted schooner which was caught in a bitter December blizzard on the twenty-third in 1896. The captain was trying to make port for Christmas. He had gotten in too close to the beach and could not get off. When he set both anchors, they dragged. Before the night was over, the blizzard would smash the *Orcutt* to bits on the outer bar at Chatham.

As the storm worsened, the lifesavers at the Chatham Station were helpless; they could not launch their boat in the wild seas and they were across the harbor from the beach opposite the schooner. Orleans, although a few miles up the beach, was in the best position to go to her aid. Unfortunately the storm was so thick that Orleans apparently did not yet know about the wreck. The telephone lines were down from Chatham to Orleans. In desperation, the Chatham Station reached Highland Light by telegraph. Highland, in turn, reached the telegraph at the rail station at Orleans with the crucial "Ship Ashore!" message.

From there, a local resident named Henry Cummings hand carried the word several miles through deep snow to the home of Benjamin Sparrow, superintendent of the district. Mr. Sparrow had a direct phone line to the station from his house and his lines were not down. At eleven p.m. the message was received at the Orleans Life Saving Station.

The Life Savers set out immediately with the life boat, mortar to fire lines out to the vessel and a lifebuoy. They had a slow trek through the deep snow on the beach. The horse hauling the boat became exhausted and the men had to help out. When they finally reached the spot across from the wreck, the frozen life savers could barely see the stricken vessel and only then when the driven snow would let up briefly.

She was too far out to fire a line and the men could not even approach the waterline, the sea was so ferocious. That night the *Orcutt* broke up. It was later said that the vessel was "...the only wreck on Chatham shores within the memory of man, where men on shore, knowing the wreck was there, were unable to recover the bodies either dead or alive."

Pieces of the ship the size of a small house were seen on the beach the next morning. Some of these pieces of wreckage had one inch iron bolts twisted in knots by the force of the stormy ocean. All nine crew members of the *Orcutt* lost their lives. There was considerable controversy amongst the government bureaucrats in the following months concerning the inability of the Orleans crew to help the men of the *Orcutt*.

The men of Chatham and Orleans who spend their lives on the sea knew the efforts that the life saving crew took to make the rescue. Mr. Sparrow, in pushing five miles through snow, permanently damaged his eyesight and other station members were frostbitten from their efforts. After some debate, there was a new lifesaving station built on the outer beach. This new station was called Old Harbor Station and it, too, was manned by strong, skillful men who saved the lives of those in peril on the sea.

The Old Harbor Station is now gone, dismantled and moved several decades ago, but the bones of the *Calvin B. Orcutt* still snag the nets of the winter flounder fisherman, reminding them of one of the worst wrecks in Chatham's history.

Throughout the northeast in the winter time, regardless of the weather, the life saving patrolman would trek the beach and

The launching and landing of a life boat during a rescue was performed by strong and skilled men. These photographs were taken during a training session, but the procedure was usually necessitated during periods of high surf. Many times a rogue wave would overturn the boat and spill the life savers into a winter sea. The crews were trained to enter the lifeboat quickly, keep their eyes on the man at the helm and respond to his orders with speed and power. *Photo courtesy Paul Morris, Nantucket MA*

keep a sharp eye for ships in or near distress. The men from adjacent stations would patrol from their station to a "halfway house" and there they would swap "checks," or small brass emblems. They would then continue back toward their respective stations. In this manner the beach was completely covered by the patrols. When a patrol sighted a vessel in trouble but not yet wrecked, the crews of these stations would work hard to save her and her crew. Often, they would go out to a vessel to help assist the captain and crew as this excerpt from the 1899 Annual Report of the United States Life Saving Service relates:

"American Schooner Richard S. Leaming... Anchored near Handkerchief Lightship during a S.W. Gale and parted both anchor chains. She then made sail and ran before the gale across Pollock Rip Shoals and while running as close to shore as possible in order to keep in smooth water, she grounded on Orleans Beach at eleven p.m. The north patrol discovered her, at once burned a Coston light and then hastened to the station to notify the life saving crew. The surfboat was transported by horse along the beach about two miles to a point abreast of the stranded schooner where the surfmen launched and went on board. The master and crew were thoroughly exhausted and suffering from the intense cold; the sails were all blown away, she was a mass of ice from rail to rail and the pumps were frozen up. Keeper sent her crew below, took charge, and, at the masters request, dispatched a surfman ashore with a telegram to the owners. At high water the next morning she floated, and the keeper anchored her with the only remaining anchor, a small kedge, which failed to hold, and she began to drift seaward. Keeper made a signal for assistance to a tug near by, with a tow of barges. The tug anchored the barges and the master of the schooner quickly closed a bargain to be towed to Vineyard Haven. Tug towed her to the barges, where she made fast to the after end of the tow. Life-savers set to work at pounding the ice off her decks, heaving in the chain that was dragging overboard, thawing out her pumps, and making her as shipshape as possible. They left her just before sundown, and had a very hard pull against a westerly gale back to station, where they arrived with the surfboat looking like a small iceberg, and with several surfmen frost-bitten."

THE LOSS OF THE *JASON*

One of the greatest examples of heroism in the United States Life Saving Service is the action of Captain Eldridge, and the

In a blinding snowstorm in December 1893 the full rigged ship *Jason* struck the outer bar at Truro, Cape Cod. The shredding of the heavy canvas sails could be heard as far as ten miles away that night. The sea broke the iron ship in half. The *Jason* was located with magnetometers and surveyed in 1988. *Photo courtesy William P. Quinn, Orleans, MA*

crew of the Monomoy Life Saving Station, during the "Monomoy Disaster" in 1902. The Lifesavers repeated similar incidents over the years but there were also times that frustrated them when men from a wreck could not be rescued either because of weather or the violence of a wreck. The wreck of the *Jason* was one example.

The *Jason* was an iron sailing vessel on a voyage from Calcutta to Boston. On December fifth, 1893, the life saving crew at Nauset, Massachusetts, spotted her. There was a fearful storm blowing out of the northeast and sleet was falling into the hissing surf. They immediately telephoned the other stations to be on the lookout for a vessel offshore. All the stations along Cape Cod hitched up their horses and were on full alert, should the unfortunate ship hit their section of shore.

At half past seven in the evening, the north patrol of the Pamet station saw wreckage on the beach. Towards the east, he could hear heavy canvas sails snapping and shredding on the wind over the din of the storm. He burned his Coston signal to let the wrecked sailors know they had been seen and help was on the way. He had no way of knowing that twenty-four of her crew of twenty-five had already died in the wreck.

The lifesavers brought the mortar and life boat to the beach immediately. Upon arrival they found a man washed up on the beach barely alive. This man, Samuel Evans, was freezing and senseless. They brought him to the station and as he revived, he told the life savers that as soon as the vessel had struck, she broke in half and all the others had washed overboard and drowned. He remembered being knocked overboard by a big wave, but nothing else. Evans was the only survivor of one of the worst wrecks to occur on these shores.

THE FORMATION OF THE COAST GUARD

In 1915 the two maritime rescue services, the seaborne Revenue Cutter Service and the land based Life Saving Service were brought together to form the United States Coast Guard. The Life Saving Stations were turned into Coast Guard Stations and they practiced "through the surf" life saving techniques into the 1950s.

The author's father had the following recollection of the Coast Guard just after it was formed to include the Life Saving Service:

Throughout the decades of 18th, 19th and 20th centuries, men have used the seaways to smuggle one form of contraband or another to the Northeast. This engraving of the late 1800's depicts a Revenue Service steam cutter bearing down on one such band as they heave their outlaw cargo over the side. Today the Coast Guard's responsibility includes deterring smuggling in U.S. waters. *From Harper's Weekly*

"The Coast Guard Station in 1925? I remember it well. But you must appreciate that you will be looking at it through the eyes of a ten year old boy, because that's how old I was then.

"My family had a small cottage next to the Nauset Coast Guard Station and most of my days were spent watching the Coast Guard activities or sitting around the stove and chatting with the crew members.

"I remember the Coast Guard Station as being a wonderful place. There was no electricity, no telephone, no plumbing at that time. The only mechanized equipment was a Caterpillar tractor which was used to tow the surfboat through the sand and down to the ocean. They stopped using horses years earlier.

"The place was always kept scrupulously clean. The exterior of the low building was white with green trim. As you entered the building through a low door, there was a short hallway. To the right was the small storage area for brooms and mops, and 'inside outhouse' as we used to call it.

"To the left was the kitchen with a highly polished combination coal and kerosene stove. There was always a pot of hot coffee and the makings of hot chocolate on that wonderful old cooking stove.

"The crew consisted of a captain (whose official rank was Chief Boatswain's Mate) and nine surfmen. Surfmen were numbered one to nine in the order of their length of service. Surfman #1 was First Mate and took over as captain if the latter was ill or absent.

"Beyond the kitchen was the living-dining room with a large dining table and several wooden chairs. It was a bit austere by today's standards, but still quite comfortable. When meals were not being served, the men would play cards or checkers on the big table.

"There were three doors in that room. One led to the kitchen, another to the captain's room and office and the third to the upstairs sleeping quarters. These were dormitory style with neat gray wool blankets on the beds.

"Adjoining the captain's office was the Boat House, a part of the main building. Inside this was kept the surfboat and oars, the tractor, the breeches buoy cart and all the ropes, life jackets and equipment necessary to the whole operation.

"One of the crutches of a person's memory is his sense of smell. I remember the redolence of that old building as though it were yesterday: the coffee, and chocolate brewing on the stove, the smell of kerosene and the tarry smell of the ropes and lines. Add a whiff of Edgeworth pipe tobacco and an apple and you have it! An indefinite aura that defies the computer.

"Each Tuesday morning at nine was Boat Drill. The surfman were assigned the duty according to his number. At a given signal, the tractor would be cranked and started, hitched to the boat carriage and the trek to the surf edge would begin. The tiny sand road was about 1/8 of a mile from the launching point.

"Once the boat had been beached at the edge of the surf, it would be pushed by the men, four on each side, into the first great wave that came crashing in. The Captain, or Number One Surfman, would be the helmsman, steering with an oar at the stern of the boat. After launch, the men would put their back to the oars for about one hour and then land the boat and the entourage would return to the station.

"On Thursday morning at nine would be breeches buoy drill. A mast had been erected about two hundred yards from the station yard. This mast had two arms at the top which extended like a Y at 45 degree angles.

"A small cannon would fire a shot from the yard, across the arms, and the Number Six Surfman, acting as crew of a distressed vessel, would haul increasingly heavy lines and secure them until the line was strong enough to carry a man's weight. The breeches buoy would then be hauled from the yard to the mast and a few lucky youngsters, acting as crew from a distressed vessel, would be hauled ashore. I used to look forward with great anticipation to this event in the hopes that I would be allowed to climb the mast and ride 'to shore and safety'.

"While this apparatus may sound inept and clumsy, it was surprisingly effective and was used when the seas were too rough to permit a boat launching.

"Most of the Coast Guardsmen, as I remember them, were kindly, brave and modest people. Old local names predominated. Captains Abbott Walker, George Nickerson, Henry Daniels, Wilbur Chase and Ralph Ormsby. I remember them well, God bless 'em."

Shipwrecks are not as frequent along these shores now as they were during the height of the years of the Life Saving Service but, like the *Eldia*, ashore on Cape Cod in the 1980's, they do occur. The lifesaver's tasks are still carried on with bravery and courage by the Coast Guard but the days of the lifeboat launched through the surf, the lyle gun, Coston signal, breeches buoy and often repeated heroic rescues on the beach, are past.

The lifesaving stations were austere but effective quarters for the men who spent many months patrolling the beaches and watching for shipwrecks. These huts also contained all the apparatus used in effecting a rescue including a lifeboat and cart (often with a horse to pull it over the sand), line throwing guns, lines and breeches buoy. The crew of the Highland Live Saving Station posed for this picture in front of their station with the crew of the wrecked barge *Manheim* in April of 1915.

5 Steam and Sail,
Storms and Collisions

During the latter part of the 19th and beginning of the 20th century, the northeast saw its highest level of coastal shipping. Hundreds of steamers, multimasted sailing vessels and luxurious yachts could be seen sailing up and down the coast every day. Unfortunately, the expansion of rail services and the development of the internal combustion engine brought a slow decline to this seagoing activity by the late 1930s. During this turn-of-the-century period, the region saw its largest number of recorded shipwrecks per year.

At this point nearly everything moved by sea. At one time or another, some component of manufactured goods and much of the raw commodities consumed by the American public was transported by sail or steamship. Even much of the commuting was done by sea. Travel to other northeastern cities for either business or pleasure was often done by passenger steamer. The Fall River Line had many vessels that traveled to New York and the Joy Line had a frequent Boston to New York run. To the north the Portland line had several passenger steamers. These were shallow draft vessels and often driven by side paddle wheels. The designs were more suited to rivers and lakes where the fetch was not as great as along the northeastern seaboard. The misapplication of this design did not become strikingly apparent until the fall of 1898.

THE *PORTLAND* GALE OF 1898

As can be seen in the computer generated graphs of shipwrecks in Appendix C, the largest number of shipwrecks to occur in one year in the entire history of the region happened during 1898. Ninety per cent of the shipwrecks that year took place in just three days.

On the evening of November twenty-eighth that year, a storm raged over the northeastern United States. In Provincetown,

By first light on Monday, November 28th the beaches at Truro were littered with the unquestionable evidence that the steamer *Portland* had sunk with all on board. *From the author's collection*

Massachusetts a man was trudging along the outer beach. His name was John Johnston and he was a lifesaver. As he fought the icy wind and snow that night, he walked by the surf that was pounding the shoreline and carefully studied the beach after each receding wave. There was flotsam of many kinds washing in and out with the surf but his well trained eye was looking for a special kind of debris, the kind that meant a ship and her crew were in danger. He saw something ahead of him in the dim light of evening on the beach. It had been thrown up high by the waves and on inspecting it, he though it to have little significance. It was an empty ice cream can from a creamery in Maine. Before long he found another and then a third along his beat. Then a different looking piece of flotsam caught his eye and he grabbed it from the surf. This was just the type of debris that he was trained to look for but he never wanted to find. It was a life preserver marked "Stmr. PORTLAND." He began running to the station house to report to the captain and alert the other stations.

This November gale in 1898 when Johnston found the life preserver was the most severe storm to hit the region in most men's memory. One of the few other bad storms during the 1800s was a storm that was in fact a closely spaced series of three storms, called the Triple Hurricanes of 1839 (see Chapter 3). Over 160 people lost their lives during the three storms, and for decades any given period of high winds was compared in strength to the 1839 storms. After the gale of 1898, little mention was given to the earlier "Triple Hurricanes".

The storm during which Johnston found this historic flotsam took the region completely by surprise. Blowing snow and winds that reached over 90 miles per hour destroyed roads, sections of railroad and whole buildings near the seashore. Over 400 vessels were sunk during the storm with as many lives lost. Many ships and their crews that left port just before the gale struck were never heard from again.

One ship, a passenger steamer, sank off the region during the storm and took over 160 lives with her. The significance of this event becomes clear when we realize that in this incident alone, as many lives were lost as in all the Triple Hurricanes of 1839.

Thanksgiving, 1898, was on November twenty-fourth. It was a typical fall in the region, with crisp weather and bright skies. Although there had been a few snow flurries in the north, no snow had stuck to the ground yet. In the late 19th century, as they do today, many people visited their relatives for family holidays. Thanksgiving that year was no exception as friends and relatives shared the holiday in Boston and other metropolitan areas.

On the Friday following the holiday, the weather in the northeast continued to hold clear and cool. In Boston Harbor the usual passenger steamers and freight-carrying schooners were traversing the harbor islands as they entered and left the large port. But a low pressure area in the form of a cyclonic storm had been moving north off the eastern seaboard. Its outer edges brushed New York on Friday evening. Various telegrams generated in New York hinted that some bad weather might be bound for Boston over the weekend. It was not known at the time, but this cyclonic storm was very severe for this time of the year. It was not reported before touching New York, because any vessel and crew offshore which ran into it probably did not survive the storm, and only its outer edge touched the Long Island Shore. At the same time, a low pressure area was progressing eastward from the lakes region headed for central Massachusetts.

None of this was realized in Boston, however, and on Saturday morning the weather was "bright and fare" with a light west wind. During that day the coastal communities in the region carried on business as usual. The sky began to gray in midafternoon. At India Wharf several steamers were boarding passengers. People destined for a sea voyage trickled onto the wharf as dusk approached.

By five p.m. the sky was more threatening and seemed to warn of an approaching squall, but with seeming indifference, the steamer *Kennebec* left on her passenger run to the north. Some of the men on the waterfront discussed the bad turn in the weather and, as the temperature dropped, they expected snow flurries.

The steamer *Portland*, also lying at India Wharf, was loading passengers for her eight hour run to Portland, Maine. The passengers boarding the steamer *Portland* were from varied walks of life. Mrs. Elmira Timmons was a widow who lived in Malden, Massachusetts. Her son bade her goodbye as she boarded, on her way to visit relatives in Portland, Maine. Susan Kelly was a teacher in Auburn, Maine, returning there from a Thanksgiving vacation with her family in Dorchester. Married in July, Walter Bemis and his bride had spent the Thanksgiving holiday with his father in Dorchester and were returning to their home in Auburn, Maine. E. Dudley Freeman, a prominent attorney in Maine, and member of the Governor's Council, boarded the *Portland* to return to his home in Yarmouth, Maine. Families, too, boarded the big white steamer. Charles H. Thompson, manager of a grocery store in Woddfords, Maine boarded with his wife and little daughter.

Leonard Dora of Saco, Maine had been in Boston for a week and was returning home. Mr. Dora was occasionally absent-minded and as he entered the cabin assigned to him on the steamer, he realized that he had left all his luggage in the hotel at which he stayed in Boston. The captain of the *Portland* assured him that there was plenty of time to retrieve his bags. On his way to the hotel, however, Leonard stopped to see several friends.

Of the many people boarding the waiting steamer, more than a few cast a wary glance at the darkening sky and some even expressed the fear of seasickness to friends who were seeing them off, but most put their trust in the captain and the steamship line and settled into their cabins. In all, over one hundred passengers boarded the ship, helped by the sixty or so crew members that would see to the most comfortable trip as possible.

Captain Hollis Blanchard of the *Portland* had recently been promoted from pilot but had many years of experience on the water. The sistership to the *Portland* was the *Bay State* which was in the city of Portland, Maine readying to make its evening run down to Boston. Captain Blanchard spoke by telephone to Captain Dennison of the *Bay State* that afternoon. During this conversation, Captain Dennison told Blanchard that he intended to stay in port until the weather became less threatening. In contrast, Blanchard said that he intended to keep to his schedule.

Later, the head of the Portland Steamship Authority in Portland, Maine telephoned Boston with a message for Blanchard to hold at the dock until at least nine p.m. due to possible bad weather.

The Boston - Maine steamer *Portland* of the Portland Steam Packet Company was one of the most luxurious coastwise steamers on the east coast. With accommodations for over 500 people, she was well appointed and boasted a main saloon almost as long as the vessel herself. The steamer traveled at 12 - 14 knots, making the run between Portland and Boston in just over nine hours. *From the author's collection*

There is, however, a question of Captain Blanchard ever receiving this message because the *Portland* slipped her lines and pulled away from the wharf at about seven-twenty that evening. Leonard Dora, having been delayed by his visit with friends, arrived at the wharf minutes later and saw the slowly disappearing stern of the steamer as it headed out towards the harbor islands. Prematurely, he cursed himself for being so absent-minded as to miss the steamer.

At the beginning of its voyage, when the *Portland* passed Deer Island Light, Blanchard saw the steamer *Kennebec*, which had left Boston a few hours earlier, heading in to the protection of the harbor. Her captain felt that it would be wise seamanship to hold in Boston for the night. A little farther out, near the Grave's Light, Captain William Rioux of the steamer *Mt Desert* was just completing his run to Boston as he passed the outward bound *Portland*. He looked back to see when the *Portland* would turn around. He watched as the stern of the Maine bound steamer disappeared in the snow falling from the darkening sky.

The weather began to rapidly deteriorate after the *Portland* rounded Deer Island Light. Blanchard became more and more apprehensive about his decision to leave as he headed towards Thatcher's Island. The captain of a fishing schooner called the *Maude S* reported seeing the steamer pass him at nine-thirty p.m. in the snowy night off Gloucester.

The wind increased in strength with each passing hour and with it the snow fell heavier. Although she was heading into the sea, the steamer was making about 11 knots and was on course. Blanchard had her at full speed in hopes of making Portland before the blow got any worse. After rounding Thatcher's Island and putting the rocky coast of Cape Ann behind him, he felt the full force of the storm waves. His new course towards Portland put the wind and sea on his starboard quarter and the seas here were more than she could take. The severe rolling of the 240 foot steamer would first lift one paddle wheel out of the water and then the other, making the ship quite unmanageable.

Many of the passengers on board were soon seasick. The crew had fastened down anything movable hours earlier. Just after ten p.m. Captain Blanchard felt the *Portland* shudder with the impact of huge waves and realized the mistake he had made. He had to turn back. He did not dare to turn the ship here, north of Gloucester's rocky shore. Although he knew his approximate position, he could not see any lights on shore through the driving snow.

The Eastern Steamship Corporation's passenger side wheeler *Bay State* survived the gale of 1898. She was the sister ship to the *Portland* and she remained in Portland Harbor when the weather started to turn bad on that fateful Thanksgiving weekend. She was not as lucky 18 years later when she went aground in dense fog off the Maine coast on September 23, 1916. *Photo courtesy William P. Quinn, Orleans MA*

We know from repeated sightings that night that Blanchard turned the big steamer about 50 degrees to bring her on an easterly heading. He had wanted to put more distance between the steamer and the shore before turning for a downwind run into the protection of Boston. Suddenly something broke loose in the ship and destroyed part of the vessel's main electrical wiring. The *Portland* went dark. Now Blanchard's apprehension was transformed into real fright. He was frightened for himself and the 160 odd men, women and children in his care. They were all huddled, seasick, in their darkened cabins.

After a few miles of steaming, the seas grew in height and the wind increased in intensity. The sea was so wild now, and the waves so big, that he felt he could not turn the ship around for a southwest run into port. Such a maneuver would surely capsize the boat when the waves were directly abeam. Blanchard then turned the ship up to its original course into the wind to ease the beating that she was taking. Although he was now making little progress, he headed the Portland a few points to the east of the wind. This action, he hoped, would keep him from being blown onto the rocky north shore of Boston.

At eleven p.m. Blanchard saw a red flare off his bow. He heaved the *Portland*'s helm over and narrowly missed the fishing schooner *Grayling* which was also bobbing in the wind whipped seas. With the wind and snow whistling through the broken windows in the *Portland*'s upper deck and the monstrous waves punishing her hull, Blanchard and the crew prayed that they could survive the storm. The passing of the night within the wave-torn, rocking hull of the steamer must have seemed an eternity.

The constant pounding of the sea slowly broke fittings loose on the outside of the ship. Three and four decades later, fisherman would find these fittings in the middle of Massachusetts Bay as they hauled their bottom trawls.

In the weeks that followed the November twenty-sixth sailing of the steamer *Portland*, there were many reports of sightings of the steamer. There are a several indisputable facts, however, that bear retelling.

The *Portland* battled waves generated by two weather disturbances which collided off to the southeast of Cape Cod and stalled there that night and the following day. The weather at the Blue Hill Observatory in Canton, Massachusetts, reported the highest winds at 55 miles per hour and similar winds were reported at the Boston Observatory, but in Provincetown the winds reached over 90 miles per hour before destroying the wind measuring instruments there. Mrs. Small, the wife of the lighthouse keeper of the Highland Light, left an oral history in the care of the Provincetown Library, which she reported that the wind pressure was so forceful during the storm that it ripped the mantelpiece off the wall of the keeper's house.

The sea churned furiously for 36 hours breaking high up on the shores of the region. In Portland, Maine, however, the highest wind recorded was 44 MPH. If the steamer that bore that city's name had left Boston an hour or two earlier, she likely would have made port before sunrise.

We do know that the *Portland* made it through the night. At 6:00 a.m. on Sunday, there was a lull in the storm as the "eye" passed over the middle of Massachusetts Bay. Almost as quickly as it came, the lull passed with the sky clouding over, and the fury raged again for another 24 hours.

On Sunday, November twenty-seventh, the *Portland* and her

fragile human cargo finally succumbed to the force of this, the worst storm in memory, sinking somewhere north of Cape Cod. No one survived.

On Sunday night, almost 24 hours to the minute after the *Portland* left India Wharf, John Johnston found the creamery cans and the life preserver with the steamer's name written on it. He had hoped that it had been blown off the steamer by accident, and that the big boat was still afloat, but these were only the first signs of the great steamer's demise.

Within four hours the beach near high head in Truro was heaped with the wreckage of the ship. The first of twenty eight bodies came ashore at three-thirty a.m. on Monday morning, along with other wreckage from Race Point to Chatham. Over the next three weeks, bodies and flotsam rose from the *Portland's* grave and floated ashore on Cape Cod. Life Saving Service reports show that the men in its service were psychologically exhausted from the ghastly job of pulling body after body from the surf each night. The storm rapidly became known, as it is to this day, as the "Portland Gale."

We will not know what happened in those final hours until the remains of this great vessel are examined. The largest piece of wreckage that came ashore was only 30 feet in length, and no part of the main hull was ever found. All the wreckage located was from the upper decks, including the main and spare steering wheels and much of the woodwork that made up the cabins of the ship.

For one reason or another, the ship probably could not be kept into the sea. As soon as she fell into the trough of the waves with the sea directly abeam, the force of the giant combers destroyed her upper works in a matter of minutes. It is thought that Captain Blanchard did not make the progress that he had hoped. With the steamer's bow a few points east of the wind, the steamer had been pushed farther and farther to the southeast until she was well offshore when the end came.

The loss of the steamer *Portland* has been one of the most controversial marine mysteries in the history of the region. There are disputed reports of the vessel being sighted or heard on Sunday morning off Highland Light. Many people have searched for the *Portland*, including the Government and two prominent Boston newspapers. None successfully located the vessel's remains. After deep bottom trawling became a popular fishing method at the turn of the century, draggers brought up many artifacts from the ship

ABOVE: The Portland gale of 1898 devastated the northeast coast. Over 400 vessels were wrecked in the storm. The *Albert Butler* was driven ashore on Cape Cod only yards from the bulk of the wreckage of the steamer *Portland*. **BELOW**: The sea's destructive force on a shipwreck laying exposed to the coast can be seen in this photograph of the *Albert Butler* a few weeks after she was wrecked in the Portland Gale. *Photos from the collection of William P. Quinn, Orleans MA*

from a variety of areas north of Cape Cod. Most of these were torn from the steamer or her wreckage as it floated in the storm that day in 1898.

In the Pilgrim Monument Museum in Provincetown there are many artifacts exhibited which were recovered from the beach after the gale. In the Historical Museum at Highland Light in Truro there is a model of the steamer and other artifacts from the ship.

It was also proposed that there might have been treasure on board the *Portland* for her routine voyage to Maine but these treasures are only in the imagination of those who talk of them. The *Portland* carried general freight to the state of Maine three times a week and had no capacity for carrying cargo of great value. The steamer carried only the treasure of frail human lives that were lost when she went down.

The wrecking of the *Portland* marked a change in the practice of coastwise passenger shipping in the region. From that point on, a duplicate passenger list was always left on shore when a passenger vessel left port. In a disaster, therefore, those on shore would know who was on board. It also marked a change in the design of coastal passenger steamers. Paddle wheel steamers, like the *Portland*, were of shallow draft which, while allowing passage up into Maine's rivers, did not make for good handling in heavy seas. The *Portland* was replaced by the *Governor Dingly* in 1899 followed by the *Calvin Austin* in 1903 and the *Governor Cobb* in 1906. These vessels were of the propeller type rather than the paddle wheel, had a deeper draft and were more enclosed, thus allowing for more seaworthiness in the unpredictable and often wild waters of the northeast.

In 1989 the author and colleagues located the remains of the *Portland* in over three hundred feet of water. A thorough survey of the site is planned. This may give us a better understanding of what caused her to sink, and tell us what Captain Blanchard might have tried to do to save her from the ravages of the worst gale to hit New England in man's memory - *The Portland Gale of 1898.*

"NEVER ON A BRITISH VESSEL"

Near the turn of the century steam power continued to gain headway on the coastal and seagoing market. Although some of the largest coastal schooners were built in the first decade of the new century, by 1910 it became clear that sail could not compete as before. Steam freighters could carry more cargo and passengers at considerably lower cost than sailing vessels. Steamers were more predictable as well, being able to continue at a good speed even in calm weather.

Foreign steamers and domestically owned vessels, were plying the northeast United States, working between New York, Boston, the Maritimes and Europe. There were many strandings of both sail and steam vessels, and collisions were frequent in this competitive seaway. The collisions brought about numerous court cases where it seemed every captain insisted that the fault lay solely with the "other vessels." This was actually reflected in a number of government reports as well.

We can see in tables A and B that during the year 1906 collisions and strandings were the cause of most accidents, and that the collisions reported for that year were often the fault of no one but the "other" fellow. One such collision happened before the 1906 reports, and was typical of many collision situations.

On the evening of January twenty-second, 1900, the New England sky was clear and cool. There was a brisk wind. The British steamer *Ardandhu* had left New London, Connecticut after taking on the largest marine cargo to ever leave that port, including six thousand bales of hay, gold specie for Nova Scotian banks and odd lots of merchandise for Cuba. It was a new run for the vessel, originating in New York and putting in to New London and Halifax before continuing to Havana.

Built seven years earlier by Workman, Clark and Company in Belfast, Ireland, she was a relatively young vessel. The steel two masted steamer, owned by the Clark and Service Company of Glasgow, was now leased by the Munson Steamship line of New York. Captain Dundas felt secure with the strength and speed of his vessel. She had a questionable history, but the captain was proud of her and the crew he commanded.

This particular evening the wind was fresh from the southwest and did not hamper the vessel's speed as it steamed into the outer reaches of Vineyard Sound, just south of Cape Cod. The night-piercing beacon of Gay Head Lighthouse could be seen off the starboard bow and the village lights from the Elizabeth Islands were several miles to port. The area surrounding these islands was often called "the graveyard" because of the many ships that had been drawn to their death by the swift and deceptive currents here. It was now past midnight, but Captain Dundas stayed on the bridge. Although the night was clear, in a few hours the *Ardandhu* would have to pass through the most treacherous waters of the entire

CAUSE	NUMBER OF VESSELS
Foundered	30
Stranded	134
Collided	177
Capsized	1
Explosion	3
Fire	52
Ice	1

TABLE A

NATURE OF VESSEL CASUALTIES ON THE GULF AND ATLANTIC COASTS
DURING FISCAL YEAR 1906.

Data Source: *United States Life Saving Annual Report 1906*

CAUSE OF COLLISION	NUMBER OF VESSELS
Accidental	12
Bad Management	7
Carelessness	2
Error in Judgment	1
Error of Pilots	2
Fault of other Vessel	60
Fault of Tug towing	8
Fog	26
High, Baffling Winds	4
Misunderstanding Signals	7
Snowstorm	6
Tides and Currents	3
Unavoidable	5
Want of proper Lights	1
Miscellaneous	3
Unknown	30

TABLE B

NATURE OF VESSEL COLLISIONS ON THE GULF AND ATLANTIC COASTS
DURING FISCAL YEAR 1906

Data Source: *United States Life Saving Annual Report 1906*

ABOVE: Some collisions on the northeast's seaways were caused by floating derelicts such as this abandoned schooner. BELOW: The *Harry Knowlton* is shown after a collision with the steamer *Larchmont* where over one hundred people froze in the winter waters off Rhode Island in 1907.

voyage. These waters would include shoals with names such as Hedgefence, Tuckernuck, Halfmoon, Handkerchief and the most dangerous of all -- Pollock Rip. The captain had already lost several days due to fog after leaving New York, and then another day in New London while waiting for freight. He hoped to make up for lost time. Captain Dundas would guide the 281 foot, 1401 ton steamer on the first leg of this new route himself. However, the treacherous shoals and swirling currents were not to be the *Ardandhu's* undoing.

Only two years earlier, en route from Jamaica to New York with a cargo of island rum and seven passengers, a fire had broken out in the third hold. Passengers had panicked and had to be held at bay with revolvers in order to keep them from boarding the lifeboats. With the fire temporarily contained and the cargo of rum moved out on deck away from the flames, the steamer had limped along in an effort to reach New York. Entering the outer reaches of the harbor, a thick fog had enveloped the injured ship. Suddenly, through the mist, another large vessel had been sighted dead ahead. The captain of the *Ardandhu* had steered his ship across the bow of the unknown steamer, avoiding collision by only twenty feet.

Less than two years later, while entering Boston Harbor, the *Ardandhu* had collided with and sank the *Two-Forty*, a fishing schooner. Although Captain Dundas had been in charge at the time, his ship had been in the control of Horace Folger, a Boston pilot. The accident took place between Castle Island and channel buoy number seven. Four lives were lost from the fishing vessel.

These thoughts had slipped from the captain's mind as he spotted another large freighter heading down Vineyard Sound on this starry January night. As the distance between them lessened, Captain Dundas recognized the ship as the Metropolitan Line steamer *Herman Winter* making its usual run to New York from Boston. The *Winter's* lights were visible in the clear night air.

The crew of the *Ardandhu* were unaware of these events. Chief Engineer James Henderson of Glasgow, had received a cable in New York the week before. It had told of his wife's good health after giving birth to a baby boy. He had talked often when his watch was over, with his fellow crew members about his plans for his wife and new baby in Scotland. He had planned to take the next available ship out of Halifax, Nova Scotia and visit them in his homeland. He was talking to second mate Fred Dowe of Boston that evening of this new addition to his family. Dowe had followed the chief engineer down into the engine room as the latter checked the huge triple-expansion engines before turning the watch over to the assistant engineer.

Then, in the middle of Vineyard Sound, with the *Herman Winter* just off his starboard bow, Captain Dundas heard the blasting whistle of the Metropolitan Liner. Thinking that this was an indication that the *Winter* was turning to port, the skipper of the *Ardandhu* cursed this inconvenience as he spun the great wheel putting his vessel hard to port. He was surprised at seeing the other vessel turning to starboard -- definitely on a collision course. He watched in horror as the two ships moved towards each other. He did not realize that the *Winter's* captain had signaled only one blast on the whistle, indicating a turn to starboard. For the second time in its career, the *Ardandhu* cut across another ship's bow. This time she did not survive.

Too late for any corrective action, the two vessels came together with a grinding crash. It was three-forty-five a.m. and most of the thirty-one crewmembers were asleep. When the *Herman Winter's* steel bow cut into the *Ardandhu* amidships and well into the engine room, the shock of the crash jolted the crew from their bunks.

Realizing the severity of damage to his vessel, Captain Dundas reached the main deck at the same time as most of the crew. Lines were thrown to them from the bow of the *Winter*, and they scurried up the ropes to safety. The captain, seeing that there was no one left on the deck of the rapidly settling ship, was the last to leave. The *Herman Winter* had been damaged but the water tight bulkheads were holding and she stayed afloat. The two steel steamers were locked together momentarily. Mate John Lee, realizing that Henderson and Dowe had not reached safety, climbed back down to the sinking *Ardandhu*. He quickly made his way among the twisted wreckage trying to find the two men. He called for them through the darkness, but when he heard the ships beginning to separate, he abandoned his desperate mission and again climbed to the safety of the *Winter's* decks.

The *Ardandhu* settled stern first, her watertight compartments in the bow still holding air. The bow floated for a time before the big ship sank to her final resting place eighty feet down in Vineyard Sound.

The *Herman Winter* proceeded to Vineyard Haven to land the surviving crew members of the *Ardandhu*. The following day, when asked by the reporter if there was a confusion of signals, the chauvinistic Captain Dundas replied, "Young man, signals are never misunderstood on a British vessel!" It seemed to the proud old captain that things always went properly on any vessel flying the Union Jack, but, actually, the *Ardandhu's* final night on Vineyard Sound had ended a short and checkered career.

WRONG CAPTAIN, WRONG VESSEL

As big steel steamers became more and more frequent on the coastal route of the northeast, collisions between sailing vessels and these mechanized ships increased.

An example of a collision on the freight route, involving one of the approximately 500 four-masted schooners that carried freight along the East coast, is that of the Kennebunkport built schooner *Sagamore*.

The *Sagamore* was built in Maine in 1891 by Charles W. Ward. Launched in May of that year, her birth was witnessed by most of the town. A launching in the town of Kennebunkport was

One of the most bizarre shipwreck incidents in the northeast took place when the captain of the Steamship *Edda* was inadvertently taken hostage by the schooner *Sagamore* in May 1907. The schooner's long bowsprit swung over the bridge of the steamer and pulled off the Norwegian Captain. As the men of the *Sagamore* and the steamer's Captain boarded the schooner's yawl boat, the *Sagamore* slipped into fourteen fathoms of water. *From the author's collection*

reason enough for children to be excused from school and most of the town merchants closed shop for an hour or two as well. When the *Sagamore* slipped into the water that sunny day, her launching wave was big enough to travel to the opposite river bank and soak a few youngsters watching from under a neighbor's porch. The *Sagamore* was a large vessel, displacing 1,415 tons. She was one of the larger vessels built in this port, and was equipped with three big centerboards rather than a deep keel, to allow access to some of the shallower ports along the coast.

She was a handsome vessel and sailed well. On May eleventh, 1907, Captain Treffrey was carrying 2,200 tons of coal from Newport News, Virginia to Boston. She had a smooth voyage up the East Coast, off New York and then in through the race in order to avoid the treacherous Nantucket Shoals. The night was clear as Treffery passed Gay Head Light on Martha's Vineyard to starboard and Cuttyhunk and the Islands to port. As he rounded West Chop at the tip of Martha's Vineyard he saw a few other vessels in the area. He eased sail a bit and steered a steady course. Treffrey had been a skipper for many years with experience both at sea and on the inshore waterways. Dead ahead he saw a tug and several barges heading east also. Farther up the sound he could see the lights of a steamer apparently headed south.

As one looked from the helm of one of these vessels down the deck and on ahead, it was truly an awesome sight. The *Sagamore's* deck alone was over two hundred feet in length and it took some good sailing to predict her course changes as the tide or wind tried to deflect her from a set course.

Heading in the other direction was the Norwegian steamer *Edda* carrying plaster rock from Nova Scotia to New York. Captain Meidell, of the *Edda*, was not very familiar with the waters of the sound but knew he would shortly be passing the long string of barges he could see heading his way. The tug and each of the towed vessels had navigational lights illuminated. He put the *Edda* on a course that would keep him close, but clear of the barge tow. As the tug steamed past the *Edda* with the current behind it, Meidell suddenly realized what he thought was the last schooner barge in the tow was a separate vessel not connected to the other barges. It was on a different course. He swung the big steamer's wheel to change course. This separate vessel was the big schooner *Sagamore*.

On the *Sagamore* Captain Treffrey studied the steamer's actions as it neared the tug in front of him. He suddenly realized that the steamer was planning on passing the tug and barges very

closely. This would be too close for it to clear the *Sagamore* as well.
Treffery, being pushed by a three knot tidal current, swung the helm
of the *Sagamore* to try to avoid the looming steamer.

Meidell saw the schooner in front of him begin to change
course thereby putting the two vessels on a collision course. He
ordered the engine room command for Full Astern. The answering
bell from the engine room confirmed receipt. Although events seem
to happen quickly during disasters at sea, in reality the huge vessels
involved move and change courses relatively slowly. It was this time
lag that allowed Meidell to go out onto the bridge wing of the *Edda*
as the big triple expansion engine rumbled and shook in the massive
effort to start turning the propeller in the opposite direction. He
watched helplessly as the gap between the two vessels closed. The
Edda slammed into the port bow of the *Sagamore* splintering the
heavy oak and pine timbers.

On board the *Sagamore*, someone had shouted to the crew
below. The rest had braced themselves for the collision that was
imminent. When the big steamer drove into the bow of the
schooner, it smashed the lashings of the 5000 pound bow anchor
which fell to the bottom of the sound with a rattling of anchor chain.
Suddenly, as if by magic, the steamer began to back away. The
schooner, still being pushed by the current, followed the retreating
steel steamer. As the two vessels moved down current, the
Sagamore, now anchored to the seabed, began to turn on her axis.
As she turned, her fifty foot bowsprit swept across the side of the
Edda and brushed the bridge wing of the Norwegian ship.

Stunned, the captain of the *Edda* stood outside his pilot
house watching the aftermath of the collision. The huge schooner,
which his great steel prow had splintered, began to turn as the *Edda*
backed away. Suddenly, he saw a broken bowsprit and tangled mass
of rigging coming towards him out of the darkness. He tried to duck
below the railing but a loop of hemp rigging caught his arms and
pulled him away.

Captain Meidell hung on to that rope for dear life. He had
been swept off his ship and now looking below him, all he could see
were the cold waters of Vineyard sound. He clambered up the lines
hanging about him and grabbed onto the huge bowsprit. Assessing
his situation, he knew that he had to get onto the deck of the
schooner and so made his way down the bowsprit onto the deck of
the *Sagamore*. He looked down the sound and saw his ship still
backing astern almost 1/4 mile away. He rapidly came to three
realizations. First, he was on another vessel with which he had just

collided. Second, his own vessel was going full astern with no captain and no one at the helm. Third, the vessel he was on was sinking. This woke him out of his stupor as he began to go towards the stern of the schooner to find her captain.

In the immediate aftermath of the collision, all the crew of the *Sagamore* had run to the stern where Treffrey was instructing them to lower the longboat and prepare to abandon the mortally wounded schooner. Suddenly out of the darkness of the foredeck emerged a tall uniformed figure in a captain's hat. All of the crew of the *Sagamore* momentarily stopped what they were doing and stared at this apparition. Captain Treffery ordered the men back to the task of abandoning ship and told this stranger to get aboard the longboat.

On the long row to shore, Meidell introduced himself to the captain and crew of the *Sagamore*. No one has recorded the words exchanged in the little ship's dory that night in the aftermath of one of the strangest collisions on the northeast coast.

Many vessel losses during this period of decline of the sailing vessel were due to stiff competition that occurred between shipowning companies. Some of the older vessels were not in the best state of repair simply from economic reasons. The old trade of carrying freight by coal was being threatened by the many schooners being converted to schooner barges. The vessels were towed by a tugboat and might number four to six in a tow. Their total capacity was considerably larger than the single schooners under sail and the total tow could be manned by fewer men.

Quarried stone, ore and lumber was freighted by barge more and more, putting a heavy burden on the schooner owners to push their prices lower and keep older vessels in service longer.

THE STORM OF 1914

January 1914 brought a storm to New England that was as severe a winter storm as had hit in many years. Although it did not take the toll on shipping that others had, it dealt a bad blow to the maritime trade of hauling coal because two big five-masted coal schooners were lost off Boston.

The *Fuller Palmer* and the *Grace A. Martin* were both lost during that storm, and the *Prescott Palmer* was blown out to sea and had to be abandoned in a sinking condition more than one week later, as she limped back to the Maine coast. Interestingly enough, the *Grace A. Martin* was the second largest five-masted schooner, measured in gross tonnage, and the *Fuller Palmer* was the third largest, both measuring over three hundred feet in length. The age of these behemoths was not very great, and there were many big vessels that out lived them. The only reason for their sinking was the severity of the storm.

Another schooner, the *John Paul*, was lost in this gale, but little is said of her, because she was only one of hundreds of three-masted schooners sunk in storms off New England. Her story is typical of the hardships and uncertainty the crews of these vessels experienced as the ships got older and their strength waned.

The *John Paul* was built in Franklin, Maine in 1891, at the shipyard of John Paul Gorden. Mr. Gorden, who lived in the town of Franklin, was a reasonably traveled man during his time. He was a "49-er," traveling to the western part of the country during the gold rush days and returning to Maine shortly after the Civil War. He was well-to-do, and a respected townsperson.

Franklin, Maine had several actively producing stone quarries during this time, some near the estuaries and inlets that so characterize the Maine coastline. These stone quarries provided a major export commodity, and many shallow draft vessels came up the inlets to carry the huge stone blocks to major Atlantic ports.

Some sixty or more ships were built in Franklin during the 1800's, and some of these were constructed at Gordon's Shipyard on a spit of land still known today as Shipyard Point. In 1890 he built his largest ship for his brother, Orlando Foss. Late in June of 1891, this fine new ship stood on the ways at Gordon's Shipyard.

The launching of a new ship was an important event for all involved. Interestingly enough, a ship in those days was insured only during the building process and when safely afloat. During that brief moment of her "birth," as she traveled down the ways, most insurance policies were void. If the ways collapsed under a new ship, the yard had a very expensive repair bill.

Since the *John Paul* was the largest ship ever built at Gordon's yard, the ways had been carefully scrutinized before the laying of her keel. Most of the town turned out for the momentous event. A launching was an important occasion and this was a big ship by Franklin's standards. She was 137 feet long, 32 feet wide and had a draft of 12 feet. Built of oak and pine and fastened with bronze, she was schooner rigged and boasted three tall masts.

As the chocks were knocked from beneath her with heavy mallets, everyone held their breaths as the *John Paul* slid down the ways and eased into the water. A loud cheer came up from the

The freight schooner *John Paul* was a money making investment for all concerned. Her only real accident before the last voyage was a collision with a steamer. She is shown above after putting into Savannah, Georgia for repairs to her bow. *From the author's collection*

crowd, and Mr. Gordon admired the new ship that carried his name on her quarterboards. She looked like a moneymaker.

She was registered in Hancock, a neighboring town, and in her time she saw five captains. Orlando Foss, for whom she had been built, skippered her for six years. He was followed by Captain Harold Foss in 1897, Captain Boyd Foss in 1902, Captain John Rutledge in 1906, and finally Captain E. J. Hutchenson in 1910.

It was said that she was a fine ship, that she sailed well, handled easily and was always a profit maker for those involved. There were many wooden schooners that had fewer credits to their name. However, the last voyage of the *John Paul* ended, as so many others off the New England shore, with the captain and crew struggling to keep her afloat against terrible odds.

Before the January storm set began in 1914, Captain Hutchenson was sailing down the coast. The weather glass on the cabin wall had dropped steadily since mid-morning, and he glanced at it occasionally as he entered the daily report in the ship's log. This instinctively concerned the captain. He was an experienced seafarer from Deer Isle, Maine, and had learned to respect such signs. The voyage had been blessed thus far with fair skies and light seas. Although it had been cold, the southwest wind filled the sails and the waves gently stroked the schooner's hull. Sailing up past Jeffrey's Bank, off Gloucester, Massachusetts, the first mate had the *John Paul's* course set for New York. Her cargo was stone blocks, quarried in Stonington, Maine, bound for transfer in New York. The ship's set course would bring her by the outer side of Cape Cod, through the narrow channel north of Nantucket Island, through Vineyard Sound, and then past Block Island into the shelter of Long Island Sound.

The *John Paul* had worked the coastal trade to ports as distant as Cuba for over two decades. She had a fine record for a ship of her size. Having seen many rugged voyages in her twenty three years, the ship was strong. Nonetheless, Captain Hutchenson preferred to see his four hundred mile journey end before any major winter storm set in.

The sky remained clear and the wind had not picked up, though by 2200 hours that evening, the weather glass had dropped further still. Realizing then that a winter storm was nearer than he had earlier surmised, the captain pulled out his charts to study the various ship havens south of Cape Cod and how the currents would affect his progress to them. He now hoped to get through the rugged ship channel at Pollock Rip before the weather turned sour. The currents there were treacherous in strong winds. Looking over his well used charts, the captain was immersed in the warm glow of his cabin's oil lamps. The after house provided comfortable shelter from the bitter chill of the winter night.

By the next morning the *John Paul* would have passed through Pollock Rip and into the teeth of a January gale.

On Monday morning, at Woods Hole, Massachusetts, thirty miles from Pollock Rip Channel, the usual work was going on aboard the Revenue Cutter *Acushnet*. The southwest wind had died and there was talk on the waterfront of stormy weather approaching, but chipping paint and overhauling standard gear inside the warm, coal heated *Acushnet* seemed the order of the day. However, by 0900 hours a wind had sprung up out of the northeast and grew stronger within the hour. The increasing wind whipped the waves and sent a freezing mist down Vineyard Sound. The wireless at the Woods Hole Station had crackled occasionally during the morning, but now more and more communications were being received, from vessels in need. A schooner off Chatham with a distress flag in its rigging was being tended by boats from the Old Harbor Life Saving Station. Another vessel in trouble off Hyannis had a steam tug at her side providing assistance. By 1100 hours the northeast wind had increased to gale force.

Captain Slatterly of the Cutter *Acushnet* knew that a wind from the northeast with this force meant the imminent storm would churn the sound for three solid days. He sipped his morning coffee as he looked over the weekly list of vessels expected to traverse Nantucket and Vineyard Sounds in the next few days.

A chilling blast of cold air interrupted his concentration as Mate Robinson entered the bridge. Pulling the door closed behind him, he said that the station had just received a message from the Tarpaulin Cove Lighthouse, suggesting that a vessel, blowing its whistle out in Vineyard Sound, was in distress.

Putting his steaming mug of coffee down on the chart table, Captain Slatterly told Robinson to prepare to get underway, and blew the whistle that alerted his crew and ordered up steam. He had a sound knowledge of New England weather and knew that three long days of hard work were at hand. What he did not know is that for those three days the men of the *Acushnet* would get hardly any sleep as they battled for their own survival on the cold winter seas while saving weather beaten ships and the lives of the men who sailed them.

With near hurricane winds roaring out of the northeast and short fetched waves in Nantucket Sound, Captain Hutchenson of the *John Paul* was seriously concerned for his ship and crew. He had entered Pollock Rip at 0600 hours with a fair tide, but at the approaches to Nantucket Sound, the tide had turned and the storm he had foreseen began to howl. Before passing the *Cross Rip Lightship* in the center of the sound, heavy seas began to take their toll of the aging *John Paul*. The constant pounding of the waves on the wooden schooner's hull began to weaken her seams. When water levels in the holds began to increase, he ordered the crew to start pumping. He knew now that the leaks could only get worse until they could find a safe haven. Increasing the burden of his ship was the freezing, wind driven spray which coated the rigging and decks with heavy ice. This caused the schooner to ride lower and lower in the water, leaving her at the mercy of the head tide. To combat the ice in the rigging, the crew now had the endless job of breaking the ice with sledges and axes to lighten the schooner's load.

At one point, the cargo of quarried stone blocks shifted, causing the *John Paul* to list badly to port. The Cook, John Thorr of New York, had long since secured the galley. It was far too rough even to keep coffee warm, so he turned his efforts to chopping ice from the rails. Working alone in the bow, his oilskins provided little protection from the bitter spray-laden wind. He was cold to the point of numbness, but he knew that their survival depended upon all the men working together to get them through this storm alive. He had faith in Captain Hutchenson as did the rest of the crew. The vessel pitched and heaved under Thorr's feet as he swung his heavy hammer against the accumulation of ice. An unexpected wave hit the hull; Thorr lost his footing on the slippery deck and fell, crashing into the forward wall. Half an hour later, First Mate Frank Hardy found him there covered with frozen spray. He shook him and dragged him into the protection of the cabin. Thorr was still alive.

Although not directly responsible for saving the crew's lives on the *John Paul*, the Revenue and later Coast Guard Cutters were responsible for many at-sea rescues in the early 1900's. The *Acushnet*, pictured above, was a hard working vessel that was put to sea during bad winter storms to save lives and ships. *Photo courtesy William P. Quinn, Orleans MA*

Captain Hutchenson and most of his crew were from Maine, and accustomed to bitter winters. They had witnessed storms worse than this. He never doubted that they would see this storm through, even with the old schooner under constant pounding, and the men working hour after hour at the pumps. Tarpaulin Cove, twenty miles to the west, would provide the needed safe haven for the *John Paul* and her crew, and he believed they could make it if the storm did not get worse. Slowly, it did.

Captain Slatterly of the Cutter *Acushnet* assured himself that the whistling tugboat that had been reported in distress had found the safety of Tarpaulin Cove as he saw her dropping anchor there and removing her distress signal from the mast. He headed the *Acushnet* into the wind, blowing down Vineyard Sound, knowing that any vessel taken unaware by the storm might need help. He spotted several vessels and spoke with their crews. Many requested to have their progress reported to their owners by the Revenue Service wireless. The six masted schooner of the Lawrence Fleet, the *Edward J. Lawrence* of Portland Maine, requested reporting, and farther down the sound, the captain of the *Wyoming*, the largest schooner ever built, shouted to the *Acushnet's* crew that she was covered with ice and leaking some, but otherwise OK.

At 1405 hours, Slatterly spotted a three masted schooner with a distress flag in her rigging and proceeded to her assistance. Her skipper shouted through the storm that she was the *John Paul* of Hancock, Maine, leaking badly, and that her cargo had shifted. Slatterly could not make out everything the captain said, but could see that she was listing and that her decks were ice covered.

The crew of the cutter passed a 900 foot, heavily tarred, manila hawser to the *John Paul* over the stormy seas, and once it was secure, began the tow with the sea on their starboard forward quarter. After several hours of towing in low visibility, Captain Slatterly had made little headway. The burden of the *Paul* was growing as the schooner settled lower and lower due to her increasing weight.

By 1800 hours it had grown dark, and although they had been fighting the storm for over three hours, the cutter had traveled little more than half a mile. Captain Slatterly ordered her to half speed for fear of breaking the hawser. The seas were high and at times, the huge propeller of the *Acushnet* would rise out of the water, spinning wildly before biting into the next wave.

The crew of the cutter was continually monitoring the tow, and they knew they would get no sleep that night, as they battled the elements to pull the *John Paul* to the aptly named Vineyard Haven Harbor. The sea continuously pushed the *Paul* downwind of the cutter, and the *Acushnet* would have to slacken up on the tow in order to reposition herself in relation to the stricken schooner. The icy spray kept visibility to fewer than one hundred feet, but Slatterly knew the sound well and kept his position in the shipping channel.

At approximately 2300 hours, the *Acushnet's* mate, who occasionally brought the searchlight around to the *Paul*, noticed a longboat tied off at the stern of the schooner. This was a common practice of ship captains when they believed their vessel was going

Taking any large vessel under tow is never a small job. It requires careful planning and good timing. In contrast to the sea conditions when the *John Paul* was under tow, the *Sintram* is shown above being pulled off Hawes Shoal near Martha's Vineyard, on November 15, 1921. Although successfully towed free of the shoal, she sank in a collision four days later.

to sink. By tying a small boat off on a tether, a captain assures himself of a floating lifeboat should his ship go down.

On the *John Paul*, Captain Hutchenson and his crew were huddled in the stern and had abandoned all efforts at pumping and chipping ice. The men had fallen, one by one, from exhaustion or frostbite. The level of water in the holds had been rising, even during pumping. With the wisdom gained on the sea for many years, Captain Hutchenson came to the difficult realization that his vessel was sinking, and that all attempts to save her were futile. The strong ship that he and three others before him had proudly commanded for years along the Atlantic seaboard was dying a violent death. She struggled against waves which beat against her huge sides with tremendous force. He was proud of his ship's struggle to stay afloat, but he knew the storm was too powerful and unceasing, and that she would lose. Now his more urgent task was to save the lives of his crew. He ordered Hardy to pull his mattress from the aft cabin, pour kerosene on it and ignite it on the cabin roof, hoping that the flames would show as a final signal to the cutter that they were abandoning ship. He then hauled the lifeboat in against the churning sea and attempted to get his men into it. With difficulty, the crew, taking the unconscious cook, managed to man the lifeboat. Captain Hutchenson jumped aboard last and let the line out to the end, and they swung into line at the end of the tow.

Suddenly aware that he did not know the exact water depth where they were, Captain Hutchenson feared that the line connecting the lifeboat with the doomed *John Paul* might be too short and would pull the lifeboat down if she sank. The cutter probably would not be able to find them in the dark before they froze to death in the wintry sea, so he cut the line. In a sense, he had severed the umbilical, his only connection with his vessel and the life saving crew of the *Acushnet*. However, his decision was timely, for minutes later, the *John Paul* slipped beneath the waves, settling upright on the bottom of the cold Atlantic, still carrying her cargo of granite blocks. Only her masts, which stood slightly above the surface, marked her position now.

The long boat drifted seaward. The wind driven spray and choppy seas filled the boat, despite the disheartened crew's constant attempts to bail with small buckets. They knew that with their present direction and drift, soon they would drift out to sea and never have a chance to be rescued. The temperature was 10 degrees below zero. The icy water surrounded the body of John Thorr lying in the bottom of the lifeboat as he succumbed to the cold. The men used their remaining strength to keep the tiny boat afloat as they continued drifting farther out to sea.

Suddenly the lights and bell of a ship were off the bow of the lifeboat, very close to them. They began to shout and yell with renewed strength. They had miraculously drifted within yards of the *Cross Rip Lightship*, the only ship anchored within 100 square miles, but they were swiftly passing the Lightship and would soon be past, again with little hope of rescue.

Upon hearing the cries of the *John Paul's* crew, the watch aboard the lightship moved quickly to call hands on deck and heave a line to the little life boat. The line landed true and was made fast by the schooner crew.

Aboard the *Acushnet*, Captain Slatterly had the nine hundred foot hawser cut by ax as soon as he realized the *John Paul* was going to sink. He then swung the *Acushnet* around and headed toward the masts and rigging standing above the waves. He had expected to find the lifeboat floating above the wreck, but as the cutter's spotlight played over the area, there was no sign of it. He searched the area downwind of the wreck, with lookouts stationed, but found no boat or bodies. He abandoned the search when the wireless operator informed him of several other ships in distress to the west of their present position.

The crew of the *Acushnet* would work for three more days and nights before they would be able to return to Woods Hole for refueling. At that time, the vessel would be badly iced up and the crew exhausted from lack of sleep.

As the *John Paul's* lifeboat heaved and pitched alongside the Lightship, it was apparent to all that the transfer of these half frozen men would be difficult. Captain E.B. Phillips commanded the Lightship and he handled the rescue expertly. The stricken men were carefully assisted aboard one at a time. His own men risked their lives each time one of the *Paul's* crew was lifted aboard to safety. The transfer took more than half an hour, and when the Lightship's crew went down for the cook's body, Captain Phillips ordered them to leave it in the lifeboat and tie the lifeboat to the stern of the Lightship. The seas whipped furiously as the crew of the Lightship wrapped the freezing sailors in blankets in the coal heated wardroom and gave them hot coffee. By morning the lifeboat had broken free, carrying the body of John Thorr seaward, and was never seen again.

As a last resort, the captain may order his crew into the dory to leave a sinking vessel. This two masted schooner in the Atlantic was abandoned in the same manner as the *John Paul* which was sunk in the January gale of 1914. *Photo courtesy Paul Morris, Nantucket MA*

It was necessary to get some of the sailors to the hospital because of frost bite injuries, and the Lightship's tender, *Anemone*, took them ashore on the following day, where they were admitted and treated at the Mariner's Hospital.

After the storm had passed, Captain Hutchenson said that they all owed their lives to the crew of the *Acushnet*, but that they would surely have been lost, if the watch and crew of the *Cross Rip Lightship* had not acted with the speed and precision they had bestowed on the small band of men who had witnessed the last voyage of the *John Paul*.

Similar stories were repeated during other winter wrecks in this and other storms throughout the northeastern United States, where older ships and their crews were unable to win the battle against a relentless sea.

6   The Keepers Of The Seaways

Over the years, lighthouses have guarded the northeast coast since the first ones were built in the 1700's. Many of these lighthouses have witnessed tragic shipwrecks right at their doorsteps. One of these guardians of the coast, the Monomoy Lighthouse at Cape Cod's elbow, has seen numerous gales and wrecks but the actual loss of some vessels could not be seen until the aftermath of a storm. The loss of the great *Wyoming* was one such occurrence.

THE *WYOMING*

Built by Percy and Small in Bath, Maine, and launched in December of 1909, the *Wyoming* was the largest wooden sailing vessel ever to carry a cargo. Donald McKay's *Great Republic* was larger by 825 tons when built; however, she burned before she could carry a cargo. The *Wyoming* measured 329.5 feet in length, 50.1 feet in beam, and had a draft of 30.4 feet. Her masts were 30 inches in diameter and were 182 feet in length including her top masts. No wooden sailing ship had ever carried a greater load (6,004 tons) at one time. She was deemed the most luxurious six master afloat, having steam heat and even a telephone system on board.

On March tenth, 1924, she left Hampton Roads, Virginia, laden with coal. Captain Charles Gleason had every sail drawing the fresh breeze to start the voyage to the northeast. The *Wyoming* had the company of another big schooner, the *Cora F. Cressey*, which was a five master also built by Percy and Small. She was loaded with coal from Sewall's Point, Virginia, for Searsport, Maine. They were within sight of one another for most of the first day and night. On March eleventh, both vessels encountered headwinds and anchored off Monomoy Point to wait for more favorable winds. The *Wyoming* dropped anchor on a smooth sand bottom about five miles due east of Monomoy and the *Cressey* five miles further east. Late that afternoon the northeast wind began to pick up. Captain C. N.

The five masted *Cora F Cressy* escaped sinking in the storm that took the great *Wyoming*. One of the last big hulls still in existence, the *Cressy* was purchased in the 1930s by Bernard Zahn of Medomunk, Maine. It now rests in the river outside his estate reminding us of a lost era of the sailing vessels that moved commodities throughout the eastern United States. *Photo courtesy William P. Quinn, Orleans MA*

Publicover of the *Cressey* decided to make a run for it, shortened sail, weighed anchor and sailed east into deep water. Days later, she arrived in Boston with shredded sails and leaking, having taken a severe beating from the Nor'easter.

A few miles north of Monomoy Point, the keeper of the Morris Island Station, Captain Tyler, had his watchmen keep an eye on the *Wyoming* as long as the weather was clear. As night set in, Captain Gleason of the *Wyoming* was able to check his position and see that his anchors were not dragging by taking sights on the Monomoy Point Lighthouse. But as the gale increased, the wind drove salt spray high off the water obscuring any view of shore. The keeper of the Monomoy lighthouse lost sight of the big six master in the thickening weather.

The March gale was fierce. The rugged lightship *Pollock Rip*, stationed a few miles from the *Wyoming* anchorage, barely survived being pushed onto the shoals to the lee. Nearby, bell buoy no. 1, although weighted with a 6,500 pound anchor, was dragged into shore during the night.

On the following day, five masts rose out of the water east of

The *Wyoming* was the largest wooden vessel ever to carry a cargo. Donald Mckay's *Great Republic* was larger in tonnage, but she burned before she could load a cargo. The six masted schooners represented the culmination of wooden, freight carrying, sailing vessels. Although their lifespan was short due to hogging and other construction limitations, a few, like the Bath built *Ruth E Merrill*, sunk in 1924, had working lives of over 20 years. *Photo courtesy William P. Quinn, Orleans MA*

the Monomoy Lighthouse. Two were from where the *Wyoming* had been anchored, but three masts were several thousand yards to the leeward. The *Wyoming* was nowhere to be seen. At first no one associated either wreck with the big schooner. Later, it was reported that large pieces of the stern of the *Wyoming* were positively identified as being ashore at Nantucket Island. It was then decided that the *Wyoming* and another unidentified two master schooner had been lost. For more than a week following the gale, due to bad weather, the set of two masts were not identified with the *Wyoming*. Then, after close examination it was realized that both pieces of wreckage were part of the same vessel. She had broken in half during that terrible storm. What happened during that long night will never be known but the wild pitching of the big schooner surely struck fear in the hearts of her crew as they felt her fight to stay together in the stormy seas. All thirteen of the crew perished when she sank.

Some coast men believe that she struck bottom in the trough of a huge wave that fateful night and broke her back suddenly. Others believe that she turned broadside to the sea with the changing tide, waves destroying her cabins and hatch covers, and filled with water. She then would have broken up after sinking.

The masts, visible from the lighthouse, marked the tragic end of the last voyage of one of the great coastal schooners in maritime history. Her cargo of coal has washed up on the shore of Monomoy over the decades. Pieces collected along the shore have fired the stove in the lighthouse keeper's main room. There is little else left of the largest sailing vessel that once carried the greatest load in one voyage.

Lightships have been a part of New England maritime history since the early 1800s. Manning the lightships was necessary, and life aboard these vessels was lonely, at times tedious and very often dangerous. When storms created hazardous sailing and drove most coastal vessels into a safe port, the men aboard the lightships had to weather the blow through, for this was a time when their services were most needed. As ships were caught in storms, they needed the guidance of the lightships to get them safely into port. During severe storms, the men on the lightships would lose sight of land as visibility was cut down by rain or snow and the wind on the waves.

A good example of a storm of this sort was the gale of 1924 just described. During this storm the *Pollock Rip* Lightship, # 73, was stationed off the southeast corner of Cape Cod. She had her storm anchor set against the ferocious wind, but the storm grew to intense fury. The men on board were aware that if the anchor dragged, the wind would blow their vessel into the shoal waters of Pollock Rip and she would pound to pieces. They also knew that no one could survive such a wrecking. The commander of the Lightship had the engines started and put them ahead at full speed while the ship was at anchor. During the storm the men were not sure if this would keep the ship away from the shoals, but as the storm abated they saw that they were still on station. The force of the engines had been just enough to overcome the storm's force and keep the anchor from dragging.

THE HURRICANE OF 1944

The *Pollock Rip* Lightship was built in 1901 and in 1924 she was rather young by lightship standards. After this storm she was taken off station and repaired in the yards at Boston.

The following year, she was renamed the *Vineyard* Lightship and stationed at the southern end of Vineyard Sound where

Buzzards Bay and the new Cape Cod Canal shipping channel began. For many years in that position, she guided passing ships on their courses and kept them away from the treacherous reefs at Cuttyhunk Island.

She remained on station for two decades, removed only for occasional maintenance as required. The men who manned her were Coast Guardsmen well trained in maritime safety procedures.

One of the greatest hazards of Lightship Service was the possibility of being rammed in the fog. An example discussed often among these men was the loss of the Lightship Number 117 named the *South Shoals* Lightship. She was stationed off the Nantucket Shoals in the approach lanes to New York. In order to find their

Lightship duty is lonely by nature. An added danger compounded this loneliness when the Radio Direction Finder (RDF) was developed in the early 1900s and transmitters were placed on lightships. Ships being navigated with RDF followed the beacon towards its source. One foggy morning on May 15, 1934, the *Nantucket* was hit by the White Star liner *Olympic* as it followed the RDF signal. The *Nantucket* sank within minutes, taking 7 of her crew with her. *Drawing by Paul Morris, Nantucket MA*

way when navigating in foggy weather, many mariners were using the newly invented Radio Direction Finders and homing in on the signals transmitted by the lightships.

On May fifteenth, 1934, the huge ocean liner *Olympic* was completing its voyage from European ports when it encountered fog at the approach to New York. The Radio Direction Finder gave a bearing to the lightship and the big liner followed its course.

Aboard the lightship, when fog set in, around the clock watch kept a sharp ear for any vessels. When the watch heard the liner cutting the water, an alarm was shouted for the crew to come out on deck. Simultaneously he rang the big fogbell harder and harder as the *Olympic's* engines grew louder, but the watchmen on the liner did not hear the bell in time. Everything happened so quickly that the whole crew of the lightship did not have a chance to get up on deck. The *Olympic* sliced through the lightship. Water poured through the ripped hull plates and sank her within minutes. Seven men died as Lightship Number 117 sank in 40 fathoms to a cold grave in the foggy Atlantic.

As a result of this tragic accident, the British government donated a special Lightship to the United States Lightship Service. She was double armored and designed to withstand collisions of this sort. She stood as a memorial to the brave men who died on Number 117 for many years at the approach to New York.

This tale was told and retold to any new recruits to the Lightship Service, and helped to keep them on their toes when the watch called all personnel onto the deck.

The year 1944 brought a number of bad fall storms to the northeast coast, but the worst occurred in September. Bad weather was forecast on the radio all day on September thirteenth. The forecast called for hurricane force winds to hit the coast, and as a result many coastal communities were evacuated.

The crew of the *Vineyard* Lightship radioed to Providence, Rhode Island headquarters and asked if they should put into New Bedford during the predicted gale. The response was that they should stay on station in the event that any vessels headed up the coast might need guidance towards safe ports.

The men aboard the Lightship prepared to weather the gale and tied down anything movable. They lengthened scope on her main anchor in anticipation of high seas. They left her spare anchor lashed to the rail as insurance, to be set if needed. The storm roared out of the south on the fourteenth of September. Weather records show that, in the region of the Lightship, the wind speed reached 100 mph. The sea was driven by the wind into a wild fury of foam and froth atop 20 foot high seas. During the storm, visibility dropped to only a few feet. People on shore could only imagine the struggle of those on board the 43 year old Lightship as it fought the seas tugging on its massive anchor chain.

When the storm abated and the visibility improved, the people on shore scanned the horizon but the bright red Lightship was nowhere to be seen. There was hope that she had broken free as so many Lightships did when there were bad storms. On April fourth, 1859, a similar Lightship stationed in the same place drifted out to sea for thirteen days, covering hundreds of miles before she was towed into port. But after the September 1944 gale, signs of wreckage and a few bodies found on the shore of Buzzards Bay confirmed the *Vineyard* Lightship's loss to the sea. All twelve crew members had perished in the storm.

DISCOVERING THE *VINEYARD* LIGHTSHIP

For almost two decades, the loss of the *Vineyard* remained a mystery, but this wreck marked a turning point in underwater archaeology when on September second, 1963, Doctor Harold Edgerton of the Massachusetts Institute of Technology and shipwreck researcher Bradford Luther of Fairhaven, Massachusetts, visited the area of the Lightship in the research vessel *Hilgard*. "Doc," as he is affectionately called, brought a prototype sonar with him in hopes of locating the remains of the *Vineyard* Lightship. This new sonar was designed not to look down at the seabed but rather out away from the path of the search vessel.

Certainly a revolutionary idea, this sonar was not without its skeptics. Doc had a long list of remarkable inventions to his credit including the electronic flash used by every photographer in the world today. Each of his inventions were born of innovative and forward thinking ideas. Even though the new sonar was unlike anything ever used for remote sensing underwater, there were those on board who knew too much about Doc to be skeptical.

Captain Luther had researched the wreck thoroughly, and provided the team with a two square mile search area. He was prepared to dive on any targets Doc's new invention might discover. Luther was anxious to determine exactly how and why she sank.

They began their search where the lightship was last stationed and towed the sonar in a northerly direction. They had hoped to follow the possible path of the Lightship if she had dragged her anchor down-wind that fateful night. They crossed hundreds of yards of flat bottom with no wrecks visible but faith in Doc and his machine did not falter. Luther checked and rechecked his bearings against the research. Suddenly, Doc got a reading of what he felt might be wreckage on the seafloor. Excitement aboard the *Hilgard* was running high as a small buoy was thrown overboard. Doc made several more passes imaging the "anomaly" repeatedly. The captain of the *Hilgard* notified the explorers that they were losing sunlight and the sea conditions were deteriorating. A storm was brewing. As difficult as it was, all on board agreed that they would have to wait for another day to see what Doc's sonar had found.

The wind blew hard for the next few days and when the weather abated, Brad's buoy was gone. Doc returned and after a short time, had the same anomaly located. A second buoy was thrown over as Doc showed the crew the details of the sonar record.

Brad Luther was not waiting for the details and he tugged on his wetsuit ready to identify the mysterious target. The skipper positioned the boat near the buoy and Captain Luther went overboard with a splash. As he swam down the buoy line, the bright daylight faded away melting into darker and darker shades of blue green. He looked at his depth gauge as he passed the 25 foot mark. The current pulled at him as he continued his descent past the 30, 40 and 50 foot marks. Upon passing 60 feet his eyes became accustomed to the eerie gloom and he stopped suddenly on the descent line.

There lying on the flat sandy bottom of Buzzards Bay was a steel shipwreck. He had descended onto the stern of the wreck and could see the huge steering quadrant of the ship below him. As he looked toward the bow, the wreckage faded into the gloom of the depths. This remarkable new invention of Doc Edgerton's had worked beautifully. Brad was ecstatic, but he was more concerned with the question, "Had Doc found the *right* wreck?"

Captain Luther swam over the stern of the growth-covered ship's skeleton, passing by the huge fog bell still in its iron bracket. He could see the remains of a mast stub on deck.

He swam out over the sand off the port side of the wreck and came upon what he was hoping for. There, sitting in the sand, was the top of the six foot diameter mast head light which for so many years had shined its warning to passing sailors to stay away from the nearby reefs. The thick fresnel glass lens was still intact. This was confirmation that the wreck which Doc's sonar had "seen" was indeed the Lightship.

Swimming back to the wreck, Brad made his way to the bow. Over the side he found a chain with very little slack in it emerging from the hawse pipe. It went down to the Lightship's mushroom storm anchor which was resting on the sand near the hull. Suddenly, Brad realized how the Lightship had succumbed to the sea.

This, the second spare anchor, which was originally lashed to the rail, had broken free of its ties during the height of the gale and swung down into the side of the lightship tearing open the steel hull plates. The hole in the hull was large enough for Brad to put his arm through.

The mystery of the lightship was solved. The crewmen probably scrambled to the chain locker to try and stop the sea from flooding into the ship. In the last moments they must have realized that the hole was too big to seal.

In the following weeks Brad and his associates brought the Lightship's bell to the surface and donated it to the Coast Guard. It was set up as a memorial to the brave men who died when the *Vineyard* sank.

Doc's invention was developed further at the instrument firm of Edgerton Germenhausen and Grier. It has been refined over the years into a very sophisticated imaging system that can graph highly accurate "pictures" of the seafloor, detailing features only imagined in the 1960s. It is used by archaeologists, oil companies and research organizations in their daily work at sea. The Lightship, as it turns out, is only one of Doc's numerous shipwreck finds. He continued with the new sonar to discover wreck after wreck in the far corners of the world. He has located wrecks in the Mid East, South America, the Caribbean and many areas in Europe.

The men of the Lightships have kept watch over the shipping channels for over 100 years. Many lives have been saved by them as in the adventure of the crew of the schooner *John Paul* outlined in an earlier chapter.

By mid-twentieth century, as in so many aspects of modern life, machines had become very reliable and replaced men for these dangerous duties. In the late 1970's the last manned lightship in the U.S. was the *Nantucket* in the New York approach channel. As the 1980's arrived it was replaced by a 40 foot Large Navigational Buoy (LNB) which will autonomously broadcast the weather and sea conditions 24 hours per day without a risk of human life even during the worst of hurricanes. Lightship duty has become a thing of the past but the men who manned them will never be forgotten.

Jean Colladon performed an experiment in 1826 to determine the speed of sound in water. *Courtesy Oceanus Magazine*

7   Locating Lost Ships

In the past four decades major technological advances have made the process of locating shipwrecks a far easier process than it has ever been. Historically, there are key specific breakthroughs in the development of these undersea search technologies. In the 1930's, development of the underwater sound projector and receiving hydrophone actually set the stage for major acoustic developments of the 60's and 70's. In the 1950's, developments in radio technologies led the way for the design of very precise navigation systems. During the same period, Dr. Harold Edgerton perfected a reliable still camera system for use in the deep ocean. During World War II, research and development in magnetic sensing opened the way for developing the sophisticated magnetometers that we have today.

Several tools used in searching for shipwrecks are common to all serious search operations, whether they are for a deep water wide search area target like the *Titanic* or a small vessel in much shallower water. These include: navigations systems, magnetic sensing systems, acoustic systems and optical viewing systems.

NAVIGATION SYSTEMS

One of the crucial achievements of any search operation is the ability to navigate. At sea where winds and ocean currents affect a search vessel's path, this ability is even more important. Navigation during ocean search operations is important because success almost always depends upon systematic search and it usually requires that the search vessel cover predetermined, theoretical "track lines", each adjacent but parallel to the last. During the search, if the lines are followed carefully, a search area can be covered effectively. However, if the search vessel strays from this track, that line must be searched again to eliminate the possibilities of gaps or "holes" in the search area. If there are holes in the search area, it cannot be eliminated as not containing the target.

Navigation systems can be very simple and still perform the required function, or they can be very complex and provide extreme accuracy. On the simpler end of the scale, there are numerous methods of navigation using tools that were not originally designed for that purpose; nonetheless, they can be effective. Out of sight of land and without LORAN, GPS or other radio navigation systems for example, a perfectly adequate navigation system can be devised by placing a buoy and radar reflector at the center of the search area. This can be the base center and can be tracked using radar. But some of the more acceptable and commonly used systems include specific tools designed for track line navigation.

Very basic navigation which can be useful in near shore areas are the hand bearing compass and the sextant. Many underwater sites have been successfully located using these simple tools, and they should not be underestimated. Years ago the author and colleagues located many wrecks several miles offshore using only a hand bearing compass as a navigational tool.

A more accurate system is a LORAN (LOng RAnge Navigation) receiver which receives the transmissions of land based, government operated, radio beacons. LORAN C receivers can position the search vessel with a repeatability of about 75 meters on the surface of the ocean.

The transmitted signals that the LORAN receives originate from a "master" and several "slave" stations known as a LORAN chain. The time difference (TD) between the received signals is measured by the LORAN receiver and displayed in microseconds. Most LORAN receivers also compute latitude and longitude from the measured TDs but only the highest quality receivers provide acceptable accuracy and update rates in this calculation. As a result, survey navigation using LORAN is generally performed based on TDs rather than latitude-longitude calculations.

LORAN has a range of close to one thousand miles from the land based beacons. Outside this region of coverage, surveyors must rely on underwater acoustic networks, moored buoy marked positions or satellite based navigation systems. Acoustic nets are very expensive and best used in deep water. Often moored buoys provide the best navigation but are easiest to deploy in shallow waters. Satellite systems will become employed more often for surveys outside of LORAN range as more satellites are deployed.

Instead of using land based transmitters, satellite navigation systems use signals transmitted from orbiting satellites to determine position. Since the system is 'line of sight" and the signals do not travel over large land masses, the accuracy of these systems is very good. There are two types of satellite navigation systems that can be used for shipwreck search in deep water out of LORAN range.

The transit satellite system has been in use since the early 1960's. It receives the transmitted signals from 5 satellites in polar orbit at an altitude of about 600 miles. The orbits allow the transit satellites to cover the entire globe but the low altitude provides a very narrow area of coverage on each pass. This system relies on the Doppler shift of the received signal as the satellites rise above, and fall below, the horizon. The system can provide an accurate fix when the satellite is between 15° and 75° above the horizon. Although the receiver will acquire a fix about every ninety minutes, not all of the fixes are usable. To make up for this long delay in position updates most receivers can also use heading, speed and drift data to calculate a dead reckoning plot. As a result of the low update rates this type of navigation is used only as a last resort in shipwreck search.

The Global Positioning System (GPS) is currently being developed to solve most of the existing problems experienced with the transit system. GPS is planned to have far greater coverage and better accuracy when it is fully deployed. The system will have a total of eighteen satellites in orbit at an altitude of 10,000 miles. There will be at least four different satellites available to any receiver at every location on earth at all times. The GPS system works in a manner similar to LORAN C. The satellites all transmit a coded signal containing the satellites position and time. The GPS receiver interprets the signals from four satellites and calculates the ships position based on the time of signal arrival and the satellite's positions. For non-military applications, undifferentiated GPS will be accurate to about 30 meters. Because the GPS coverage will be continuous, there will be no need to generate a dead reckoning plot. However at the present time not all satellites have been deployed and coverage is not complete. The system is not expected to be fully operational until the mid 1990's.

When using a wide swath search system such as a side scan or multibeam sonars, LORAN or GPS can be sufficient navigation tools. However, when using a narrow search tool such as the echosounder, magnetometer or remotely operated vehicle, an HF, microwave or laser positioning system is preferred. These navigation systems are far more accurate than LORAN or satellite navigators but have limited ranges. A further limitation to the laser system is that its performance is impacted by atmospheric conditions and their range is drastically reduced in limited visibility. These high accuracy, shorter range systems usually rely on local stations set up near the search site. Navigation with these systems is typically based upon signal travel time between stations mounted on the survey vessel and the shore stations. By this method, the systems can provide very accurate navigational fixes of less than a meter. After the survey, the stations are usually dismantled. These shore stations must be precisely positioned or "surveyed in" and their exact locations recorded. Any resulting navigational readouts from the search are based on ranges from these stations. Recording the location of these shore stations is extremely important.

IMAGING SONARS

Oceanographers, marine geologists and archaeologists depend heavily on sound energy to transform the things we cannot see underwater into numbers, graphs and pictures that provide us with an approximation of what exists. The instruments that transmit and receive these sound pulses have become sophisticated and very accurate since their early stages of development. Almost all of these systems rely on an accurate prediction of the speed of sound underwater.

In September, 1826 early sound speed measurements were made by Daniel Colladon in lake Geneva (see illustration). He started a stop watch when he saw the flash from the second boat (about 16 kilometers away) and stopped it when he heard the signal of the bell (the striking of the bell generated the flash) about ten seconds later through the long trumpet. This method was crude but effective. The results were within one tenth of one percent of today's accepted values of the speed of underwater sound.

In the early 1930's specialized ceramics were developed that greatly aided the technique of transmitting and receiving sound underwater. These ceramics eventually became the main components of today's "transducers" and, coupled with electronics and a chart recorder they resulted in the present day depth sounder. This instrument is useful in locating shipwrecks and other objects that protrude from the seafloor. The depth sounder aims an acoustic pulse directly down to the seabed from the surface vessel. When this pulse strikes the seabed, sound waves are reflected back to the vessel. When the reflected sound is received by the transducer, it is converted to an electronic signal. This signal is traced on a chart recorder. The chart recorder contains circuitry to time the

Acoustic imaging is one of the most effective methods of remotely imaging the seafloor in search of shipwreck remains. In the illustration above, the survey vessel tows a side scan sonar which images wide swaths of the seabottom as it is towed over the search area. The sonar outputs carefully formed beams of sound which reflect off the ocean bottom and return to the towed transducer assembly. These signals are sent up the towcable to the shipboard recorder, processed and displayed. The resulting records are remarkably accurate pictures of the seafloor and any targets laying on it. Simultaneously, the survey vessel uses a vertical sounder to inspect the bottom for protrusions or inclines that may rise up in front of the towfish. *Illustration courtesy EG&G Inc.*

difference between the outgoing and incoming pulses. This process is repeated many times per minute and the charted line is an accurate trace of the topography of the seabed. The topography, or bathymetry as it is properly known, is changed by shipwrecks and other objects that rise above the bottom. These objects can be imaged by the depth sounder as the surface vessel passes directly over them.

One of the primary limitations of the depth sounder as a search instrument is that it senses only those objects that are directly below the vessel. Unless care is taken during a depth sounder survey, it is possible to miss a large target. For example, if the target wreck is 10 meters in width and the search track lines are 12 meters apart, unbeknownst to the researcher, the surface vessel could pass along a track parallel to the wreck to one side of the wreck and on the next parallel track, to the other. As a result of this possibility, the researcher using a depth sounder as a search tool must keep his track lines very close together. This, of course will drastically increase the time to search any given area. Nevertheless, the depth sounder is a valuable tool for imaging the seabed and was the forerunner of the more sophisticated sub bottom profiler and side scan sonar, which are crucial tools for shipwreck search.

Since the invention of the depth sounder, sonar systems have made great strides in imaging the sea bottom, objects resting on it and objects buried beneath it. Two of the most advanced systems in underwater sonar imaging are the side scan sonar and the sub bottom profiler. The first of these to be developed was the sub bottom profiler.

As is true in imaging with most reflected wave energy, lower frequencies will usually result in greater transmission range at the expense of lower resolution in the resulting information. This is also true with acoustic subsea imaging systems. The sub bottom profiler was designed as an extension of depth sounder technology, but it uses lower frequencies. These low frequency acoustic pulses will penetrate the seafloor and send back reflections from objects such as buried shipwrecks. This technique has been used for several decades to locate buried cultural sites and shipwrecks around the world. "Doc" Harold Edgerton has done successful searches with his profilers in the Caribbean, Mediterranean and the Pacific ocean since he first designed a sub bottom profiler in the 1950's.

A major limitation to the sub bottom, however, is the same as the depth sounder: it propagates acoustic energy in a cone that is directed straight down from the surface vessel and surveys can

ABOVE: The Steamer *Yankee* was built in 1892. She had a sixteen-year career, including service as a cruiser in the Spanish-American War. In 1908 she struck Spindle Rock off Westport, and filled. Salvage attempts managed to tow the stricken vessel only a few miles to the mouth of New Bedford Harbor, Massachusetts. She settled there resisting further salvage attempts. Since she sank directly in the path of shipping traffic, the Government dynamited the wreck extensively. *Photo courtesy William P. Quinn, Orleans, MA* **BELOW**: The remains of the steamer *Yankee* as she existed in the early 1980's was a 200 foot by 75 foot mass of tangled iron. This sonar record shows the extent of the wreck as it lies in 50 feet of water in Buzzards Bay, Massachusetts. Although visibility is often limited on the wreck, the *Yankee* is a popular dive site. *Sonar record courtesy American Underwater Search and Survey*

require many successive passes in a relatively small area. In 1963, Doc Edgerton performed a remarkable experiment with his newly designed "Sub Bottom Profiler" in a small bay in Massachusetts. In a search for a shipwreck, he turned the profiling transducer, or sensor, on its side, so that it transmitted and received its acoustic beam 90 degrees out to the side of the surface vessel's path. As a result, the vessel traveled along a specific track line, and the acoustic beam was projected at a right angle to the track. This provided information from the seabed many meters away from the vessel. This experiment provided the groundwork for the development of the side scan sonar, which has revolutionized seabed imaging. The side scan has been useful to shipwreck search techniques and seabed imaging worldwide.

In the following decades, the method of acoustically imaging to the side of a vessel's path became remarkably refined. Beam pattern adjustment, along with carefully engineered chart writing techniques and sound frequency experimentation, has resulted in systems that almost photographically image the seabed hundreds of meters out from a search vessel's path. This means, in effect, that in a search for a large shipwreck, a researcher can carefully cover an area of seabed 3/5's of a mile wide with one pass of the surface vessel.

Since Doc's first experiment in side looking imaging, the side scan sonar has become a versatile tool for archaeologists, treasure hunters, salvagers, military organizations, and search and rescue groups. As well, it has demonstrated its ability to locate important shipwrecks. Recent successes include the *H.M.S. Breadalbane* , on the bottom in the high Arctic for 130 years, the Vanderbilt yacht, *Alva*, which sank in a collision off New England in 1891, the *H.M.S. Edinburgh*, lost during World War II with five tons of gold aboard, and the famous liner *Titanic* sunk in over 12,000 feet of ocean water.

In basic principle, the modern side scan sonar utilizes a series of very short, high frequency, acoustic pulses beamed across the seabed. The pulses are reflected from the sea floor and from objects on it to produce an image on a chart recorder that today approaches aerial photography in coverage and sharpness of detail. While one hard copy of these images is being made in real time, all of the data can be simultaneously recorded on magnetic or optical storage media, allowing reexamination and special image processing at a later time.

Three components make up the basic side scan sonar system commonly used for shipwreck search. The recording unit which produces the graphic records, typically contains tuning controls as well as the printing mechanism and paper. The component containing the transducers and signal conditioning circuitry is called a "towfish." Towing, instead of hull mounting, the transducer array has a number of advantages other than keeping the system portable. It also puts the transducer array near the bottom where a higher resolution image is obtained and decouples the array from the ships motion providing a stable imaging point for the final record of the sea bottom. A lightweight electromechanical cable for shallow operations, or an armored one for deeper towing, connects the towfish to the recorder. The side scan sonar system is portable enough to be quickly mobilized from vessels of almost any size.

The side scan is available in different frequencies, each for use in different applications. Lower frequencies such as 25, 27 or 50 kHz will propagate further underwater, covering a larger area. However, due to the longer wavelengths, they provide a lower resolution image. As a result, although they can provide a swath of 3 kilometers or more in width, these lower frequencies are only used to image large targets. In contrast, the higher frequency systems available include a 400 kHz sonar that can resolve objects just a few inches in size. These high resolution systems can only cover an area of a few hundred meters in width and so are usually used to search for heavily deteriorated shipwreck sites where maximum resolution is required.

MAGNETIC SEARCH EQUIPMENT

Another valuable tool used for shipwreck search is the proton precession magnetometer. There are several different types of instruments that will sense ferrous and non-ferrous metals underwater, but the proton precession magnetometer is one of the more useful tools for shipwreck search.

The earth's magnetic field is present at all points around the globe. It has a specific strength and polarity in any given area. Different places have different field strengths but typically these values do not change over short distances unless there is a concentration of iron or other ferrous metals in one location. In principle, the marine search proton precession magnetometer senses the strength of the earth's field as it is towed with the sensor near the seabed. This data is sent up the tow cable, to the deck unit. The circuitry in the deck unit then amplifies this information and provides a readout to the operator in units of total field strength.

ABOVE: On June 28, 1942, the freighter *Steven R. Jones* was carrying a cargo of seven thousand tons of coal from Norfolk, Virginia to Boston, Massachusetts. As she cruised through the Cape Cod Canal, she struck rocks and sank, completely blocking the passage. BELOW: Since the canal was crucial to the northeast's coastal traffic during the war, the *Jones* had to be removed expediently. It took 28 days and seventeen tons of explosives to flatten the wreck to the floor of the canal. *Photos courtesy William P. Quinn, Orleans, MA*

Each pulsing and subsequent readout is performed at the rate of about 30-60 times per minute. If the data is simultaneously plotted on a graph, a trace can easily be followed by the operator.

The earth's magnetic field is locally changed by any ferrous object. The amount of change is proportional to the amount of ferrous iron and the size of the object. Towing the magnetometer sensor over a large ferrous object will drastically change the sensor readings. This change is typically expressed in units called Gammas.

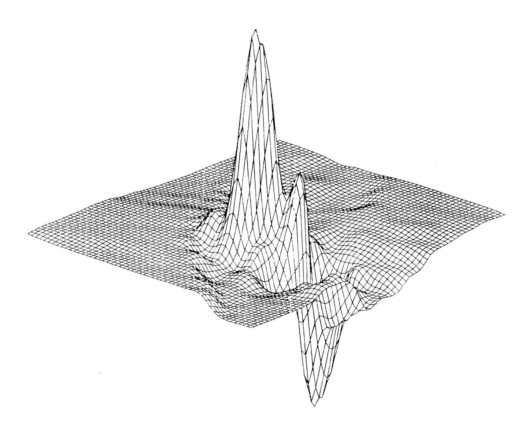

After the Army Corps of Engineers dynamited the wreck of the *Steven R. Jones* in the Cape Cod Canal in the summer of 1942, coastal shipping was able to pass through and avoid U-Boats lurking off the coast. The floor of the canal is extremely rugged preventing simple sonar detection. To locate the central portion of the wreckage, a magnetometer was the search tool of choice. On successive survey runs, magnetic data was logged directly to computer. Later data processing resulted in an isometric projection shown above, outlining the extent of the wreck of the *Jones*. *Data courtesy American Underwater Search and Survey, Ltd.*

The magnetometer is most frequently used for locating buried or heavily deteriorated sites that would not be detected by an active search tool such as sonar. The magnetometer also provides a sizably wider search swath than a sub bottom profiler, and can often detect objects buried too deeply for the sub bottom profiler to image. However, one of the drawbacks of the magnetometer is that the field deviation induced by ferrous objects lessens with the inverse square, and sometimes the inverse cube, of the distance between the sensor and the object. If a 5000 pound anchor provided a field deviation of several hundred gamma at 5 meters from the sensor, the same anchor might only provide a 20 or 30 gamma deviation 15 meters from the sensor. This can present a problem greater than simply limiting the magnetometer's range. For example, a group of 5 cannon, each weighing 1800 pounds, buried 8 meters into the seabed, might provide the exact same reading as a steel oil drum weighing 75 pounds buried just under the surface. As a result, with only a magnetometer used for shipwreck search, positive target identification becomes extremely difficult without uncovering all the targets encountered.

REMOTELY OPERATED VEHICLES

Once a target is located, it needs to be evaluated and identified if possible. The depths of most near-shore wrecks are shallow enough to survey using simple SCUBA or surface supplied diving equipment, but many wrecks are in water too deep for these simple diving methods. In the past, in order to survey a wreck in water deeper than 75 meters, expensive mixed gas diving equipment or costly manned submersibles were required to spend sufficient time on the bottom to gather the required data. In the early 1980's, however, small, inexpensive remotely operated submarines were designed. These subs, called Remotely Operated Vehicles (ROVs) are able to transmit high resolution color television pictures from depths of 300 meters, over its tether cable, to the surface ship where the surveyor can sit comfortably and pilot the sub using a television monitor.

These ROVs are very valuable for classifying targets that are either too deep for conventional diving or may have dangerous cargoes on board. Although the small ROVs do not have the capability for heavy work or maneuvering in high currents, they often can give the search team the information needed for further work on the site.

ABOVE: On the clear night of February 11, 1907, the steamer *Larchmont*, shown above, collided with the schooner *Harry P. Knowlton*. The *Larchmont* sank rapidly with the loss of over 350 lives. *Photo courtesy William P. Quinn, Orleans MA.* **BELOW**: This side scan record of the steamer shows one stack on a boiler is still standing and the filigree pattern covering her port paddle wheel can be seen in the sonars acoustic shadow. *Data courtesy EG&G Washington Analytical Service Center.*

The ROVs are valuable tools for underwater site inspection even though they are constrained by the cables that connect them to the surface ship. Multi-conductor cables allow the transmission of power and control to the ROV while carrying the returning system status and television images back to the operator. By using a complex, or "smart", tether, the ROV remains reasonably simple in design and function. This allows for a low cost and easily maintainable vehicle. More expensive and more capable vehicles used for shipwreck survey have a single conductor, "dumb" tether, which is usually very low profile and thus presents a small cross section to the water column. This can be a considerable advantage in inspecting shipwrecks in high current environments. These designs however require a smarter vehicle which is often more difficult to maintain and repair. Although more expensive, the UUV (unmanned, untethered vehicle) have the ultimate freedom of no tether at all. These vehicles are valuable for traveling long distances from the mother ship. They can also dive to shipwreck sites through a variety of bottom obstructions without the risk of tether hangup. The UUV is typically battery powered and either preprogrammed, acoustically controlled or a combination of the two for each individual mission.

In almost any serious shipwreck search most of these technologies play a key role. The search for the *Titanic* is an example of an undersea search effort that utilized high technology equipment to locate a difficult target. The search and its success is clear evidence of the progress that has been made in underwater search technologies.

DEEP WATER

The complexity of underwater search and identification operations increases dramatically with increases in water depth. While small vessels and lightweight equipment can be mobilized easily for continental shelf depth searches, large vessels and heavy underwater equipment must be used in deep water operations. In terms of expense and technology, the differences between shallow and deep water operations can be compared to those between a transatlantic jetliner flight and a space shuttle mission. One of the major difficulties encountered in deep search operations concerns controlling the towfish which carries sonar or imaging systems. To reach the ocean floor in five thousand meter depths, the ship may require over ten or fifteen thousand meters of tow cable due to the catanary induced in the cable by towing. These long lengths of cable often prevent real-time control of the instruments at the bottom. If the surface ship turns around to proceed in the opposite direction, it may take several hours before the towfish responds to the directional change. Although recent developments in fiber optic technology and more sophisticated electronics are giving better control of these underwater search systems, deep water operations still require skilled personnel and very sophisticated instrumentation. Recently, combinations of towed vehicles with ROVs attached have been successfully used on search operations, giving the survey team the ability to record very high resolution images of deep water sites.

Plans to locate the *Titanic* began almost ten years before she was found in 1985. During the early 1970's in Woods Hole, Massachusetts, a group headed by Dr. Robert Ballard began to put together the evidence surrounding the sinking, and surmised that she could be located and surveyed. Working with National Geographic Magazine, Ballard and Geographic Staff Photographer Emory Kristoff set up a plan for the search. They began to test the most sophisticated ocean floor survey equipment that had been designed to date. They surveyed shallower areas of the northwestern Atlantic to see if the surface vessel, the navigation systems and the search sensors could be integrated into a deep water search program.

During one test, with a major portion of the search equipment towed near the seafloor, heavy seas caused the towing assembly to snap and the search equipment fell to the seafloor in over one thousand meters of ocean water. Much of this equipment was made up of prototype designs and could not be easily and quickly replaced. The cost of the equipment was high, but the cost to recover it by submarine was even higher. It remains on the deep ocean seafloor to this day.

After this accident, the team realized that technology had not yet come of age for the deep water search for the *Titanic* but this did not sway the explorers. They quietly went back to the drawing board with the ultimate patience of men with a purpose.

The original search package had included acoustic positioning, television and still cameras along with a search sonar for locating targets. During the later 1970's the scientists knew that even if they had found the *Titanic* they might well have lost their underwater sensors. The sensor package had contained television and still cameras, and they would have had to get so close to their underwater targets that the cameras could possibly have snagged on any obstruction. Usable visibility ranges, even with the most powerful light, were only 5 to 10 meters in the deep ocean. There would be a high risk to the system when photographing any target with the camera suspended at the end of thousands of feet of tow wire. Ballard knew of such accidents. In 1975, inventor Dr. Harold Edgerton, in his enthusiasm to get sharp close up pictures of the wreck of the *Monitor*, lost his camera system. The cameras snagged on the wreck and Doc was unable to recover them for almost two years. The *Monitor*, sunk in the 1860's was lying in only 240 feet of water compared to the abyssal depth of the *Titanic*.

Ballard and Kristoff knew that they had to design a better imaging system, one that could be towed high up off the seabed to be sure that it would not hang into the wreck when and if it was located.

The first plans had been laid for the search in 1975, and over the next eight years the team tested and integrated a multitude of television and still camera systems. Slowly, technology advanced and with help from Ballard and Kristoff, systems were tested, redesigned and retested. By 1984 the team was getting usable television images from an incredible 30 to 40 meters off the seabed. These high altitude search systems would be able to "fly" high enough so that they were not susceptible to getting snagged in seafloor debris or shipwrecks.

Concurrent to their testing period, the two men were also watching the progress of underwater designers who were coming up with further remarkable advances. One of these advances was the design of small, fast unmanned submarines equipped with a television camera and three thrusters or motors to maneuver it in small places. These vehicles, called remotely operated vehicles or "ROVs" were not a new idea, but existing designs were limited in their abilities and very expensive. And most of the existing designs were quite large and designed for major subsea tasks such as trans-atlantic cable burial or repair work on offshore oil rigs.

Ballard realized that it would be this type of system, a remote machine, that would explore the inside of the *Titanic* when she was found. First she had to be located.

Ballard had a long standing relationship with a French research organization, and it was decided that they would perform the search as a team. During the summer of 1985, the multinational team set out to explore the deep near the last reports of the great liner.

Both teams had their most sophisticated side scan sonar systems and magnetometers. They both utilized navigational positioning satellites that whirled overhead beaming information that was valuable for positioning the search vessels in the proper areas. The French were first on the site, and after they eliminated a large portion of the search area, Ballard's team continued the survey. Ballard's high altitude imaging systems were working perfectly, transmitting television from the cameras just off the seafloor over thousands of meters of cable to the monitors on board the search vessel. After many hours of laborious search, without warning, the image of a huge boiler came into view on the television screen.

Since the team had done their research by studying all of the aspects of the ship and her construction, they immediately knew that this was one of the *Titanic's* boilers. Further search work in the area proved successful as they followed the telltale field of various bits and pieces of the huge ship. Finally, they came upon the hulk herself.

In the following year Ballard prepared an ROV of his own design. Working with a staff of experts, he designed this ROV to be operated out of a deep diving submersible. The reason was that at these great depths a submersible pilot will not risk the life of the crew in physically tight spaces. If the manned submersible were to get snagged herself in four thousand meters of water, only a few sister subs exist in the world that could be mobilized for the rescue. However, if the remote sub could be carried piggyback to the wreck site and then deployed, it could squeeze in all the tight spots without risking the manned sub's crew.

Dubbed Jason Jr., the little robot was similar to the other recent designs except for one crucial difference: it could go far deeper and withstand the crushing pressures of the ocean that surround the *Titanic's* hull. None of the other ROVs designed so far could fit this requirement and still maneuver into the tight spots that might be found on the *Titanic*.

In August of 1986 the team again went out and dived with the deep submergence manned submarine ALVIN. Jason Jr. was carried in a cradle on the front of ALVIN, and sent back pictures to the men in the ALVIN, detailing the condition of the ship after 74 years on the sea bottom.

In a series of nerve wracking but carefully calculated operations, the pilot settled softly to the deck of the rusted wreck and adjusted her ballasting to make the submarine about 65 Kg heavy. The ALVIN is usually perfectly neutral when she cruises just above the seafloor. The pilot and crew then sat back and waited. Thoughts rambled through their minds of the emergency procedures that would have to be undertaken if the *Titanic's* deck suddenly gave way and the ALVIN became trapped, wedged in the steel jaws of a hole in the old decking. They waited for several minutes, listening and feeling if the deck showed any signs of collapsing. Then the ALVIN pilot gave the go-ahead to Martin Bowen, the passenger in the ALVIN whose task was to pilot Jason Jr. Martin fired up the

ROV from within the ALVIN, and sent her off on her reconnaissance missions to tour the liner, her staterooms and ballrooms.

The television pictures that were sent back from the ROV were remarkably clear as it maneuvered inside the shipwreck. The resulting film footage was published in National Geographic Magazine and made into a television special. This search and survey expedition was truly a milestone in the technology of wreck location, in that it showed that great depths and large search areas were no longer a limitation for search programs.

With technology in undersea exploration increasing at a faster rate every decade, major obstacles to locating and mapping shipwrecks are disappearing. As shown with the location and photo imaging of the *Titanic*, we are approaching an era when we will be able to explore virtually any shipwreck regardless of depth or expanse of search area. Someday, the remains of the *Royal Tar,* more of the Penobscot Fleet, and vessels like the *Wyoming* may be found so that generations to follow will be able to learn much more about earth's maritime history than we or our forebears were able to do.

Appendices

APPENDIX A
REGIONAL NEWSPAPER RESEARCH SOURCES

Newspapers are one of the most readily available sources of shipwreck information available to the maritime historian. Although, in the rush to get the news into print, many newspapers printed erroneous information in the first reports of a maritime accident, these errors were often corrected in follow up stories. Newspapers that carried maritime news and their dates of publication to 1956 are listed in the following appendix. If the publication was sporadic, a year of last publication is not given.

Portland, ME	Gazette	1798-1824
Portland, ME	Eastern Argus	1803-1921
Portland, ME	Advertiser	1831-1909
Portland, ME	Transcript	1837-1910
Portland, ME	Press Herald	1862-1956
Portland, ME	Express	1882-1956
Rockland, ME	Courier Gazette	1846-1956
Rockland, ME	Tribune	1855-1897
Portsmouth, NH	New Hampshire Gazette	1756-Spor.
Boston, MA	News Letter	1704-1776
Boston, MA	Gazette	1719-1798
Boston, MA	Evening Post	1735-1775
Boston, MA	Advertiser	1768-1876
Boston, MA	Columbian Centinel	1790-Spor.
Boston, MA	Commercial Gazette	1795-1840
Boston, MA	Daily Advertiser	1813-Spor.
Boston, MA	Commercial & Shipping Lst	1843-1886
Boston, MA	Herald	1846-1956
Boston, MA	Globe	1872-1956
Newport, RI	Mercury	1758-1956
Newport, RI	Daily News	1846-1956
Newport, RI	Advertiser	1850-1864
Newport, RI	Evening Bulletin	1863-1956
Newport, RI	Journal	1867-1928
Providence, RI	Gazette	1762-1825
Providence, RI	Patriot	1802-1834

Providence, RI	American	1808-1833
Providence, RI	Republican Herald	1828-1873
Providence, RI	Journal	1829-1956
Providence, RI	Evening Press	1859-1884
Providence, RI	News	1891-1906
Providence, RI	News Tribune	1891-1956
Bridgeport, CT	Standard	1854-1918
Bridgeport, CT	Post	1883-1956
Bridgeport, CT	Herald	1890-1956
Hartford, CT	Connecticut Courant	1764-1914
Hartford, CT	American Mercury	1784-1833
Hartford, CT	Hartford Courant	1837-1956
Hartford, CT	Evening Post	1858-1920
New Haven, CT	Connecticut Journal	1767-1835
New Haven, CT	Columbian Register	1812-1911
New London, CT	Connecticut Gazette	1763-1844
New London, CT	Day	1881-1956
New York, NY	Gazette	1725-1744
New York, NY	Mercury	1752-1768
New York, NY	Daily Gazette	1788-1795
New York, NY	Globe and Commercial	1797-1923
New York, NY	Commercial	1815-1926
New York, NY	Journal Of Commerce	1827-1892
New York, NY	Herald	1835-1924
New York, NY	Tribune	1841-1906
New York, NY	Herald Tribune	1841-1956
New York, NY	Times	1851-1956
New York, NY	Evening Mail	1867-1924
New York, NY	Maritime Register	1869-1956
New York, NY	Press	1887-1916
New York, NY	Evening Journal	1896-1956

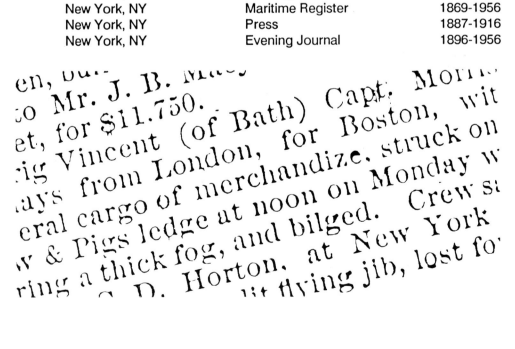

APPENDIX B
NORTHEASTERN LIFE SAVING STATIONS

There were 12 life saving districts in the early part of the service. These 12 districts incorporated most of the US seaboard and the Great Lakes. Within these twelve districts there were 243 stations by 1893. They were all manned by men whose tasks were to save the lives of wrecked sailors and prevent the loss of property and lives if humanly possible. The northeastern seaboard was included in the jurisdiction of Districts One, Two and Three and, by 1893, contained 75 Life Saving Stations.

These stations, while fully manned during the winter months, were out of commission from springtime until September 1 each year and occupied only by the keeper. During the other months though they held a contingent of men and equipment to meet most any disaster. During the first few months of the winter season the stations would be manned by a basic crew and two more lifesavers would be added in November as the severity of the northern winters began to threaten coastwise shipping.

During the time periods when there were no shipwrecks and the weather was clear, the life savers would complete detailed records concerning the most recent shipwrecks within their jurisdiction. Needless to say most of these records were very accurate and can be used to this day to relocate wrecks that have long since disappeared beneath Atlantic waters. However, in order to determine where these wrecks lie, since their location is frequently given in relation to a station, the locus of these stations must be determined. Although these locations changed from time to time, each year's Life Saving Report provides that data.

The shore line has changed also over the past decades but the location names given for these Life Saving Stations below are the locations as they are now known rather than the names which they had in the past. At various times over the duration of the Service, there were more stations than these in the northeast and some of the ones listed were not used at various times. But in general, these life saving stations provided fairly complete coverage of all parts of the region. They and their crews were very effective in protecting shipping and those whose lives were at stake on a shipwreck.

NAME OF STATION	LOCALITY	POSITION
Quoddy Head	Carrying Pt Cove ME	44 48 40 x 66 58 50
Cross Island	Machaisport ME	44 36 00 x 67 17 00
Crumple Island	Jonesport ME	44 26 40 x 67 35 50
Cranberry Isles	Little Cranberry Isl. ME	44 15 20 x 68 12 50
White Head	White Head Island ME	43 58 40 x 69 07 50
Hunniwells Beach	Kennebeck River ME	43 44 40 x 69 46 50
Fletchers Neck	Biddeford Pool ME	43 26 30 x 70 20 30
Rye Beach	Rye NH	42 59 30 x 70 45 20
Plum Island	Newburyport MA	42 48 30 x 70 49 00
Davis Neck	Annisquam MA	42 40 10 x 70 40 20
Fourth Cliff	Scituate MA	42 09 30 x 70 42 10
Gurnet	Duxbury MA	42 00 10 x 70 36 10
Manomet Point	Manomet MA	41 55 30 x 70 32 40
Race Point	Provincetown MA	42 04 10 x 70 14 20
Peaked Hill Bar	Provincetown MA	42 04 30 x 70 09 10
High Head	Provincetown MA	42 03 40 x 70 06 30
Highland	Truro MA	42 02 50 x 70 04 20
Pamet River	Truro MA	42 00 00 x 70 01 10
Cahoons Hollow	Wellfleet MA	41 56 40 x 70 00 00
Nausett	Eastham MA	41 50 30 x 69 56 40
Orleans	Orleans MA	41 45 30 x 69 56 00
Chatham	Chatham MA	41 43 10 x 69 55 40
Monomoy	Monomoy Island MA	41 36 00 x 69 59 50
Coskata	Great Pt. Nantucket MA	41 22 00 x 70 01 20
Surfside	Southern Nantucket MA	41 14 30 x 70 05 00
Muskeget	Muskeget Island MA	41 20 10 x 70 19 20
Narragansett Pier	Narragansett RI	41 26 00 x 71 27 20
Point Judith	Point Judith RI	41 21 40 x 71 29 00
Watch Hill	Watch Hill RI	41 18 20 x 71 51 30
New Shoreham	Eastern Block Island RI	41 10 20 x 71 33 30
Block Island	Western Block Island RI	41 09 40 x 71 36 40
Eatons Neck	Eatons Neck NY	40 57 10 x 73 24 00
Montauk Point	Montauk NY	41 04 00 x 71 51 30
Ditch Plain	Southern Montauk NY	41 02 10 x 71 54 30
Hither Plain	Southern Montauk NY	41 01 30 x 71 57 50
Napeague	Nepeague Harbor NY	40 59 45 x 72 02 40
Amagansett	Amagansett NY	40 58 00 x 72 08 20
Georgica	East Hampton NY	40 56 40 x 72 11 40
Mecox	Bridgehampton NY	40 54 10 x 72 18 00
Southampton	Southampton NY	40 52 10 x 72 23 40
Shinnecock	Shinnecock Bay NY	40 50 40 x 72 27 50
Tiana	Tiana Beach NY	40 49 40 x 72 31 30
Quogue	Quogue NY	40 48 20 x 72 36 00
Petunk	Petunk NY	40 47 30 x 72 39 00
Moriches	Westhampton Beach NY	40 46 30 x 72 43 10

NAME OF STATION	LOCALITY	POSITION
Forge River	Fire Island NY	40 44 30 x 72 49 00
Smiths Point	Great South Beach NY	40 44 00 x 72 52 20
Bellport	Great South Beach NY	40 42 40 x 72 55 50
Blue Point	Great South Beach NY	40 40 40 x 73 01 20
Lone Hill	Fire Island NY	40 39 40 x 73 04 20
Point Of Woods	Ocean Beach NY	40 38 50 x 73 08 10
Fire Island	Fire Island Inlet NY	40 37 40 x 73 13 20
Oak Island	Eastern Oak Island NY	40 38 10 x 73 17 40
Gilgo	Western Oak Island NY	40 37 20 x 73 22 20
Jones Beach	Tobay Beach	40 36 40 x 73 26 20
Zachs Inlet	Tobay Beach NY	40 36 10 x 73 28 50
Short Beach	Jones Beach NY	40 35 30 x 73 31 20
Point Lookout	Point Lookout NY	40 35 10 x 73 35 40
Long Beach	Long Beach NY	40 34 40 x 73 39 00
Far Rockaway	Averne NY	40 35 30 x 73 44 00
Rockaway	Rockaway NY	40 35 30 x 73 47 20
Rockaway Point	Rockaway Point NY	40 34 10 x 73 51 50
Coney Island	Manhatten Beach NY	40 34 20 x 73 56 20

APPENDIX C
GRAPHS OF NORTHEASTERN SHIPWRECKS

Analysis of shipwreck incidents over an area as large as the northeastern United States can provide the researcher with insight into relationships between shipwrecks. By working with a chronology of shipwreck incidents, battles, storms and congested seaways can be clearly defined. One can also examine the trends of our maritime history and gain an understanding of the health of the industry through this type of chronology. The three graphs on the following pages exhibit some interesting trends.

Graph A depicts shipwreck incidents over the entire northeast region from 1606 to 1956. More wrecks than average for their period occurred a number of times. The storm of 1635, in which the *Angel Gabriel* was lost, is evident during the early years. During the 1700's, the more notable years for ship losses were during the revolutionary period centered around 1778 and 1779. As shipping became more common in the region during the early part of the 1800's, the notable periods include The War Of 1812 and the Triple Hurricanes of 1839.

By far the largest number of shipwrecks in the region occurred during the year 1898. A factor which contributed to this is the large number of vessels that sailed in the northeast at the time but it is significant that over 70% of these ships sank on one day, November 27th. This is the date of the great "Portland Gale" and the ships that sank include the famous steamer *Portland*. Graph B demonstrates the percentage of wrecks during the year 1898, by month.

In graph A it can be seen that 1907 was another year that had numerous shipwrecks. Shipwrecks, that year, are examined by month in Graph C. In contrast to the year 1898, 1907 had few bad storms. Most of the wrecks in 1907 appear to have been primarily due to collisions and founderings. As a result, the incidents are spread out through the year. It can be seen in Graph C that most of the shipwrecks occurred in the fall and winter. This was common for most years in the northeast and it shows why lifesaving stations were manned for the season starting in the month of September.

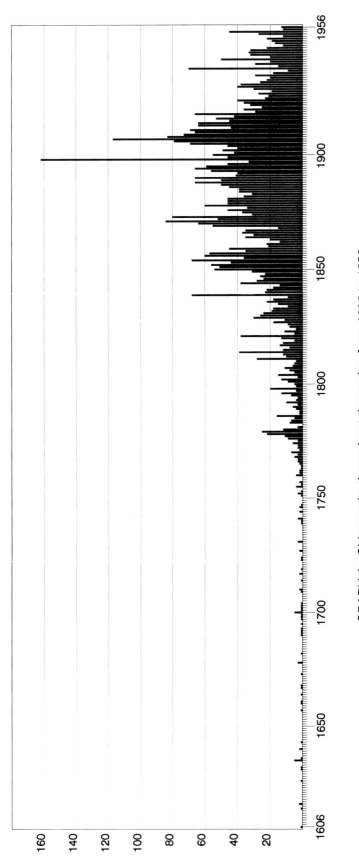

GRAPH A: Shipwrecks throughout the region from 1606 to 1956

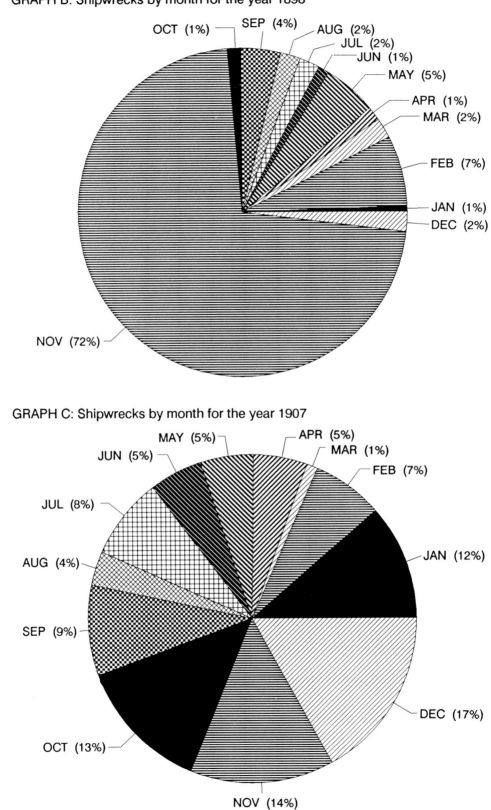

GRAPH B: Shipwrecks by month for the year 1898

OCT (1%) SEP (4%) AUG (2%)
JUL (2%)
JUN (1%)
MAY (5%)
APR (1%)
MAR (2%)
FEB (7%)
JAN (1%)
DEC (2%)
NOV (72%)

GRAPH C: Shipwrecks by month for the year 1907

MAY (5%) APR (5%)
MAR (1%)
JUN (5%)
FEB (7%)
JUL (8%)
JAN (12%)
AUG (4%)
SEP (9%)
DEC (17%)
OCT (13%)
NOV (14%)

APPENDIX D
A CHRONOLOGY OF VESSELS LOST
IN THE NORTHEASTERN UNITED STATES

When researching historic events in the United States it is often necessary to rely upon sources that do not document all the factors concerning the event. This is particularly true when researching shipwrecks. For very early shipwrecks, historical personal diaries were often more accurate than newspapers. During colonization and immediately after the Revolution, newspapers in the northeastern United States were published sporadically. It was not until the mid and late 19th century that full reports of shipwrecks were published in newspapers with reasonable accuracy. But even in the 19th century, many newspaper reports were sketchy and a researcher may have to carefully study and analyze the evidence to determine the correct details surrounding a ship loss. Sometimes, in reporting a ship's sinking, different newspapers gave different reports of the vessel's name, captain or country of registry. The researcher thus finds himself recording all the available data, correct and erroneous, until further research provides the true facts. For large research projects where thousands of incidents are compiled, the computer can be very helpful in sorting out multiple entries and incorrect data. For the following list, the computer has been a tremendous asset in identifying and qualifying multiple and erroneous data.

In developing a computerized database to investigate historical events it is important not to underestimate the value of recording a large number of parameters for each event in order to take full advantage of the data after compilation. Only the most important parameters of each shipwreck are included in the following list due to space limitations. However, the database with which they were analyzed contains a field each for: vessel name; day, month and year of loss; vessel type; where and when built; registry; general location; exact location; cargo; captain's name; lives lost; lives saved; primary source of the data; voyage; and general comments. The computer can arrange this data in different ways for analysis. For instance, the data can be arranged to compare the number of shipwrecks per year in different areas, the number of shipwrecks in the entire region by day, month or year, and numerous other arrangements. This capability allows examination of shipwreck events from a number of perspectives.

The list in this appendix is a compilation of shipwrecks over ten gross tons having occurred in the northeastern United States from the early 1600's through 1956. The vessels are listed chronologically. In the event of more than one wreck on the same date, they are listed alphabetically by name. The list includes vessels that were totally lost on this coast in continental shelf depths and shallower. A vessel has been included in the list if there was no indication that it was salvaged, or there is an indication that it was partially salvaged and some or part of the wreck was left on site. If research shows a vessel was completely salvaged after being wrecked, it was not included in the list.

Very often, early newspapers were in error in their first reports of a shipwreck. However, during compilation, information of questionable accuracy was omitted. For instance, if more than one day was reported for the loss of a vessel and further research did not eliminate the duplicity, only the month and year were listed. If different months were reported then only the year was listed. In the event multiple reports of the same incident with two different ship names occurred for a vessel, they may both be listed if research did not provide the true identity of the vessel.

In the list, the name of the vessel is provided first name first. In the event that a vessel's name is not presently known it is listed as "Unidentified". If research indicated that a vessel was not named, it is listed as "(Unnamed)". The place where the vessel was lost is given as the general location indicated by research. Once the researcher has the name and the date of loss of a vessel, further information such as latitude and longitude coordinates or specific distances from known landmarks can usually be found in the data sources available in libraries and maritime museums in the region of the vessel loss.

Reports of shipwrecks often give different descriptions of the type of vessel involved in the loss. The reports may provide a description of the vessel by indicating either rig, propulsion method or primary use. For instance a report of a ferry boat sinking may give no indication of whether it was powered by sail, steam, man or horse. On the other hand, a report may describe a schooner sinking without indicating whether it was a freighter, pilot boat or a lightship. Making research even more challenging, many terms for types of vessels had different meanings in different periods. For instance, today the term "Sloop" refers to a single-masted vessel usually with a length of less than 35 meters. However, in the early 1700's a "Sloop" was often a three-masted warship with up to 16 guns. From the eighteenth century onwards it has been customary to describe a sailing vessel's construction by the type of rig it carries but to apply these recent meanings to earlier craft can be misleading.

The sources for the information contained in the list include local historical records, personal diaries, many of the newspapers listed in Appendix A, American Lloyd's, United States List Of Merchant Vessels, United States Annual Life Saving Service Reports and American and European naval records. The vessel types used in the list are taken from the source material and abbreviated. These abbreviations are explained in the following key:

Vessel Type By Construction

Bark — *Barque*: A sailing vessel with at least three masts of which only the mizzen mast carried a fore and aft rig with the remaining masts carrying a square rig. When constructed of wood, these vessel were typically between 200 and 600 tons with a crew of about 14 men.

Bge — *Barge*: A vessel without propulsion power, designed for carrying raw materials and most often towed or otherwise propelled by a second vessel. Many early barges had sea-going hull types but after the mid nineteenth century, most barges were built for the coastal trade with a shallow draft, hard chine and squared bow.

Bgtn — *Brigantine*: In the early 1700's, a two-masted sailing vessel with square rig on both masts. After the early 1800's, the term was used to describe a two-masted sailing vessel with only the main mast carrying the fore and aft rig.

Bktn — *Barkentine*: A sailing vessel with three or more masts similar in size and construction to the barque but with only the foremast square rigged. The remaining masts carried a fore and aft rig.

Brig — *Brig*: A two-masted square rigged sailing vessel with the main mast carrying a large fore and aft sail in addition to the square rig. This design was very popular in the early 1800's. The common tonnage was between 150 and 350. The brig was used as a naval vessel by European and American Navies and could be armed with as many as 20 guns.

Ctbt   *Catboat*: A single-masted sailing vessel designed with a shallow draft, wide beam and a centerboard. Near the turn of the last century, large catboats were used in the coastal trade.

Cnlb   *Canalboat*: A sail, oar or horse powered vessel of light construction, shallow draft and generally less than 150 gross tons. These were designed to carry cargo along the tributaries, river and canals in the northeast.

Corv   *Corvette*: In the eighteenth century the corvette design was three-masted and similar to a small frigate. They were fast sailers and typically displaced about 600 tons. The corvette could carry up to 32 cannon and a crew as large as 100 men

Frgt   *Frigate*: Usually a three-masted naval vessel of between 750 and 1400 tons. In the eighteenth century the larger frigates carried up to 64 guns and were some of the faster warships. With the introduction of iron plating in the nineteenth century the displacement of the larger frigates rose to over 5000 tons.

Galy   *Gally*: During the late 16th and early 17th centuries, a vessel that could be powered solely by man powered oars. The gally was represented by a number of different designs throughout history, but later construction usually included one or more masts that carried sufficient sail for propulsion.

Ktch   *Ketch*: A two-masted vessel typically capable of transporting up to 50 tons of commodity. The mast arrangement had the taller mast stepped in the forward portion of the vessel and the shorter mast stepped aft, but ahead, of the rudder post.

Pink   *Pinke*: A coastal sailing vessel with three masts usually square rigged. The pink design was about 250 tons displacement and could be found in the region as late as the early 1800's.

Pinn   *Pinnace*: A small armed vessel of about 25 meters in length with three masts. During the 1700's these sailing vessels were used much like the later frigates.

Sch   *Schooner*: A vessel of two or more masts all carrying a fore
        and aft rig. The four and five-masted schooner became the
        backbone of the northeast's coastal freight trade after the
        1860's. In total there were over five hundred four-masted
        schooners which sailed on the east coast between that time
        and the mid 1900's.

Sbge   *Schooner-Barge*: A schooner rigged vessel, most commonly
        with three masts designed for carrying raw goods or
        commodities. This craft was invariably towed by a tug boat
        along with other schooner-barges. This design was popular
        during the late nineteenth and early twentieth centuries
        when steam powered tow-boats came of age. Although the
        schooner barges rarely used their sails, the design proposed
        that, given the proper wind, they could raise sail and lighten
        the load on the towing vessel.

Ship   *Full Rigged Ship*: A sailing vessel with a minimum of three
        masts all of which carried a full square rig. In the 1800's this
        design became the most widely used in the world. There
        were numerous three and four-masted ships and one with
        five masts.

Shlp   *Shallop*: A small one or two-masted sailing vessel which
        could be rowed. In the 1700's the shallop was used to load
        water and supplies aboard a larger vessel. However, large
        shallops were built in excess of 35 tons. When they began to
        be used for cargo carrying, the term was often confused with
        sloop.

Slp   *Sloop*: A small sailing vessel of the Royal Navy in the
        seventeenth and eighteenth centuries. Armed with up to 16
        guns, these vessels had either two or three masts with a
        variety of sailing rigs from ketch to three-masted, square
        rigged ships. From the late nineteenth century the sloop
        design was represented by a single-masted sailing vessel.

Snow   *Snow*: A two-masted sailing vessel very similar to a brig in
        design. The snow was popular in the eighteenth and
        nineteenth centuries. Along with slight modifications in
        vessel design, the term was replaced by brig in the mid
        nineteenth century.

Sub   *Submarine*: A submersible vessel. Submarines were powered by man in the early experimental days of the 1800's. By the twentieth century the submarine design was developed to the point where diesel and batteries became the power source of choice.

Yawl   *Yawl*: A two-masted sailing vessel with the larger mast stepped well forward and the smaller mizzen stepped aft of the rudder post. This smaller sail was usually used only as steadying canvas.

Vessel Type By Power Or Propulsion

Els   *Electric Screw*: A propeller driven vessel in which the main engine rotates generators which drive electric motors to turn the propellers. This design became very popular during the second quarter of the twentieth century. With this design the engine speeds remained constant while vessel speed changes were very smooth through electrical control of the motors.

St   *Steamer*: A steam powered vessel using a boiler most often fired by coal or wood.

Sts   *Steam Screw*: A propeller driven vessel with a steam engine as it's primary power. The propeller was used by some early steamers but then overshadowed by the use of paddle wheel drives on many passenger vessels. At the end of the last century, when steel hull construction became commonplace, most coastal steamers were equipped with propellers.

Stp   *Steam Paddle*: A paddle wheel driven vessel with a steam engine as it's primary power. Most of the paddle wheel steamers in the northeast were of the side wheel version which was better adapted to coastal waters than the stern wheel design.

Ols   *Oil Screw*: A propeller driven vessel equipped with a diesel engine as it's primary power.

Gas   *Gasoline Screw*: A propeller driven vessel equipped with a gasoline engine as it's primary power.

Nas   *Naptha Screw*: A propeller driven vessel equipped with a naptha engine as it's primary power.

Vessel Type By Primary Task

Fery   *Ferry*: A vessel designed to carry persons, goods and vehicles across rivers and coastal waterways.

Ltsp   *Lightship*: A vessel with the primary task of maintaining a lighted beacon in or near a shipping channel or shoal waters. Early lightships were equipped with masts and could sail to their stations. In later years the masts were used only to mount the light and the vessels were mechanically powered. By the end of the 1970's most of the lightships in the northeast were replaced by large, automated buoys.

Pckt   *Packet*: A sailing vessel originally designed to carry mail on the transatlantic during the nineteenth century. The packets were not large, usually measuring less than 1000 tons but were heavily constructed in order to survive the Atlantic in a variety of weather conditions.

Prvt   *Privateer*: A privately owned warship with the official sanction to attack the commerce of the enemy. Usually these vessels were merchant ships but some privately owned vessels were constructed solely for the purpose of "privateering".

Drge   *Dredge*: A vessel used for removing sediment from channel areas. Some dredges were much like a barge in hull design while others were designed with a sea going hull. Dredges have been built in all sizes and those used near the turn of the century were often steam or diesel powered.

Ycht   *Yacht*: A sail or engine powered vessel for the use of pleasure boating. In the late nineteenth century, very large and luxurious yachts were constructed.

DATE LOST	TYPE	NAME	WHERE LOST
1606			
October	Shlp	(Unnamed)	Nantucket Sound, MA
1614			
January	Ship	*Tijger*	New York, NY
1616			
		Unidentified	Chatham, MA
	Ship	Unidentified	Marshfield, MA
1626			
		Sparrow Hawk	Orleans, MA
1631			
February 18		Unidentified	Nahant, MA
1632			
	Pinn	Unidentified	Long Island, NY
1635			
August 6	Slp	Unidentified	Plymouth, MA
August 6	Slp	Unidentified	Plymouth, MA
August 15	Ship	*Angel Gabriel*	Pemiquid Harbor, ME
August 15	Bark	Unidentified	Gloucester, MA
August 15	Slp	*Watch And Wait*	Off Thatchers Island, MA
1636			
		Unidentified	Long Island, NY
1640			
	Pinn	*Make Shift*	Off Long Island, NY
		Unidentified	Southampton, NY
1643			
	Pinn	Unidentified	Hell Gate, NY
1657			
September 9		*Prins Maurits*	Fire Island, NY
1660			
		Unidentified	Easthampton, NY
1664			
		Unidentified	Nantucket, MA

DATE LOST	TYPE	NAME	WHERE LOST
1667			
		Unidentified	Elizabeth Islands, MA
1668			
March 22	Ship	*John & Lucy*	Montauk, NY
1673			
July 5		*Exploration*	Nantucket, MA
1678			
	Ship	Unidentified	Montauk, NY
September		Unidentified	Nantucket, MA
November	Ship	Unidentified	Nantucket Shoals, MA
1682			
November 28	Ship	Unidentified	Boston, MA
1690			
		Unidentified	Portsmouth, NH
1691			
May		*Dolphin*	Nantucket Shoals, MA
1692			
		Unidentified	Nantucket Shoals, MA
1693			
December 17	Slp	Unidentified	Off Scituate, MA
1694			
	Ship	*Conception*	Northeast Coast
1695			
	Ship	*Halcyon*	Jones Inlet, NY
1697			
September 28	Ship	*Providence*	Hull, MA
1698			
March		Unidentified	Sandwich, MA
1699			
		Adventure	Off Long Island, NY

DATE LOST	TYPE	NAME	WHERE LOST
1700			
		Captain Bell	Montauk, NY
	Ship	*Cibila*	Boston, MA
	Galy	*Essex*	Salem, MA
	Ship	*Magnifico*	Boston, MA
	Ship	*Margarette*	Cape Ann, MA
1701			
November 23	Slp	*Mary*	Montauk, NY
1702			
January 31	Brig	*Mary*	Marblehead, MA
1703			
November 3	Ship	*John Of Exon*	Boston, MA
1704			
	Ktch	*Society*	Long Island, NY
1709			
December 25	Ship	*Solebay*	Boston, MA
1710			
July 7	Ship	*Herbert*	Long Island, NY
December 11	Ship	*Nottingham Gally*	Boone Island, ME
1714			
October 12	Slp	*Hazard*	Cohasset, MA
1717			
April 25	Pink	*Mary Anne*	Orleans, MA
April 26	Ship	*Whidah*	Wellfleet, MA
1719			
		Unidentified	Eastern Long Island, NY
1723			
July 29	Slp	Unidentified	East Hampton, NY
1724			
March 5	Brig	Unidentified	Nantucket, MA
1727			
	Slp	Unidentified	Boston, MA
March 27		Unidentified	Gloucester, MA

DATE LOST	TYPE	NAME	WHERE LOST
1731			
		Anne	Marthas Vineyard, MA
		John & Mary	Boston, MA
		Unidentified	Eastham, MA
1739			
March 6	Snow	*Marblehead*	Salisbury, MA
1740			
December 17		Unidentified	Nahant, MA
1741			
		Grand Design	Mt Desert, ME
	Fery	*Thomas Jones*	Long Island Sound
	Slp	Unidentified	Grand Manaan, ME
1744			
January 17	Ship	*Astrea*	Portsmouth, NH
October 30	Slp	Unidentified	Nantucket Sound, MA
1746			
	Slp	Unidentified	Nantucket, MA
November 5	Slp	*Africa*	Vineyard Haven, MA
1747			
		Don	Mt Desert, ME
1751			
December 26	Ship	*Bumper*	Boston, MA
1752			
	Brig	*Halifax*	Block Island, RI
	Ship	*Palatine*	Block Island, RI
	Frgt	*San Jose*	Off New London, CT
1753			
		Unidentified	New London, CT
1755			
	Slp	*Martha & Hannah*	Block Island, RI
	Snow	*Union*	Provincetown, MA
February 24	Sch	Unidentified	Nahant, MA
December 16	Snow	*Jamaica Packet*	Rockaway, NY
1756			
January 1		Unidentified	Nantucket, MA

DATE LOST	TYPE	NAME	WHERE LOST
1757			
February 6		Unidentified	Nahant, MA
August 12		*Clinton*	Nomansland Island, MA
1760			
		Adventure	Lower Bay, NY
		Claremont	Cape Cod, MA
		Friends Adventure	Portsmouth, NH
December	Slp	Unidentified	Nantucket, MA
1761			
	Ship	*City Of Werry*	New York, NY
December 6	Slp	Unidentified	Nantucket, MA
1762			
		Mary	Boston, MA
		Unidentified	Cape Cod, MA
1763			
	Sch	*Marey*	Montauk Point, NY
1764			
July 10	Slp	*H M Chalever*	New York, NY
1765			
	Brig	*Golden Grove*	Block Island, RI
April 1	Sch	*Newport*	Setauket, NY
1766			
		Pembroke	Nahant, MA
February 8	Brig	Unidentified	Nahant, MA
November 10		Unidentified	Marblehead, MA
December 29	Sch	Unidentified	Nantucket, MA
1767			
		Betsey	Provincetown, MA
	Ship	*Britannia*	Merrick Beach, NY
November 18	Slp	Unidentified	Marblehead, MA
1768			
		Hawke	Boston, MA
	Slp	Unidentified	Off The Northeast Coast
	Slp	Unidentified	Off The Northeast Coast
December 4	Brig	Unidentified	Boston, MA
December 4	Brig	Unidentified	Cape Ann, MA
1769			
		Elizabeth	Long Island, NY
March	Slp	Unidentified	Billingsgate, MA

DATE LOST	TYPE	NAME	WHERE LOST
July 19	Slp	*Liberty*	Newport, RI
1770			
	Slp	*Albany*	Triangle Ledges, ME
	Ship	Unidentified	Brookhaven, NY
	Ship	Unidentified	Bridgehampton, NY
January		Unidentified	Nantucket, MA
June 22	Sch	(Unnamed)	Salem, MA
October 19		Unidentified	Long Island Sound
October 19		Unidentified	New London, CT
October 20	Brig	(Unnamed)	Marblehead, MA
October 20	Sch	(Unnamed)	Marblehead, MA
October 20	Slp	(Unnamed)	Marblehead, MA
November	Slp	Unidentified	Nantucket, MA
1771			
March 20	Brig	Unidentified	Quogue, NY
November 7		*Greyhound*	Ipswich, MA
1772			
		London	Newport, RI
March 21	Sch	Unidentified	Nahant, MA
June 9	Sch	*Gaspee*	Pawtuxet, RI
December 26	Sch	Unidentified	Boston, MA
1773			
		Hope	Staten Island, NY
	Ship	Unidentified	Provincetown, MA
June 17		Unidentified	Marblehead, MA
1774			
		Scripio	Portsmouth Harbor, NH
January	Brig	Unidentified	Nantucket, MA
June 10	Sch	*Lowden*	Nantucket, MA
November 21	Slp	(Unnamed)	Marblehead, MA
November 21	Slp	(Unnamed)	Marblehead, MA
November 21	Slp	(Unnamed)	Marblehead, MA
December		Unidentified	Buzzards Bay, MA
December		Unidentified	Buzzards Bay, MA
December		Unidentified	Buzzards Bay, MA
December 26		*George*	Portsmouth, NH
1775			
February 15	Sch	*Halifax*	Machias, ME
May 27	Sch	*Diana*	Boston, MA
November 25	Ship	*Jupiter*	Gloucester, MA
1776			
	Ship	*Carteret*	Jones Beach, NY
		Generous Friends	Coney Island, NY
	Prvt	*Revenue*	Hempstead, NY
	Slp	*Sally*	Provincetown, MA
	Corv	Unidentified	Coney Island, NY

DATE LOST	TYPE	NAME	WHERE LOST
	Sch	Unidentified	Marblehead, MA
March 6	Ship	*Sally*	Montauk, NY
March 11		*Stakesby*	Gloucester, MA
June	Ship	*Friendship*	Truro, MA
December 26		*George*	Portsmouth, NH

1777

	Ship	*Congress*	Hudson River, NY
		Diamond	New York, NY
	Ship	*Montgomery*	Hudson River, NY
		Neptune	Newburyport, MA
		Triton	Point Judith, RI
	Ship	Unidentified	Marthas Vineyard, MA
	Ship	Unidentified	Wallabout Basin, NY
	Brig	*Wilkes*	Eastham, MA
August 27	Slp	*Oliver Cromwell*	Sakonnet, RI
November 10		*Syren*	Point Judith, RI
December 24	Ship	*HMS Mercury*	Off New York, NY

1778

	Ship	*Falcon*	Narragansett Bay, RI
	Ship	*Flora*	Narragansett Bay, RI
	Ship	*Jenny*	Staten Island, NY
January 26	Slp	Unidentified	Lynn, MA
February 11	Ship	*Liverpool*	Long Island, NY
May 5	Sch	Unidentified	Cuttyhunk, MA
May 6	Ship	Unidentified	Falmouth, MA
July	Galy	*Spitfire*	Seaconnet, RI
August 1	Galy	*Alarm*	Seaconnet, RI
August 4	Slp	*Morning Star*	New York, NY
August 5	Ship	*Cerberus*	Narragansett Bay, RI
August 5	Galy	*Pigot*	Freeborns Creek, RI
August 6	Ship	Unidentified	Off Goat Island, RI
August 6	Ship	Unidentified	Off Goat Island, RI
August 7	Slp	*Kingfisher*	Seaconnet, RI
August 7	Ship	*Juno*	Narragansett Bay, RI
August 7	Ship	*Lark*	Narragansett Bay, RI
August 8	Ship	*Grand Duke*	Off Goat Island, RI
August 15	Ship	*Orpheus*	Narragansett Bay, RI
December	Ship	*Rose*	Staten Island, NY
December 8	Ship	*HMS Somerset*	Provincetown, MA

1779

	Ship	*Colpoys*	Long Island, NY
	Ship	*James & William*	Hell Gate, NY
	Brig	*Middletown*	Sag Harbor, NY
	Ship	*Minerva*	Westerly, RI
		Unidentified	Rockaway Bay, NY
		Unidentified	Rockaway Bay, NY
March 11	Prvt	*Defense*	New London, CT
August 13	Brig	*Defense*	Stockton, ME
August 14	Brig	*Active*	Penobscot River, ME
August 14	Ship	*Black Prince*	Penobscot River, ME
August 14	Ship	*Charming Sally*	Penobscot River, ME
August 14	Ship	*Defiance*	Penobscot River, ME
August 14	Slp	*Diligent*	Penobscot River, ME
August 14	Ship	*General Putnam*	Penobscot River, ME

DATE LOST	TYPE	NAME	WHERE LOST
August 14	Brig	*Hazard*	Penobscot River, ME
August 14	Ship	*Hector*	Penobscot River, ME
August 14	Ship	*Monmouth*	Penobscot River, ME
August 14	Ship	*Revenge*	Penobscot River, ME
August 14	Ship	*Sky Rocket*	Penobscot River, ME
August 14	Ship	*Springbird*	Penobscot River, ME
August 14	Brig	*Tyrannicide*	Penobscot River, ME
August 14	Ship	*Vengence*	Penobscot River, ME
August 14	Ship	*Warren*	Penobscot River, ME
September	Slp	*Hannah*	Bucks Harbor, ME

1780

		Betsey	Lower Bay, NY
	Ship	*Patience*	Long Island, NY
	Ship	Unidentified	Isles of Shoals, NH
	Ship	Unidentified	Isles of Shoals, NH
	Ship	Unidentified	Isles of Shoals, NH
	Ship	*Watt*	Long Island, NY
February 12	Sch	*Nancy*	Portland, ME
March 2	Ship	*Mercury*	Long Island, NY
June		Unidentified	Butlers Point, NY
July 25	Ship	*Blonde*	Corlears Hook, NY
September 13	Frgt	*Lexington*	East River, NY
November	Ship	*Magnifique*	Boston, MA
November 3	Frgt	*Hussar*	Hell Gate, NY

1781

	Ship	*Mars*	Block Island, RI
	Slp	*Rover*	Off New York, NY
January 23	Ship	*Culloden*	Long Island, NY
April 14	Ship	*Royal Oak*	New York, NY
August 26	Slp	*Swallow*	Long Island, NY

1782

January 21	Ship	*Blonde*	Nantucket Shoals, MA

1783

		Elizabeth	Long Island, NY
		Saint James	Staten Island, NY
	Ship	*St Helena*	Castine Harbor, ME
October 9		Unidentified	Boston, MA
October 9		Unidentified	Boston, MA
October 9		Unidentified	Boston, MA
November 25	Ship	*Erfprins*	Off Cape Ann, MA

1784

		Fanciculetta	Nantucket Shoals, MA
		Julius Caesar	Cape Cod, MA
		Peace And Plenty	Cape Cod, MA
	Fery	Unidentified	New York Bay, NY
January 15	Fery	Unidentified	East River, NY
January 15		Unidentified	Long Island, NY
July		Unidentified	Nantucket, MA

ABOVE: The German barque *Francis*, shown above, wrecked on Cape Cod on December 26, 1872. Another ship, the *Peruvian* wrecked within a few miles on the same night. Here, a salvage schooner is alongside the *Francis* as her cargo of block tin and sugar is removed. She became a total loss. *Photo from the collection of William P. Quinn, Orleans MA.*   **BELOW**: In one of the great tragedies of the northeast, the steamer *City of Columbus* sank in the frigid waters off Martha's Vineyard on January 18, 1884. She struck the rock shoal known as Devils Bridge. Over 100 people lost their lives after the captain, thinking she would still float, backed the steamer off the shoal and into deeper water. *From the author's collection.*

DATE LOST	TYPE	NAME	WHERE LOST
1785			
		Nuestra Senora	New York, NY
		Ross	Boston, MA
January	Sch	*Dolphin*	Oyster Bay, NY
September 29	Ship	*Alstromer*	Governor's Island, NY
December 25	Sch	Unidentified	Damariscove, ME
1786			
	Brig	*Peggy*	Montauk Point, NY
	Slp	Unidentified	Boston Harbor, MA
		Unidentified	Damariscove, ME
	Sch	Unidentified	Boston, MA
January 23		*Cicero*	Hull, MA
March	Slp	Unidentified	Chatham, MA
March	Sch	Unidentified	Elizabeth Islands, MA
March	Slp	Unidentified	Elizabeth Islands, MA
March	Brig	Unidentified	Elizabeth Islands, MA
April 1	Sch	Unidentified	Marblehead, MA
April 1	Sch	Unidentified	Salem, MA
July 31	Brig	Unidentified	Nantucket Shoals, MA
August	Ship	*Mariann*	Long Island, NY
December 4	Brig	*Lucretia*	Boston, MA
December 4	Slp	*Thomas*	Marshfield, MA
December 9	Slp	Unidentified	Duxbury, MA
1787			
	Slp	Unidentified	Bangs Island, ME
March 4		*Minerva*	Marshfield, MA
1788			
		Betsy And May	Long Island, NY
January 26	Slp	Unidentified	Lynn, MA
1789			
		Mary & Ann	Plum Island, MA
	Ship	*Nancy*	Portland Head, ME
		Sally	Coney Island, NY
December 12	Brig	Unidentified	Salem, MA
1790			
January 8	Sch	*Frederick*	Off York, ME
January 27	Sch	Unidentified	Newburyport, MA
March 16	Sch	*Abigail*	Thatchers Island, MA
December	Brig	*Sally*	Eatons Neck, NY
December 12	Sch	Unidentified	Salem, MA
1791			
		Hopewell	Boston, MA
February	Slp	*Sally*	Winter Harbor, ME
March 21	Brig	Unidentified	Salem, MA

DATE LOST	TYPE	NAME	WHERE LOST
1792			
	Ship	*Columbia*	Cape Cod Bay, MA
	Ship	*Eliza*	Long Island, NY
	Ship	*George*	Long Island, NY
	Ship	*Marretta*	Cape Cod, MA
	Ship	*Rodney*	Cape Cod, MA
January 14		Unidentified	Plum Island, MA
October 13	Sch	Unidentified	Salem, MA
October 13		Unidentified	Cape Ann, MA
November	Slp	Unidentified	Cape Ann, MA
November 28	Brig	Unidentified	Lynn, MA
1793			
		Gertrude Maria	Off Scituate, MA
August 8	Slp	*Southaven*	Long Island Sound
October 17		*Sally*	Nantucket, MA
November	Slp	Unidentified	Nantucket, MA
1794			
		Fanny	Marthas Vineyard, MA
February 2		*Good Intent*	Nantucket, MA
November	Sch	Unidentified	Hull, MA
1795			
	Ship	*Clarissa*	Nantucket, MA
		Neptune	Long Island, NY
March 13	Ship	Unidentified	Salem, MA
November 25	Slp	Unidentified	Nantucket, MA
November 25		Unidentified	Nantucket, MA
December 8	Brig	*Peggy*	Nahant, MA
December 17	Fery	Unidentified	East River, NY
1796			
January 6	Brig	Unidentified	Gardiners Bay, NY
January 7	Ship	*Margaret*	Salem, MA
January 11	Brig	*John*	Salem, MA
January 11		Unidentified	New York, NY
January 11	Ship	Unidentified	New York, NY
January 11	Ship	Unidentified	New York, NY
January 11	Ship	Unidentified	New York, NY
January 11	Ship	Unidentified	New York, NY
January 11	Ship	Unidentified	New York, NY
January 11	Ship	Unidentified	New York, NY
January 11	Ship	Unidentified	New York, NY
December		*Julian*	Nantucket, MA
1797			
		Enrique	Long Island, NY
		Three Sisters	Cape Cod, MA
January	Sch	*Mary*	Damariscove, ME
February 27	Ship	*Betsey*	Off The Northeast Coast

DATE LOST	TYPE	NAME	WHERE LOST
1798			
	Ship	*Charming Betsey*	Marthas Vineyard, MA
	Ship	*Commerce*	Nantucket Shoals, MA
	Ship	*Delight*	Cape Cod, MA
		Jenny	New York Bay, NY
January	Slp	Unidentified	Damariscotta, ME
January 4	Ship	*Grand Turk*	Cushing's Point, ME
April 2	Fery	Unidentified	East River, NY
August 14		*Sally*	Nantucket, MA
October 24	Sch	*Sukey*	Cape Ann, MA
November 10	Sch	*Susannah*	Cape Ann, MA
November 20	Sch	*Rachel*	Truro, MA
November 26	Sch	Unidentified	Portland Head, ME
November 30		Unidentified	Truro, MA
November 30		Unidentified	Truro, MA
November 30		Unidentified	Truro, MA
November 30		Unidentified	Truro, MA
November 30		Unidentified	Truro, MA
November 30		Unidentified	Truro, MA
November 30		Unidentified	Truro, MA
November 30		Unidentified	Truro, MA
November 30		Unidentified	Truro, MA
December 10	Sch	Unidentified	Nahant, MA
December 17	Sch	Unidentified	Portland Head, ME
1799			
		Unidentified	Eastham, MA
January 12	Brig	*Weazle*	Cape Cod Bay, MA
February 15	Slp	Unidentified	East River, NY
December 15		Unidentified	Manchester, MA
1800			
	Bark	*Algae*	Long Island, NY
	Brig	*Braganza*	Eastern Long Island, NY
		Columbia	Off Whitehead, ME
		Delight	Marthas Vineyard, MA
	Ship	*Experiment*	Off New York, NY
	Brig	*Marcellus*	Eastern Long Island, NY
		Syracuse	Brookhaven, NY
	Brig	Unidentified	Brookhaven, NY
	Ship	*Forrester*	Long Island, NY
January 17	Brig	*Ocean*	Long Island, NY
August	Sch	*Three Friends*	Eastern Long Island, NY
October	Sch	*Fair America*	Eastern Long Island, NY
October 18	Ship	*Charles*	Nantucket Sound, MA
December	Sch	*Polly*	Long Island, NY
1801			
	Ship	*Ann*	Brookhaven, NY
	Ship	*Thomas*	New York, NY
	Ship	*Traveler*	Long Island, NY
February 14	Ship	*Portland*	Nantucket, MA
March 17	Sch	*Sally*	Southern Long Island, NY
April 10	Slp	Unidentified	Nantucket, MA
May	Fery	Unidentified	East River, NY
May 1	Sch	Unidentified	Salem, MA

DATE LOST	TYPE	NAME	WHERE LOST
December 31	Sch	*Mary Anne*	Orleans, MA

1802

	Ship	*Astrea*	Cape Cod, MA
	Ship	*Mary*	Lower Bay, NY
	Ship	Unidentified	Gardiners Island, NY
January 11	Ship	*Minerva*	Boston, MA
January 23	Slp	Unidentified	Plum Gut, NY
February 21	Ship	*Catherine Ray*	Long Island, NY
February 22	Ship	*Brutus*	Truro, MA
February 22	Ship	*Ulysses*	Provincetown, MA
June 2	Bgtn	*Ann*	Southern Long Island, NY
August	Brig	*Mary*	Nantucket, MA
November		Unidentified	Plum Island, MA
December	Sch	Unidentified	Nantucket, MA
December 15	Brig	*Elizabeth*	Hull, MA

1803

January		Unidentified	Nantucket, MA
February 4	Ship	*Aurora*	Nantucket, MA
November	Slp	*Hero*	Off New England

1804

	Ship	*Nelly*	Long Island, NY
		Unidentified	Cohasset, MA
January 1	Brig	*Little Jane*	Nepeague, NY
January 5	Brig	*Alert*	Salem, MA
January 8	Slp	Unidentified	Ram Island, NY
January 26	Sch	Unidentified	Gardiners Point, NY
February 24	Sch	*Gladiator*	Gardiners Island, NY
April 7	Brig	*Apollo*	Trundy's Reef, ME
October 9	Sch	*Dove*	Ipswich, MA
October 9	Slp	*Hannah*	Cohasset, MA
October 9	Slp	*Mary*	Cohasset, MA
October 15	Ship	*Protector*	Off Truro, MA
November 12	Brig	Unidentified	Nantucket, MA
November 12	Brig	Unidentified	Nantucket, MA
December 14	Slp	*Juno*	Boston, MA
December 24	Ship	*Alert*	Boston, MA

1805

January 16		*Cato*	Long Island, NY
January 31	Ship	*Perseverence*	Elizabeth Islands, MA
March 18	Ship	*Oneida*	Easthampton, NY
October 16	Slp	Unidentified	Newburyport, MA
December 30		*Eliza*	Nantucket, MA

1806

		Edward	Long Island, NY
January 6	Sch	Unidentified	Westhampton, NY
January 6	Brig	*Veroni*	Westhampton, NY
January 10	Ship	*Ann & Hope*	Block Island, RI
March 24	Ship	*Confidence*	Cape Cod Bay, MA
November 4	Sch	*Redbridge*	Providence, RI
November 9	Brig	*Lucretia*	Westhampton, NY

ABOVE: In this classic shipwreck photograph, the two masted schooner *Plymouth Rock* is shown ashore at Provincetown MA on April 11, 1888. In the foreground are the frame tops and planking of the *Hannah Shubert* wrecked two years earlier. *Photo from the collection of William P. Quinn, Orleans MA.* **BELOW**: With improvements in diving equipment in the mid 1800's many sunken ships were salvaged only after considerable effort. Here the hull of the schooner *Garfield White* is repaired prior to being raised by a salvage team which includes a hard hat diver, surface crew and an unusual diver support vessel. *Photo courtesy Paul Morris, Nantucket MA.*

DATE LOST	TYPE	NAME	WHERE LOST
November 14	Sch	*Antelope*	Easthampton, NY

1807

	Ship	*Brutus*	Block Island, RI
		Cordelia	Scituate, MA
		Mississippi	Lower Bay, NY
		Nereus	Long Island, NY
March 1	Ship	*Howard*	Cape Ann, MA
March 1	Sch	*Little Sally*	Salem, MA
March 25		*Selby*	Off Manhattan, NY
July 12	Sch	*Charles*	Richmonds Island, ME
November	Ship	*Cato*	Nantucket, MA
November	Slp	*Packet*	Nantucket, MA
December	Ship	*Alexander*	Southampton, NY

1808

		Flora	East River, NY
January 29		*Little George*	Off Long Island, NY
October 28	Sch	*Active*	Off Truro, MA
December	Brig	*Betsey*	Westhampton, NY
December 20	Brig	*Fox*	Easthampton, NY
December 20	Sch	*Wilson*	Southampton, NY

1809

January 15	Sch	Unidentified	Nantucket, MA
January 18	Ship	*Trial*	Long Island, NY
February 20		*True American*	Upper Bay, NY
October 28		*Fahlum*	Off Cedar Island, NY
December	Sch	*Dolly*	Southampton, NY

1810

March	Ship	*Hudson*	Moriches, NY
September 15	Sch	*Sally*	Off Southampton, NY
November 10		*Cincinnati*	Governor's Island, NY
November 10		Unidentified	Moriches, NY

1811

	Ship	*Abeona*	Cape Cod, MA
	Ship	*Alknomack*	Marthas Vineyard, MA
	Ship	*Florenza*	Cape Cod, MA
	Ship	*Four Brothers*	Cape Cod, MA
	Ship	*Neutrality*	Cape Cod, MA
	Ship	*Newcastle*	Cape Cod Bay, MA
	Ship	*Olive Branch*	Long Island, NY
February 23		*Caroline*	Nantucket, MA
March 6	Ship	*Thistle*	Long Island, NY
November 20	Brig	*Success*	Marshfield, MA
December 20	Slp	Unidentified	Nantucket, MA
December 23	Ship	*Maria Louisa*	Gardiners Island, NY
December 23	Slp	*Rosette*	Long Island, NY
December 23	Slp	*Traveler*	Eatons Neck, NY
December 23	Ship	Unidentified	Long Island, NY
December 24		*Black Rock*	Manhasset, NY
December 24		*General Gates*	Governors Island, NY
December 24		*Maybelle*	Long Island, NY

DATE LOST	TYPE	NAME	WHERE LOST
December 24	Slp	Unidentified	Nantucket, MA
December 24		Unidentified	Long Island, NY
December 24		Unidentified	Long Island, NY
December 24		Unidentified	Long Island, NY
December 24		Unidentified	Long Island, NY
December 24		Unidentified	Long Island, NY
December 24		Unidentified	Long Island, NY
December 24		Unidentified	Long Island, NY
December 24		Unidentified	Long Island, NY
December 25	Ship	*Maria L Stowell*	Gardiners Island, NY

1812

DATE LOST	TYPE	NAME	WHERE LOST
		Jupiter	Off Orient, NY
		Unidentified	Cape Cod Bay, MA
January 3		*Alfred*	Cape Ann, MA
January 18	Ship	Unidentified	Nantucket Sound, MA
January 21	Brig	*Lydia Whittlesey*	Sakonnet, RI
February		*Osprey*	Off New London, CT
June 12		*Egeria*	Long Island Sound
September 17	Slp	*Defiance*	Salem, MA
December	Slp	Unidentified	Nantucket, MA
December 21	Ship	*Sir Sidney Smith*	Off Nantucket, MA

1813

DATE LOST	TYPE	NAME	WHERE LOST
	Ship	*Amazon*	Nomansland Island, MA
		Ann	Barrington, RI
	Brig	Unidentified	Bellport, NY
January		*Queen*	Nantucket, MA
January 7	Sch	Unidentified	Nantucket, MA
January 14	Ship	*Sagunta*	Isle of Shoals, NH
March 23	Slp	Unidentified	Cuttyhunk, MA
April 7	Brig	*London Packet*	Nantucket, MA
April 27	Ship	*Princess*	Cape Cod, MA
April 28	Ship	*Whampoa*	Narragansett Bay, RI
May 13		Unidentified	Manchester, MA
September		Unidentified	Fire Island, NY

1814

DATE LOST	TYPE	NAME	WHERE LOST
	Ship	*Liverpool Trader*	Penobscot River, ME
	Slp	*Woodcock*	Fire Island, NY
January 18	Slp	*Two Brothers*	Falmouth, MA
February	Sch	Unidentified	Nantucket, MA
March	Ship	Unidentified	Manchester, MA
March 7	Prvt	*Mars*	New York
March 11	Slp	Unidentified	Nantucket, MA
May 22	Sch	Unidentified	Nantucket, MA
June	Sch	*Independence*	Scituate, MA
June	Sch	*James*	Scituate, MA
June	Sch	*Lucy*	Scituate, MA
June	Sch	*Revival*	Scituate, MA
June		Unidentified	Cape Ann, MA
June 14	Slp	*Diligence*	Ipswich, MA
June 14	Slp	Unidentified	Ipswich, MA
June 14	Sch	Unidentified	Saco, ME
June 14	Brig	Unidentified	Saco, ME
June 14	Sch	Unidentified	Saco, ME
June 14	Sch	Unidentified	Saco, ME

DATE LOST	TYPE	NAME	WHERE LOST
June 14	Sch	Unidentified	Saco, ME
June 25	Sch	*Nordkoping*	Nantucket, MA
July 15	Brig	*George Washington*	Southampton, NY
August	Sch	*Westerwick*	Nantucket, MA
September 3	Slp	*Adams*	Hamden, ME
October 10	Ship	*Douglas*	Nantucket, MA
November 1		*Decatur*	Hampden, ME
November 1		*Kutsoff*	Hampden, ME
November 1		Unidentified	Hampden, ME
November 1		Unidentified	Hampden, ME
November 1		Unidentified	Hampden, ME
November 1		Unidentified	Hampden, ME
November 1		Unidentified	Hampden, ME
November 1		Unidentified	Hampden, ME
November 1		Unidentified	Hampden, ME
November 1		Unidentified	Hampden, ME
November 1		Unidentified	Hampden, ME
November 1		Unidentified	Hampden, ME
November 1		Unidentified	Hampden, ME

1815

	Ship	*Nelson*	New York Bay, NY
January 17	Brig	*Sylph*	Long Island, NY
April	Brig	Unidentified	Nantucket, MA
July	Brig	*Live Oak*	Shinnecock Point, NY
September 23	Ship	*Friendship*	Staten Island, NY
September 23		*Matchless*	Boston, MA
September 23	Brig	*Orion*	Montauk, NY
September 23		Unidentified	Patchogue, NY
October 28	Slp	Unidentified	Nantucket, MA
October 28	Ship	*Vidette*	Long Island, NY
December	Brig	*Leda*	Southampton, NY
December 16	Sch	*Susannah*	Nantucket, MA

1816

	Ship	Unidentified	Shinnecock, NY
	Ship	Unidentified	Long Island, NY
		Unidentified	Long Island, NY
	Slp	Unidentified	Long Island, NY
		Unidentified	Long Island, NY
	Ship	Unidentified	Long Island, NY
October	Slp	*Anion*	New London, CT
October	Slp	*Two Brothers*	Trumans Beach, NY

1817

		Dispatch	Boston, MA
January 16	Sch	*Arnold*	Salem, MA
January 18		*Fox*	Marthas Vineyard, MA
February	Slp	*Morgiana*	Fireplace Point, NY
February 24	Ship	*Union*	Salem, MA
March	Brig	*Friendship*	Montauk, NY
March 25		*Mary*	Darien, CT
March 25	Slp	*Mistletoe*	Off New England
April	Sch	*Lydia*	Long Island, NY
May 14		*Commerce*	Portsmouth, NH
June 15	Slp	*Mary*	Nantucket Shoals, MA

DATE LOST	TYPE	NAME	WHERE LOST
October 16		*George*	Off New London, CT
October 18	Brig	*William Todd*	Nantucket, MA
December 12	Brig	Unidentified	Marblehead, MA

1818

		Mary Ann	Cape Cod, MA
February		*Albion*	Coney Island, NY
April 10	Sch	*Rambler*	Cape Ann, MA
April 21	Sch	*Angler*	Salem, MA
September 9	Sch	Unidentified	Nantucket, MA
September 9	Sch	Unidentified	Nantucket, MA
November		*Warren*	Cape Cod, MA
December	Ship	*Governor Hopkins*	Brentons Reef, RI
December 2	Sch	*Brittania*	Salem, MA
December 2	Slp	Unidentified	Salem, MA
December 6	Bark	*Sarah & Susan*	Cohasset, MA
December 20	Ship	*Cicero*	Marthas Vinyard, MA

1819

		Montgomery	Sakonnett Point, RI
February 10	Brig	*Mary*	Point Judith, RI
May 15	Ship	*Amazon*	Newport, RI
May 25	Sch	*America*	Block Island, RI
December 3	Slp	*Katherine*	Off Cape Cod, MA

1820

	Brig	*Massachusetts*	Eastham, MA
January	Slp	*Nautilus*	Sandwich, MA
January	Slp	Unidentified	Nantucket, MA
January 3		Unidentified	Nantucket, MA
January 3		Unidentified	Nantucket, MA
January 10	Sch	Unidentified	Nantucket, MA
January 10	Sch	Unidentified	Nantucket, MA
January 17		*Helen*	Southampton, NY
January 17	Sch	*Union*	Gloucester, MA
July	Ship	*Atlas*	Nantucket, MA
November 11	Sch	*Two Brothers*	Block Island, RI
December 25	Ship	*Rolla*	Eastham, MA
December 30	Brig	*Mary Jane*	Point Judith, RI

1821

		Albert	Long Island, NY
January 4	Brig	*Catherine*	Nantucket, MA
February 16		*Paragon*	Cape Ann, MA
March 1	Sch	*Randolph*	Block Island, RI
September 3	Ship	*Two-Catherines*	Narragansett Bay, RI
September 3		Unidentified	Rockaway, NY
September 3		Unidentified	Rockaway, NY
September 3		Unidentified	Rockaway, NY
September 3		Unidentified	Rockaway, NY
September 3	Sch	*William*	Nantucket, MA
September 4	Sch	*Gloriana*	Bellport, NY
September 4	Ship	Unidentified	Long Island, NY
September 4	Ship	Unidentified	New York, NY
September 4	Ship	Unidentified	New York, NY
September 4	Ship	Unidentified	New York, NY

ABOVE: The *Alva* was William K. Vanderbilt's private yacht. When she was built in 1886 she was the most expensive yacht afloat. Six years later she was anchored in fog on a voyage from Bar Harbor to Newport. The steamer *H.F.Dimock* emerged from the dense mist and cut deep into the yacht. The *Alva* sank within minutes. **BELOW**: With her top masts showing above the water, the yacht was deemed to be a hazard to navigation and dynamited by the government. In this photograph, a small salvage schooner is supporting dive operations to remove her brass steam engine while Sunday yachts of a more moderate genre sail in to view the shipwreck. *Photos courtesy Peabody Museum of Salem.*

DATE LOST	TYPE	NAME	WHERE LOST
September 4	Ship	Unidentified	New York, NY
September 4	Ship	Unidentified	New York, NY
September 4	Ship	Unidentified	New York, NY
September 4	Ship	Unidentified	New York, NY
September 4	Ship	Unidentified	New York, NY
September 4	Ship	Unidentified	New York, NY
September 4	Slp	Unidentified	New York, NY
September 4	Fery	Unidentified	New York, NY
September 4	Ship	Unidentified	New York, NY
September 4	Ship	Unidentified	New York, NY
September 4		Unidentified	Bellport, NY
September 4		Unidentified	Bellport, NY
September 4		Unidentified	Bellport, NY
September 4		Unidentified	Bellport, NY
September 26	Sch	Victory	Nantucket, MA
November 5	Ship	Savannah	Fire Island, NY

1822

February		Florenzo	Marshfield, MA
April 14	Ship	Speculator	Sakonnet, RI
May 7		Favorite	Edgartown, MA
July 1	Sch	Maria Louisa	Duxbury, MA
December 18	Ship	Maria Caroline	Narragansett Bay, RI

1823

	Sch	Ligera	Montauk, NY
January 1	Slp	Venus	Block Island, RI
March 9	Slp	Two Sisters	Nantucket, MA
March 31		Cashier	Nantucket, MA
April 1	Brig	Rebecca-Ann	Gloucester, MA
September 28	Slp	Victory	Mattituck, NY
October	Sch	Sammual Tyler	Nantucket, MA
November 6	Slp	Express	Point Judith, RI

1824

January 20		Federal George	Scituate, MA
January 24	Slp	Sabine	Block Island, RI
May 15	St	Aetna	New York, NY
December 25	Ship	Nestor	Fire Island, NY

1825

	Ship	Improve	Nantucket, MA
January 22	Slp	Aurora	Narragansett Bay, RI
March 6	Ship	Improvement	Nantucket, MA
May 10	Brig	Diana	Nantucket, MA
August 13	Sch	Dromo	Newport, RI
November 2	Brig	Clio	Nantucket, MA
December 9	Sch	Unidentified	Nantucket, MA
December 29	Brig	Sylvester Healy	Gardiners Island, NY

1826

January	Slp	Fair American	Shinnecock, NY
March 20	Sch	Susan	Montauk, NY
March 23	Sch	Midas	Block Island, RI
July 18	Slp	Rose Three	Sakonnet, RI

DATE LOST	TYPE	NAME	WHERE LOST
August 22	Stp	*New York*	Petite Manan, ME
October 7	Slp	*Marietta*	Mattituck, NY
October 29	Sch	*Nellie*	Nantucket, MA
November 21	Brig	*Rival*	Scituate, MA
November 22	Sch	*Hope*	Off Cape Cod, MA

1827

	Ship	*Maine*	Eastham, MA
	St	*Oliver Ellsworth*	East River, NY
January	Slp	*Consolation*	Gardiners Island, NY
January 17	Sch	*Almira*	Barnstable, MA
January 20	Sch	*Polly & Lucy*	Cape Ann, MA
April 16	Sch	*Globe*	Cuttyhunk, MA
April 16	Sch	*Strong*	Block Island, RI
April 24	Slp	*Fulton*	Block Island, RI
April 24	Sch	*New Hope*	Point Judith, RI
September	Slp	*Wave*	Plum Gut, NY
September 6	Sch	*Unidentified*	Gloucester, MA
September 20	Slp	*David Porter*	Eatons Neck, NY
October 26	Sch	*Fame*	Beverley, MA
November	Slp	*Eliza Ann*	Southold, NY
November	Slp	*Planet*	Nantucket, MA
November 9	Brig	*Francis Miller*	Nantucket, MA
November 9	Sch	*Independence*	Nantucket, MA
December 16	Slp	*Traveller*	Nantucket, MA

1828

	Brig	*Mars*	Easthampton, NY
January 21	Slp	*Henry*	Newport, RI
February 23	Brig	*Angenoria*	Canoe Place, NY
March 19		*Ann Maria*	Rock Lighthouse, NY
April	Sch	*Sally*	Nantucket, MA
May 15	Sch	*Francis*	Isle of Shoals, NH
July	Brig	*John Harris*	Nantucket, MA
November 2	Ship	*Superior*	Wellfleet, MA
November 7	Slp	*Morning Star*	Newport, RI
December 3	Slp	*Polly*	Nantucket, MA
December 14	Brig	*Packet*	Nantucket, MA
December 18	Sch	*Fair Play*	Cape Ann, MA

1829

	Sch	*Unidentified*	Nantucket, MA
	Sch	*Unidentified*	Nantucket, MA
January 2	Slp	*Enterprise*	Plum Island, NY
January 2	Sch	*Unidentified*	Plum Island, NY
February 9	Sch	*Mary Ann*	Block Island, RI
February 14	Brig	*Thomas*	Easthampton, NY
February 20	Sch	*Harriet & Eliza*	Eastham, MA
February 22	Brig	*Diamond*	Elizabeth Islands, MA
February 24	Slp	*Caroline*	Hyannis, MA
February 25	Sch	*Hannah Jane*	Truro, MA
February 26	Brig	*Ann Eliza*	Nantucket, MA
February 27	Brig	*Jachin*	Boston, MA
February 27	Sch	*Superior*	Block Island, RI
March 3	Sch	*Lafayette*	Marblehead, MA
March 5	Brig	*Elizabeth & Ann*	Nahant, MA
March 5	Brig	*Persia*	Gloucester, MA

DATE LOST	TYPE	NAME	WHERE LOST
March 7	Sch	*Dewitt Clinton*	Wellfleet, MA
March 10	Sch	*Atlantic*	Dennis, MA
March 18	Sch	*Greek*	Easthampton, NY
March 20	Sch	*Spring-bird*	Eastham, MA
March 22	Sch	*Ann*	Nantucket, MA
March 22	Sch	*Ranger*	Nantucket, MA
March 23	Sch	*Panama*	Wellfleet, MA
March 23	Brig	*William & Henry*	Cape Cod Bay, MA
April 24	Brig	*Telemachus*	Eastham, MA
June 4	Stp	*Fulton*	Brooklyn, NY
July	Sch	*Adelia*	Bridgehampton, NY
October 21	Slp	*Chelsea*	Block Island, RI
October 31	Sch	*Sarah*	Thatchers Island, MA
December	Sch	*Velocia*	Nantucket, MA

1830

DATE LOST	TYPE	NAME	WHERE LOST
		Lucy Ellen	Quogue, NY
	Brig	*Vinyard*	Long Island, NY
January 25	Ship	Unidentified	Fire Island, NY
March	Sch	*Lincoln*	Quogue, NY
April 8	Slp	*William*	Thatchers Island, MA
August 17	Sch	*Friendship*	Marthas Vineyard, MA
August 17	Sch	*Leopard*	Wellfleet, MA
August 26	Slp	*Abel Hoyt*	Elizabeth Islands, MA
August 26	Sch	*Adeline*	Eastham, MA
August 26	Sch	*Cyrus*	Wellfleet, MA
August 26	Sch	Unidentified	Chatham, MA
August 26	Brig	Unidentified	Chatham, MA
September 16	Brig	*Belvidere*	Off Provincetown, MA
October		*Herald*	Gloucester, MA
October 11	Sch	*Francis*	Hyannis, MA
November 11	Sch	*Harmony*	Chatham, MA
November 25	Brig	*Echo*	Wellfleet, MA
November 25	Sch	*Friendship*	Rockport, MA
November 28	Sch	*Minerva*	Gloucester, MA
December	Brig	*Miles Standish*	Nantucket, MA
December 6	Brig	*Algerine*	Rock Harbor, MA
December 6	Sch	*Caroline*	Nantucket Sound, MA
December 6	Brig	*Cynthia*	Rock Harbor, MA
December 6	Slp	*Louisa*	Nantucket, MA
December 6	Brig	Unidentified	Eastham, MA
December 8	Sch	Unidentified	Nantucket, MA

1831

DATE LOST	TYPE	NAME	WHERE LOST
January	Brig	*Socrates*	Wellfleet, MA
January 17	Sch	*Volant*	Sandwich, MA
January 22	Sch	*Boliva*	Nantucket Sound, MA
January 29	Brig	*Planet*	Wellfleet, MA
January 31	Sch	*Climax*	Wellfleet, MA
January 31	Sch	*Volunteer*	Provincetown, MA
February 2	Slp	*Ortolan*	Chatham, MA
April 6	Sch	*Lorenzo*	Nantucket Sound, MA
April 8	Sch	*Lady Hope*	Cape Ann, MA
April 9	Sch	*Warrior*	Block Island, RI
May 14	Stp	*Washington*	Milford, CT
July 24	Sch	*Speculator*	Coney Island, NY
November 7	Sch	*Amelia*	Off Provincetown, MA
November 7	Sch	*Francis*	Truro, MA

DATE LOST	TYPE	NAME	WHERE LOST
November 7	Sch	*Tonkey*	Chatham, MA
November 22	Sch	*Newcomb*	Block Island, RI
November 29	Sch	*Olive Branch*	Chatham, MA
November 30	Sch	*Hazard*	Truro, MA
December 1	Sch	*Success*	Chatham, MA
December 4	Ship	*President*	Romer Shoal, NY
December 10		Unidentified	Thatchers Island, MA
December 12	Sch	*Packet*	Nantucket, MA
December 21	Brig	*George Henry*	Chatham, MA
December 21	Sch	*Turk*	Chatham, MA

1832

	Ship	Unidentified	Hempstead, NY
January 5	Sch	*Rapid*	Provincetown, MA
January 28	Brig	*William Henry*	Nantucket, MA
February 9	Brig	*Java*	Eastham, MA
February 10	Brig	*Fitz Owen*	Rockport, MA
March	Brig	*Pacific*	Eastham, MA
March 11	Sch	*William*	Narragansett Bay, RI
May 21	Sch	*Sarah*	Pollock Rip, MA
May 31	Brig	*James McCoy*	Nantucket, MA
June 30		Unidentified	Cape Ann, MA
July 6	St	*Ohio*	New York, NY
July 21	Brig	*Splendid*	Truro, MA
September 4	Sch	*Mark*	Block Island, RI
October 20	Slp	*William*	Buzzards Bay, MA
November 12	St	*Martha Ogden*	New York, NY
December	Sch	*Babcock*	Easthampton, NY
December 8	Sch	*Richmond*	Provincetown, MA
December 8	Ship	*Warren*	Provincetown, MA
December 22	Slp	*Galen*	Cuttyhunk, MA

1833

January 10	Sch	*Arcade*	Buzzards Bay, MA
January 11	Slp	*Collector*	Narragansett Bay, RI
January 31	Sch	*Cherub*	Point Judith, RI
February 1	Sch	*Mechanic*	Cohasset, MA
March 4	Ship	*Sagamore*	Block Island, RI
May 16	Ship	*Ruth & Mary*	Block Island, RI
May 28	Brig	*Florida*	Nantucket, MA
October 2	Brig	*Amelia Charlotte*	Truro, MA
November	Slp	*Gazette*	Shelter Island, NY
November	Slp	*Imperial*	Plum Gut, NY
November	Sch	*Jane Ann*	Fishers Island, NY
November 9	Sch	*Panams*	Block Island, RI
November 11	Slp	*Napoleon*	Truro, MA
December	Slp	*Irene*	Hell Gate, NY
December 7	Sch	*Wareham*	Narragansett Bay, RI
December 8	Sch	*Polly*	Gloucester, MA
December 15	Brig	*Owhyhee*	Chatham, MA
December 17	Sch	*Ann Isabella*	Gloucester, MA

1834

	Brig	Unidentified	Smith Point, NY
February 26	Brig	*Norna*	Nantucket Shoals, MA
March 21	Sch	*Gem*	Nantucket, MA
July	Brig	*John Bergen*	Patchogue, NY

ABOVE: Out from the Canadian Maritimes, the bark *Kate Harding* ran ashore on Cape Cod during a northeast gale on November 30, 1892. The ship had so much damage below the waterline that she was declared a total loss and never floated again. *Photo from the collection of William P. Quinn, Orleans MA.* **BELOW**: When the *Gluckauf*, whose name means "Good Luck", was launched in June 1886, she was one of the earliest "tankships", able to carry bulk oil across the Atlantic. She is often referred to as the "the grandmother of the modern tanker". She stranded on Long Island, on March 29, 1893. *Photo courtesy Paul Morris, Nantucket MA.*

DATE LOST	TYPE	NAME	WHERE LOST
October 23	Sch	*Brookville*	Nantucket, MA
October 23	Sch	*Talma*	Nantucket, MA
November 22	Brig	*Ganges*	Nantucket, MA
November 26	Slp	*Fox*	Elizabeth Islands, MA
December 4	Sch	*Live Oak*	Elizabeth Islands, MA

1835

	Stp	*William Peacock*	Ripley, NY
January	Sch	*Warrior*	Barnstable, MA
January 6	Sch	*Hyperon*	Nantucket, MA
February 26	Sch	*Martha*	Chatham, MA
March 18	Slp	*Eloisa*	Watch Hill, RI
March 22	Sch	*Catherine*	Truro, MA
April 16	Sch	*Orleans*	Nantucket Sound, MA
April 18	Stp	*Chief Justice Marshall*	New Haven, CT
April 28	Sch	*Hellespont*	Gloucester, MA
April 28	Sch	*Maine*	Provincetown, MA
May 29	Brig	*Triumph*	Montauk, NY
June	Slp	*Catherine Maria*	Off Greenport, NY
June	Slp	*Morning Star*	Orient, NY
August 7	Brig	*John*	Nantucket, MA
December 16	Sch	*Sarah Ann*	Provincetown, MA

1836

January	Brig	*Henrietta*	Quogue, NY
February 4	Brig	*Regulator*	Plymouth, MA
February 5	Slp	*Reaper*	Nantucket, MA
May 26	Sch	*Amethyst*	Chatham, MA
May 26	Sch	*Eliza*	Nantucket, MA
June 11	Sch	*Pallender*	Nantucket, MA
June 20	Brig	*Eligible*	Bridgehampton, NY
July 12	Sch	*Sophronia*	Gloucester, MA
August 9	Sch	*Arms*	Truro, MA
August 23	Stp	*General Jackson*	New York, NY
September 28	Stp	*Independence*	Bangor, ME
October	Brig	*Solon*	Pollock Rip, MA
October	Stp	*Ticonic*	Hallowell, ME
October 11	Sch	*William Wallace*	Nantucket Sound, MA
October 12	Sch	*Mercator*	Block Island, RI
October 14	Brig	*Rising Sun*	Nantucket, MA
October 21	Stp	*Royal Tar*	Off Vinalhaven, ME
October 27	Stp	*Tom Thumb*	Boone Island, ME
November 21	Bark	*Bristol*	Far Rockaway, NY
November 21	Sch	*Lexington*	Narragansett Bay, RI
November 25	Brig	*Albion*	Nantucket, MA
December 17	Brig	*Shamrock*	Lynn, MA

1837

	Brig	*Ceylon*	Nantucket, MA
January 2	Bark	*Mexico*	Hempstead, NY
January 3	Ship	*Tamarac*	Islip, NY
January 6	Sch	*George*	Off Provincetown, MA
February	Brig	Unidentified	Southold, NY
February 8	Brig	*Bon Pere*	Moriches, NY
February 20	Brig	*Ellsworth*	Hull, MA
February 23	Ship	*Mercury*	Pollock Rip, MA
March 20	Brig	*Trio*	Boston, MA

DATE LOST	TYPE	NAME	WHERE LOST
June 20	Sch	*Deborah*	Elizabeth Islands, MA
June 30	Sch	*Triton*	Nahant, MA
September 12	Sch	*Warsaw*	Nantucket, MA
November 1	Sch	*Isabella*	New York, NY
November 14	Sch	*Betsey*	Provincetown, MA
November 14	Sch	*Columbus*	Block Island, RI
December	Brig	Unidentified	Cohasset, MA
December 9	Brig	*Curlew*	Salem, MA
December 29	Stp	*Carolina*	Schlosser, NY

1838

		Florida	Damariscotta, ME
		Franklin	New York, NY
	Brig	*J Palmer*	Brenton Reef, RI
May 18	Sch	*Ariel*	Nantucket, MA
May 24	Brig	*Tom Cringle*	Southampton, NY
May 31	Stp	*New England*	Off Boone Island, ME
November 10	Brig	*Helen*	Nantucket, MA
November 25	Sch	*Potomac*	Long Island Sound
November 30	Sch	*Splendid*	Buzzards Bay, MA

1839

	Sch	*Oxford*	Chatham, MA
		Sevo	Thatchers Island, MA
		Unidentified	Eastham, MA
		Unidentified	Coney Island, NY
		Unidentified	Coney Island, NY
		Unidentified	Coney Island, NY
January 26	Sch	*Abigail & Eliza*	Gloucester, MA
February 2	Slp	*Harvard*	Truro, MA
March 3	Brig	*Lucy Ann*	Truro, MA
April 18	Sch	*Mary*	Nantucket Sound, MA
May	Ship	*Edward Quesnel*	Napeague Beach, NY
June 4	Slp	*Emily*	Block Island, RI
June 15	Sch	*Emperor*	Southampton, NY
July		*John Mckeon*	Off New York
July 4	Fery	*Sampson*	New York Bay, NY
July 28		*Gratitude*	New York, NY
August 4	Sch	*New Union*	Chatham, MA
August 30	Sch	*Lion*	Nantucket, MA
August 30	Brig	*Nelson*	Nantucket, MA
August 30	Sch	*Prospect*	Marthas Vineyard, MA
September 5	Slp	*George*	Eastham, MA
December	Sch	*Elizabeth*	Sagaponack, NY
December	Sch	Unidentified	Off Cape Cod, MA
December 4	Bark	*Perzagno*	Essex, MA
December 5	Brig	*Charles Wells*	Hull, MA
December 13	Sch	Unidentified	Off Cape Cod, MA
December 15	Sch	*Amethyst*	Wellfleet, MA
December 15	Sch	*Antioch*	Cohasset, MA
December 15	Sch	*Boston*	Gloucester, MA
December 15	Sch	*Brillant*	Gloucester, MA
December 15	Sch	*Caledonia*	Wellfleet, MA
December 15	Brig	*Carrabassett*	Truro, MA
December 15	Sch	*Catherine Nichols*	Nahant, MA
December 15	Sch	*Charlotte*	Gloucester, MA
December 15	Sch	*Columbia*	Gloucester, MA
December 15	Sch	*Coopers Fancy*	Gloucester, MA

DATE LOST	TYPE	NAME	WHERE LOST
December 15	Brig	*Democrat*	Nantucket Sound, MA
December 15	Slp	*Eagle*	Gloucester, MA
December 15	Sch	*Eliza & Betsey*	Gloucester, MA
December 15	Sch	*Enterprise*	Cohasset, MA
December 15	Sch	*F Severs*	Gloucester, MA
December 15	Sch	*Fame*	Gloucester, MA
December 15	Sch	*Favorite*	Gloucester, MA
December 15	Slp	*Independence*	Provincetown, MA
December 15	Sch	*Industry*	Gloucester, MA
December 15	Brig	*Maria*	Wellfleet, MA
December 15	Sch	*Mary Gould*	Gloucester, MA
December 15	Sch	*Milo*	Gloucester, MA
December 15	Sch	*Neutrality*	Gloucester, MA
December 15	Sch	*Paul Jones*	Marblehead, MA
December 15	Slp	*Portland*	Gloucester, MA
December 15	Sch	*Robert Raikes*	Cohasset, MA
December 15	Sch	*Saint Cloud*	Gloucester, MA
December 15	Sch	*Sally*	Gloucester, MA
December 15	Sch	*Sally And Mary*	Gloucester, MA
December 15	Sch	*Sarah*	Gloucester, MA
December 15		*Sea Flower*	Marblehead, MA
December 15	Sch	*Shakespeare*	Provincetown, MA
December 15	Sch	*Splendid*	Gloucester, MA
December 15	Brig	*Unidentified*	Truro, MA
December 15	Sch	*Unidentified*	Wellfleet, MA
December 15	Sch	*Unidentified*	Wellfleet, MA
December 15		*Unidentified*	Rockport, MA
December 15		*Unidentified*	Rockport, MA
December 15	Sch	*Volant*	Gloucester, MA
December 15	Sch	*Walrus*	Rockport, MA
December 16	Brig	*Austin*	Provincetown, MA
December 16	Brig	*Rideout*	Provincetown, MA
December 16	Sch	*Scio*	Wellfleet, MA
December 21	Sch	*Charles*	East Thomaston, ME
December 22	Sch	*Charlotte*	Hull, MA
December 22	Sch	*Deposite*	Ipswich, MA
December 22	Bark	*Lloyd*	Hull, MA
December 22	Brig	*Pocohantas*	Plum Island, MA
December 22	Brig	*Richmond Packett*	Gloucester, MA
December 22	Sch	*Tremont*	Hampton Beach, NH
December 22	Sch	*Triumph*	Jeremys Point, NH
December 23	Sch	*Thetis*	Gloucester, MA
December 27	Brig	*Aladdin*	Gloucester, MA
December 27	Sch	*Leader*	Salem, MA
December 28	Sch	*Elizabeth Ann*	Provincetown, MA
December 28	Brig	*Imogene*	Provincetown, MA

1840

	Sch	*J Tolman*	Chatham, MA
	Sch	*Martha Steward*	Easthampton, NY
	Pckt	*Recide*	Eatons Neck, NY
	Sch	*Rispah*	Chatham, MA
	St	*Unidentified*	New York, NY
January 3	Bark	*Norfolk*	Provincetown, MA
January 13	Stp	*Lexington*	Long Island Sound
January 31	Brig	*Emolument*	Nantucket, MA
January 31	Sch	*Talmon*	Chatham, MA
March 7	Sch	*Rosilla*	Nantucket Sound, MA
March 13	Sch	*Prospect*	Ipswich, MA

DATE LOST	TYPE	NAME	WHERE LOST
March 22	Sch	*William*	Eastham, MA
March 26	Brig	*Tariff*	Cohasset, MA
March 29	Sch	*Nile*	Block Island, RI
March 29	Brig	Unidentified	Fire Island, NY
May 3	Sch	*Triton*	Nantucket, MA
June 6	Sch	*Hope & Susan*	Nantucket, MA
September 9	Sch	*Washington*	Newport, RI
September 27	Sch	*Lafayette*	Pollock Rip, MA
October 24	Ycht	*Catarina*	Glen Cove, NY
November 5	Sch	*Rodney*	Barnstable, MA
November 16	Sch	*Benevolence*	Newport, RI
November 22	Sch	*Brighton*	Nantucket Sound, MA
November 22	Slp	*William Frederick*	Block Island, RI
December 7	Sch	*Susan & Amelia*	Rock Harbor, MA
December 21	Slp	*Otho*	Off Provincetown, MA
December 22	Sch	*Chickatabut*	Narragansett Bay, RI
December 31	Sch	*Peru*	Wellfleet, MA

1841

DATE LOST	TYPE	NAME	WHERE LOST
	Brig	*Favorite*	Hull, MA
March 12	Stp	*President*	Off New England
April 24	Slp	*Only Daughter*	Nantucket, MA
April 24	Sch	Unidentified	Nantucket, MA
April 27	St	*Henry Eckford*	New York, NY
April 30	Slp	*Warsaw*	Cohasset, MA
April 30	Sch	*William*	Rockport, MA
August 9	Stp	*Erie*	Silver Creek, NY
September 30	Sch	*Almira*	Block Island, RI
October		*Forest*	Provincetown, MA
October		*Gov. Kingston*	Eastham, MA
October		*Mary Ann*	Eastham, MA
October		*Nautilus*	Eastham, MA
October 2	Sch	*Harvest*	Nantucket, MA
October 2		*Orb*	Nantucket, MA
October 2	Slp	*Platina*	Nantucket Sound, MA
October 2	Sch	*Tremont*	Nantucket Sound, MA
October 2		Unidentified	Nantucket, MA
October 3	Sch	*Byron*	Nantucket Sound, MA
October 3	Sch	*Clifford*	Rockport, MA
October 3	Sch	*Eliza Ann*	Gloucester, MA
October 3	Sch	*Garnet*	Truro, MA
October 3	Slp	*George Frederic*	Rockport, MA
October 3	Slp	*Granite*	Rockport, MA
October 3	Slp	*Hanson*	Rockport, MA
October 3		*Helen Mar*	Rockport, MA
October 3		*Jack Downing*	Annisquam, MA
October 3	Sch	*Liberty*	Nantucket Sound, MA
October 3		*Maine*	Scituate, MA
October 3		*Native*	Rockport, MA
October 3		*Pearl*	Rockport, MA
October 3	Sch	*Rob Roy*	Rockport, MA
October 3		*Traveller*	Rockport, MA
October 3	Sch	*Washington*	Rockport, MA
October 4	Sch	*Miller*	Hull, MA
October 30	Stp	*Bunker Hill*	Saybrook, CT
November	Sch	*Charles & Henry*	Old Field Point, NY
November 8	Sch	*Crusader*	Ipswich, MA
November 20	Brig	*Constantia*	Scituate, MA
November 24	Slp	*Confidence*	Point Judith, RI

ABOVE: The three masted *Howard W. Middleton* grounded in a thick fog at Scarborough, Maine in 1897. Salvage efforts were unsuccessful before nature took it's course on the hull. Her remains are typical of the many shipwrecks exposed to the elements on the northeast coast. **BELOW:** One of the larger wrecks on Fisher's Island is that of the *SS Olinda* which went ashore on the south side of the island on June 11, 1895. When she was accidentally run on the rocks, she was under the control of a Fall River pilot. *Photo courtesy Paul Morris, Nantucket MA.*

DATE LOST	TYPE	NAME	WHERE LOST
December 17	Ship	*Mohawk*	Hull, MA
December 17	Sch	*Saloon*	Cape Ann, MA

1842

DATE LOST	TYPE	NAME	WHERE LOST
	Ship	*Plato*	Montauk, NY
		San Jacinto	New York, NY
	Brig	Unidentified	Chatham, MA
January 1	Sch	*Atoniette*	Block Island, RI
February 16	Sch	*Ruby*	Gloucester, MA
March 2	Brig	*Brutus*	Chatham, MA
April 14	Ship	*Louis Philippe*	Mecox, NY
April 17	Slp	*Fame*	Gloucester, MA
May		*Lively*	Wellfleet, MA
June 13	Sch	*Reindeer*	Newport, RI
June 24	Sch	*William & John*	Block Island, RI
November		*Milo*	Isle of Shoals, NH
November 17	Slp	*Euphrates*	Sakonnet, RI
November 27	Ship	*Joseph Starbuck*	Nantucket, MA
November 30	Bark	*Isadore*	Ogunquit, ME
November 30	Sch	*Pequot*	Sakonnet, RI
November 30	Sch	Unidentified	Point Judith, RI
December 30		*Maine*	Cohasset, MA

1843

DATE LOST	TYPE	NAME	WHERE LOST
	Sch	*Concord*	Narragansett Bay, RI
		Fly	New York, NY
	Slp	*J G Meyers*	Hyannis, MA
	Bark	*Mohawk*	Hyannis, MA
February 5	Sch	*Delight In Piece*	Sakonnet, RI
February 9	Slp	*Herald Lake*	Block Island, RI
March 6	Sch	*Maize*	Nantucket Sound, MA
March 17	Sch	*Thomas*	Nahant, MA
March 23	Ship	*Francis & Lovell*	Pollock Rip, MA
March 28	Slp	*Meridian*	Gloucester, MA
September 3	Stp	*John W Richmond*	Hallowell, ME
October 20	Slp	*Briliant*	Gloucester, MA
November 27	Sch	*Mary Francis*	Nantucket, MA
December 28	Sch	Unidentified	Chatham, MA

1844

DATE LOST	TYPE	NAME	WHERE LOST
	Sch	*Aid*	Chatham, MA
	Sch	*Carribean*	Chatham, MA
	Brig	*Cumberland*	Truro, MA
	Sch	*Diskau*	Chatham, MA
	Brig	*Francis & Louisa*	Eastham, MA
	Slp	*Hannah & Maria*	Eastham, MA
	Sch	*Lexington*	Chatham, MA
	Sch	*Plover*	Chatham, MA
		Unidentified	Vineyard Sound, MA
		Unidentified	Vineyard Sound, MA
		Unidentified	Vineyard Sound, MA
January 5	Sch	*Mexico*	Nantucket, MA
January 7	Sch	*Martha Robinson*	Vineyard Haven, MA
January 12	Slp	Unidentified	Point Judith, RI
January 13	Sch	*Charles Thompson*	Quonochontaug, RI
March	Brig	*Rebecca C Fisher*	Shinnecock, NY

DATE LOST	TYPE	NAME	WHERE LOST
March 30	Sch	*Australian*	Cohasset, MA
August 7	Slp	*Champion*	Point Judith, RI
August 21	Sch	*Maluina*	Chatham, MA
September 19	Sch	*Extra*	Newport, RI
September 29	Slp	*Bulletin*	Sakonnet, RI
September 29	Brig	*General Wayne*	Narragansett Bay, RI
September 29	Brig	*Mars Hill*	Block Island, RI
October 7	Brig	*Tremont*	Hull, MA
October 23	Stp	*Robert Fulton*	Sturgeon Point, NY
November 5	Sch	*Thames*	Nantucket, MA
November 12	Brig	*Osceola*	Truro, MA
November 25	Slp	*Charles*	Nantucket, MA
November 25	Sch	*Fair Play*	Nantucket, MA
November 27	Sch	*Addison*	Nantucket, MA
December 7	Sch	*Harriet*	Off Nantucket, MA
December 8	Sch	*Exile*	Scituate, MA
December 8	Sch	*Non Pareil*	Provincetown, MA
December 11		*Fawn*	Gloucester, MA
December 11	Ship	*Massoit*	Hull, MA
December 17	Sch	*Helen Mar*	Cape Ann, MA
December 18	Sch	*Litchfield*	Nantucket, MA
December 22	Bark	*Charlie Hickman*	Forge River, NY

1845

	Sch	*Maria Hill*	Chatham, MA
	Brig	*Pactolus*	Chatham, MA
	Sch	*Rappahannock*	Eastham, MA
		Robert Peel	Metinic Island, ME
	Sch	*W Hawes*	Nantucket Sound, MA
January	Ship	*Unidentified*	Isle Au Haut, ME
January 13	Slp	*Huntress*	Narragansett Bay, RI
January 14	Sch	*Maria*	Eastham, MA
January 14	Brig	*Marine*	Scituate, MA
February 4	Brig	*Emerald*	Gloucester, MA
February 4	Sch	*Marietta*	Hyannis, MA
February 4	Sch	*Texas*	Hyannis, MA
February 6		*Reeside*	Lloyds Neck, NY
February 12	Pckt	*Sheffield*	Gilgo Bar, NY
February 13	Bark	*La Plata*	Lower Bay, NY
March 12		*Unidentified*	Deer Island, ME
March 19	Sch	*Jasper*	Nantucket, MA
May		*Reform*	Off New York, NY
May 8	Slp	*Fame*	Marthas Vineyard, MA
May 16	Sch	*Unidentified*	Pollock Rip, MA
May 22	Sch	*Royal Tar*	Thatchers Island, MA
July 18	Ship	*Centurion*	Nantucket Shoals, MA
July 29	Sch	*Margaret*	Chatham, MA
October 15	Brig	*Mariner*	Nantucket, MA
October 17	Sch	*Meridian*	Nantucket, MA
November 11	Sch	*Cato*	Gloucester, MA
November 11	Sch	*Garnet*	Cape Ann, MA
December 16	Bark	*Zamorer*	Plymouth, MA

1846

	Brig	*Orcott*	Eastham, MA
	Brig	*Saint Thomas*	Eastham, MA
January 17	Slp	*Laureate*	Portsmouth, RI
January 30	Bark	*Oregon*	Eastham, MA

DATE LOST	TYPE	NAME	WHERE LOST
March 14	Ship	*Earl Of Eglington*	Nantucket, MA
March 17		*Susan*	Southampton, NY
May 10	Sch	*Waldo*	Marthas Vineyard, MA
June 19	Sch	*Samuel*	Chatham, MA
September 15	Brig	*William*	Nantucket, MA
October 17	Brig	*Sutlej*	Cuttyhunk, MA
October 22	Sch	*Charles Henry*	Chatham, MA
November	Brig	*Lincoln*	Marthas Vineyard, MA
November	Ship	Unidentified	Cranberry Islands, ME
November 1	St	*Rhode Island*	Huntington, NY
November 9	Sch	*Eliza*	Rockport, MA
November 21	Brig	*Old Colony*	Nantucket Shoals, MA
November 21	Sch	Unidentified	Nantucket, MA
November 23	Sch	*Susan & Jane*	Nantucket, MA
November 26	Stp	*Atlantic*	Fishers Island, NY
November 27	Sch	*Boston Packet*	Truro, MA
November 27	Sch	*Elizabeth*	Nantucket, MA
December 8	Brig	*Rolla*	Canoe Place, NY
December 18	Sch	*Mary Howard*	Gloucester, MA
December 18	Brig	*Melazzo*	Cohasset, MA

1847

		Ashland	Southampton, NY
	Sch	*Harvard*	Eastham, MA
		Walcott	Nantucket, MA
January 19	Brig	*Orissa*	Chatham, MA
January 23	St	*Alexandre La Valle*	Southampton, NY
February 18	Ship	*Jenny Lind*	Cohasset, MA
March 3		Unidentified	Montauk, NY
March 21	Bark	*Cactus*	Truro, MA
March 23	Brig	*Baltic*	Truro, MA
May	Bark	*Isidore*	Trundy's Reef, ME
May 2	Slp	*Hudson*	Buzzards Bay, MA
May 22	Sch	*Susan*	Cape Ann, MA
June 11	Sch	*Rio Grande*	Gloucester, MA
August 4	Sch	*Banner*	Matinicus Island, ME
August 18	Sch	*Two Marys*	Block Island, RI
September 4	Brig	*Oreco*	Vineyard Sound, MA
September 25	Sch	*Surplus*	Hull, MA
September 30	Ship	*Auburn*	Long Island Bch, NY
October 12	Sch	*Edward*	Narragansett Bay, RI
October 15	Brig	*N F Frothingham*	Wellfleet, MA
November 5	Sch	*Commerce*	Chatham, MA
November 14	Brig	*Reo*	Newport, RI
November 25		*Alabama*	Minots Ledge, MA
November 28	Sch	*Nancy*	Off Nantucket, MA
November 29	Sch	*May*	Falmouth, MA
December 16	Ship	*Louise Phillipe*	Nantucket, MA
December 18	Sch	*Malvina*	Cohasset, MA

1848

	Sch	*Cyrus Chamberlin*	Eastham, MA
	Brig	*E O Holt*	Chatham, MA
	Brig	*Isabella*	Chatham, MA
	Sch	*Margaret Ann*	Chatham, MA
	Sch	*Oneco*	Nantucket, MA
	Slp	*Rough & Ready*	Chatham, MA
January 8	Sch	*Lion*	Vineyard Sound, MA

DATE LOST	TYPE	NAME	WHERE LOST
January 15	Bark	*Natchez*	Marshfield, MA
March	Sch	Unidentified	Montauk, NY
May 10	Slp	*General Mercer*	Long Island Sound
June 12		*George & Alfred*	Nantucket Sound, MA
June 28	Sch	*Emeline*	Eastham, MA
September 15	Sch	*President*	Thatchers Island, MA
September 18	Ship	*Rough & Ready*	Marshfield, MA
October 1	Brig	*Oceanus*	Scituate, MA
October 18	Sch	*Two Sisters*	Cape Ann, MA
November	Sch	Unidentified	Westhampton, NY
November 5	Brig	*Sirico*	Scituate, MA
November 19	Slp	*Reformation*	Narragansett Bay, RI
November 20	Ship	*Clara*	Truro, MA
December 21	Sch	*Van Buren*	Eastham, MA
December 27	Sch	*A P Fielding*	Provincetown, MA
December 27		*Lowell*	Cape Ann, MA

1849

	Brig	*Dracut*	Eastham, MA
	Sch	*Gold Hunter*	Chatham, MA
	Sch	Unidentified	Chatham, MA
	Brig	*Warner*	Eastham, MA
January 2	Brig	*Spartan*	Cuttyhunk, MA
January 2		*Wyoming*	Nantucket, MA
January 13	Sch	*Susan Benjamin*	Orleans, MA
February 9	Bark	*Kate Kearney*	Chatham, MA
February 17	Sch	*Matilda*	Nantucket Shoals, MA
February 18	Bark	*Oscar*	Scituate, MA
March 3	Ship	*Franklin*	Wellfleet, MA
March 3		Unidentified	Montauk, NY
March 27	Sch	*Charles*	Gloucester, MA
April 2	Brig	*Ontario*	Rockport, MA
May 31	Ship	*London*	Wellfleet, MA
October		*Levi Woodbury*	Boone Island, ME
October 7	Brig	*St John*	Off Cohasset, MA
October 7	Sch	Unidentified	Provincetown, MA
October 12	St	*Spitfire*	New York, NY
October 13	Brig	*Lelolla Leoiah*	Pollock Rip, MA
October 14	Slp	*Juno*	Off Rhode Island
October 22	Sch	*America*	Block Island, RI
October 24	Sch	*Amazon*	Nantucket Shoals, MA
October 25	Stp	*New World*	Point Washington, NY
December 3	Sch	*Sarah Hamilton*	Eastham, MA
December 7	Sch	*Atlantic*	Off Cape Cod, MA
December 8	Slp	*Clementine*	Cape Ann, MA
December 19	Sch	*Minnisota*	Eastham, MA
December 19	Sch	*Post Boy*	Gloucester, MA
December 20	Sch	*Java*	Rye Beach, NH
December 30	Sch	*Splendid*	Off Seguin Island, ME

1850

	Sch	*Flash*	Chatham, MA
	Sch	*Golden Rule*	Wellfleet, MA
	Sch	*Juno*	Hyannis, MA
	Sch	*Palo Alto*	Chatham, MA
	St	*Resolute*	New York, NY
	Sch	*Seraph*	Chatham, MA
	Brig	*Majestic*	Moriches, NY

ABOVE: Kennebunkport, Maine produced many strong, seaworthy, commercial sailing vessels. Unfortunately, the three masted schooner *Louis V. Place*, shown here after launching, had only a few years of service before she wrecked with the loss of six men. **BELOW**: In February 1895, she stranded near Moriches, Long Island, forcing her crew into the rigging. By the second day, six men had succumbed to the winter winds. When the heavy seas abated, the Life Saving Service was finally able to get a lifeboat to the wreck and rescue the survivors. *Photo from the collection of William P. Quinn, Orleans MA.*

DATE LOST	TYPE	NAME	WHERE LOST
	Brig	*Mount Vernon*	Wellfleet, MA
		Persian	Moriches, NY
	Brig	Unidentified	Wellfleet, MA
	Brig	Unidentified	Wellfleet, MA
	Brig	*Victory*	Provincetown, MA
January 10	Slp	*Triumph*	Nantucket, MA
February	Ship	*Ivanhoe*	Nantucket Shoals, MA
February 10	Brig	*Minerva*	Gilgo, NY
March 1	Sch	*Eleanor*	Nantucket Sound, MA
March 4	St	*Charter Oak*	New York, NY
March 12	Sch	*Franklin*	Nantucket Shoals, MA
March 13	Sch	*Covenent*	Provincetown, MA
March 15	Sch	*Athalia*	Truro, MA
March 21	Sch	*Dolphin*	Nantucket, MA
March 21	Sch	*Hattie Maria*	Nantucket, MA
March 25		*Fredrick*	Penobscot Bay, ME
March 25	Slp	*Napolean*	Falmouth, MA
April	Slp	*Pilot*	Cape Cod Bay, MA
April 2	Brig	*Ellen Maria*	Marthas Vineyard, MA
April 4	Sch	*Pearl*	Gloucester, MA
April 5	Brig	*L'Essai*	Hull, MA
April 6	Brig	*Hayward*	Truro, MA
April 8	Sch	*Anti*	Thatchers Island, MA
April 14	Slp	*Rienz*	Watch Hill, RI
May 6	Ship	Unidentified	Montauk, NY
May 13	Sch	*Essex*	Scituate, MA
June 2	Brig	*Watchman*	Fisher's Island, NY
June 7	Sch	*Convoy*	Chatham, MA
June 14	Brig	*Lucy*	Long Island Sound
June 22	Stp	*Warren*	New York, NY
June 23	Brig	*Salon*	Cutler, ME
June 26	Sch	*Steeprock*	Off Shore, ME
July 13	Sch	*David Ames*	Pollock Rip, MA
July 14	Sch	*Myrtle*	Nantucket, MA
July 19	Sch	*Charles L Vost*	West Quoddy Head, ME
July 19	Bark	*Elizabeth*	Fire Island, NY
July 19	Sch	*Philosopher*	Nantucket, MA
July 19	Sch	Unidentified	Quoddy Head, ME
July 19	Sch	*William Penn*	Cutler, ME
July 27	Sch	*Peerless*	Vineyard Haven, MA
July 29	Sch	*Hercules*	Grand Manan Channel, ME
October 26	Sch	*Magdalia*	Nantucket Sound, MA
October 27	Sch	*Yonke Hero*	Cape Ann, MA
October 31	Sch	Unidentified	Chatham, MA
November	Sch	*Extra*	Crane Neck, NY
November 17	Sch	*Homer*	Nantucket, MA
November 17	Bark	Unidentified	Nantucket, MA
November 19	Sch	*Eliza Hupper*	Nantucket, MA

1851

	Sch	*Haven*	Truro, MA
	Sch	*Lightfoot*	Chatham, MA
March 1	Brig	*Jane*	Nantucket, MA
April	Sch	*Barrington*	Salem, MA
April	Sch	Unidentified	Marshfield, MA
April 8	Sch	*British Queen*	Portsmouth, NH
April 15	Ship	*Columbus*	Nantucket Sound, MA
April 16	Sch	*Augusta*	Wood Island, ME
April 16	Sch	*Boston Packet*	South Boston, MA

DATE LOST	TYPE	NAME	WHERE LOST
April 16	Ship	*Columbus*	Barnstable, MA
April 16	Sch	*Crown*	Portsmouth, NH
April 16	Brig	*Elizabeth*	Marshfield, MA
April 16	Brig	*Esther*	Nauset Beach, MA
April 16	Sch	*Exchange*	Boston, MA
April 16	Sch	*Fredonia*	Plymouth, MA
April 16	Sch	*Frowley*	Boston, MA
April 16	Sch	*Marianne*	Truro, MA
April 16	Sch	*Pearl*	Boston, MA
April 16	Brig	*Primrose*	Cape Ann, MA
April 16	Sch	*Token*	Gloucester, MA
April 16	Sch	*Uncus*	Nantucket, MA
April 16	Sch	Unidentified	Truro, MA
April 16	Sch	*Volunteer*	Clarks Island, ME
April 16	Sch	*Wave*	Hull, MA
April 16	Brig	*Wellamo*	Scituate, MA
April 17	Sch	*Thistle*	Kittery, ME
April 18	Sch	*Eagle*	Truro, MA
April 30	Sch	*C M Walton*	Sakonnet, RI
May 13	Sch	*Post Bay*	Chatham, MA
June 27	Bark	*Henry*	Mecox, NY
August 7	St	*Trojan*	New York, NY
August 25	Ship	*Catherine*	Amagansett, NY
August 25	Sch	*Harriet*	Block Island, RI
August 25	Sch	*Superior*	Block Island, RI
August 27	Sch	*Union*	Vineyard Haven, MA
September 6	Slp	*Julia Ann*	Rockport, MA
September 13	Slp	*Fame*	Off Shore, RI
September 21	Sch	*Franklin*	Chatham, MA
September 21	Brig	*Partridge*	Scituate, MA
September 21	Bark	*Ulster*	Cohasset, MA
November 20	Sch	*Oread*	Gloucester, MA
November 21	Brig	*Exile*	Nahant, MA
November 30	Brig	*Hope*	Thatchers Island, MA
December 1	Brig	*Lucy Ellen*	Nantucket, MA
December 1	Sch	*Mary George*	Nantucket, MA
December 1	Brig	Unidentified	Nantucket, MA
December 15	Sch	*Wellington*	Nantucket, MA
December 18	Ship	*British Queen*	Nantucket Sound, MA

1852

DATE LOST	TYPE	NAME	WHERE LOST
		Commerce	Off New York, NY
	Sch	*Fellowship*	Narragansett Bay, RI
	Sch	*James A Boyd*	Chatham, MA
	Sch	*Martha C Titus*	Sagaponack, NY
	Brig	*Sallie*	Pollock Rip, MA
	Sch	*Thatcher Fanton*	Marthas Vineyard, MA
January 6	Sch	*Caroline*	Barnstable, MA
January 23	Sch	*James A Paine*	Chatham, MA
January 23	Sch	*North Star*	Chatham, MA
February 12	Ship	*Constantine*	Babylon, NY
February 12	Ship	*Shanunga*	Nantucket, MA
February 17	Brig	*Sunny Eye*	Vineyard Sound, MA
February 18	Brig	*Ellen Maria*	Quonochontaug, RI
February 28	Sch	*George Evans*	Cape Ann, MA
April	Brig	*Colonia*	Provincetown, MA
April 6	Brig	*Maria*	Cohasset, MA
April 6	Brig	Unidentified	Off Provincetown, MA
April 8	Brig	*Marriel*	Cohasset, MA

DATE LOST	TYPE	NAME	WHERE LOST
April 9	Sch	*Louisa*	Nantucket, MA
April 13	Bark	*Gay Head*	Duxbury, MA
April 13	Sch	*Mary*	Cape Ann, MA
April 18	Brig	*Margaret*	Eastham, MA
April 19	Bark	*Jane Duffer*	Chatham, MA
April 19	Brig	*Romp*	Chatham, MA
April 19	Sch	*Sarah*	Chatham, MA
April 20		*Inez*	Provincetown, MA
April 20	Bark	*Josephia*	Truro, MA
April 20	Bark	*Queen*	Provincetown, MA
April 20	Sch	Unidentified	Provincetown, MA
April 20	Sch	Unidentified	Provincetown, MA
April 21	Sch	*Chalcedony*	Marshfield, MA
April 21	Brig	*Marcus*	Scituate, MA
May 17	Sch	*Mary Chilton*	Cuttyhunk, MA
June 9	Brig	*A Dunbar*	Cuttyhunk, MA
June 9	Sch	*Betsey*	Chatham, MA
July 22	Stp	*Alice*	Bridgeport, CT
July 28	Stp	*Henry Clay*	Riverdale, NY
August 4	Sch	*Union*	Nantucket, MA
September 10	Stp	*Reindeer*	Malden, NY
September 28	Ship	*Amulet*	Off Long Island, NY
October 19	Sch	*Mary Elizabeth*	Vineyard Haven, MA
October 21	Brig	*Roscoe*	Marthas Vineyard, MA
November 13	Sch	*Frances*	Thatchers Island, MA
November 16	Sch	*Henry*	Cape Ann, MA
December 3		*Yankee*	New York, NY
December 9	Brig	*Callao*	Chatham, MA
December 14	Sch	*Vonda-Vandia*	Chatham, MA
December 24	Bark	*Forest Prince*	Nantucket, MA

1853

	Sch	*Benjamin H Hold*	Nantucket Sound, MA
	Brig	*Cordelia*	Eastham, MA
	Brig	*Lemontine*	Narragansett Bay, RI
	Sch	*Mary A Taylor*	Chatham, MA
	Brig	*Monte Christo*	Eastham, MA
	Brig	*Virginia*	Chatham, MA
January 3	Sch	*Charles Appleton*	Nantucket, MA
January 4	Sch	*I O Of O F*	Nantucket, MA
February 17		Unidentified	Nepeague, NY
March 1	Sch	*Narcissa*	Off Provincetown, MA
March 1	Sch	*Sarah Lewis*	Marthas Vineyard, MA
March 1	Bark	*Vernon*	Scituate, MA
March 1	Sch	*William Bacon*	Vineyard Sound, MA
May		*Ocean Nymph*	Provincetown, MA
June 25	Sch	*Boxer*	Chatham, MA
July	Sch	*R B Glover*	Newport, RI
August 24	Sch	*Orient*	Chatham, MA
August 25	Sch	*Susan M Young*	Easthampton, NY
August 26	St	Unidentified	New York, NY
September 24	Slp	*Cabinet*	Millers Place, NY
September 28	Sch	*Emily B Souder*	Sakonnet, RI
October 7	Sch	*Othello*	Chatham, MA
October 27	Brig	Unidentified	Provincetown, MA
November 4	St	*James Rumsey*	New York, NY
November 23	Sch	*N & L Wasson*	Chatham, MA
November 24	Sch	*Drinkwater*	Nantucket, MA
November 24	Brig	*Madison*	Nantucket, MA

DATE LOST	TYPE	NAME	WHERE LOST
November 24	Sch	*Rebecca Fogg*	Nantucket, MA
December 8	Stp	*Montague*	New York, NY
December 16	Ship	*Abby Pratt*	Nantucket Shoals, MA
December 23	Sch	*W W Dyer*	Vineyard Haven, MA
December 24	Sch	*J C Calhoun*	Vineyard Sound, MA
December 27	Ship	*White Squall*	New York, NY
December 29	Sch	*Amaranth*	Duxbury, MA
December 29	Sch	*Eben Sawyer*	Plymouth, MA
December 29	Bark	*Ida*	Provincetown, MA
December 29	Sch	*Willow*	Nantucket Sound, MA
December 29	Sch	*Yarmouth*	Nantucket Sound, MA
December 30		*Marine*	Eastham, MA

1854

DATE LOST	TYPE	NAME	WHERE LOST
	St	*Jacob Bell*	Hudson River, NY
	Sch	*Telegraph*	Vineyard Sound, MA
	Sch	*Wasp*	Provincetown, MA
	Sch	*Willow*	Marthas Vineyard, MA
January	St	*Ericsson*	North River, NY
January	Sch	*Ina*	Plymouth, MA
January	Sch	*Philidelphia*	Plymouth, MA
January 2	Sch	*Mozelle*	Newport, RI
January 12	Brig	*Royal Southwick*	Vineyard Sound, MA
January 13	Brig	*Eleanor*	Nantucket Sound, MA
January 20	Brig	*Clio*	Scituate, MA
January 20	Brig	*Velasco*	Duxbury, MA
January 20	Sch	*Woodell*	Marshfield, MA
February 3	Sch	*Rattle Snake*	Block Island, RI
February 6	Sch	*Alfred*	Wellfleet, MA
February 6	Bark	*Amanda*	Marshfield, MA
February 6	Brig	*Czarina*	Chatham, MA
February 9	Sch	*William*	Vineyard Haven, MA
March 1	Sch	*Russell*	Plymouth, MA
March 19	Sch	*Golden Hunter*	Nantucket Sound, MA
May 2	Sch	*Forrester*	Wellfleet, MA
May 2	Sch	*Maize*	Chatham, MA
May 13	Sch	*D Lumbard*	Narragansett Bay, RI
May 15		*Montezuma*	Jones Beach, NY
May 15	Sch	*President*	Block Island, RI
June 29	St	*Buffalo*	New York, NY
July 17	Stp	*Franklin*	Center Moriches, NY
July 28	Stp	*Agawan*	East Haddam, CT
July 28	Sch	*Boston*	Orient Point, NY
August 3	Sts	*M K Wilson*	Saybrook, CT
August 16	Stp	*May Queen*	Staten Island, NY
August 18		*New England*	Nantucket, MA
September 7	Sch	*Statesman*	Block Island, RI
September 10	Sch	*Fame*	Cape Ann, MA
September 29	Sch	*Tallent*	Cape Ann, MA
October 9	Sts	*Mohawk*	Saybrook, CT
November	St	*Traveler*	Long Island Sound
November	Brig	Unidentified	Scituate, MA
November 1	St	*Champion*	Matinecock Point, NY
November 7	Ship	*Virgin Mary*	Long Island, NY
November 15		Unidentified	New York, NY
November 15		Unidentified	New York, NY
November 15		Unidentified	Long Island, NY
November 15		Unidentified	Long Island, NY
November 15		Unidentified	Long Island, NY

ABOVE: The paddle wheel steamer *Portland* was lost in a gale off Cape Cod on November 27, 1898. Over 160 people lost their lives when the steamer became storm-bound and went to pieces. Entitled *LOSS OF THE STEAMER PORTLAND ON PEAKED HILL BAR*, this picture was drawn with some imagination since it is felt that no lifeboats could ever be launched in such a storm. *Courtesy Allie Ryan Collection, Maine Maritime Academy.* **BELOW:** Many ships were engaged in the fruit trade between Cuba and the northeast during the first quarter of the 1900s. On March 27, 1901, the Norwegian steamer *Gwent* went ashore at Long Beach N.Y. She had fruit and passengers from Cuba bound for New York. *Photo courtesy Paul Morris, Nantucket MA.*

DATE LOST	TYPE	NAME	WHERE LOST
November 15		Unidentified	Long Island, NY
November 15		Unidentified	Long Island, NY
November 22	Sch	*Sarah & Maria*	Cape Ann, MA
November 24	Stp	*Ocean*	Boston, MA
December	Sch	*Helana*	Narragansett Bay, RI
December	Sch	*William Henry*	Narragansett Bay, RI
December 1	Sch	*Susan*	Cape Ann, MA
December 3	Sch	*Boston*	Marshfield, MA
December 3	Brig	*Lafayette*	Scituate, MA
December 3	Brig	*Lamarting*	Narragansett Bay, RI
December 3	Sch	*Two Brothers*	Chatham, MA
December 20	Brig	*Samuel Cambell*	Scituate, MA

1855

	Sch	*Jane Pindle*	Elizabeth Islands, MA
	Sch	*Mary E Mchale*	Quonochontaug, RI
	Sch	*Mecklenburg*	Vineyard Haven, MA
	Sch	*R B Pitts*	Elizabeth Islands, MA
	Sch	*Tryall*	Point Judith, RI
January 17	Brig	*Maritimay*	Chatham, MA
January 20	Ship	*Favorite*	Salem, MA
March 10	Sch	*A Damon*	Scituate, MA
March 10	Bark	*California*	Chatham, MA
March 10	Bark	*Edisto*	Eastham, MA
March 10	Ship	*Hudson*	Brewster, MA
March 10	Sch	*Hutoka*	Provincetown, MA
March 10	Sch	*Morning Star*	Barnstable, MA
April 10	Brig	*Boston*	Nantucket, MA
May 3		*John*	Falmouth, MA
May 20	Sch	*Charles*	Barnstable, MA
June 28	Ship	*Robert*	Wickapogue, NY
August 12	Sch	*Judis Ward*	Offshore RI
September	Sch	*William*	Scituate, MA
October 25	Brig	*St George*	Cuttyhunk, MA
December	Bark	Unidentified	Montauk, NY
December 11	Sch	*Horace Nichols*	Vineyard Sound, MA
December 17	Ship	*Ontario*	Nantucket, MA
December 29		*Sarah & Ellen*	Newport, RI

1856

	Bark	*John Gilpin*	Cape Cod Bay, MA
	Brig	*R H Moulton*	Vineyard Haven, MA
	Bark	*San Jacinto*	Chatham, MA
	St	*Shephers Knapp*	New York, NY
	Sch	*Silver Bell*	Marthas Vineyard, MA
	Bark	*Tammany*	Vineyard Haven, MA
January	Fery	*Columbus*	Battery, NY
January 6	Sch	*George Savery*	Wellfleet, MA
January 13	Sch	*Josephine*	Gloucester, MA
February 3	Bark	*Gem*	Newport, RI
February 11	Sch	*Mary C Ames*	Nantucket, MA
February 27	Sch	*Louisana*	Cape Ann, MA
March	Brig	Unidentified	Amagansett, NY
March 24	Brig	*Clements*	Narragansett Bay, RI
March 25	Brig	*Daniel Webster*	Amagansett, NY
April 3	Sch	*D W Dickson*	Newport, RI
May 9		*David Parker*	Sandwich, MA

DATE LOST	TYPE	NAME	WHERE LOST
June 14	Stp	*E I Dupond*	Jamaica, NY
August	Sch	*M S Hall*	Cohasset, MA
August 21	Sch	*Mary Snow*	Annisquam, MA
August 21	Sch	Unidentified	Cape Ann, MA
August 21	Sch	*William Henry*	Ipswich, MA
September 18	Sch	*Julia Ann Staples*	Chatham, MA
September 21	Sch	*Mist*	Cape Ann, MA
September 30	Sch	*Shark*	Nahant, MA
October 6		*Chalcedony*	Nantucket, MA
October 28	Sch	*Splendid*	Nantucket, MA
November 2		*Charles Simmons*	Nantucket Sound, MA
November 2		*Lyonnais*	Nantucket, MA
November 10	Sch	*Thatcher Taylor*	Nantucket Sound, MA
November 23	Sch	*Fly*	Nantucket, MA
November 29	Bark	*Solomon Piper*	Chatham, MA
November 30	Sch	*Sarah*	Nantucket, MA
December	Sch	*Belcher*	Off Provincetown, MA
December	Sch	*Charles Prindle*	Brewster, MA
December 2	Sch	*Copier*	Chatham, MA
December 5	Sch	*Fair Trader*	Chatham, MA
December 5	Sch	*Tribune*	Off Provincetown, MA
December 10	Brig	*Vernon*	Vineyard Haven, MA
December 14	Brig	*Flying Cloud*	Montauk, NY
December 15	Brig	*Brazilian*	Nantucket Sound, MA
December 17	Stp	*Flushing*	Machias, ME
December 21	Bark	*Jenny Lind*	Provincetown, MA
December 22	St	*Knoxville*	New York, NY

1857

DATE LOST	TYPE	NAME	WHERE LOST
	Bark	*Chester*	Chatham, MA
	Brig	*E P Sweet*	Wellfleet, MA
	Sch	*Maria*	Nantucket Shoals, MA
	Brig	*Pilgrim*	Vineyard Sound, MA
	Bark	*Sinbad Sultan*	Eastham, MA
	Brig	*Susan*	Marthas Vineyard, MA
	Brig	*Yankee*	Elizabeth Islands, MA
January		*Irene*	Moriches, NY
January 10		*Sylph*	Off Fire Island, NY
January 18	Sch	*Harp*	Rockport, MA
January 18		*Liberator*	Rockport, MA
January 18	Ship	*Orissa*	Eastham, MA
January 18	Bark	*Tedesco*	Swampscott, MA
January 18	Sch	*Trader*	Gloucester, MA
January 18		*Washington*	Off Shore, NY
January 19		*California*	Cohasset, MA
January 19	Sch	*Geneva*	Scituate, MA
January 19	Brig	*Judge Hathaway*	Scituate, MA
January 19	Bark	*New Empire*	Cohasset, MA
January 19	Sch	*Rough & Ready*	Block Island, RI
January 19	Brig	*Swan*	Ipswich, MA
February	Slp	*Clinton*	Narragansett Bay, RI
February 13	Stp	*Chelsea*	Saugerties, NY
March 2	Ship	*Delaware*	Hull, MA
March 2	Brig	*Lorana*	Hull, MA
March 2	Brig	*Odessa*	Hull, MA
March 4	Stp	*East Boston*	Boston, MA
March 4	Brig	*Ellen Maria*	Eastham, MA
April 19	Sch	*Tiberius*	Chatham, MA
June 1	Bark	*General Taylor*	Nantucket, MA

DATE LOST	TYPE	NAME	WHERE LOST
July 2		Priscilla	Gloucester, MA
July 22	Sch	Cion	Ipswich, MA
August 15	St	J N Harris	Faulkners Island, CT
October 15	Bark	John Swasey	Nantucket, MA
October 15	Bark	Parodi	Block Island, RI

1858

DATE LOST	TYPE	NAME	WHERE LOST
	Sch	B F Sparks	Elizabeth Islands, MA
	Bark	Danial Webster	Falmouth, MA
	Sch	E F Lewis	Chatham, MA
	Sch	Golden Gate	Pollock Rip, MA
	Sch	Lion	Chatham, MA
	Sch	Lookout	Chatham, MA
	Sch	Mary Ann	Chatham, MA
	Sch	Mary F	Eastham, MA
	Sch	Seraph	Wellfleet, MA
February 2	Bark	N G Highborn	Nantucket, MA
February 16	Sch	Eben Atkins	Chatham, MA
February 20	Ship	John Milton	Montauk Point, NY
March 21	Sts	Palmetto	Block Island, RI
April	Sch	Isaac Acborn	Nantucket, MA
April	Sch	Roanoke	Marthas Vineyard, MA
April	Sch	Unidentified	Marthas Vineyard, MA
April 13	Ship	Mountain Wave	Scituate, MA
April 20		Westervelt	New York, NY
May 4	Sch	A L Hardy	Montauk, NY
May 13	Sch	Unidentified	Amagansett, NY
June 17	Sch	A W Eldridge	Vineyard Haven, MA
July 3	Sch	Adrian	Chatham, MA
July 4	Sch	Emily C Horton	Watch Hill, RI
September 10	Sch	Serra Nevada	Gloucester, MA
September 16	Sch	Peru	Vineyard Sound, MA
September 18	Ship	Unidentified	Off Montauk, NY
November	Sch	Pearl	Narragansett Bay, RI
November 6	Stp	Petrel	North River, NY
November 28	Sch	Glide	Cohasset, MA
November 30	Sch	Banner	Narragansett Bay, RI
December 3	Sch	Ostrich	Narragansett Bay, RI
December 5	Sch	William Eliason	Quonochontaug, RI
December 9	Sch	Welcome Relief	Block Island, RI
December 20	Sch	Sally Badger	Scituate, MA
December 27	Ship	Joseph Walker	New York, NY

1859

DATE LOST	TYPE	NAME	WHERE LOST
	Sch	Boston	Chatham, MA
	Sch	G Stratton	Cuttyhunk, MA
	Sch	James Farewell	Chatham, MA
	Ship	Nantucket	Elizabeth Islands, MA
	Sch	Oneco	Buzzards Bay, MA
	Brig	Unidentified	Sagaponack, NY
January 7	Brig	Thomas & Edward	Cuttyhunk, MA
January 8	Sch	Oregon	Cohasset, MA
January 10	Sch	R L Kenny	Duxbury, MA
January 14	Sch	Samuel Castner	Narragansett Bay, RI
January 28	Ship	Roebuck	Cohasset, MA
February 3	Bark	Vernon	Nahant, MA
February 12	Sch	Chieftain	Chatham, MA
February 14	Sch	Hope	Provincetown, MA

DATE LOST	TYPE	NAME	WHERE LOST
February 18	Sch	*Richmond*	Newport, RI
February 20	Stp	*Black Warrior*	Rockaway Point, NY
February 26	Sch	*Start*	Narragansett Bay, RI
February 28	Sch	*Elizabeth Lord*	Scituate, MA
March	Slp	*Henry*	Narragansett Bay, RI
March 3	Brig	*Brooklin*	Narragansett Bay, RI
March 3	Sch	*H F Payton*	Narragansett Bay, RI
March 6	Sch	*Uncas*	Newport, RI
March 9	Brig	*M S Cousins*	Provincetown, MA
March 23	Ship	*Shooting Star*	Nantucket, MA
March 31	Sch	*Lonsdale*	Newport, RI
March 31	Sch	*Sarah Bright*	Narragansett Bay, RI
March 31	Sch	*Susan & Mary*	Nantucket, MA
April 1	Sch	*Gazelle*	Vineyard Haven, MA
April 1	Sch	*Sarah*	Nantucket, MA
April 3	Sch	*Sarah Elwell*	Vineyard Haven, MA
April 23	Sch	*Jenny Lind*	Provincetown, MA
May 15	Sts	*Curlew*	Point Judith, RI
May 20	Sch	*William Tyson*	Nomansland Island, MA
May 21	Sch	*Londonderry*	Block Island, RI
September 21	Sch	*Francis Newton*	Block Island, RI
September 22	Sch	*John Bull*	Thatchers Island, MA
November 13	Brig	*Harvard*	Nantucket Shoals, MA
November 29	Sch	*Emerald*	Off Chatham, MA
December 3	Sch	*Susan*	Quogue, NY
December 4	Sch	*Prudence*	Gloucester, MA
December 4	Brig	*Solicitor*	Southampton, NY
December 4	Sch	*Victoria*	Ipswich, MA
December 5	Sch	*Magellan Cloud*	Annisquam, MA
December 25	Sch	*Sarah Woodbridge*	Nantucket, MA
December 27	Sch	*Caroline*	Nantucket, MA

1860

	Sch	*Anne*	Chatham, MA
	Sch	*Maryland*	Napeague, NY
		Sarah S Bird	Off New York
	Bark	*Unidentified*	Chatham, MA
January 28	Ship	*John J Boyd*	North River, NY
February 16	Brig	*Susan*	Nantucket Sound, MA
February 18	Brig	*Ocean Bell*	Gardiners Island, NY
March 9	Brig	*Ewan Crerar*	Boston, MA
May 9	Sts	*Hornet*	Peekskill, NY
August 15	Stp	*New Era*	New York, NY
September 22	Sch	*Neptunes Bridge*	Vinalhaven, ME
October 6	Sch	*Angeretta*	Rockport, MA
October 14	Brig	*James Davis*	Nantucket, MA
October 18	Sch	*Almedia*	Block Island, RI
November 2	Sch	*Round Pond*	Elizabeth Islands, MA
November 21	Sts	*James H Elmore*	New York, NY
November 23	Sch	*Caroline*	Falmouth, MA
November 23	Sch	*Mogul*	Buzzards Bay, MA
December 2	Sch	*Gulnair*	Watch Hill, RI
December 13	Stp	*Clifton*	Port Ewen, NY
December 27	Ship	*Emperor*	Chatham, MA

1861

		Republic	Ragged Island, ME
January 23	Sch	*Rebecca*	Gloucester, MA

Within months after grounding on an exposed part of the Massachusetts coast in 1898, the bark *Harriet S. Jackson* became buried in sand. The hull became exposed in the mid 1980's. This side scan sonar record shows the remaining portions of the *Jackson*, including her keelson and frames, protruding from the seafloor. *Sonar Record courtesy American Underwater Search and Survey, Ltd.*

DATE LOST	TYPE	NAME	WHERE LOST
February 2	Sch	*North State*	Point Judith, RI
February 8	Sch	*Doreas Ireland*	Nomansland Island, MA
February 11	Sch	*R R Freeman*	Elizabeth Islands, MA
February 12	Brig	*Velocipede*	Nantucket, MA
February 16		*Telegraph*	Gloucester, MA
March		*Saint Cloud*	Eastham, MA
March 21	Sch	*D P Gale*	Cape Ann, MA
March 30	Sch	*Unidentified*	Cape Ann, MA
March 30	Sch	*Unidentified*	Cape Ann, MA
April 6	Sch	*Edith May*	Cape Ann, MA
June 8	Brig	*Jaffa*	Nantucket, MA
July 24	Stp	*Eagles Wing*	Narragansett Bay, RI
September 21	Sch	*William H Sheldon*	Block Island, RI
September 25		*Nathanial Coggswell*	Scituate, MA
October		*Joseph A Smith*	Long Island Sound
November		*Unidentified*	Quogue, NY
November 2	Ship	*Maritana*	Boston, MA
December 2	Brig	*May Queen*	Nantucket, MA
December 8		*Patrick Henry*	Rockport, MA
December 27	Sch	*Howell Cobb*	Ipswich, MA

1862

		Edwin Forrest	Off Long Island, NY
January 10	Brig	*Lewis*	Southampton, NY
January 27	Brig	*Elba*	Watch Hill, RI
February	Sch	*Helen*	Plum Island, NY
February 3	Sch	*Emma*	Montauk, NY
February 25	Sch	*Antelope*	Long Island Sound
February 25	Sch	*Meteor*	Plum Island, NY
August 8	Slp	*Star*	Newport, RI
October		*Unidentified*	Nepeague, NY
October 16	St	*Union Star*	New York, NY
October 23	Slp	*Lafayette*	Seal Island, ME
November 8	Sch	*Boston*	Cape Ann, MA
December 4	Sch	*Iowa*	Rockport, MA
December 31	Sts	*Caledonia*	Provincetown, MA

1863

		William J Romer	Off New York
January 14	Sch	*Eben Sawyer*	Watch Hill, RI
February		*Mary E Hiltz*	Marblehead, MA
February 22	Sch	*Target*	Narragansett Bay, RI
April 7	Stp	*Walpole*	Minots Ledge, ME
April 21	Bark	*Elwine Fredricke*	Nantucket, MA
June 21		*Byzantium*	Off New England
June 21	Bark	*Goodspeed*	Off New England
June 22	Sch	*E Ann*	Off New England
June 23		*Ada*	Off New England
June 25	Bark	*Village*	Damariscove, ME
June 27	Sch	*Caleb Cushing*	Off Portland, ME
July	Sch	*Unidentified*	Montauk, NY
August 27	Sch	*L B Meyers*	Nantucket, MA
September	St	*Augusta*	Hell Gate, NY
October 22	St	*Oregon*	New York Harbor, NY
October 26	Brig	*Scotland*	Nantucket, MA
November 18	Bark	*Mesopotamia*	Ponquogue Light, NY
December 2	Sch	*Louisa H Endicott*	Warwick, RI
December 5	St	*Isaac Newton*	Hudson River, NY

DATE LOST	TYPE	NAME	WHERE LOST
1864			
	Sch	*Cross Rip Lightship*	Marthas Vineyard, MA
		S J Waring	Stonybrook, NY
January		Unidentified	Vineyard Sound, MA
February 22	Sts	*Bohemian*	Broad Cove, ME
February 26	Sch	*Wonder*	Montauk, NY
March	Sch	*Triumph*	Nantucket Sound, MA
April 30	Sch	*Amelia*	Point Judith, RI
June 8	Brig	*Normandy*	Point Judith, RI
June 30	Sch	*Adelaide*	Point Judith, RI
July 17	Sch	*Mary*	Narragansett Bay, RI
July 18	Sch	*Mavilletta*	Block Island, RI
July 24	Sch	*Gazette*	Thatchers Island, MA
August	Slp	*Unknown*	Hempstead Hrbr, NY
August 4	Sch	Unidentified	Ipswich, MA
August 10	Sch	*Etta Caroline*	Seal Island, ME
August 11	Bark	*Bay State*	Off New York, NY
August 11	Sch	*Carrie Estelle*	Off New York, NY
August 13	Sch	*Lammot Du Pont*	Off New York, NY
August 14	Sch	*Floral Wreath*	Off Monhegan Island, ME
August 14	Sch	*Magnolia*	Off Monhegan Island, ME
August 15	Sch	*Howard*	Off New England
August 16	Sch	*Leopard*	Off New England
August 16	Bark	*P C Alexander*	Monhegan Island, ME
August 16	Sch	*Pearl*	Monhegan Island, ME
October 1	Sch	*Charlotte*	Pollock Rip, MA
October 2	Sch	*Flora*	Rockport, MA
October 12	Sch	*Sarah N Mcdonald*	Nepeague, NY
November 1	Sch	*Goodspeed*	Off New England
November 25	Stp	*Francis Skiddy*	Staats Landing, NY
December	Brig	*Swordfish*	Hull, MA
December 8	Sch	*William Penn*	Hell Gate, NY
December 9	Sch	*Eliza Helen*	Gloucester, MA
December 10	Sch	*Lion*	Nahant, MA
December 23	Sch	*H E Bishop*	Gloucester, MA
December 24	Brig	*Denmark*	Gardiners Island, NY
1865			
	Brig	*Humbolt*	Newport, RI
	Sch	Unidentified	Newport, RI
January 6	Sts	*Piedmont*	Cape Elizabeth, ME
January 10	Sch	*General Marion*	Easthampton, NY
January 17	Ship	*Sir Jon Franklin*	Rockport, MA
February	Brig	*Merganser*	Montauk, NY
March 16	Sch	*Daniel C Higgins*	Rockaway, NY
April 18	Brig	*Adelma*	Watch Hill, RI
May 10	St	*E L Clark*	East River, NY
June 6	Sts	*Potomac*	Casco Bay, ME
July		*Edwin*	Isle of Shoals, NH
August 5	Stp	*Arrow*	New York, NY
August 13	Slp	*Planter*	Hell Gate, NY
August 25	Sch	*Industry*	Gloucester, MA
September 8	Sch	*Champion*	Nantucket, MA
September 19	Brig	*Vincennes*	Ipswich, MA
October 12	Sch	*Boston Packet*	Rockport, MA
October 19	Brig	Unidentified	Nantucket Sound, MA
October 21	Sch	*Evelyntreat*	Nantucket, MA

DATE LOST	TYPE	NAME	WHERE LOST
November 3	Sch	*Chief*	Hell Gate, NY
November 24	Sch	*Larch*	Gloucester, MA
November 27	Sch	*W Carleton*	Smiths Point, NY
December	St	*Alleghaney*	Gilgo Beach, NY
December		*D Alveit*	Montauk, NY
December	Slp	*Miami*	North Haven, NY
December 5	Sts	*Neptune*	Long Island, NY
December 16		*Nifidelos*	New York Harbor, NY
December 22	Sch	*Haynes*	Nantucket, MA
December 25	Ship	*Newton*	Nantucket, MA
December 29	Stp	*Commonwealth*	Groton, CT

1866

	Sch	*Abraham Leggett*	Easthampton, NY
		Evening Star	Off New York, NY
		Laura Jane	Portland Head, ME
	Bark	*Trojan*	Newport, RI
January 3	Sch	*Johanna Ward*	Far Rockaway, NY
January 7	Sch	*Texas*	Montauk Point, NY
January 8	St	*Mary A Boardman*	Romer Shoals, NY
January 10	Sch	*Christiana*	Nantucket Sound, MA
January 21	Sch	*Adelaide*	Marthas Vineyard, MA
January 26	Sts	*Western Port*	Duxbury, MA
February	Brig	*Vincent*	Cuttyhunk, MA
February 8	Brig	*F W Gnade*	Chatham, MA
March 28	Sts	*Marcena Johnson*	Holbrook Island, ME
April	St	*City Of Norwich*	Huntington, NY
April 24	Sch	*Samuel Colt*	Nantucket, MA
May	Brig	*Arcturus*	Falmouth, MA
May		*Clarion*	Newport, RI
May 4	Sch	*Flora*	Marthas Vineyard, MA
May 22	Sts	*Uncle Sam*	Georges Islands, ME
June 18	Bark	*Winslow*	Nantucket Sound, MA
July 3	Sch	*Exchange*	Hell Gate, NY
July 4	Sch	*James And Lucy*	Newport, RI
July 23	Sch	*Ellen*	Cape Ann, MA
September 18	Sch	*Mary Francis*	Gloucester, MA
October 1	St	*Tempest*	New York, NY
November		*Boxer*	Gloucester, MA
November		*James Seward*	Rockland, ME
November 12	St	*T A Knickerbocker*	New York, NY
November 17	Brig	*Flying Scup*	Rockaway, NY
December 1	Ship	*Kate Dwyer*	Off Fire Island, NY
December 1	St	*Scotland*	Fire Island, NY
December 7	St	*J D Secor*	Blackwells Island, NY
December 24	Bark	*C B Hamilton*	Point Judith, RI
December 24	Brig	*C C Van Horn*	Nantucket, MA
December 25	St	*Commodore Brady*	Peconic, NY
December 27	Bark	*Christiane*	Off New York, NY
December 27	Stp	*Commodore*	New York, NY

1867

	Sch	*Cross Rip Ltship*	Nantucket Shoals, MA
		Guy Mannering	Matinicus Island, ME
	Sch	*Helen Gifford*	Patchogue, NY
	Sch	*Nellie Doe*	Narragansett Bay, RI
		Nettle	New York, NY

DATE LOST	TYPE	NAME	WHERE LOST
	Sch	Unidentified	Narragansett Bay, RI
	Brig	Unidentified	Newport, RI
	Brig	Unidentified	Newport, RI
		Unidentified	Long Island, NY
		Unidentified	Long Island, NY
January	Brig	Dawn O'the Day	Off Cohasset, MA
January	Sch	Julia Ann	Hull, MA
January	Sch	Shooting Star	Plymouth, MA
January 17	Sch	Juliet	Gloucester, MA
January 22	St	Enterprise	North River, NY
January 25	Bark	Velma	Plymouth, MA
February 9	Bark	White Squall	Wellfleet, MA
March 9	Sch	William Bell	Amagansett, NY
April 2	Sch	H A Barnes	Rikers Island, NY
April 29	Brig	Hound	Rockaway, NY
May 2	Ship	Hibernian	Fulton Ferry, NY
May 22	Sch	Fanny Bagley	Nantucket, MA
June 21		Reaper	East River, NY
July 23	Slp	Vienna	Hell Gate, NY
July 28		L R Ogden	Hell Gate, NY
July 30	Slp	Guilford	Nantucket, MA
August	Sch	Waterwitch	Ragged Island, ME
August 17	Bark	Tragan	Newport, RI
September 30	Sch	Ada F Lowe	Rockport, MA
October 10	Sch	Arabian	Montauk, NY
October 21	St	Amsterdam	Montauk, NY
November 23	Brig	Charles Levett	Stonybrook, NY
November 30	Sch	Volant	Hampton Bays, NY
December 13	Slp	Maria	Davids Island, NY

1868

DATE LOST	TYPE	NAME	WHERE LOST
	Ship	Emily B Souder	Southampton, NY
	Sch	Unidentified	Newport, RI
February 21	Stp	Huntington	Hunters Point, NY
May 15	Sch	E C Knight	Hell Gate, NY
May 24	St	Oceanus	New York, NY
June 8	Sch	Sarah L	Point Judith, RI
June 27	Sch	Bloomer	Rockport, MA
July 17	Brig	Eliza	Nantucket, MA
August 7	Ship	Expounder	Wellfleet, MA
August 7	Brig	Guiding Star	Wellfleet, MA
September 5	Sch	Washington	Hell Gate, NY
October 17	Sch	J B Meyers	Nantucket, MA
October 26	Stp	Kings County	Hunters Point, NY
December 7	Sch	Cygnet	Gloucester, MA

1869

DATE LOST	TYPE	NAME	WHERE LOST
February 26	Ship	Harry Bluff	Nantucket Shoals, MA
March 6		Josiah Johnson	New York Bay, NY
April 2	Sts	Harvest	Off Point Judith, RI
May 8	Sch	Sallie Smith	Huntington, NY
June	Brig	Nigate	Gardiners Island, NY
June 8	Brig	Birdie	Fire Island, NY
July 20		Harriet Livesley	Elizabeth Islands, MA
July 28	Sch	Transit	Newport, RI
August		Ignazio	Brewer, ME
August 2	Slp	Eliza Jane	Newport, RI
August 8	Sch	Adelia Kelly	Boston, MA

ABOVE: The three masted schooner *Joseph Luther* was under tow out of the Kennebec River in Maine on January 21, 1901, when the tow line parted and she drifted onto Whaleback Ledge. A wreck in an exposed position such as this gives the crew little protection. The crew of the *Luther* spent a few anxious hours before being rescued by lifesavers. **BELOW:** The *Acara* went ashore in a stiff southwest blow at Jones Inlet, NY on March 1, 1902. The sea took a rapid toll on the ship as she sheared in half forward of the engine room. Sixty-one people were saved but the ship became a total loss. *Photo from the collection of William P. Quinn, Orleans MA.*

DATE LOST	TYPE	NAME	WHERE LOST
August 8	Bark	*Pacific*	Narragansett Bay, RI
August 8	Sch	*Patriot*	Stockton, ME
August 20	Sch	*Albion*	Vineyard Haven, MA
August 28	Sch	*D C Smith*	Kennebunk, ME
August 30	Ship	*Robin Hood*	Bakers Island, MA
September		*Alabama*	York, ME
September		*Rambler*	Portland, ME
September 4	Sch	*Winslow*	Gloucester, MA
September 8	Sch	*Andes*	Boothbay, ME
September 8	Sch	*Clara W McConville*	Stockton, ME
September 8	Sch	*F I Perkins*	Boothbay, ME
September 8	Sch	*Helen Eliza*	Off Peaks Island, ME
September 8	Sch	*Issac Van Zant*	Fall River, MA
September 8	Sch	*Jane Eliza*	Camden, ME
September 8	Sch	*Ossuna*	Narragansett Bay, RI
September 8	Sch	*Teaser*	Bristol, RI
September 8		*Thistle*	Deer Island, ME
September 8	Sch	*Yankee Lass*	Off New England
September 8	Slp	*Young Raven*	Gloucester, MA
September 13	Sch	*Mary Millness*	Montauk, NY
September 24		*Betsey Ames*	Whitehead, ME
September 27	Sch	*Baltic*	Handkerchief Shoal, MA
October		*Roam*	Lubec, ME
October 4	Sch	*Emma*	Calais, ME
October 4	Sch	*Lookout*	Lubec, ME
October 4	Sch	*Nellie Grant*	Wood Island Harbor, ME
October 5	Sch	*Velocity*	Deer Island, ME
October 8		*Exemplar*	Off New England
October 10	Brig	*Charles W King*	Moriches, NY
October 11		*Blue Bird*	Widows Island, ME
October 15	Bark	Unidentified	Fire Island, NY
October 16	Sch	*Rassilla B*	Bliss Bay, ME
October 24	Sch	*George Ormerod*	Off New England
November		*S T King*	Chatham, MA
November 9	Sch	*Pilot*	Isle of Shoals, NH
November 10	Sch	*Abraham Lincoln*	Off Cape Cod, MA
November 17	Sch	*Addie Cowen*	Hampton, NH
November 17	Sch	*Decatur*	Rye Harbor, NH
November 20	Sch	*Alice R*	Gloucester, MA
November 20	Sch	*Eben Herbert*	Eastport, ME
November 20	Sch	*Lucy Robinson*	Kittery Point, ME
November 20	Sch	*Slendid*	Jewells Island, ME
December	Brig	*Golden Lead*	Skiffs Island, MA
December		*Ocean Star*	Nantasket, MA
December 4	Sch	*Eva*	Old Orchard Bch, ME
December 16		*Lacon*	Moose Neck Harbor, ME
December 18	Ship	*Kendrick Fish*	Calais, ME
December 21	Brig	*Meteor*	Point Judith, RI
December 24		*Seth & William*	Cape Ann, MA
December 31		*Catherine Wilcox*	Marblehead, MA

1870

January 2	Sch	*Ann*	Small Point Harbor, ME
January 2	Sch	*Ida L Small*	Belfast, ME
January 10	Brig	*Beauty*	East Chop, MA
January 20	Sch	*Statesman*	Rockaway, NY
January 26	Sch	*Emma C Verrell*	Chatham, MA
February	Brig	*Meteor*	Point Judith, RI
February 15	Sch	*Nevita*	Off New England

DATE LOST	TYPE	NAME	WHERE LOST
February 19	St	John P Sleight	Port Ewen, NY
February 25	Sch	Benjamin Butler	Off New York, NY
March	Sch	Connecticut	Hell Gate, NY
March	Sch	Hickory	Off Bedloes Island, NY
March	Brig	Highland	Off New England
March 9	Sch	Trenton	Fishers Island, NY
March 10	Sch	Leila	Nantucket, MA
March 13	Bark	Aloha	New Bedford, MA
March 13	Sch	Trojan	Scituate, MA
March 14	Sch	Austerlitz	Off New England
March 16	Sch	Ariadne	Dutch Island, CT
March 17	Sch	Senator	New Haven, CT
March 18	Sch	Ida Hudson	Hell Gate, NY
March 25	Sch	Thomas Potter	Staten Island, NY
May 2	Sch	Cruiser	Ogunquit, ME
May 7	Stp	Shippan	Stamford, CT
June 3	Sch	Lehman Blew	Montauk, NY
June 13	Sch	Samuel Cartner	Block Island, RI
June 15	Sch	Susan Ross	Off Monhegan Island, ME
June 16	Sch	Mary Rich	Southampton, NY
June 30	Sts	Palmella	New York, NY
July	Brig	Topaz	Moriches, NY
July 29	Sch	S H Woodbury	Marthas Vineyard, MA
August	Sch	Algoma	Calais, ME
August 2	Bark	Nellie Fenwick	Off Block Island, RI
August 4	Sch	Emiline	New Harbor, ME
August 7	Sts	Parthenia	Falkner Island, CT
August 10	Slp	Charles Clements	Hell Gate, NY
August 20	Sch	Mary Brown	Off Boston, MA
August 27	Sch	Ann Flower	Port Jefferson, NY
August 30	Brig	Poinsett	Nantucket, MA
September 3	Sch	Hartford	Narragansett, RI
September 4	St	Alice Rosa	Ipswich, MA
September 4	Bark	Arthur Kinsman	Nantucket Shoals, MA
September 15	Sch	Henrietta	Scituate, MA
September 15	Sch	Henry	Off Marblehead, MA
October 7	Brig	Cecile	Boston Harbor, MA
October 20	Bge	W H Gattrick	Milford, CT
October 26	Sch	James Newton	Fall River, MA
October 30	Sch	Montrose	Cape Cod, MA
October 31	Sch	Amanda Powers	Newport, RI
November 1	Sch	Pinta	Off Montauk Point, NY
November 2	Sch	T C Lyman	Hell Gate, NY
November 7	Brig	Mary Curley	Fishers Island, NY
November 22	Slp	Exertion	North River, NY
November 22	Sch	Watchman	Off Thatchers Island, MA
November 23	Slp	Annie	Rockaway Beach, NY
November 30	Slp	Reindeer	Nantucket, MA
December	Sch	Tryall	Hudson River, NY
December 1	Sch	Cameo	Brewster, MA
December 2	Sch	N & D Scudder	New York, NY
December 5	Sch	Pacific	Off Cranberry Islands, ME
December 12	Ship	Liebich	Bakers Island, MA
December 15	Sch	Nellie Staples	Race Point, MA
December 18	Sch	Wm. Penn	Off New England
December 20	Sch	Edward Collyer	Hell Gate, NY
December 23	Sch	R W Genn	Hull, MA
December 26	Sch	Stars And Stripes	Boston Harbor, MA
December 27		Elizabeth & Helen	Cornfield Light, CT

DATE LOST	TYPE	NAME	WHERE LOST
1871			
January	Sch	*Lottie G White*	Yarmouth, MA
January	Sch	*White Rover*	Ipswich, MA
January 21	Bark	*Black Brothers*	Winter Quarter Shoals, NY
January 23	Sch	*Metamora*	Glen Cove, NY
January 23	Sch	*New Zealand*	Narragansett Bay, RI
January 26	Sch	*Ella*	Triangle Rocks, CT
January 30	Sch	*Ocean Star*	Off Cape Cod, MA
February	Sch	*Oliver Spelman*	Saybrook, CT
February 1	Bark	*Rosina*	Moriches, NY
March 3	Sch	*Adelbert*	Dickens Reef, RI
March 3	Slp	*Planter*	West Haven, CT
April 12	Sch	*S C Loud*	Off Block Island, RI
April 13	Sch	*Suliote*	Portsmouth, NH
May 31	Bark	*Rhea*	New York, NY
June 2	Brig	*Lizzie Billings*	Nomansland Island, MA
June 3	Ship	*Pacific*	Narragansett Bay, RI
June 4	Sch	*Fearless*	Bridgeport, CT
June 6	Sch	*Soyder And Munson*	Port Jefferson, NY
June 10	Sch	*Daring*	Rockland, ME
June 12	Sch	*A E Carll*	Block Island, RI
June 29	Brig	*T W Chelsey*	Lttle Hope Island, RI
July 8	Sch	*Charles*	Point Judith, RI
July 8		*M A Longbery*	Hell Gate, NY
July 18		*Charles F Beebe*	Vineyard Sound, MA
July 18	Sch	*Oscar C Acken*	Hell Gate, NY
July 19	Bge	*J W Andrews*	Bridgeport, CT
July 26	Sch	*Robert Emmett*	Nauset, MA
July 29	Slp	*Thomas Ransen*	Hell Gate, NY
July 30	Stp	*Westfield*	New York, NY
August 3	Sts	*William Tibbets*	Nashawena Island, MA
August 21		*Juno*	Hell Gate, NY
August 28	Sch	*C D Hallock*	Long Island Sound
August 31	Sch	*Kate Church*	Ravenswood, NY
September 14	Sch	*Sarah*	Roamer Shoal, NY
September 28	St	*Delaware*	Pot Cove, NY
September 29	Sch	*D C Hulse*	Astoria, NY
October 16	Ship	*Wild Rover*	Jones Inlet, NY
October 29	Sch	*Mary H Banks*	Nantucket, MA
November 5	Sch	*Emma Johnson*	Rockport, MA
November 18	Brig	*Caroline Grey*	Moriches, NY
November 22	Stp	*City Of New London*	Norwich, CT
November 25	Bark	*J H Mclaren*	Lower Bay, NY
December	Brig	*James Landels*	Two Rivers, ME
December 6	Ship	*Mesopotami*	Southampton, NY
December 8	St	*Wilson D Reed*	East River, NY
December 17	Bark	*Sydenham*	Jones Inlet, NY
1872			
January 8	Brig	*Mountain Eagle*	Off New England
January 17	Sch	*Richard Bullwinkle*	New London, CT
January 20	Sch	*Idaho*	Trundys Reef, ME
January 27	Sts	*Nautilus*	Welfleet, MA
January 30	Sch	*Abby H Brown*	Scituate, MA
February	Sch	*Warren Blake*	Off New England
February	Bark	*Robert Fletcher*	Moriches, NY
February 10	Sch	*Antecedent*	Eatons Neck, NY

DATE LOST	TYPE	NAME	WHERE LOST
February 16	Brig	*Anna Eldridge*	Fire Island, NY
March 4	Bark	*Mary C Dyer*	Stonehorse Shoal, MA
March 6	Sch	*Clara Belle*	Provincetown, MA
March 9	Sch	*Dirigo*	Off Block Island, RI
March 12	Bark	*Gaetano*	Chatham, MA
March 12	Sch	*S P M Taske*	Provincetown, MA
April 1	Sch	*Belle*	Hell Gate, NY
April 9	Sch	*Breeze*	Rockaway, NY
April 9	Sch	*Telegraph*	Cuttyhunk, MA
April 15	Sch	*Abby Morton*	Hell Gate, NY
April 22	Sch	*Frances Ellen*	Hell Gate, NY
May 1	Sch	*Henry Cole*	Hell Gate, NY
May 2	Sch	*William R Knapp*	Hell Gate, NY
May 6	Sch	*Trimmer*	Astoria, NY
May 10	Sch	*William Butman*	Hell Gate, NY
May 17	Sch	*Elizabeth Segar*	Shipann Point, CT
May 19	Bark	*Lakema*	Jones Inlet, NY
May 27	Sts	*Harry Bumm*	New York, NY
May 28	St	*Emperor*	Seal Island, ME
June 5	Sch	*Doris*	Salisbury Beach, MA
June 5	Sch	*Edinburg*	Gloucester, MA
June 5	Sch	*Fanny Fern*	Odiornes Point, NH
June 5	Sch	*General Marion*	Highlands, MA
June 5	Sch	*Georgia*	Plum Island, MA
June 5	Sch	*Jane*	Cape Ann, MA
June 5	Sch	*M M Freeman*	Rockport, MA
June 5	Sch	*Sun*	York Harbor, ME
June 5	Sch	*Ulla*	Gloucester, MA
July 30	Brig	*Roslyn*	Hunters Point, NY
July 30	St	*Seneca*	New York, NY
August	Sch	*Kate Robinson*	Point O Woods, NY
August 3	Sch	*Signal*	Matinicus Island, ME
August 6	Sch	*James M Freeman*	Warren, RI
August 17	Sch	*Florida*	Off Newburyport, MA
August 21	St	*Cathcart*	College Point, NY
August 23	Slp	*Brandywine*	Hell Gate, NY
August 24	Slp	*George B Bloomer*	Astoria, NY
August 28	Sch	*C L Hulse*	Hell Gate, NY
August 30	Sch	*Boston*	Rye, NH
August 30	Sts	*Metis*	Off Watch Hill, RI
September 1	St	*Nevada*	New London, CT
October	Sch	*Superior*	Highland, MA
October 12	Sch	*Kate Gordon*	Long Island Sound
October 22	Sch	*Frank N Freeman*	Cuttyhunk, MA
October 24	Sch	*William Walworth*	Annisquam, MA
November 2	Sch	*North Pacific*	Napatree Point, RI
November 6	Sch	*Mary Elizabeth*	New London, CT
November 29	Sch	*Pearl*	Off City Island, NY
November 29	Sch	*Santa Maria*	Rockport, MA
November 30	Sch	*Allen Middleton*	East Of Fire Island, NY
December 1	Sch	*Charles A Moller*	Lower Bay, NY
December 1	Brig	*Mary Givan*	Nashawena, MA
December 12	Sch	*Frances Cummings*	Rockport, MA
December 15	Slp	*G J Demorest*	Hell Gate, NY
December 20	Stp	*Andrew Fletcher*	Staten Island, NY
December 23	Sch	*Magellan*	Hart Island, NY
December 26	Bark	*Francis*	Truro, MA
December 26	Bark	*Kadosh*	Hull, MA
December 26	Ship	*Peruvian*	Provincetown, MA
December 27	Brig	*Altavela*	Libby Islands, ME

Near the turn of the century ferry boat overcrowding was commonplace. Very often excursion vessels were packed with far more passengers than could be accommodated by the vessels lifeboats. The *General Slocum* was one such vessel when it burned and sank in New York on June 15, 1904, killing over 1000 men, women and children. Later the wreck was partially salvaged and the main hull of the wreck was removed from the site of the tragedy. The *Slocum* accident becomes more tragic when it is realized that most of those who lost their lives were school children on a day outing. *Photo courtesy Paul Morris, Nantucket MA*

DATE LOST	TYPE	NAME	WHERE LOST
1873			
January	Sch	Addison Gilbert	Portland, ME
January	Sch	Sarah A Hammond	Moriches, NY
January	Sch	Waterfall	Boston, MA
January 1	Sch	Wilie Perry	Conanicut, RI
January 3	Sts	Sir Francis	Hampton Beach, NH
January 13	Sch	R H Dexter	Mt Desert, ME
January 17	Sch	Arctic	Wells Beach, ME
January 17	Sch	Franklin Melanson	Long Island Sound
January 24	Sch	Maud Muller	Deer Island, MA
January 26	Sch	Charles A Grenier	Hell Gate, NY
February 17	St	Norwich	Off New York, NY
March	Sts	Grace Irving	Off Duxbury, MA
March	Sch	Helene	Hull, MA
March 4	St	Braux	Plum Island, NY
March 7	Sch	Island Belle	Wards Island, NY
March 16	Sch	Clara E McConville	Narragansett Bay, RI
March 20	Bark	Celeste Clark	Pollock Rip, MA
March 20	Bark	Josephine	Scituate, MA
March 20	Sch	Kimball	Cuttyhunk, MA
March 29	Slp	Ellen Butler	Black Point Bay, CT
March 31	Brig	Cecile	Cuttyhunk, MA
April	Sch	Gipsey	Niantic, CT
April 1	Sch	Willie B Wilbur	Off Highland, MA
April 12	Sch	J T Strickland	Brentons Reef, RI
May 3	Sch	Edward	Marshfield, MA
May 3	Sch	George Gilman	Yarmouth, MA
May 4	Sch	J B Meyers	Cape Porpoise, ME
May 13	St	Hope	Hell Gate, NY
June		Belvidere	Newport, RI
June 17	Sch	Tabitha & Hannah	Hell Gate, NY
June 18	Sch	S H Cady	Long Island, NY
July 8	Sch	Patron	Hell Gate, NY
July 30	St	Easby	East River, NY
August 14	Sch	Briton Cook	Hudson River, NY
August 23	Sch	Alpha	Astoria, NY
August 27	Sch	Sophie Parker	Gloucester, MA
September 7	St	Vixen	Hell Gate, NY
October 3	Sch	Benjamin Baker	Gloucester, MA
October 8	Sch	Emblem	Cape Ann, MA
October 20	Sch	Connaught Ranger	Gloucester, MA
October 25	Sch	Leon	Hell Gate, NY
November 14	Slp	Gold Leaf	Astoria, NY
November 17	Sch	Robert Raikes	Nahant, MA
December	Sch	Florence V Turner	Lloyd Neck, NY
1874			
		James Rommel	Provincetown, MA
	Sch	Minnie	Off Boston, MA
January 5	Sch	Eliza S	Gloucester, MA
February	Sch	Experiment	Ponquogue, NY
February 13	Sch	Rodney Parker	Roamer Shoals, NY
February 18	Bge	Joseph E Dow	Hell Gate, NY
March 19	St	R S Carter	East River, NY
March 20	Sch	Elizabeth B	Hell Gate, NY
March 25	Sch	Crescent Lodge	Cape Ann, MA

DATE LOST	TYPE	NAME	WHERE LOST
April 17	Brig	*Aroostook*	Nauset, MA
May	Sch	*Sarah M Saunders*	Nantucket Sound, MA
May 24	Sch	*Arrow*	Off Glen Cove, NY
May 26	Sts	*Enterprise*	Fishers Island, NY
May 30	St	*Idaho*	Fire Island, NY
June 13	Bge	*Ohio*	East River, NY
June 24	Slp	*Caroline*	Battery, NY
July 7	Sch	*Annie E Friend*	Thatchers Island, MA
July 13	Sch	*China*	East River, NY
August 9	Sch	*V M Barkalew*	Eatons Neck, NY
August 22	Sch	*Martha Jane*	Hell Gate, NY
September 2	Sts	*Young America*	Oak Orchard, NY
October 14	Sch	*John Randolph*	New York, NY
November	Brig	*Alfaretta*	Hell Gate, NY
November 2	Sch	*Susan & Jane*	York Ledges, ME
November 17	St	*Lilly*	Hell Gate, NY
November 29	Sch	*Anthony Burton*	Cow Bay, NY
November 30	Sch	*Webster Kelly*	Jones Inlet, NY
December	Sch	*Fanny Fern*	Hell Gate, NY
December	St	*May Queen*	Cow Bay Flats, NY
December 11	St	*L Markle*	Off Randalls Island, NY

1875

DATE LOST	TYPE	NAME	WHERE LOST
	Sch	*David & Benjamin*	Narragansett Bay, RI
		G W Blunt	Long Island, NY
	Yawl	Unidentified	Off New York
January 16	St	*Sentinel*	New York, NY
January 25	Sch	*Henry Seavey*	Point Judith, RI
February	Sch	*Oakwood*	Whitestone, NY
February 7	Sch	*Eliza Pharo*	Bedloes Island, NY
February 15	Bge	*Jacob*	New York, NY
February 25	St	*Vicksburg*	Fire Island, NY
March	Sch	*Birkmyre*	Isles of Shoals, NH
March	Brig	Unidentified	Isles of Shoals, NH
March 2		*George Osborn*	Negro Ledge, ME
March 4	Bark	*Giovanni*	Provincetown, MA
March 4	Sch	*Sea Lion*	Rockport, MA
March 11	Bge	*Gladiator*	Execution Rocks, NY
March 12		*Amelia*	Hog Island, NY
March 15	Sts	*Mary*	New York, NY
March 20	Stp	*Thomas E Hulse*	New York, NY
April 30	St	*Vulcan*	Bedloes Island, NY
May 2	Sch	*Irving*	Nantucket, MA
June		*Belle Of The Bay*	Block Island, RI
August 8	Sts	*Dirigo*	Portland, ME
September 28	Sch	*Florida*	Chatham, MA
September 28	Sch	*L A Watson*	Chatham, MA
October 5	Sch	*D W Clark*	Provincetown, MA
October 24	Sch	*Mary Cobb*	Chatham, MA
October 27	Sch	*Emily H Naylor*	Southampton, NY
October 30	Sch	*Ocean*	Gloucester, MA
November 10	Brig	*Machias*	Cape Ann, MA
November 12	Bark	*Starr King*	Plymouth, MA
November 18	Sch	*Charles Amory*	Provincetown, MA
November 18	Sch	*Edgar Baxter*	Fire Island, NY
November 19	Sch	*Robin*	Narragansett Bay, RI
November 30	Sts	*Marigold*	New York, NY
December 1	Stp	*Sunny Side*	West Park, NY
December 26	Sch	*Bill Baxter*	Shinnecock, NY

DATE LOST	TYPE	NAME	WHERE LOST
December 29	Sch	*Dawning Day*	Chatham, MA

1876

DATE LOST	TYPE	NAME	WHERE LOST
	Sch	*Alfred Huddle*	Narragansett Bay, RI
	Sch	*Caroline & Cornelia*	Narragansett Bay, RI
	Brig	Unidentified	Moriches, NY
January 2	Sch	*Marcus Hunter*	West Hampton Bch, NY
January 6	Sch	*Emma L Porter*	Chatham, MA
January 30	Sch	*J B Woodbury*	Chatham, MA
February 15	Sch	*Citizen*	Gloucester, MA
February 19	Sch	*Glenwood*	Provincetown, MA
February 19	Sch	*Horatio Babson*	Provincetown, MA
March 16	Sch	*J C Thompson*	Southampton, NY
March 17	Sch	*E & L Marts*	Provincetown, MA
March 22	Sch	*Ida B Silsby*	Fire Island, NY
March 26	St	*Great Western*	Great South Bch, NY
March 26	Sch	*Jacob C Thompson*	Shinnecock, NY
April 4	Sch	*Helen G Holway*	Great South Beach, NY
April 4	Sch	*Isabella*	Truro, MA
April 5	Sch	*Jennie Lind*	Rockport, MA
April 5	Sch	*Mary Augusta*	Block Island, RI
May 7	Sch	*Kattie E Wheeler*	Pollock Rip, MA
May 27	Sch	*Catherine W May*	Block Island, RI
May 27	Sch	*Henry J May*	Block Island, RI
June 9	Sch	*Ocean Traveller*	Pollock Rip, MA
June 9	Sch	*Richard W Tull*	Pollock Rip, MA
July 20		*F A Colcord*	Whitehead, ME
July 30	Sch	*Elizabeth English*	Chatham, MA
August 17	Sch	*Golden Eagle*	Vineyard Sound, MA
September 28	Sch	*Capitol*	Provincetown, MA
October 1	Sch	*William Capes*	Nantucket, MA
October 6	Brig	*Cementhia Hopkins*	Truro, MA
October 6	Brig	*H A Frost*	Truro, MA
October 15	Sch	*Niantic*	Montauk, NY
October 16	Sts	*Louis*	Coney Island, NY
October 19	Bark	*R H Purinton*	Nantucket Shoals, MA
October 21	Sch	*Saxon*	Gloucester, MA
October 22	Sch	*October*	Cape Ann, MA
October 31	Sch	*Mazzeppa*	Gloucester, MA
November	Slp	*W E Hulse*	Jones Inlet, NY
November 18	Sch	*S E Trafton*	Duxbury, MA
November 19	Sch	*Annie C Cook*	Long Island, NY
November 30	Sch	*Mary Louise*	Nantucket, MA
December 3	Sch	*Cherub*	Off Truro, MA
December 10	Sch	*David Aprague*	Montauk, NY
December 11	Ship	*Circassian*	Mecox, NY
December 12	Sch	*Kate Grant*	Rockaway, NY
December 16	Sch	*Thomas Hull*	Eastham, MA
December 18	Sch	*Ellie L Smith*	Eastham, MA

1877

DATE LOST	TYPE	NAME	WHERE LOST
	Sch	*Jennie C Russ*	Hell Gate, NY
January 2	Sch	*Massachusetts*	Provincetown, MA
January 2	Sch	*Walter Irving*	Provincetown, MA
January 17	Sch	*Perit*	Chatham, MA
January 24	Sch	*James Lawrence*	Jones Inlet, NY
February 18	Sch	*Abby Morton*	Port Jefferson, NY
March 9	Bark	*William F Marshall*	Nantucket, MA

DATE LOST	TYPE	NAME	WHERE LOST
March 14	Sch	Sophie	Block Island, RI
March 17	Sch	Jonathon May	Orleans, MA
March 17	St	Rusland	Off Staten Island, NY
March 21	Bark	Papa Luigi C	Nantucket, MA
March 31	Sch	Flying Fish	Newburyport, MA
March 31	Sch	Queen Of The Bay	Newburyport, MA
May 14	Sch	Clara B Chapman	Chatham, MA
May 16	Sch	Marietta Tilton	Nantucket Sound, MA
June 10	Sch	Caroline Kienzie	Block Island, RI
June 14	Sch	L M Lamond	Block Island, RI
June 19	Sch	Czar	Chatham, MA
July 1	Sch	Ann Maria	Ipswich, MA
July 6	Sch	Ceylon	Gloucester, MA
July 14	Sch	Mary	Eatons Neck, NY
July 16	Sch	William S Scull	Block Island, RI
July 19	Sch	Adelaide Aldridge	Long Island, NY
July 20	Sch	Bayudrici	Block Island, RI
August		Belle	Portsmouth, NH
August	Sch	Venus	Point Judith, RI
August 14	Sch	Goddess	Eastham, MA
August 31	Brig	Idalia	Montauk Point, NY
October 5	Sch	Armstrong	Tiana, NY
December 3	Sch	Josephine	Plum Gut, NY
December 6	Sch	General Conner	Jones Beach, NY
December 14	Sch	Francis Hatch	Chatham, MA
December 15	Sch	Elizabeth Edwards	Flat Beach, NY

1878

		Caledonia	Machias Bay, ME
		Romeo	Metinic Island, ME
January 3	Sch	Addie P Avery	Truro, MA
January 3	Sch	Fredrick Fish	Pollock Rip, MA
January 3	Sch	J G Babcock	Eastham, MA
January 3	Sch	Miles Standish	Truro, MA
January 3	Sch	Pow-Wow	Truro, MA
January 3	Sch	Sea Lion	Eastham, MA
January 4	Sch	Granite State	Orleans, MA
January 4	Sch	Julia Newell	Cape Ann, MA
January 5	Brig	Sarah M Loring	Lucy's Inlet, NY
January 8	Sch	Rachal Vanaman	Narragansett Bay, RI
January 10	Stp	Ulysses	Rockland, ME
January 16	Sch	Edna Harwood	Truro, MA
January 28	Bark	Fredrik	Westhampton, NY
January 31	Sch	Nellie Bloomfield	Off City Island, NY
February 2	Sts	Hunter	New York, NY
February 11	Brig	Carrie Winslow	New York Bay, NY
February 23	Sch	J F Dunton	Block Island, RI
March 20	Sch	Enterprise	Annisquam, MA
March 21	Sch	Highlander	Pollock Rip, MA
March 24	Sch	Ann H Hickman	Long Island, NY
March 29	Sch	John Farnum	Nantucket, MA
April 20	Sch	John Mashon	Ipswich, MA
April 26		Cameo	Metinicus Island, ME
May		Bonanza	Plymouth, MA
May	Sch	Lizzie	Off Oyster Bay, NY
May 5	Ship	John Clark	Great Head, ME
May 25	Sch	Union	Nantucket, MA
June 1		Dr J P Whitbeck	East River, NY
June 15	Sts	Leopard	Thatchers Island, MA

ABOVE: On October 12, 1906, the four masted schooner *Helen B. Crosby* struck Bay Ledges off Rockland, Maine. She was carrying 3000 tons of coal and the cargo's weight broke her in half. *Photo from the collection of William P. Quinn, Orleans MA.* **BELOW**: Constructed of steel and often sailing northeast waters, the *Thomas W. Lawson* was the largest pure sailing vessel the world has known. She also had the distinction of being the only seven masted schooner. Unfortunately, she did not handle well. In an incident that has become legend amongst the British inhabitants of the Isles of Scilly, she wrecked in those treacherous waters on the island of Annet on December 14, 1907. *Photo courtesy Paul Morris, Nantucket MA.*

DATE LOST	TYPE	NAME	WHERE LOST
June 18	Sch	*Sea Bird*	Cape Ann, MA
July 5	Sch	*Oronoco*	Cape Ann, MA
July 20	Ycht	*Mohawk*	New York, NY
July 26	Bark	*Guila D*	Nantucket, MA
August		*Lizzie & Mamari*	Matinicus Island, ME
August 14	Sch	*Armenia*	Narragansett Bay, RI
September 1	Sch	*Rebecca W Hudell*	Block Island, RI
September 27	Sch	*Water Lily*	Provincetown, MA
October 9	Sch	*Alida*	Point Judith, RI
October 12	Slp	*Ace Of Clubs*	Marthas Vineyard, MA
October 12	Sch	*Albert Steele*	Nantucket, MA
October 12	Sch	*Alvarado*	Nantucket, MA
October 12	Sch	*Clara Smith*	Nantucket Sound, MA
October 12	Sch	*Union*	Nantucket, MA
October 13	Sch	*Joseph Story*	Chatham, MA
October 13	Sch	*Tunis Depew*	Chatham, MA
October 17	Sch	*Greenbury Willy*	Rockaway Beach, NY
October 18	Sch	*Lucy Clark*	Provincetown, MA
November		*Riverdale*	Thatchers Island, MA
November 5	Sch	*Gazelle*	Jones Inlet, NY
November 22	Sch	*William Hill*	Rockport, MA
November 26	Sch	*Frank Wilson*	Gloucester, MA
November 28	Sch	*Charlie Cobb*	Manchester, MA
November 28	Sch	*William Carroll*	Ipswich, MA
December 15	Stp	*Union*	New York, NY
December 18		*E E Johnson*	Thatchers Island, MA
December 19	Sch	*Eliza A Hooper*	Jones Inlet, NY
December 21	Sch	*J M Morales*	Provincetown, MA
December 22	Sch	*James A Potter*	Southampton, NY

1879

DATE LOST	TYPE	NAME	WHERE LOST
		Abraham Leggett	Off New York
January 3	Sch	*E A Hooper*	Block Island, RI
January 3	Sch	*Nellie*	Chatham, MA
January 4	St	*Vindicator*	Blue Point, NY
January 14	Stp	*George T Oliphant*	New York, NY
January 24	Sch	*Scud*	Orleans, MA
January 26	Sch	*Snow Bird*	Chatham, MA
February 23	Sch	*C B Paine*	Great South Beach, NY
March 31	Sch	*Anna D Price*	Off Plymouth, MA
March 31	Sch	*Convoy*	Nantucket Sound, MA
March 31	Sch	*Emma*	Nantucket Sound, MA
March 31	Sch	*Emma G Edwards*	Nantucket, MA
March 31	Sch	*J W Hall*	Nantucket Sound, MA
March 31	Brig	*Manzanilla*	Nantucket, MA
April 1	Sch	*William Cargill*	Nantucket, MA
April 4	Sch	*Sarah J Fort*	Provincetown, MA
May		*Trenton*	Deer Island, ME
May 12	Sch	*Alexander*	Block Island, RI
May 12	Sch	*Sparkling Wave*	Pollock Rip, MA
May 17	Sts	*Ashland*	Point Judith, RI
June 1	Sch	*City Of Gloucester*	Chatham, MA
July 4	Slp	*Nettie*	Promised Land, NY
August 16	Sch	*George W Andrews*	Ponquogue, NY
August 17	Slp	Unidentified	Ipswich, MA
August 21		Unidentified	Sag Harbor, NY
August 21		Unidentified	Sag Harbor, NY
August 21		Unidentified	Sag Harbor, NY
August 21		Unidentified	Sag Harbor, NY

DATE LOST	TYPE	NAME	WHERE LOST
November 14	Sch	*Bay Queen*	Rockport, MA
November 18	Sch	*Greyhound*	Ipswich, MA
November 20	Sch	*L V Ostrum*	Freeport, NY
November 21	Sch	*Hector*	Long Island, NY
December 16	Sch	*Open Sea*	Watch Hill, RI
December 21	Sch	*T J Trafton*	Marshfield, MA
December 21	Sch	*Trellis*	Chatham, MA
December 22	Brig	*Black Swan*	Chatham, MA

1880

	Brig	*Brilliant*	Fire Island, NY
	Sch	*Columbia*	Off Fire Island, NY
	Bge	*Cuba*	Montauk, NY
	Stp	*Rhode Island*	Narragansett Bay, RI
	Sch	*Unidentified*	New York, NY
	Sch	*Wave Crest*	Off Provincetown, MA
January 9		*Madeira*	Quoddy Light, ME
January 17	Bark	*Thor*	Rockaway, NY
February 2		*Mary E Nason*	Jones Inlet, NY
February 3	Sch	*Carl D Lothrop*	Provincetown, MA
February 3	Brig	*Guisborough*	Crab Meadow, NY
February 3	Sch	*Juno*	Provincetown, MA
February 3	Sch	*Stephen Harding*	Off New York, NY
February 3	Sch	*Winifred J King*	Gloucester, MA
February 5	Sch	*Riverside*	Thatchers Island, MA
February 7	Sch	*Maggie A Fisk*	Provincetown, MA
February 13	Sch	*Leander Knowles*	Pollock Rip, MA
March		*Harp*	Green Island, ME
March 3		*Challange*	Petite Manan, ME
March 28	Sch	*West Wind*	Nantucket, MA
March 28	Sch	*Zicavo*	Scituate, MA
April 5	Sch	*Ralph Howes*	Shinnecock Inlet, NY
April 20	Sch	*Aspinwall*	Fire Island, NY
April 20	Sch	*William Aspinwall*	Long Island, NY
April 29	St	*Narragansett*	Shinnecock, NY
May 7	Sts	*Alice M*	Chatham, MA
May 29	Slp	*Wave*	Block Island, RI
June 11	Sch	*Illinois*	Point Judith, RI
June 11	Sts	*Narragansett*	Canfield Point, NY
June 19	Stp	*Adelaide*	New York, NY
June 23	St	*City Of New York*	East River, NY
June 28	Stp	*Seawanhaka*	East River, NY
August 16	Sch	*Estella*	Wellfleet, MA
September 8	Sch	*Franklin*	Ipswich, MA
September 10	Sch	*Wellington*	Plymouth, MA
October	Sts	*P W Sprague*	New York, NY
October 8	Ctbt	*Bride Of The Mine*	Jones Inlet, NY
October 20	Sts	*S W Schuyler*	Block Island, RI
October 23	Brig	*Kate Upham*	Fishermans Island, ME
October 24	Bark	*W A Holcomb*	Long Beach, NY
November 8	Slp	*Equator*	Fire Island, NY
November 11	Sch	*Addie Ryerson*	Whitehead Island, ME
November 20	Slp	*Bee*	Gloucester, MA
November 30	Slp	*C E Trumbull*	Provincetown, MA
December 1	Brig	*Nellie*	Fishers Island, NY
December 30	Bark	*Idaho*	Moriches, NY

DATE LOST	TYPE	NAME	WHERE LOST
1881			
	Slp	*Cornelia*	Cousins Island, ME
	Sts	*Gordon*	Portland, ME
		Unidentified	Pollock Rip, MA
January	Sch	*J W Carver*	Nantucket Sound, MA
January 2	Sch	*Mary E Turner*	Rockaway, NY
January 7	Bark	*Josie T Marshall*	Oak Island, NY
January 7	Sch	*Loretta Fish*	Shinnecock Inlet, NY
January 9	Sch	*Nevins Floyd*	Great Neck, NY
January 12	Brig	*Lije Houghton*	Off Nantucket, MA
January 23		*Culloden*	Long Island, NY
January 29	Sch	*Alfred Keen*	Provincetown, MA
January 30	Sch	*U B Fisk*	Nantucket, MA
February 4	Sch	*William*	Plymouth, MA
February 10	Brig	Unidentified	Marthas Vineyard, MA
February 14	Bark	*Hazard*	Nantucket, MA
February 17	Ship	*Star Of India*	Bedloes Island, NY
February 28	Bark	*Brothers*	Gloucester, MA
February 28	Sch	*Walter B Chester*	Moriches, NY
March 1	Bark	*August*	Roamer Shoals, NY
March 1		*Carrie S Webb*	Roamer Shoals, NY
March 2	St	*H G Lapham*	East River, NY
March 4	Bark	*Ajace*	Rockaway Shoals, NY
March 4	Slp	*J R Brown*	Rockaway Bay, NY
April 15	Sch	*Ganges*	Duxbury, MA
April 15	Sch	*J G Huntingdon*	Chatham, MA
April 27	Sts	*Totten*	Fishers Island, NY
April 30	Sch	*Palladium*	Off Rhode Island
May 16	Sch	*Issac P Hazard*	Eatons Neck, NY
May 29	Sch	*Julia Elizabeth*	Watch Hill, RI
June 8	Sch	*Dauntless*	Ipswich, MA
July 13	Sch	*Cant Come It*	Ipswich, MA
August 5	Sch	*Elizabeth Sinnick*	Block Island, RI
August 5	Sch	*John T Manson*	Block Island, RI
August 6	Sch	*Roamer*	Block Island, RI
August 6	Sch	*Tillie E*	Point Judith, RI
August 24	Sch	*Charlotte Jameson*	Nantucket, MA
September 19	Brig	*Clara J Adams*	Provincetown, MA
October 4	Sts	*A H Glover*	Provincetown, MA
October 4	Sch	*G F Hathaway*	Pollock Rip, MA
October 4	Sch	*Malabar*	Nantucket, MA
October 4	Sch	*R Baker Jr*	Nantucket, MA
November 4	St	*Lancaster*	Easthampton, NY
November 21	Brig	*Bonnie / Leslie*	Nantucket, MA
November 25	Sch	*Nellie Chase*	Pollock Rip, MA
December 4	Sch	*Richard Morrell*	Long Island Sound
1882			
	Bark	*Scotia*	West Quoddy Head, ME
	Sch	*Smith*	Narragansett Bay, RI
January 1	Sch	*Sarah W Blake*	Point Judith, RI
January 4	Sch	*Monmouth*	Watch Hill, RI
January 11	Sch	*A F Ames*	Provincetown, MA
January 11	Sch	*J H M*	Long Island, NY
January 17	Sch	*Jessie Y Baker*	Plum Island, MA
January 23	Sts	*H P Farrington*	Haverstraw, NY
January 27	Ship	*Margaretha*	Great South Beach, NY
January 31	Sch	*Louise Rathborne*	Scituate, MA

DATE LOST	TYPE	NAME	WHERE LOST
February 1	Sch	*Bucephalus*	Hull, MA
February 1	Sch	*Fanny A Pike*	Boston, MA
February 1	Sch	*Nellie Walker*	Hull, MA
February 4	Sch	*Bunker Hill*	Thatchers Island, MA
February 10	Sch	*Thomas Harrison*	Pollock Rip, MA
February 18	Sch	*John D Buckalew*	Montauk, NY
February 22	Sch	*Cora*	Ipswich, MA
March 23	Slp	*Dispatch*	Off New York
March 27	Stp	*Thomas Cornell*	Hudson River, NY
March 30	Slp	*Kate Cannon*	Eaton's Neck, NY
June 1	Bark	*J S Winslow*	Nantucket Shoals, MA
June 10	Slp	*Alice*	Fire Island, NY
June 24	Sch	*S D Hart*	Chatham, MA
July 13	Sch	*Rennie J Carlton*	Nantucket Shoals, MA
July 14	Stp	*C Vanderbuilt*	Esopus Meadows, NY
July 18	Sch	*Young Fraser*	Smiths Point, NY
September 8	Sch	*Copia*	Rockaway Point, NY
September 12	Sch	*Mary Shields*	Chatham, MA
September 15	Sch	*W P Richie*	Cape Ann, MA
October 12	Sch	*Cuckoo*	Point Judith, RI
October 15	Bge	*Manhattan*	Watch Hill, RI
October 21	Slp	*Hannah Ann*	Hell Gate, NY
October 26	Sch	*Antoinette Aiken*	Nantucket, MA
December 1	Bge	*Jennie Phinney*	Short Beach, NY
December 3	Sch	*Pallas*	Eastham, MA
December 9	Bge	*Water Lilly*	Forge River, NY

1883

		Barbra Singleton	Brant Rock, MA
	Sch	*J D Strickland*	Newport, RI
January 10	Bark	*Friedricke*	Orleans, MA
February 28	Sch	*Providence*	Chatham, MA
March 24	Sch	*Samuel Gilman*	Cape Ann, MA
March 25	Sch	*Warren Gates*	Point Judith, RI
April 11	Sch	*Copy*	Eaton's Neck, NY
April 11	Sch	*Estella Day*	Eaton's Neck, NY
April 11	Sch	*Marietta Smith*	Eaton's Neck, NY
April 11		*Oscar F Hawley*	Eaton's Neck, NY
April 16	Sch	*Sarah Babcock*	Fishers Island, NY
May 11	Sch	*T S Mclellan*	Pollock Rip, MA
May 18	Stp	*Granite State*	Goodspeed Landing, CT
June 7	Sch	*Annie Whiting*	Block Island, RI
June 26	Sch	*Clarabell*	Cape Ann, MA
June 28	Brig	*Martha A Berry*	Chatham, MA
August 20	St	*Riverdale*	Hudson River, NY
September 2	Sch	*Milo*	Plymouth, MA
September 13	St	*Independence*	East Short Beach, NY
September 25	Bge	*(Unnamed)*	Watch Hill, RI
October 29	Sch	*Vesta*	Block Island, RI
October 31	Sch	*Rose Brothers*	Nepeague, NY
November 2	Sch	*Annis*	Eastham, MA
November 13	Sch	*Winnie*	Long Island, NY
November 16	Sch	*Lucy Morgan*	Montauk, NY
November 16	Sch	*William Garrison*	Chatham, MA
November 21	Sch	*Island Belle*	Nepeague, NY
November 26	Sch	*Effort*	Chatham, MA
November 29	Sch	*Amazon*	Provincetown, MA
December 3		*Columbia*	New York, NY
December 19	Brig	*Ellen Maria*	Watch Hill, RI

ABOVE: With over five hundred, four masted schooners carrying freight up and down the east coast, many "4-stickers" wrecked in the northeast. On July 1, 1909, the *Alice E. Clark* grounded off Islesboro, ME. Salvage efforts were in vain, however, and within six months the sea broke her up. *Photo courtesy Paul Morris, Nantucket MA.* **BELOW**: On September 9,1909, the 246 foot wooden schooner barge *West Virginia* sank northeast of Nantucket. As can be seen in this sonar image of the wreck, as if viewed from directly above, all that now remains protruding above the sand is a few feet of ribs, planking and her keelson running through her bilge from stem to stern. In spite of her low profile above the sand, the wreck manages to provide a haven for five to ten pound lobster year round. *Record courtesy American Underwater Search and Survey, Ltd..*

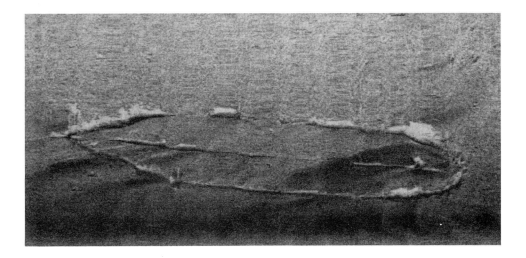

DATE LOST	TYPE	NAME	WHERE LOST
1884			
		Elna	Portland, ME
		G & B Morse	Portland, ME
	Sch	*Sunbeam*	Gloucester, MA
January 1	Sch	*Julia*	Long Beach, NY
January 3	Sch	*Adrianna*	Block Island, RI
January 6	Sch	*Lucy E Friend*	Smiths Point, NY
January 18	Sts	*City Of Columbus*	Marthas Vineyard, MA
February 2	Sch	*S C Noyes*	Block Island, RI
February 29	Brig	*Fleetwing*	Chatham, MA
February 29	Slp	*Hattie J*	Lone Hill, NY
March 24	Brig	*Augusta*	Block Island, RI
March 30	Sch	*Ella M Johnson*	Ipswich, MA
March 30	Sch	*William Mailer*	Provincetown, MA
March 31	Sch	*Vashti R Gates*	Nantucket, MA
April	Slp	*Exel*	Long Island Sound
April	Sch	*Nellie B*	Plum Island, NY
April 3	Sch	*Robert B Smith*	Provincetown, MA
April 3	Sch	*Viking*	Wellfleet, MA
May 8	Stp	*City Of Portland*	Mussel Ridge Channel, ME
May 10	Sch	*Julia A Tate*	Point Judith, RI
May 28	Sch	*Advance*	Ipswich, MA
June 12	St	*Bermuda*	Amagansett, NY
July 4		*Gulf Of St Vincent*	Lone Hill, NY
August 2	Stp	*Eagle*	Milton, NY
September 22	Sch	*Starlight*	Cape Ann, MA
September 23	Sch	*Lettie S Reed*	Cape Ann, MA
September 25	Sch	*Gussie Blaisdell*	Ipswich, MA
October 9	Sch	*E L Rowe*	Cape Ann, MA
October 18	Sch	*Commander*	Provincetown, MA
October 18	Sch	*Guard*	Watch Hill, RI
October 20	Sch	*Curtis Tilton*	Jones Inlet, NY
November 14	Sch	*Alexander Harding*	Far Rockaway, NY
December 15	Brig	*Mary E Mallett*	Cuttyhunk, MA
December 20	Sch	*Carrie M Richard*	Provincetown, MA
December 21	St	*Oliveto*	Forge River, NY
December 22	Sch	*Warren Sawyer*	Nantucket, MA
December 24	Sts	*New Castle City*	Nantucket Shoals, MA
1885			
		Empire	Portland, ME
		Mary Powers	Isle Au Haut, ME
	Sch	*Newcomb*	Casco Bay, ME
	Sch	*Unidentified*	Deer Island, ME
January 12	Sch	*Avlona*	Bellport, NY
January 24	Stp	*Saint John*	New York, NY
January 26	Sch	*Hopvine*	Gloucester, MA
January 28	Sch	*Australia*	Cape Elizabeth, ME
February 10	Brig	*Julia Norton*	Cape Ann, MA
February 10	Sch	*S M Thomas*	Point O' Woods, NY
February 12	Sch	*Lyndon*	Nantucket Sound, MA
February 15	Sch	*Charles A Ropes*	Nantucket Sound, MA
February 15	Sch	*Dolly Varden*	Marthas Vineyard, MA
February 15	Sch	*Sammy Ford*	Nantucket Sound, MA
March 10	Sch	*Bertha J Fellows*	Chatham, MA
March 12	Sch	*Saint Mary*	Nantucket Sound, MA
March 28	Sch	*Harriet*	Ipswich, MA

DATE LOST	TYPE	NAME	WHERE LOST
March 29	Sch	French Van Guilder	Nantucket, MA
April 4	Sch	Mary Doane	Truro, MA
April 21	Sch	Alice Oaks	Nantucket, MA
May 16	Sch	Champion	Mussel Ridge Chnl., ME
May 31	Sch	B D Haskins	Eastham, MA
July 16	Sts	Perkiomen	Off Chatham, MA
August 18	Sch	Tantamount	Pollock Rip, MA
August 25	Sch	Oregon	Nantucket, MA
October 13	Sch	Virginian	Plum Island, MA
October 26	Sch	Unidentified	Nantucket, MA
November 2	Sch	Clara Fletcher	Gloucester, MA
November 5		Almon Bacon	Point Judith, RI
November 28	Sch	Moses Webster	Pollock Rip, MA
November 30	Sch	Mollie Porter	Watch Hill, RI
December 1	Brig	Anita Owen	Hull, MA
December 6	Sch	Grecian	Chatham, MA
December 9	Sch	Austin Locke	Nantucket, MA
December 9	Sch	Hettie J Dorman	Shinnecock, NY
December 12	Bge	Perseverance	Provincetown, MA
December 25	Sch	Mott Haven	Off Rhode Island
December 25	Sch	Willie De Wolf	Block Island, RI

1886

DATE LOST	TYPE	NAME	WHERE LOST
	Sch	White Foam	Hyannis, MA
January 6	Bark	Ibis	Pollock Rip, MA
January 8	Sch	Leventer	Provincetown, MA
January 9	Sch	Allen Greene	Point Judith, RI
January 9	Sch	Clio Chilcott	Watch Hill, RI
January 9	Sch	Isaac Carlton	Scituate, MA
January 9	Sch	Joel Cook	Scituate, MA
January 9	Sch	Lookout	Truro, MA
January 9	Sch	Mattie D	Newport, RI
January 9	Sch	Mollie Trim	Boston, MA
January 9	Sch	Nimble	Provincetown, MA
January 10	Sch	T B Witherspoon	Nantucket, MA
January 10	Sch	Unidentified	Montauk, NY
January 31	Sch	Sophie Kranz	Provincetown, MA
February	Sts	Hilton Castle	Off Fire Island, NY
February	Sch	Lizzie M Dean	Montauk, NY
February 3	Sch	Mary A Killen	Scituate, MA
February 10	Stp	Cambridge	Port Clyde, ME
February 10	Sch	Lizzie Haskell	Plum Island, MA
February 15	Sch	Lucy A Blossom	Watch Hill, RI
February 25	Sch	Orianna	Gloucester, MA
March	St	Idlewild	Port Jefferson, NY
March 9	Sch	Hannah Shubert	Provincetown, MA
March 14	Sts	Oregon	Off Moriches, NY
March 14	Sch	Unidentified	Off Moriches, NY
March 22	Brig	Emily T Sheldon	Provincetown, MA
March 30	St	Europa	Quogue, NY
March 31	Sch	Pereaux	Quogue, NY
April 6	Sch	Beta	Ipswich, MA
April 15	Sch	C W Lock	Watch Hill, RI
May 3	Sch	A N Clark	Gloucester, MA
June	Sch	Bucco	Narragansett Bay, RI
June 24	Brig	James T Abbott	East Hampton, NY
August 25	Sch	Julia E Pratt	Nantucket, MA
August 29	Stp	Daniel Drew	Kingston Point, NY
September 7	Sch	Hattie A White	Shinnecock, NY

DATE LOST	TYPE	NAME	WHERE LOST
October 10	Sch	*Wild Pigeon*	Block Island, RI
November	Sch	*Long Island*	Sea Cliff, NY
November 13	Sch	*Franklin*	Ipswich, MA
November 25	Bge	*Toronto*	Watch Hill, RI
November 29	Stp	*Bridgeport*	Rikers Island, NY
December 1	Sch	*Mary Natt*	Point Judith, RI
December 2	Bark	*H C Sibles*	Pollock Rip, MA
December 24	Bark	*Annie C Maguire*	Cape Elizabeth, ME
December 26	Sch	*Sarah Purves*	Huntington Bay, NY
December 30	Brig	*Christina Moore*	Lloyds Neck, NY
December 30	Sch	*Richard K Fox*	Orleans, MA

1887

	Sch	*Alvina Campbell*	Montauk, NY
		D W Hammond	Portland, ME
	Sch	*Phantom*	Off Fire Island, NY
January 3	Bktn	*Lotus*	Long Beach, NY
January 6		*Flying Dart*	Lockes Point, NH
January 12	Sch	*Carrie W*	Truro, MA
January 15	Sch	*Afton*	Cranberry Islands, ME
February	Sch	*William L Bradley*	Vineyard Sound, MA
February 10	Sch	*Rising Star*	Rye, NH
February 20	Sch	*Harry A Barry*	Point Judith, RI
February 28	Sch	*Daniel Webster*	Eatons Neck, NY
March 6	Stp	*City Of Chicago*	Westhampton, NY
March 15	Sch	*J H Eells*	Eastham, MA
March 19	Sch	*A W Thompson*	Willets Point, NY
March 25	St	*Scotia*	Great South Beach, NY
March 31	Sch	*Sedona*	Libby Island, ME
April 1	Sch	*Pathfinder*	Block Island, RI
April 2	Slp	*Anna T*	Nepeague, NY
April 2	Sch	*Oceana*	Duxbury, MA
April 2	Sch	*Rose Brothers*	Nepeague, NY
April 5	Sch	*Cora Etta*	Off Nantucket, MA
April 10	Sch	*R A Lindsay*	Rockaway, NY
May 11	Sch	*Ozelia*	Whalesback Ledge, ME
May 27	Sch	*Alexandria*	Pollock Rip, MA
June 6	Sts	*Achilles*	Block Island, RI
June 8	Sch	*Avon*	Eatons Neck, NY
June 22	Bark	*Georgietta*	Block Island, RI
July 3	Bark	*R A Allen*	Chatham, MA
July 6	Sch	*Hudson*	Green Island, ME
August 4	Sch	*Jennie A Cheney*	Watch Hill, RI
August 12	Sch	*Caroline Young*	Ipswich, MA
August 15	Sch	*Nathan Clifford*	Boothbay, ME
August 26	Sch	*Ocean Spray*	Block Island, RI
August 31	Bge	*H B Hussey*	Pollock Rip, MA
September 17	Sch	*A G Blair*	Mt Desert, ME
September 20	Sch	*Light Wing*	Scituate, MA
September 26	Sch	*Eva C Yates*	Fire Island, NY
September 27	Sch	*Joseph G Stover*	Orleans, MA
November 1	Sch	*William E Barnes*	Eastham, MA
November 3	Sch	*John E Sanford*	Newburyport, MA
November 10	Sch	*Maggie J Smith*	Narragansett Bay, RI
November 10	Sch	*Mystery*	Jerrys Point, NH
November 11	Sch	*Helen Mar*	Pollock Rip, MA
November 11	Sch	*John Linsey*	Pollock Rip, MA
November 17	Sch	*George & Albert*	Wood Island, ME
December 1	Sch	*Abby Wasson*	Pollock Rip, MA

DATE LOST	TYPE	NAME	WHERE LOST
December 18	Sch	*Lewis A King*	Montauk, NY
December 24	Sch	*George Temple*	Roamer Shoals, NY
December 31	Sch	*Mary A Drury*	Point Judith, RI

1888

		Ellen R	Buzzards Bay, MA
		Flora	Quoddy Head, ME
	Sch	*Lamartine*	East Bay, NY
		Maud S	Penobscot Bay, ME
		Unidentified	Point Judith, RI
January	Sch	*Ida E Latham*	Baiting Hollow, NY
January	Sch	*Riverside*	McGlatherly Island, ME
January 2	Sch	*William H Jordan*	Block Island, RI
January 17	Sch	*Sylvester*	Gloucester, MA
February 11	Sch	*Agnes R Bacon*	Marshfield, MA
February 25	Sch	*Nellie Bowers*	Richmonds Island, ME
March 3	Brig	*John Welsh Jr*	Point Judith, RI
March 11		*Edmund Driggs*	Bay Ridge, NY
March 11		*Ezra Nye*	New York, NY
March 11	St	*Governor*	New York, NY
March 11	Sch	*Mary Heitman*	New York, NY
March 11		*Phantom*	New York, NY
March 11	Bge	Unidentified	East Neck, NY
March 12	Slp	*Cornelia A Lowndes*	Nepeague, NY
March 23	Sch	*Ella*	Chatham, MA
March 28	Ship	*Canonbury*	Off Nantucket, MA
April 10	Sch	*P A Lindsay*	Rockaway Point, NY
April 11	Sch	*Plymouth Rock*	Provincetown, MA
April 27	Sch	*W A Crocker*	Long Cove Harbor, ME
May 2	Sch	*Anita*	Point Judith, RI
May 28	Sch	*Ventura*	Calais, ME
June 1	Sch	*Marietta Smith*	Nepeague, NY
June 25	Bark	*Chattanooga*	Marshfield, MA
July	Sch	*C W Loche*	Portsmouth, NH
July 4	Sch	*Mower*	Matinicus Island, ME
July 8	Sch	*Meteor*	Block Island, RI
July 11	Sch	*Wreath*	Bass Harbor, ME
July 12	Sch	*F H Odiorne*	Chatham, MA
July 12	St	*John Rodgers*	Fire Island, NY
July 12	Sch	*Nellie D Vaughn*	Watch Hill, RI
August 6	Sch	*Quoddy*	Pollock Rip, MA
August 11	St	*Bay Ridge*	Glen Cove, NY
August 22	Slp	*Favorite*	Montauk, NY
September 9	Sch	*Isaac H Borden*	Point Judith, RI
September 20	Slp	*Ethan Allen*	Blackwells Island, NY
September 26	Sch	*Abbie P Cramer*	Ipswich, MA
September 26	Sch	*Alma*	Vineyard Haven, MA
September 26	Sch	*H A Dewitt*	Chatham, MA
October 12	Sch	*Richard Morrell*	Coney Island, NY
November 6	Sch	*J I Worthington*	Mt Desert, ME
November 10	Sts	*Iberia*	Jones Inlet, NY
November 12	Sch	*Dalas Hill*	Tenants Harbor, ME
November 14		*Goldsmith Maid*	Boston, MA
November 18	Bge	*American Lloyds*	Truro, MA
November 23	Sch	*Gertie Freeman*	Rockport, MA
November 25	Sch	*Cox & Green*	Hull, MA
November 25	Sch	*Gertrude Abbott*	Hull, MA
November 25	Sch	*John Mettler*	Cape Ann, MA
November 25	Sch	*Olive Dyer*	Jerrys Point, NH

DATE LOST	TYPE	NAME	WHERE LOST
November 25	Slp	*Target*	Rockport, MA
November 26	Sch	*Edward H Norton*	Marshfield, MA
November 26	Sch	*H C Higginson*	Hull, MA
November 26	Sch	*Mattie E Eaton*	Hull, MA
November 26	Sch	*Robert Ripley*	Gloucester, MA
December 5	Sch	*Annie E Hayes*	Buzzards Bay, MA
December 5	Sch	*Sinbad*	Mussel Ridge Channel, ME
December 7	Stp	*Maryland*	Harlem River, NY
December 10	Sch	*Hampton*	Georges Island, ME
December 27	Sch	*George W Cushing*	Richmonds Island, ME
December 28		*Katie Mitchell*	Portsmouth, NH

1889

		Quilip	Cuttyhunk, MA
		Seminole	Nantucket Sound, MA
		Unidentified	Nantucket Sound, MA
January 6	Sch	*Lillian B Jones*	Petite Manan, ME
January 9	Sts	*George Appold*	Ditch Plain, NY
January 9	Sch	*Juliet*	Boston, MA
January 19	Sch	*William Bunoughs*	Pollock Rip, MA
January 27	Stp	*Antoinette*	Nantucket, MA
February		*Bunyon*	Broad Sound, MA
March 5	Sch	*John McManus*	Wellfleet, MA
March 14		*Wingate*	Georgia, NY
March 27		*Empire State*	Narragansett Bay, RI
April	Sch	*Agnes*	Fishermans Island, ME
April 1	Bark	*Wreath*	Prospect Harbor, ME
April 4	Sch	*Anna M Nash*	Ipswich, MA
April 4	Bark	*Nellie White*	Off the Northeast Coast
April 29	Sch	*Anna B Cannon*	Cape Ann, MA
June 5	Sch	*John N Sherwood*	Watch Hill, RI
July 1	Sch	*George Killam*	West Quoddy Head, ME
July 20	Sts	*Eduardo*	Cutler, ME
July 28	Sch	*George Savage*	Jamaica Island, NH
August 2	Sch	*Magnet*	Nash Island, ME
August 14	Sch	*Lady Of The Ocean*	Watch Hill, RI
August 28	Sch	*Early Bird*	Eatons Neck, NY
September 10	Sch	*Harriet Samantha*	Gloucester, MA
September 11	Sch	*Sarah L Simmons*	Pollock Rip, MA
September 12	Sch	*Nellie V Roakes*	Chatham, MA
September 14	Sch	*Phincas Sprague*	Chatham, MA
September 16	St	*Vertuminus*	Point Lookout, NY
September 17	Sch	*Abby Thaxter*	Whitehead, ME
September 18	Sch	*Decator Oakes*	Whitehead, ME
September 19	Sch	*Brunette*	Searsport Harbor, ME
September 20	Sch	*Sarah C Pyle*	Matinicus Island, ME
September 23	Sch	*Artinius Tiwell*	Pollock Rip, MA
October 5	Sch	*Benjamin Gastside*	Pollock Rip, MA
October 12	Sch	*Sabao*	Jones Inlet Bar, NY
October 13	Sch	*Jesse Caril*	Zachs Inlet, NY
October 14	Sch	*Eurotas*	Ipswich, MA
October 15	Sch	*Eva Diverty*	Long Island Sound
October 23	Sch	*Perseverence*	Thatchers Island, MA
October 30	Sch	*Anna A Holton*	Provincetown, MA
November 3	Sch	*Paurechita*	Provincetown, MA
November 19	Bark	*Beechdale*	Point Lookout, NY
November 27	Sch	*City Of Ellsworth*	Boon Island, ME
December 3		*Three Brothers*	Gloucester, MA
December 5	Sch	*Hannah Stone*	Newburyport, MA

DATE LOST	TYPE	NAME	WHERE LOST
December 10	Sch	*Danial M French*	Watch Hill, RI
December 20	Sch	*M L St Pierre*	Whitehead, ME
December 26	Sch	*David Crowell*	Hell Gate, NY

1890

		G M Farnsworth	Pollock Rip, MA
		Ida Grover	Matinicus Island, ME
	Sch	*Julia S Bailey*	Provincetown, MA
	Sch	*Mentora*	Bucksport, ME
	Brig	*Panchita*	Provincetown, MA
		R H Shannon	Vineyard Haven, MA
	Sch	*Star Of The East*	Nantucket Sound, MA
		Unidentified	Off New York
		Unidentified	Elizabeth Islands, MA
	Sch	*W H Jones*	Rockland, ME
January		*Jane Ingram*	Prospect Harbor, ME
January 12	Sch	*Pocahontas*	Block Island, RI
January 24	Sch	*Fairfield*	Cape Small Point, ME
January 24	Sch	*Laurissa*	Machias, ME
January 25		*Ximena*	Machias, ME
February 19	Sch	*Glen*	Little Duck Island, ME
February 19	St	*John A Hadgeman*	New York, NY
March	Sch	*Belle Higgins*	Shinnecock, NY
March 6	Sch	*Abbot W Lewis*	Cape Ann, MA
April	Sch	*Bella*	Greenport, NY
April 3	St	*Panama*	Jones Inlet, NY
April 4	Sch	*Asa J Moore*	Westhampton, NY
May 1	Brig	*Charles Dennis*	Kennebunk River, ME
May 4	Sch	*W H Fredson*	Block Island, RI
May 9	Sch	*Gertrude*	Portland, ME
May 10	Sch	*Annie Sargent*	Offshore, ME
May 10	Sch	*Duroe*	Isle Au Haut, ME
May 14	Sch	*George F Edmands*	Pollock Rip, MA
May 14	Brig	*Maria W Norwood*	Great Round Shoal, MA
May 14	Sch	*R L Tay*	Chatham, MA
May 15	Sch	*Lady Of The Lake*	Block Island, RI
May 20	Sch	*Belle A Nauss*	Truro, MA
May 28	Ycht	*Yeada*	New York Bay, NY
June	Sch	Unidentified	Shinnecock, NY
June 25	Sch	*Annie J Russell*	Pears Island, ME
July 15	Sch	*Boston*	Penobscot River, ME
August		*Advance*	Lower Bay, NY
August 13	Sch	*Weybosset*	Pollock Rip, MA
August 27	Sch	*Annie E Moore*	Pollock Rip, MA
August 27	Sch	*Fred Smith*	Mosquito Island, ME
August 30	Sch	*Castillian*	Bar Harbor, ME
September 17	Sch	*Maria Adelaide*	Cuttyhunk, MA
October 7	Sch	*T B Harris*	Portland, ME
October 12	Sch	*Josiah Whitehouse*	Vineyard Sound, MA
October 17	Sch	*Asa H Pevere*	Chatham, MA
October 17	Sch	*Jane L Newton*	Chatham, MA
October 17	Sch	*Louisa Smith*	Boston, MA
October 17	Sch	*Mexican*	Annisquam, MA
October 20	Sch	*Eben Dale*	Gloucester, MA
October 20	Sch	*SS Bickmore*	Hyannis, MA
October 24	Sch	*Mabel*	Isle Au Haut, ME
October 28	Brig	*Euginie*	Jones Inlet, NY
October 29	Sch	*Mary L Varney*	Cape Ann, MA
November 7	Sch	*John Simmons*	Ipswich, MA

ABOVE: After 25 years of a successful freight carrying career, the Boston-built four masted schooner *Kenwood* was driven ashore to a total loss at Scituate MA on February 4, 1926. *Photo courtesy Paul C. Morris, Nantucket MA.* **BELOW:** Storms with blowing snow make navigating difficult even for the best skippers. The Captains of both the *Charles H. Trickey* (left) and the *Mary E. Olys* tried to sail into Cape Porpoise Harbor, Maine on January 1, 1920. In visibility less than the length of the vessels, both vessels struck ledges, sinking the schooners. They were never salvaged. *Photo from the collection of William P. Quinn, Orleans MA.*

ABOVE: In 1909, the White Star Liner *Republic* was in a collision with the *Florida* and sank south of Nantucket. With millions in gold rumored to be aboard, the *Republic* has been the target of numerous salvage operations including a major expedition by Chicago Bridge and Iron Co. in the 1930's. Her hull now lies in two pieces a few miles from the wreck of the *Andrea Doria*. *Photo from the collection of William P. Quinn, Orleans MA.* **BELOW:** Although she was not totally lost in any of her accidents, the steamer *H.F. Dimock* certainly had her share of mishaps. In 1891, she sank Vanderbilt's yacht *Alva* off Cape Cod. Eighteen years later she sank the steamer *Horatio Hall* in the same area. On February 9, 1920, she ran aground in the East River after striking a bridge. *Photo courtesy Paul Morris, Nantucket MA.*

DATE LOST	TYPE	NAME	WHERE LOST
November 8	Sch	*Anna Eliza*	Provincetown, MA
November 9	Sch	*Anna Elizabeth*	Chatham, MA
November 14	Sch	*Erie*	Damariscotta, ME
November 20	Sch	*Damon*	Chatham, MA
December	Ycht	*Jenty*	Orient, NY
December 12	Sch	*Chattanooga*	Orleans, MA
December 16	Sch	*William Emerson*	Provincetown, MA
December 19	Sch	*Carch*	Capp Island, ME
December 26	Sch	*A H Hurlburt*	Narragansett Bay, RI
December 26	Sch	*Bill Stowe*	Narragansett Bay, RI
December 29	Sch	*G Stanley*	Quoddy Head, ME
December 30	Sch	*Robert Byron*	Chatham, MA

1891

	Sch	*Expedite*	Sands Point, NY
		Unidentified	Vineyard Haven, MA
January 13	Sch	*Ada Barker*	Portland, ME
January 13	Sch	*Otter*	Bellport, NY
February 12	Sch	*James Rouke*	North Haven, ME
February 18	Sch	*Gardiner G Deering*	Cuttyhunk, MA
February 18	Bark	*Mascotta*	New York Harbor, NY
February 20	St	*James Rumsey*	New York, NY
March 2	Sch	*Fleetwing*	Negro Island, ME
March 4	Sch	*Helen*	Cape Elizabeth, ME
March 12	Sch	*Shadow*	Orleans, MA
March 13	Bark	*Umberto 1*	Roamer Shoals, NY
March 15	Sch	*Augustus Fabans*	Boothbay, ME
March 15	Sts	*Triana*	Cuttyhunk, MA
March 24	Brig	*Joseph Bannigan*	Long Beach, NY
April 2	Sch	*Nellie A Walker*	Boone Island, ME
April 9	Sch	*Nellie J Day*	Boone Island, ME
April 15	Sch	*Connecticut*	Newcastle, NH
April 19	Ship	*Lydia Skolfield*	Newport, RI
June		*Davis Brothers*	Narragansett Bay, RI
June 2	Sch	*Joseph W Fish*	Burnt Island, ME
June 4	Sch	*Seabird*	Libby Island, ME
June 9	Sch	*Richard Law*	Chatham, MA
July 4	Sch	*Alabama*	Offshore, ME
July 5	Sch	*James Nichols*	Cuttyhunk, MA
July 5	Sch	*William Boardman*	Chatham, MA
July 6	Sch	*Pavilion*	West Quoddy Head, ME
July 18	Sch	*A J Broadman*	Block Island, RI
July 25	St	*George L Garlick*	Coney Island, NY
August		*Addie Oakes*	Nantucket Sound, MA
August 19	Sch	*Lucy M Collins*	Ipswich, MA
September 24	Sch	*Harry Doremus*	Fire Island Bar, NY
September 30	Sch	*Clytie*	Metinicus Island, ME
October	Sch	*American Chief*	Gardiners Island, NY
October	Sch	*Florence Nowell*	Pollock Rip, MA
October		*Mary E Oliver*	Vineyard Haven, MA
October 7	Sch	*M M Merriman*	Pollock Rip, MA
October 22	Sch	*Hattie M Crowell*	Long Cove, ME
October 23	Sch	*Edith T Gandy*	Pollock Rip, MA
October 23	Sch	*Rose Brothers*	Block Island, RI
October 23	Sch	*S B Franklin*	Duxbury, MA
October 23	Slp	*Thomas Armstrong*	Nepeague, NY
October 23	Sch	*Vulcan*	Nantucket, MA
October 23	Slp	*Yankee Bride*	Block Island, RI
November 5	Sch	*Clara S Cameron*	Hull, MA

DATE LOST	TYPE	NAME	WHERE LOST
November 20	Sch	*Abbie H Hodgeman*	Pollock Rip, MA
November 24	Sch	*Adele Trudell*	Roamer Shoals, NY
November 29	Sch	*Albert Jameson*	Monhegan Island, ME
December 2	Sch	*Agnes Manning*	Elizabeth Islands, MA
December 5	Sch	*Trojan*	Cranberry Islands, ME
December 8	Sch	*Emma K Smalley*	Chatham, MA
December 11	Sch	*Alice M Ridgeway*	Watch Hill, RI
December 15	Sch	*Dolphin*	Boone Island, ME
December 18	Sch	*Mabel Purdey*	Machiasport, ME
December 25		*Maggie Cummings*	Watch Hill, RI
December 26	Slp	*Hornet*	Annisquam, MA
December 28	Sch	*Dudley Farlin*	Offshore, ME
December 28	Sch	*Huntress*	Browney Island, ME

1892

DATE LOST	TYPE	NAME	WHERE LOST
		Unidentified	Nantucket Sound, MA
January 6	Sts	*Gallatin*	Manchester, MA
January 7	Sch	*Mary Baker*	Cape Ann, MA
January 20	Sch	*H P Kirkham*	Off Nantucket, MA
January 25	Bktn	*Harry & Aubrey*	Long Island, NY
January 31	Sch	*W H Y Hackett*	Ipswich, MA
February	Sch	*Lucy Jones*	Nantucket Sound, MA
February 1		*Morrill Boy*	Rockport, MA
March 11	Sch	*Rob And Harry*	Cuttyhunk, MA
March 23	Sch	*Henry White*	Quonochontaug, RI
April 4	Bark	*Willy & Emmy*	Nantucket, MA
April 20	Sch	*Elizabeth M Cook*	Pollock Rip, MA
April 21	Sch	*Index*	Stage Island, ME
May		*Francis Edward*	Fairhaven, MA
May 3	Sch	*Satilla*	Great South Bch, NY
May 6		*Water Lily*	Gloucester, MA
May 13	Sch	*Alice M Leland*	Otter Island, ME
May 17		*Richard Peterson*	Georgetown Island, ME
May 26	Sch	*A Francis Edwards*	New Bedford, MA
June 13	Sch	*Jed Frye*	Plum Island, NY
June 14	Slp	*Margret E Sinclair*	Jones Beach, NY
July 3	Sts	*Alva*	Pollock Rip, MA
August 26	St	*William S Slater*	Boston, MA
September 5	Sch	*George B Marble*	Chatham, MA
September 12	Sch	*Eben Fisher*	Marthas Vineyard, MA
September 15		*Princeport*	Machias Bay, ME
October 2	Slp	*Fashion*	Newport, RI
October 21	Sch	*Eva May*	Pollock Rip, MA
October 29	Slp	*Ranger*	Block Island, RI
November	Sch	*Ada L Harris*	Nantucket Shoals, MA
November 12	Sch	*George S Tarbell*	Vineyard Sound, MA
November 16	Sbge	*Sooloo*	Pollock Rip, MA
November 16	Sbge	*Storm King*	Pollock Rip, MA
November 18	Bge	*# 16*	Rockaway Point, NY
November 30	Bark	*Active*	Truro, MA
November 30	Bark	*Kate Harding*	Truro, MA
December 2	Sch	*Ethel Emmerson*	Pollock Rip, MA
December 22	Sch	*Charlotte Fish*	Pollock Rip, MA
December 25		*Edward Cooper*	Off New York
December 27	Sch	*Esther Ward*	Chatham, MA

1893

DATE LOST	TYPE	NAME	WHERE LOST
		Break Of Day	Rockland, ME

DATE LOST	TYPE	NAME	WHERE LOST
February	Sch	John S Ames	Bellport, NY
February 6	Sch	Glenola	Jones Inlet, NY
February 10	Sch	East Wind	Point Judith, RI
February 10	Sch	John Paull	Quonochontaug, RI
February 17	Sch	Elsie Fay	Montauk Point, NY
February 19	Sch	Enos B Phillips	Hull, MA
February 20	Sch	Douglas Dearborn	Cuttyhunk, MA
February 20	Sbge	Reliance	Block Island, RI
February 22	Sch	Glenwood	Hull, MA
February 24	Brig	Aquatic	Cuttyhunk, MA
February 26	Sch	Cricket	Provincetown, MA
February 26	Sch	Menunctatuck	Watch Hill, RI
March 2	Sch	Arvesta	Narragansett Bay, RI
March 19	Bark	Altamaha	Chatham, MA
March 29	Sts	Gluckauf	Blue Point, NY
April 6	Sch	Rogers	Pollock Rip, MA
April 12	Sch	Helen R Low	Gloucester, MA
April 24	Sch	James Flanagan	Chatham, MA
May		Unidentified	Chatham, MA
May 4	Sch	Brave	Ipswich, MA
May 8	Sts	R F Loper	New York, NY
May 17	Sch	Osseo	Cape Ann, MA
May 24	Sch	Oliver Chase	Point Judith, RI
July 15	Sch	Thomas W Hyde	Pollock Rip, MA
July 23	Ycht	Olen	Marblehead, MA
August	Bge	N & W #4	Narragansett Bay, RI
August 7	Slp	Black Eagle	Montauk, NY
August 7		Wildfire	Provincetown, MA
August 11	Sch	Acacia	Pollock Rip, MA
August 21	Sch	Ethel Swift	Narragansett Bay, RI
August 21	Slp	Mary	Block Island, RI
August 24	Sch	Lotta B	Thatchers Island, MA
August 24	Bge	Lyken Valey	Southampton, NY
August 24	Sch	Multinomah	Block Island, RI
August 24	St	Panther	Southampton, NY
August 29	Sch	C Henry Kirk	Long Beach, NY
August 29	Bark	Martha P Tucker	Point Lookout, NY
September 3	Sch	Maggie Mitchell	Chatham, MA
September 8	Sch	John P Kelsey	Pollock Rip, MA
September 17	Sch	David Carll	Point Lookout, NY
October 11	Sch	Ada A Kennedy	Cuttyhunk, MA
October 21	Sch	Henry Friend	Pollock Rip, MA
November		Stephen Raymond	Hyannis, MA
November 7	Sch	Annie W Akers	Pollock Rip, MA
November 8	Sch	Edith	Monroe Island, ME
November 16	Sch	Richard B Chute	Jones Inlet Bar, NY
November 25	Sch	Franklin	Pollock Rip, MA
November 27	Sch	Louise H Randall	Smiths Point, NY
November 28		Elizabeth Emory	Chatham, MA
December	Sch	Mary Lymburner	Marthas Vineyard, MA
December 5	Ship	Jason	Truro, MA
December 5	Sch	Jefferson	Salem, MA
December 5	Sch	William G R Mowry	Block Island, RI
December 29		Perit	Chatham, MA

1894

	Sch	Albert W Smith	Orleans, MA
		City Of Portsmouth	Salem, MA
		I N Seymour	Long Island Sound

DATE LOST	TYPE	NAME	WHERE LOST
	Sch	Unidentified	Vinyard Sound, MA
January 12	Sch	Laura E Messer	Pollock Rip, MA
January 13	Sch	Ella B Kimball	Chatham, MA
January 13	Sch	Mary Williams	Nepeague, NY
January 13	Sch	Minnie C Taylor	Nantucket, MA
January 16	Sch	Fannie J Bartlett	Montauk Point, NY
January 29	Sch	Aberdeen	Cape Ann, MA
February 12	Sch	Edwin Morrison	Provincetown, MA
February 12	Sch	Fortuna	Provincetown, MA
February 13	Sch	Minnie Rowan	Cohasset, MA
February 14	St	Oliver A Arnold	New York, NY
March 10	Brig	Nellie Pickup	Block Island, RI
March 18	St	La Bretagne	Blue Point, NY
March 25	St	A C Nickerson	New York, NY
April 7	Sch	Benjamin B. Church	Sagaponack, NY
April 8	Sch	Mary A Hood	Hull, MA
April 8	Sch	Nellie	Ipswich, MA
April 8	Bark	Belmont	Provincetown, MA
April 13		Jennie M Carter	Salisbury, MA
April 13	Sch	Magnum	Scituate, MA
April 21	Bark	Elmiranda	East Hampton, NY
May 2	St	Persian Monarch	Moriches, NY
June 18	St	Canonicus	Port Richmond, NY
June 26	Bge	Shamokin	Pollock Rip, MA
July 11		Ocean Eagle	Newburyport, MA
September 2	Sch	Emta	Chatham, MA
September 2	Sch	Silver Heels	Whitehead, ME
September 5	Sch	Mary J Castner	Chatham, MA
September 6	St	Sorrento	Bellport, NY
September 10	Sch	Dora M French	Vineyard Sound, MA
September 25	Sch	Edith & May	Chatham, MA
October 6	St	City Of Albany	New York, NY
October 7	Sts	Welcome	Bagaduce River, ME
October 8	Sch	Titmouse	Thatchers Island, MA
October 10	Sch	Adeline	Gloucester, MA
October 10	Sch	L O Foster	Block Island, RI
October 10	Sch	Lana V Rose	Pollock Rip, MA
October 10	Sch	Leonessa	Narragansett Bay, RI
October 10	Sch	Light Of The East	Pollock Rip, MA
October 10	Slp	Lizzie	Block Island, RI
October 10	Sts	Majella	Point Judith, RI
October 10	Sch	Maria	Block Island, RI
October 10	Slp	Maria D	Montauk, NY
October 10	Sch	S S Scranton	Buzzards Bay, MA
October 11	Sch	Dauntless	Elizabeth Islands, MA
October 11	Sch	E K Hart	Elizabeth Islands, MA
October 11	Sch	Unidentified	Elizabeth Islands, MA
October 16	Sch	Ellen Morrison	Pollock Rip, MA
October 22	Sch	Allan	Watch Hill, RI
November 1	Sch	Yulan	Cape Ann, MA
November 5	Sch	Salmon Washburn	Huntington Bay, NY
November 6	Sch	Eddie H Weeks	Block Island, RI
November 8	Sch	Massasoit	Long Beach, NY
November 22	Sch	F Greenville Rusl.	Roamer Shoal, NY
November 24	Sch	Lettie G Howard	Truro, MA
November 25		Oriole	Fort Pond Bay, NY
November 26	Sch	Messenger	Wellfleet, MA
November 29	Sch	Royal Arch	Off Chatham, MA
December 4	Sch	Clara E Simpson	Long Island Sound
December 6	Sch	Mary B Baird	Nepeague, NY

DATE LOST	TYPE	NAME	WHERE LOST
December 26	Slp	E A Willis	Long Island Sound
December 27	Sch	Izetta	Eatons Neck, NY
December 27	Slp	Nettie	Block Island, RI

1895

DATE LOST	TYPE	NAME	WHERE LOST
	Stp	Forest City	Boston, MA
	Stp	Katahdin	Boston, MA
January 5	Sch	Job H Jackson Jr	Provincetown, MA
January 6	Sts	Sea King	Long Island Sound
January 6	Bge	Unidentified	Long Island Sound
January 6	Bge	Unidentified	Long Island Sound
January 6	Bge	Unidentified	Long Island Sound
January 6	Bge	Unidentified	Long Island Sound
January 6	Bge	Unidentified	Long Island Sound
January 13	Sch	Eva L Leonard	Newport, RI
January 13	Sch	Moss Rose	Elizabeth Islands, MA
January 14	Bge	Seth Low	Jones Beach, NY
January 26	Bge	Albert M	Point Judith, RI
January 26	Bge	American Eagle	Point Judith, RI
January 26	Bge	F A Dingee	Point Judith, RI
January 26	Sch	Leader	Gloucester, MA
February 4	St	Lamington	Great South Bch, NY
February 5		George H Warren	Off New York
February 5	Sch	T P Dixon	Marthas Vineyard, MA
February 6	Brig	Gem	Moriches, NY
February 8	Sch	John B Manning	Sayville, NY
February 8	Sch	Louis V Place	Fire Island, NY
February 8	Sch	Marblehead	Gloucester, MA
February 17	Sch	Gertie S Winsor	Provincetown, MA
February 18		Unidentified	Vineyard Sound, MA
March 12	St	F W Bosburgh	Roamer Shoals, NY
March 25	Sch	Mary H Hall	Orient Point, NY
April 7	Sch	Josiah R Smith	Vineyard Sound, MA
April 10	Sch	Lizzie W Hannum	Buzzards Bay, MA
April 10	Bge	Oneonta	Pollock Rip, MA
April 11	Sch	Henry Clay	Narragansett Bay, RI
April 14	Sch	International	Eatons Neck, NY
April 25	Sch	North Erin	Tiana, NY
May 4	Sch	Bessie Parker	Pollock Rip, MA
May 8	Slp	West Wind	Newport, RI
June 6	Sch	Rocky Glen	Pollock Rip, MA
June 11	Brig	Olinda	Fishers Island, NY
June 24	Sch	Robert Mowe	Hyannis, MA
July 25	Sch	John Lenthall	Fire Island, NY
July 26	Sch	Addie G Bryant	Pollock Rip, MA
August 5	Stcn	John Lang	Long Island Sound
September 1	Slp	Coya	Newport, RI
September 11	Sch	Ada S Allen	Cuttyhunk, MA
September 13		Mary A Heaton	Off Eastham, MA
September 18	St	Gen. A E Burnside	New York, NY
September 28	St	Harry	Off Rhode Island
September 29	Sch	Josie F	Watch Hill, RI
October 4	Sch	Nellie Pickering	Nantucket Sound, MA
October 5	Sch	Evelyn	Block Island, RI
October 17	Sch	Frank A Magee	Pollock Rip, MA
October 18	Sch	Elizabeth Levansaler	Provincetown, MA
October 23	Sch	Active	Block Island, RI
November 2	Bge	Tivoli	Pollock Rip, MA
November 13	Sch	Lillie	Boston, MA

DATE LOST	TYPE	NAME	WHERE LOST
November 23	Sch	*Cornelia Kingsland*	Roamer Shoals, NY
December 6	Sch	*Nantasket*	Pollock Rip, MA
December 11	Sch	*Carrie Easier*	Barnstable, MA
December 31	Sch	*Ellen Lincoln*	Eastham, MA
December 31	Sch	*Smuggler*	Wellfleet, MA

1896

DATE LOST	TYPE	NAME	WHERE LOST
	Sch	*Edmund*	Chatham, MA
	Sch	*Fawn*	Orleans, MA
	Bark	*Francisco*	Chatham, MA
January 13	Sch	*Fortuna II*	Off Truro, MA
January 16	Sch	*William Wilson*	Chatham, MA
January 28	St	*J W Hawkins*	Off Montauk, NY
February 8	Sch	*Alianza*	Ipswich, MA
February 11	Sch	*Belle R Hull*	Watch Hill, RI
March 2	Bark	*H J Libby*	Jones Beach, NY
March 4	Sch	*Jonathon Bourne*	Pollock Rip, MA
March 4	St	Unidentified	Montauk, NY
March 11	Sch	*Kate Scranton*	Eatons Neck, NY
March 11	Sch	*Mary A Bates*	Eatons Neck, NY
March 13	Slp	*Gracie*	Great South Bay, NY
March 15	Sch	*Clarissa Allen*	Point Judith, RI
March 19	Brig	*Water Witch*	Sakonnet, RI
May 6	Sch	*Danial B Fearing*	Wellfleet, MA
May 6	Sch	*Enterprise*	Nantucket, MA
May 7	Ycht	*Serkara*	Thatchers Island, MA
May 21	Sch	*Lewis Jane*	Chatham, MA
May 28	Sch	*War Steed*	Quonochontaug, RI
June 13	Sch	*Henry S Wyman*	Block Island, RI
July 2	Sch	*Joseph Oakes*	Cuttyhunk, MA
July 4	Bge	*# 8*	Shinnecock Inlet, NY
July 10	Sch	*J P Wyman*	Elizabeth Islands, MA
July 14	Sch	*Richard Law*	Eastham, MA
July 30	Sch	*Blue Jay*	Point Judith, RI
August 5	Sch	*Welcome R Beebe*	Wellfleet, MA
September 8	Sch	*Excelsior*	Gloucester, MA
September 13	Sch	*Silver Dart*	Truro, MA
September 14	Bark	*Monte Tabor*	Provincetown, MA
September 19	Bark	*Fantee*	Elizabeth Islands, MA
October 7	St	*William Harrison*	Grand Island, NY
October 11	Sch	*Angie*	Block Island, RI
October 16	Sch	*Alsation*	Nahant, MA
October 23	Sch	*Maggie Abbott*	Watch Hill, RI
November 15	Slp	*Wallet*	Long Island, NY
November 20	Slp	*S R Packer*	Block Island, RI
December 8	Sch	*Argo*	Nantucket, MA
December 10	St	*Clarissa Radcliffe*	Bellport, NY
December 16	Sch	*Puritan*	Scituate, MA
December 16	Slp	*Sea Serpent*	Block Island, RI
December 16	Slp	*Shaver*	Block Island, RI
December 16	Sch	*Ulrica*	Hull, MA
December 23	Sch	*Calvin B Orcutt*	Chatham, MA
December 24	Sch	*Carrie Walker*	Off Truro, MA

1897

DATE LOST	TYPE	NAME	WHERE LOST
	Stp	*Catskill*	North River, NY
January 21	Sch	*Nahum Chapin*	Quogue, NY
January 22	Bark	*Isaac Jackson*	Elizabeth Islands, MA

DATE LOST	TYPE	NAME	WHERE LOST
February 3	Bge	*Ocean View*	Block Island, RI
March 15	Bark	*Athlon*	Orient, NY
March 15	Sch	*Julia A Warr*	Wainscott, NY
April 8	Sch	*Bonita*	Off Duxbury, MA
May 2	Sch	*Ethel Maud*	Provincetown, MA
May 2	Sch	*Robert Dority*	Cape Ann, MA
May 4	Sch	*L B Gilchrist*	Amagansett, NY
May 13	Sch	*Annie Rudolph*	Off Eastham, MA
June 10	Sch	*A G Heisler*	Wellfleet, MA
June 10	Sch	*Albert Miller*	Eastham, MA
June 10	Sch	*Walter Miller*	Eastham, MA
June 14		*Edward W Schmidt*	Kennebec, ME
July 8	Sch	*Maria*	Block Island, RI
July 12	Sch	*Coree E Smith*	Pollock Rip, MA
July 14	Sch	*Ira Laffrinier*	Orleans, MA
July 21	Sch	*R L Dewis*	Marthas Vineyard, MA
August 15	Bge	*Franklin*	Rockaway, NY
August 18	Sts	*Elihio Thompson*	Pollock Rip, MA
October		*Mary B Smith*	Vineyard Haven, MA
October 1		*Idahoe*	Great Gull Island, ME
October 18	Sch	*Lodewick Bill*	Provincetown, MA
October 21	St	*James B Schyler*	East River, NY
October 21	Sch	*Nellie Lamper*	Eastham, MA
October 26	Sch	*Mary A Brown*	Block Island, RI
November	St	*John E Moore*	Roamer Shoals, NY
November 4	Sch	*Edward Mclaughlin*	Point Judith, RI
November 10	Slp	*Ella May*	Montauk, NY
November 11	Sch	*Maud H Dudley*	Watch Hill, RI
November 15	Sch	*Percy*	Block Island, RI
December 21	Sch	*Edith Bean*	Block Island, RI

1898

		Alert	Shoreham, NY
		Alida	Rockland, ME
		Carrie C Miles	Portland, ME
	Sch	*Cynthia Jane*	Gowanus, NY
		Foscolia	Off Fire Island, NY
	Sch	*Frank Beattie*	Astoria, NY
		Georgietta	Rockland, ME
		Globe	Northern Long Island, NY
	Sch	*J G Parson*	Crab Meadow, NY
	Slp	*Olive Leaf*	Port Jefferson, NY
January 31	Sch	*William Johnson*	Off Maine
February 1	Sch	*Barracouta*	Pigeon Cove, MA
February 1	Sch	*Charlie Stedman*	Rockport, MA
February 1	Slp	*Daniel Webster*	Rockport, MA
February 1	Sch	*David A Osier*	Plymouth, MA
February 1	Sch	*Defiance*	Rockport, MA
February 1	Sts	*Frank Scripture*	Rockport, MA
February 1	Sch	*George W Jewett*	Gloucester, MA
February 1	Sch	*James Holmes*	Gloucester, MA
February 1	Sch	*Marcellus*	Gloucester, MA
February 16	Sbge	*Excelsior*	Pollock Rip, MA
February 20	Ship	*Asia*	Pollock Rip, MA
March		Unidentified	Off Rhode Island
March 31	Sch	*St Elmo*	Nantucket, MA
March 31	Sch	*William Higgins*	Provincetown, MA
April 6	Stp	*Henry Morrison*	Boston, MA
April 30	Sch	*Shamrock*	Montauk, NY

ABOVE: The *Horatio Hall* was typical of the coastal steamers that ran from Boston to New York between 1880 and 1925. The *Hall* was in a collision with the *H. F. Dimock* in 1909 near the busy shipping channel at Pollock Rip Massachusetts. **BELOW:** She succumbed to the fatal blow and sank in ten fathoms of clear Atlantic water. Local wreckers stripped her of everything movable that was above the water line within a few weeks of her sinking. One facetious report said that "....even the pool table was removed." The *Hall* is a popular wreck dive in New England. *Photos from the collection of William P. Quinn, Orleans MA.*

DATE LOST	TYPE	NAME	WHERE LOST
May	Sch	Charles W Morse	Newport, RI
May 7	Sch	Alfaratta	Ipswich, MA
May 10	Sts	H W Hills	Marblehead Light, MA
May 12	Sch	Mary Miller	Point Judith, RI
May 15	Sch	Angela	Nantucket Sound, MA
May 16	Slp	Red Rover	Provincetown, MA
May 24	Ship	Troop	Forge River, NY
May 25	Sch	Laurel	Watch Hill, RI
June 2		George A Upton	Carvers Harbor, ME
June 4	Sch	Helen G Moseley	Pollock Rip, MA
July 4	Sts	Surf City	Beverley, MA
July 13	Sch	Emma M Fox	Plymouth, MA
July 29	Sch	Zenobia	Orleans, MA
August 1	Sch	Lucia Porter	Provincetown, MA
August 24	Sch	Eva Lendel	Chatham, MA
August 26		Actress	Newport, RI
September 15	Sch	Freeman	New Bedford, MA
September 16	Sch	Alice C Jordan	Nantucket Sound, MA
September 19	Sch	Fanny T	Nahant, MA
September 20	Bark	Harriet Jackson	Chatham, MA
September 24	Sch	Bon Ton	Ipswich, MA
September 26	Sch	Unidentified	Nantucket Sound, MA
October 1	Sbge	Samuel Spring	Nantucket Sound, MA
October 3	Slp	Crocodile	Quonochontaug, RI
November 12	Sch	Cinderella	Fire Island Inlet, NY
November 20	Sch	Mary F Corson	Truro, MA
November 22	Bge	Escort	Cutchogue, NY
November 22	Bge	McCauley	Peconic, NY
November 22	Bge	Nevasink	Cutchogue, NY
November 26	Sch	Carrie L Paysire	Chatham, MA
November 27	Bge	# 1	Hull, MA
November 27	Bge	# 4	Hull, MA
November 27	Sch	Abby K Bently	Vineyard Haven, MA
November 27	Sch	Abel E Babcock	Hull, MA
November 27	Sch	Addie E Snow	Provincetown, MA
November 27	Sch	Addie Sawyer	Marthas Vineyard, MA
November 27		Agnes	Provincetown Harbor, MA
November 27	Sch	Agnes Smith	Point Judith, RI
November 27	Sch	Albert L Butler	Provincetown, MA
November 27	Bark	Alexander Campbell	Block Island, RI
November 27	Sch	Aloha	Block Island, RI
November 27	Sch	Amelia Ireland	Marthas Vineyard, MA
November 27	Sch	Anna H Mason	Gloucester, MA
November 27	Slp	Anna Pitcher	Block Island, RI
November 27	Sch	Anna W Barker	Tenants Harbor, ME
November 27	Sch	Annie Lee	Rockport, MA
November 27	Bge	Beaver	Vineyard Haven, MA
November 27	Sch	Bertha E Glover	Vineyard Haven, MA
November 27	Sch	Bessie H Gross	Manchester, MA
November 27	Bge	Budget	Vineyard Haven, MA
November 27	Bge	Byssus	Vineyard Haven, MA
November 27	Sch	Calvin F Baker	Boston, MA
November 27	Sch	Canaria	Vineyard Haven, MA
November 27	Sch	Carita	Vineyard Haven, MA
November 27	Slp	Cassie	Block Island, RI
November 27	Sch	Cathie C Berry	Vineyard Haven, MA
November 27		Champion	Provincetown Harbor, MA
November 27	Sch	Charles E Raymond	Vineyard Haven, MA
November 27	Sch	Chilion	Rockport, MA
November 27	Sch	Christina Moore	Vineyard Haven, MA

DATE LOST	TYPE	NAME	WHERE LOST
November 27	Sch	Clara C Baker	Marthas Vineyard, MA
November 27	Sch	Clara Leavitt	Marthas Vineyard, MA
November 27	Sch	Columbia	Scituate, MA
November 27	Sbge	Daniel I Tenney	Barnstable, MA
November 27	Sbge	Delaware	Cohasset, MA
November 27	Sch	E J Hamilton	Vineyard Haven, MA
November 27	Sch	Edgar S Foster	Marshfield, MA
November 27	Sch	Edith Mcintyre	Vineyard Haven, MA
November 27		Ella	Provincetown Harbor, MA
November 27		Ella F Crowell	Vineyard Haven, MA
November 27	Sch	Emma	Barnstable, MA
November 27	Sts	Fairfax	Cuttyhunk, MA
November 27	Sbge	Falcon	Vineyard Haven, MA
November 27	Sch	Farmer R Walker	Provincetown, MA
November 27		Francis	Provincetown Harbor, MA
November 27	Sch	G H Hopkins	Boston, MA
November 27		G W Rawley	Marthas Vineyard, MA
November 27	Sts	George A Chaffee	Rockport, MA
November 27	Sch	George H Mills	Vineyard Haven, MA
November 27	Sch	Gloriana	Cohasset, MA
November 27	Sch	Hattie A Butler	Buzzards Bay, MA
November 27	Sch	Hector	Vineyard Haven, MA
November 27	Sch	Idella Small	Ipswich, MA
November 27		Inez Hatch	Northeast Coast
November 27	Sch	Island City	Marthas Vineyard, MA
November 27	Sch	Ivy Bell	Jerrys Point, NH
November 27	Sch	J D Ingraham	Vineyard Haven, MA
November 27	Sch	James A Brown	Vineyard Haven, MA
November 27	Sch	James Ponder Jr	Vineyard Haven, MA
November 27	Slp	Jennie	Elizabeth Islands, MA
November 27	Sch	Juniata	Cohasset, MA
November 27	Sch	King Phillip	Off Provincetown, MA
November 27	Sch	Leander V Beebe	Cohasset, MA
November 27	Sch	Leora M Thurlow	Vineyard Haven, MA
November 27	Sch	Lester A Lewis	Provincetown, MA
November 27	Sch	Lexington	Block Island, RI
November 27		Lida	Provincetown, MA
November 27	Bark	Lucy A Nichols	Cohasset, MA
November 27	Sch	Lucy Hammond	Vineyard Haven, MA
November 27	Sch	Lunet	Elizabeth Islands, MA
November 27	Sch	M E Eldridge	Vineyard Haven, MA
November 27	Sch	Marion Draper	Vineyard Haven, MA
November 27	Sch	Mertis H Perry	Marshfield, MA
November 27		Nautilus	Provincetown Harbor, MA
November 27	Slp	Nellie B	Block Island, RI
November 27	Sch	Nellie Doe	Vineyard Haven, MA
November 27	Bark	Nellie M Slade	Vineyard Haven, MA
November 27	Sch	Newburgh	Vineyard Haven, MA
November 27	Sts	Pentagoet	Off Truro, MA
November 27		Percy	Block Island, RI
November 27	Sts	Pinafore	Isle of Shoals, NH
November 27	Stp	Portland	Off Provincetown, MA
November 27	Sch	Queen Ester	Marthas Vineyard, MA
November 27	Sch	Quetay	Vineyard Haven, MA
November 27	Sch	Rose Brothers	Block Island, RI
November 27	Sch	Sadie Willcutt	Vineyard Haven, MA
November 27	Sch	Samuel W Tilton	Hull, MA
November 27	Sch	School Girl	Provincetown Harbor, MA
November 27		Sylvia	Provincetown Harbor, MA
November 27	Sch	T C Mahoney	Marblehead, MA

DATE LOST	TYPE	NAME	WHERE LOST
November 27	Sch	Unidentified	Marthas Vineyard, MA
November 27	Sch	Unidentified	Plymouth, MA
November 27	Sts	*Vigilant*	Provincetown, MA
November 27	Bge	*Virginia*	Cohasset, MA
November 27	Slp	*Vivian*	Marthas Vineyard, MA
November 27	Sch	*William Todd*	Vineyard Haven, MA
November 28		*Carrie Sayward*	Wood End, MA
November 28		*F H Smith*	Wood End, MA
November 28	Sch	*Gracie*	Cape Cod Bay, MA
November 28	Sch	*Gracie H Benson*	Boston, MA
November 28	Sch	*J M Eaton*	Rockport, MA
November 28	Sch	*William Legget*	Rockport, MA
December	Sch	*J N Ayers*	Peconic Bay, NY
December 5	Sch	*Vamoose*	Block Island, RI
December 10	St	*Governor*	Ambrose, NY

1899

		Belinda Wood	Nantucket Sound, MA
		Kendrick Fish	Portland, ME
		Unidentified	Narragansett Bay, RI
January 2		*Rovers Bride*	Quaker Head, ME
January 2	Sch	*Sebena*	Boothbay Hrbr, ME
January 31	Sch	*Charles S Briggs*	Nahant, MA
January 31	Sch	*Fanny Flint*	Pollock Rip, MA
February 8	Sch	*Robert A Snow*	Rockaway Point, NY
February 10	Bktn	*Brazil*	Moriches, NY
February 12	Sch	*E L Dow*	Nantucket, MA
February 14	Sch	*Addie M Anderson*	Narragansett Bay, RI
February 27	Sch	*May Mcfarland*	Long Beach, NY
March 5	Brig	*T Remick*	Cohasset, MA
March 7	Sch	*Hattie Paige*	Rockport, MA
March 7	Sch	*Homer D Alveson*	Fire Island, NY
March 20		*Norseman*	Marblehead, MA
April		*Lydia Jane*	Provincetown, MA
May 3	Sch	*Robert Byron*	Provincetown, MA
May 25	Sch	*Florence Pearl*	Pollock Rip, MA
June 15	St	*Argus*	Montauk, NY
June 22	Sch	*Florence*	Duxbury, MA
July 17	Sch	*Vicksburg*	Seal Harbor, ME
August 8	Sch	*Glendy Burke*	Off Fire Island, NY
August 18	Slp	*Annie*	Quonochontaug, RI
August 22	Sch	*Carrie Phillips*	Whitehead Island, ME
August 30	Sch	*Edward Rich*	Cape Ann, MA
September 3	Slp	*Pointer*	Provincetown, MA
September 11	Slp	*Arrow*	Quogue, NY
September 14	Sch	*Bramhall*	Portsmouth, NH
September 20	Slp	*Ellen*	Nepeague, NY
October 5	Sch	*Delaware*	Pollock Rip, MA
October 7	Sch	*Magnet*	Ipswich, MA
October 8	Sch	*Delia Hinds*	Mt Desert, ME
October 8	Sch	*Thomas W Holder*	Wellfleet, MA
October 13	Sch	*Romana*	Jones Beach, NY
October 14	Sts	*Nutmeg State*	Long Island Sound
October 15	Sts	*A Hallenbeck*	East Marion, NY
October 15	Bge	Unidentified	East Marion, NY
October 23	Sch	*Jennie Greenbank*	Chatham, MA
October 30	Sts	*Dolphin*	Cape Ann, MA
November 16	Sch	*Canary*	Nantucket Sound, MA
December 7	Slp	*Golden Eagle*	Provincetown, MA

DATE LOST	TYPE	NAME	WHERE LOST
December 23	Sts	*Laura Marion*	Ipswich, MA
December 26	Sch	*M J Soley*	Brig Ledge, ME
December 30	Sch	*Rabboni*	Mattituck Inlet, NY
December 31	Sch	*Carrie L Hix*	Gloucester, MA

1900

DATE LOST	TYPE	NAME	WHERE LOST
	Sch	*Anadir*	Off Point Jefferson, NY
		Clara Bella	Two Bush Island, ME
	Gas	*Don*	Ragged Island, ME
	Sch	*Maurice*	Fishers Island, NY
	Sch	*Mexico*	Newport, RI
	Sch	*Oliver W Holmes*	Chatham, MA
		Pemiquid	Monhegan Island, ME
		Unidentified	Pollock Rip, MA
January 3	Sch	*S P Hitchcock*	Moriches, NY
January 18	Sch	*Nellie J Crocker*	Schoodic Point, ME
January 23	Sts	*Ardandhu*	Elizabeth Islands, MA
January 26	Sch	*Nausett*	Watch Hill, RI
January 27	Sch	*Charles F Atwood*	Cape Ann, MA
January 27	Sch	*Helen*	Orleans, MA
February 8	Sts	*Gate City*	Moriches Inlet, NY
February 25	Sts	*Californian*	Portland, ME
February 25	Sbge	*Keystone*	Boston, MA
March 1	Sch	*Mondego*	Orleans, MA
March 11	Sch	*William P Hood*	Orleans, MA
April 1	Sch	*Minnesota*	Plum Island, MA
April 2	Sch	*Abraham Richardson*	Marthas Vineyard, MA
April 7	Sch	*Laura Robertson*	Pollock Rip, MA
April 20	Sch	*Carl Schurz*	Ipswich, MA
April 30	Sch	*Boyle*	Rockaway Point, NY
April 30	Sch	*Evelyn*	Rockaway, NY
April 30	Sch	*Kenyon*	Rockaway Point, NY
May 10	Sch	*Quivet*	Cape Ann, MA
May 31	Sch	*Herald*	Mussel Ridge Chnl., ME
June 8	Stp	*Rose Standish*	Calais, ME
June 22	Sch	*Isaac H Tillyer*	Cuttyhunk, MA
August 11		*Abiel Abbott*	Jones Inlet, NY
August 30	Slp	*Wanda*	Truro, MA
September 3	Sch	*Lizzie Smith*	Pollock Rip, MA
September 3	St	*Mosquito*	Point Lookout, NY
September 5	Sch	*Paxtang*	Ipswich, MA
September 7	Bge	*Boise Penrose*	Gloucester, MA
September 8	Sts	*John Endicott*	Hull, MA
September 16	Stp	*Stamford*	Cohassett, MA
September 20	Sch	*Eleanora V Dusen*	Gloucester, MA
October 3	Bge	*Edward Easton*	Cape Ann, MA
October 5	Slp	*Ethel*	Cape Ann, MA
October 6	Sch	*Katie G Robinson*	Provincetown, MA
October 16	Sch	*General Sheridan*	Truro, MA
October 17	Sch	*David S Siner*	Pollock Rip, MA
October 17	Bge	*Sampson*	Cohasset, MA
October 17	Sch	*Shallow-swallow*	Point Judith, RI
October 17	Sch	*W C Norcross*	Rockport, MA
October 30	Sch	*Valentine Koon*	Jones Inlet, NY
November 8	Slp	*Martha*	Block Island, RI
November 8	Sch	*Myra B Weaver*	Pollock Rip, MA
November 14	Sch	*Margaretta*	Rikers Island, NY
November 22	Stp	*J D Scott*	Off Pultneyville, NY
December 4	Slp	*Mary Emma*	Sakonnet, RI

ABOVE: Cape Elizabeth, Maine holds the bones of many vessels unlucky enough to sail too close to its reefs. On December 6, 1915, the three masted schooner *William L. Elkins* struck there. The schooner proved a total loss. *Photo courtesy Robert Beattie, Belfast , ME*. **BELOW:** In the busy ports of the northeast, not all maritime accidents involved ships. In New York, after a diver had attached slings to this milk truck, a salvage vessel pulled it out of the East River in 1913. *Photo courtesy Paul Morris, Nantucket MA*.

DATE LOST	TYPE	NAME	WHERE LOST
December 12	Sch	*Mansur B Oakes*	Gloucester, MA
December 27	Sch	*Rhode Island*	Newport, RI

1901

January	St	*Idlewild*	Brooklyn, NY
January 3	Sch	*Lilly*	Eastham, MA
January 19	Sch	*George P Davenport*	Elizabeth Islands, MA
January 19	Sch	*Percy*	Off Block Island, RI
January 21	Sch	*Electa Bailey*	Chatham, MA
March 11	Sch	*William H Oler*	Provincetown, MA
March 26	Sts	*Gwent*	Long Beach, NY
March 31	Sch	*George A Pierce*	Watch Hill, RI
April 7	Sch	*Hyena*	Gloucester, MA
April 8	Sch	*George Boutwell*	Scituate, MA
April 13	Sts	*Awashonks*	Sakonnet, RI
May	Sch	*H R Keene*	Long Beach, NY
May 23	Sch	*Polar Wave*	Block Island, RI
May 28	Slp	*Bay Queen*	Long Beach, NY
June 14	Stp	*Northfield*	New York, NY
June 28	Sch	*Lizzie M Center*	Nantucket Sound, MA
July 19	Ycht	*Venitzia*	Long Island Sound
July 23	Sts	*Ruggles*	Nyack, NY
August 17		*James Gordon Bently*	Off New York
August 17	Sch	*John T Cullinan*	Pollock Rip, MA
August 25	Sch	*Eliza A Scribner*	Oak Island, NY
September 3	Sch	*Liassa*	Chatham, MA
September 11	Sch	*Lucy W Snow*	Moriches, NY
September 12	Sch	*Saint Thomas*	Nantucket Sound, MA
September 15		*Julia A Decker*	Newburyport, MA
October 7	Sch	*Columbia*	Hull, MA
October 17	Slp	*Winona*	Nahant, MA
October 19	Sch	*Alfred W Fiske*	Pollock Rip, MA
October 22	Stp	*Elizabeth*	New York, NY
November		*Helen F Ward*	Provincetown, MA
November 7	Sch	*John S Parker*	Orleans, MA
November 8	Sch	*Addison Center*	Provincetown, MA
November 8	Sch	*Altrato*	Pollock Rip, MA
November 10	Sch	*Florida*	Wellfleet, MA
November 16	Sch	*Amanda E*	Chatham, MA
November 24	Sch	*J G Fell*	Point Judith, RI
November 27	Sch	*Lucy Belle*	Thatchers Island, MA
December	Sch	*Ringleader*	Hyannis, MA
December 8	Slp	*Shawmut*	Rockport, MA
December 8		*Douglas Haynes*	Pollock Rip, MA
December 17	Sch	*North Star*	Block Island, RI
December 28	Sch	*Maud Briggs*	Eastham, MA

1902

	Sch	*Africa*	Machias Bay, ME
		Astral	Mt Desert Island, ME
		Chewink II	Metinic Island, ME
	Sch	*Nautilus*	Chatham, MA
January 31	St	*Cajour*	Long Beach, NY
February 2	Bge	*Antelope*	Westhampton, NY
February 2	Bark	*Belle Of Oregon*	Westhampton, NY
February 2	St	*E S Atwood*	Off New York
February 2	St	*John E Berwind*	Off New York
February 3	Sch	*John F Randall*	Fire Island, NY

DATE LOST	TYPE	NAME	WHERE LOST
February 7	Sch	*Jennie C May*	Provincetown, MA
February 11	Sch	*Henry*	Provincetown, MA
February 13	Sch	*Elsie M Smith*	Orleans, MA
March 1	Sts	*Acara*	Short Beach, NY
March 5		*Amanda E*	Point Judith, RI
March 11	Sbge	*Wadena*	Pollock Rip, MA
March 12	Sts	*Continental*	Fall River, MA
March 18	Sch	*Orozimbo*	Nantucket Shoals, MA
March 18	Sch	*Sallie E Ludlam*	Pollock Rip, MA
March 19	Sch	*Elwood Burton*	Pollock Rip, MA
March 20	Sch	*Fly Away*	Off Nantucket, MA
March 21	Bktn	*Persia*	Long Beach, NY
April 10	Sch	*Thomas Borden*	Hyannis, MA
April 26	Sch	*Cornelia Soule*	Off Rockaway, NY
May 2	Slp	*Mary Seaman*	Jones Inlet, NY
May 8	Slp	*Annie*	Cape Ann, MA
May 12	Sts	*Williamsport*	Pollock Rip, MA
May 25	Sch	*Arthur Seitz*	Marthas Vineyard, MA
June 8	Sch	*Annie Laura*	Chatham, MA
June 10	Sch	*Gertie Smith*	Newport, RI
July 8	Sch	*Monticello*	Cuttyhunk, MA
July 8	Sch	*Saint Bernard*	Provincetown, MA
August 4	Sch	*Senator Grimes*	Vineyard Sound, MA
August 7	Slp	*Cant Help It*	Gloucester, MA
August 26	Sts	*Duchess*	New York, NY
September	Gas	*Stroller*	Harpswell, ME
September 18	Sch	*Dora Mathews*	Chatham, MA
October 4	Sch	*Frederick Tudor*	Cape Ann, MA
October 15	Slp	*Eagle*	Marthas Vineyard, MA
October 15	Sch	*Kate & Mary*	Quonochontaug, RI
October 25	Sch	*John Wickham*	Sakonnet, RI
November 15	Sch	*Sadie*	Cutler, ME
November 22	Sch	*Beta*	Gloucester, MA
November 29	Sch	*Phoenix*	Pollock Rip, MA
December 3	Bark	*Alice Reed*	Nepeague, NY
December 8	Sch	*Etta Stimpson*	Duxbury, MA
December 11	Sch	*Belle Wooster*	Ipswich, MA
December 17	Sch	*Frank A Palmer*	Thatchers Island, MA
December 22	Sch	*Red Wing*	Newport, RI

1903

DATE LOST	TYPE	NAME	WHERE LOST
	Brig	*D A Small*	Providence, RI
	Sch	*Edwin Collyer*	Gravesend Bay, NY
	Bge	*Harold*	Staten Sound, NY
		Kearsage	Seal Island, ME
January 18	Sch	*Emeline G Sawyer*	Chatham, MA
January 21	St	*Leyden*	Block Island, RI
January 25	Sch	*Ella Pressey*	Off Wellfleet, MA
January 25	Sch	*Francis Shubert*	Eastham, MA
January 29	Sch	*Hattie & Maggie*	Nantucket, MA
January 30	Sch	*James G Blaine*	Pollock Rip, MA
February 1	Sch	*Lyman M Law*	Truro, MA
February 20	Sch	Unidentified	Pollock Rip, MA
March 5	Sch	*Fair Deal*	Swansea, MA
March 19	Sch	*Sarah Potter*	Pollock Rip, MA
April 27	Sch	*Albert T Stearns*	Chatham, MA
May 6	Sch	*Agnes E Manson*	Nantucket, MA
May 29	Sch	*Helena Maud*	Pollock Rip, MA
June 12	Slp	*Opitsah*	Quonochontaug, RI

DATE LOST	TYPE	NAME	WHERE LOST
June 12	Sch	*Washington Thomas*	Stratton Island, ME
June 12	Bge	*Wasp*	New Bedford, MA
June 17	Sch	*Progress*	Nantucket, MA
August 5	Sch	*James Baker*	Gloucester, MA
August 10	Bge	*Abby Dunn*	Quonochontaug, RI
August 11	Bge	*Volunteer*	Narragansett Bay, RI
September	Sch	*William Clark*	Bay Ridge, NY
September 5	Sch	*Jennie R Dubois*	Off Block Island, RI
September 15	Bge	*Nora*	Block Island, RI
September 17		*Sadie & Lillie*	Pemiquid, ME
October 19	Sbge	*J B King Co # 17*	Hull, MA
October 24	Sch	*Dawson City*	Provincetown, MA
November 7	Sch	*Connecticut*	Chatham, MA
November 16	Sch	*Eben Parsons*	Nahant, MA
December 18	Bktn	*Cuba*	Montauk, NY
December 26	Bge	*General Poe*	Boston, MA
December 26	Sts	*Kiowa*	Hull, MA

1904

		Levi Hart	Pollock Rip, MA
	Slp	*Norseman*	Orrington, ME
January 2	Sch	*N Jones*	Ipswich, MA
January 3	Sch	*Belle J Neal*	Hull, MA
January 22	Sch	*Augustus Hunt*	Quogue, NY
January 23	Sch	*Alexa*	Rockaway Point, NY
January 26	Sch	*Rienzi*	Gloucester, MA
January 29	Sts	*George M Winslow*	Cuttyhunk, MA
February 8	Slp	*Startle*	Newport, RI
March 26	Sch	*Mabel Hall*	Block Island, RI
April 8	Sch	*Olivia Domingoes*	Gloucester, MA
April 16	Sch	*Albert H Harding*	Cape Ann, MA
April 24	Sch	*Buema*	Chatham, MA
May 13	Sch	*Little Jennie*	Chatham, MA
June 15	Stp	*General Slocum*	Hell Gate, NY
June 29	Slp	*Screamer*	Gloucester, MA
July 1	Bark	*Albertina*	Chatham, MA
July 2	Sch	*Viola May*	Pollock Rip, MA
July 6	Sts	*George W Humphrey*	Newport, RI
July 6	Sts	*Mabel Bird*	Salisbury, MA
August 3	Stp	*Monohansett*	Manchester, MA
August 16	Ycht	*Narika*	Point Judith, RI
September 4	Slp	*Julia E Simons*	Block Island, RI
September 8	Sch	*Fraulien*	Pollock Rip, MA
September 8	Sts	*Longfellow*	Truro, MA
September 15	Sts	*Joseph Church*	Provincetown, MA
September 15	Sch	*R S Dean*	Marthas Vineyard, MA
September 23	Sch	*George F Edmonds*	Camden, ME
October 5	Sch	*John C Smith*	Pollock Rip, MA
October 6	Sch	*Glide*	Fire Island Inlet, NY
October 13	Sch	*Wentworth*	Chatham, MA
October 14	Sch	*Elwood Burton*	Provincetown, MA
October 15	Sch	*Annie M Allen*	Manchester, MA
October 17	Sch	*Clara*	Point Judith, RI
October 19	Sch	*Annie V Bergen*	Newport, RI
November		*Columbia*	East River, NY
November 13	Bge	*C T # 5*	Long Island Sound
November 13	Sch	*Nautilus*	Gloucester, MA
November 16	Sch	*General Hancock*	Rockport, MA

DATE LOST	TYPE	NAME	WHERE LOST
November 28	Bge	*Kelsey*	New York, NY
December 14	Sch	*John Dexter*	Pembroke River, ME
December 16	Sch	*George B Ferguson*	Nantucket, MA
December 18	Sch	*Alburtis*	Fishers Island, NY
December 18	Sch	*Eliza Jane*	Chatham, MA
December 18	Sch	*Richard Leaming*	Nantucket, MA
December 25	Sts	*Drumelzier*	Long Beach, NY

1905

	Slp	*Annie E Leete*	Flushing, NY
	Sch	*Eva May*	Robbinston, ME
	Sch	*Glide*	Rockaway, NY
January 7		*Lizzie Carr*	Rye, NH
January 11		*Ray G Parrsboro*	Damariscove Island, ME
January 26	Sch	*Henry Whitney*	Newport, RI
February 4	Bge	*Atlas*	Long Island City, NY
February 22	Sch	*Eliza J Pendleton*	Off Fire Island, NY
March 19	Sts	*Spartan*	Block Island, RI
April 6	Sch	*Texas*	Block Island, RI
April 7	Sch	*George & Albert*	Sakonnet, RI
April 8	Sch	*Galatea*	Jerrys Point, NH
April 9	Sch	*Game Cock*	Stonington, ME
April 13		*Annie C Wilder*	Negro Island, ME
April 16	Sch	*Charlotte L Morgan*	Southern Island, ME
April 20	St	*A D Bache*	Newport, RI
April 26	Sch	*Harry L Whiton*	Orleans, MA
May 3	Bge	*Moonbeam*	Off Rhode Island
May 4	Sch	*John C Gregory*	Marthas Vineyard, MA
May 5	Sts	*Aransas*	Off Chatham, MA
May 13	Sch	*J Nickerson*	Johns Island, ME
May 29	Sts	*Eclipse*	Fire Island, NY
May 29	Sts	*Seaconnet*	Shinnecock Beach, NY
June 15	Sts	*Innis*	Bartletts Point, NY
June 17	Sch	*Nellie G Adams*	Nantucket, MA
June 27	Sts	*Columbia*	Off Newport, RI
June 30	Slp	*Shilo*	Narragansett Bay, RI
July 3	Sch	*Chromo*	Boston, MA
July 8	Sts	*Roys J Cram*	New Baltimore, NY
July 8	Sch	*Sarah C Smith*	Portland Head, ME
July 11	Sts	*Normandie*	Dobbs Ferry, NY
July 13	Sts	*The Senator*	Narragansett Bay, RI
July 18	Sch	*Catalina*	Rockland, ME
July 18	Sch	*L M Eaton*	Point Judith, RI
July 30	Sch	*Livonia*	Eastham, MA
August	Sch	*Caroline Augusta*	Rockaway Beach, NY
August 12	Sch	*Joe*	Petite Manan, ME
August 19	Bge	*John Neilson*	New York, NY
August 19	Bge	*William H Vanderbuilt*	New York, NY
August 20	Sch	*M C Haskell*	Pollock Rip, MA
August 22	Sch	*Marion E Rockhill*	Amagansett Bay, NY
August 25	Gas	*Thelma*	Marthas Vineyard, MA
August 28	Slp	*Astonisher*	Vineyard Sound, MA
August 30	Sch	*Alice S Hawkes*	Duxbury, MA
September	Bge	*Nimrod*	Derby, CT
September 11	Bge	*Abram Collerd*	New York, NY
September 12	Bge	*Star*	New York, NY
September 28	St	*Bridgeport*	Yonkers, NY
October 8	Sch	*Veteran*	Herring Ledge, ME

DATE LOST	TYPE	NAME	WHERE LOST
October 10	Bge	*Berkley*	New Haven, CT
October 11	Sch	*Chas H Burton*	Westfield, NY
October 11	Sts	*John McCausland*	Turkey Point, NY
October 19	St	*Nautilus*	Fishers Island, NY
October 28	Slp	*Alpha*	New York, NY
October 28	Sch	*Kentucky*	Sargentville, ME
November 1	Slp	*Idella*	Off Sakonnet, RI
November 1	Bge	*R J Wilson*	Off Bridgeport, CT
November 10	Gas	*May M*	Ipswich, MA
November 16	Sch	*Widgeon*	Block Island, RI
November 18	Slp	*Unidentified*	Narragansett Bay, RI
November 24	Slp	*Alice*	Pollock Rip, MA
November 24	Sch	*Golden Ray*	Plum Gut, NY
November 30	Sch	*Charles E Sears*	Chatham, MA
November 30	Sch	*Delawana*	Off Cohasset, MA
December		*Glen Island*	Glen Cove, NY
December	Sch	*Unidentified*	Off Bayville, NY
December 10	Slp	*Maine*	Napeague, NY
December 10	Ltsp	*Relief Lightship*	Nantucket Shoals, MA
December 16	Sts	*Alert*	Hell Gate, NY
December 16	Sch	*Blue Jay*	Block Island, RI
December 21	Ycht	*Coot*	North Haven, ME
December 27	Bge	*Unidentified*	Swash Channel, NY
December 27	Bge	*Unidentified*	Swash Channel, NY
December 31	Bge	*Baden*	Buzzards Bay, MA

1906

DATE LOST	TYPE	NAME	WHERE LOST
	Sch	*Shamrock*	Oyster Bay, NY
January 1	Bge	*N E T Co No 61*	Off Duck Island, CT
January 4	Sts	*Ariosa*	Roamer Shoal, NY
January 11	Bark	*Altona*	Pollock Rip, MA
January 17	Brig	*Atalanta*	Seal Island, ME
January 21	Sts	*Trojan*	Vineyard Sound, MA
January 24	Sch	*Stephen Woolsey*	Montauk Point, NY
January 26	Slp	*L Odin*	Jones Inlet, NY
February 2	Sch	*Yankee Maid*	Seal Island, ME
February 3	Slp	*Fortuna*	Ipswich, MA
February 10	Stp	*Charleston*	Wolf Island, ME
February 11	Gas	*Christal*	Monhegan Island, ME
February 11	Sch	*Joseph Hay*	Cuttyhunk, MA
February 21	Bge	*Dom Pedro*	New York, NY
March 1	St	*Willard*	Cape Ann, MA
March 16	Sch	*S E Davis*	Clark Island, ME
March 19	St	*H C French*	New Haven, CT
March 19	Sch	*Lady Antrim*	Marblehead, MA
March 19	Bge	*N E T Co No 10*	New Haven, CT
March 19	Cnlb	*Walter J Schloefer*	New Haven, CT
March 20	Sch	*C C Lane*	Boston, MA
March 22	Bge	*Jennie & Florence*	Oyster Bay, NY
April 4	Sts	*Wyalusing*	Hull, MA
April 10	Sch	*D Gifford*	Gloucester, MA
April 10	Sch	*Rising Sun*	Drakes Island, ME
April 10	Sch	*Sallie B*	Casco Bay, ME
April 15	Bge	*Bouquet*	Quonochontaug, RI
April 18	St	*City Of Detroit*	Staten Island, NY
April 28	Sch	*William Cambell*	Owls Head, ME
May 13	Bark	*Hattie G Dixon*	Marthas Vineyard, MA
May 30	Slp	*Elsea*	Hull, MA

DATE LOST	TYPE	NAME	WHERE LOST
June 2	Sch	Clara E Rogers	Elizabeth Islands, MA
June 3	Sts	Mary	Waddington, NY
June 28	Sch	E C Hay	New York, NY
June 30	Sch	John Cornwall	Inwood, NY
July 4	Sch	Ella G Eells	Libby Islands, ME
July 4	Sch	Kingston	Off Shinnecock, NY
July 4	Sch	Vinland	Off Rikers Island, NY
July 10	Sch	Eaglet	North River, NY
July 12	Cnlb	Mollie Barton	New York, NY
July 25	Sch	Diadem	Penobscot Bay, ME
August 1	Sts	Ailsa	Block Island, RI
August 7	Sch	George V Jordan	Pollock Rip, MA
August 10	Sch	Julia D Schmidt	Thatchers Island, MA
August 15	Sch	Maggie Todd	Watch Hill, RI
August 19	Sch	Qweene	Long Island Sound
August 20	Sch	M H Morris	Block Island, RI
August 27	Sch	M H Perkins	Cape Ann, MA
August 29	Slp	Mildred	Nantucket, MA
September 1	Sch	Annie L Henderson	Bangor, ME
September 2	Gas	Gipsy	Rockaway Point, NY
September 8	Slp	Maggie R	Marthas Vineyard, MA
September 9	Sch	Metamora	New Harbor, ME
September 17	Gas	Leslie	New Haven, CT
September 21	Gas	Water Ripple	Owls Head, ME
October 6		Gracie A	Squirrel Island, ME
October 7	Sch	Keewaydin	Greenport, NY
October 11	Sch	Ella Powell	Off New London, CT
October 11	Sch	Helen B Crosby	Penobscot Bay, ME
October 24	Sts	Hastings	Off Shippan Point, CT
October 25	Sch	Collins Howes Jr	Penobscot Bay, ME
October 5	Sch	Glenullen	Machias Bay, ME
November 4		G M Cochrane	Eastham, MA
November 7	Sch	Mopang	Marthas Vineyard, MA
November 13	Sch	M D Grace	Shinnecock, NY
November 15	Sch	Mary L Newton	Boston, MA
November 20	St	Francis B Thurber	Cornfield Lightship, CT
November 24	Gas	Gloria	Bowery Bay, NY
November 27	Sch	Jennie Pillsbury	Penobscot Bay, ME
November 29	Sch	Reindeer	Eastport, ME
December 1	Bge	Charles G Hill	Off Marlbourgh, NY
December 2	Bge	Virginian	Branford, CT
December 6	Bark	Bonny Doon	Chatham, MA
December 7	Sch	Buena Ventura	Montauk Point, NY
December 7	Sch	Ventura	Off Montauk Point, NY
December 10	Sch	William Marshall	Truro, MA
December 20	Gas	Lottie	Brooklyn, NY
December 24	Sch	Fortuna	Provincetown, MA
December 29	Stp	Patterson	North River, NY

1907

	Sch	Billow	Stonington, ME
		Edward W Murdock	Machias Bay, ME
	Bge	Expounder	Providence, RI
		Flora Condon	Vinalhaven, ME
	St	Verona	Hudson River, NY
January 4	Sch	Alice T Boardman	Hyannis, MA
January 9	Sch	Blanche Morgan	Brooklyn, NY
January 10	Bge	Delaware	Fishers Island, NY
January 10	Bge	Honesdale	Watch Hill, RI

DATE LOST	TYPE	NAME	WHERE LOST
January 10	Bge	*Hongsdale*	Fishers Island, NY
January 10	Sch	*Jessie L Boyce*	Stimpsons Island, ME
January 10	Bge	*Marvin*	Watch Hill, RI
January 19	Sch	*Maud Maloch*	Otter Point, ME
January 21	Sbge	*Montana*	Block Island, RI
January 22	Sch	*Unidentified*	Portland, ME
January 24	Sch	*A Heaton*	Boston, MA
January 24	Sch	*Addie*	Schoodic Point, ME
January 29	Sch	*Annie M Ash*	Off Fire Island, NY
February 5	Sbge	*Woodbury*	Truro, MA
February 11	Sch	*Harry P Knowlton*	Quonochontaug, RI
February 11	Stp	*Larchmont*	Off Rhode Island
February 11	Sch	*S Hale*	Off Stratford, CT
February 13	Sbge	*Pemberton*	Falmouth, MA
February 18	Sbge	*Alaska*	Provincetown, MA
February 18	Sbge	*Girard*	Truro, MA
February 27	Sch	*Morancy*	Offshore, ME
March 14	Sts	*Queen City*	Sakonnet, RI
April	Sch	*Catherine Howard*	Seguin Island, ME
April 6	Sch	*S R Lane*	Cape Ann, MA
April 13	Sch	*Nettie Cushing*	Cornfield Sand Sl, CT
April 18	Sch	*Sardinian*	Metinic Island, ME
April 22	Bge	*Susquehanna*	Off Cornfield Point, CT
April 26	Slp	*Colonel L F Peck*	Stamford, CT
May 2	Bge	*Kenneth W McNeil*	New York, NY
May 8	Sts	*Anna J Kipp*	New York, NY
May 11	Cnlb	*May*	Wards Island, NY
May 11	Sch	*Sagamore*	Vinyard Sound, MA
May 16	Sch	*Ellen M Mitchell*	Great Wass Island, ME
May 29	Bge	*Lydia Cowperthwait*	Long Island Sound
June 1		*Emily And Irene*	Great Peconic Bay, NY
June 5	Sch	*Mary Steele*	Gloucester, MA
June 11	Sch	*William Duren*	Monhegan Island, ME
June 23	Sch	*T Charlton Henry*	Fire Island, NY
June 25	Sch	*Evangeline*	Nomansland Island, MA
June 29	Sch	*Mildred A Pope*	Off Falkners Island, CT
July 2	Stp	*City Of Lawrence*	Eastern Point, CT
July 2	Cnlb	*Lizzie Evans*	Hell Gate, NY
July 5	Sch	*Maude Sherwood*	Off Provincetown, MA
July 6	Sch	*Florence*	Cape Neddick, ME
July 7	Sts	*Annie Emmons*	Nahant, MA
July 12	Nas	*Natalie Nickerson*	Nantucket Shoals, MA
July 12	Sch	*Shepherd King*	Nantucket, MA
July 15	St	*Shinnecock*	Harts Island, NY
July 28	Sts	*Wm. F Havemeyer*	New York, NY
August 11	Sch	*Idlewild*	Coney Island, NY
August 12	Sch	*Myronus*	Long Island Sound
August 12	Sch	*Traveler*	Long Island Sound
August 27	Slp	*Doris*	Petite Manan, ME
September	Slp	*Ira Palmer*	Watch Hill, RI
September 2	Sch	*James S Steele*	Marthas Vineyard, MA
September 3	Sch	*Coal King*	Montauk Point, NY
September 3	Sch	*Phineas H Gay*	Boston, MA
September 4	Bge	*Excelsior*	Watch Hill, RI
September 4	Bge	*P R R # 701*	Watch Hill, RI
September 6		*Decorra*	Nash Island, ME
September 8	Sts	*Warren*	Fall River, MA
September 13	Sch	*Julia*	Coney Island, NY
September 21	Sch	*Grace W Hone*	Penobscot Bay, ME
October 1	Bge	*Castleton*	New York, NY

DATE LOST	TYPE	NAME	WHERE LOST
October 8	Bge	Bessie J	Fall River, MA
October 8	Slp	C C Algier	Narragansett Bay, RI
October 8	Sch	Grace Choate	Mt Desert, ME
October 8	Bge	Teutonic	Greenwich, CT
October 9	Sch	R P Chase	Outer Black Rocks, ME
October 13	Sch	Demozelle	Marthas Vineyard, MA
October 14	Sch	Wasp	Nantucket Sound, MA
October 15	Sch	Carrie C Miles	Dry Roamer Shoal, NY
October 15	Sch	J S Glover	Marsh Harbor, ME
October 16	Sch	Annie Sargent	Long Island, NY
October 22	Bge	H F Hallett	Faulkners Island, CT
October 22	Bge	Prima Donna	Faulkners Island, CT
October 23	Sch	New York	Nepeague, NY
October 27	Sch	Racer	Bridgeport, CT
November 2	Sch	William Voorhis	New York, NY
November 4		City Of Birmingham	Boston, MA
November 5	Sch	Susan Stetson	Offshore, ME
November 6	Sch	Jonathon Sawyer	Cape Porpoise, ME
November 7	Sch	E Pluribus Unum	Seal Island, ME
November 9	Gas	Unidentified	Provincetown, MA
November 14	Sch	Crystal	Kill Von Kull, NY
November 14	Bge	Harriet E Winne	Plum Island, NY
November 16	Sch	Marshall Perrin	Wood Island, ME
November 17	Sch	Phoebe Ann	East River, NY
November 18	Gas	Ravenswood	College Point, NY
November 23	Sch	Lucy E	Plymouth, MA
November 24	Sch	C H Malleson	Glen Cove, NY
November 24	Sch	Mary Isabela	Reed Creek Point, NY
November 25	Sch	Cora B	Gloucester, MA
November 28	Sts	Kanawha	Brunswick, ME
December 2	St	Bunker Hill	East River, NY
December 2		Transfer #3	East River, NY
December 3	Sch	Fortuna	Portland, ME
December 4	Sch	Rebecca Shepard	Pollock Rip, MA
December 14	Bge	Alanson A Summer	Watch Hill, RI
December 14	Bge	Elk	Watch Hill, RI
December 14	Sts	Hercules	Watch Hill, RI
December 14	Sch	Ida M Silva	Plymouth, MA
December 14	Bge	James E English	Watch Hill, RI
December 14	Sch	James Parker Sr	Callenders Point, CT
December 14	Bge	John C Wyman	Watch Hill, RI
December 17	Sch	Jessie Barlow	Pollock Rip, MA
December 20	Sch	David Currie	Duck Island, CT
December 23	Bge	Ellis P Rogers	New York, NY
December 24	Sch	E Waterman	Gloucester, MA
December 30	Sch	Agnes V Gleason	Boothbay, ME
December 30	Sbge	Ida	Point Judith, RI
December 30	Bge	Jennie	Point Judith, RI
December 31	Gas	Mavourneen	Fire Island, NY

1908

	Sch	C H Mallison	Hempstead, NY
	Sch	Eastern Light	Gloucester, MA
	Sch	Modoc	Ipswich, MA
	Sch	Nil Desperandum	Penobscot Bay, ME
January 1	Sch	E M Duffield	Bridgeport, CT
January 2	Sch	Julia Davis	Fishers Island, NY
January 7	Gas	Buena	Provincetown, MA
January 7	Bge	Helen	Fishers Island, NY

Since the late 1800's every busy waterfront in the northeast has had a local diver or diving company to call on for underwater repairs or construction. The task was certainly not for the meek. The diver shown above is salvaging a barge in New York in 1911. But many of the shipwrecks that occurred in the 1800's were probed by the brave divers often working with no lights, poor, if any, communication to their tenders, and no decompression chambers to cure pressure related diseases. *Photo courtesy Paul Morris, Nantucket MA*

Along with Cape Cod and Long Island, Salisbury Beach, MA can be a treacherous lee shore. This was discovered by the captain of the *Virginian*, shown above. She was driven ashore there on June 9, 1916. All hands were rescued by the Coast Guard using a Breeches Buoy. *Photo courtesy Peabody Museum of Salem, Salem MA.*

DATE LOST	TYPE	NAME	WHERE LOST
January 27	Sch	*Matanzas*	Montauk, NY
January 27		*Winifred*	Montauk, NY
January 30	Bark	*Fredericka Schepp*	Nantucket, MA
February 1	Sch	*Julia Baker*	Milbridge, ME
February 1	Bark	*Puritan*	Patchogue, NY
February 1	Sch	*Waldron Holmes*	Point Francis, ME
February 4	Sch	*Abby Morse*	Narrascangus Bay, ME
February 8	Sch	*F L Lowell*	Rodicks Island, ME
February 10	Bge	*Addie B Bacon*	Flynns Knoll, NY
February 13	St	*Dudley Pray*	Cape Ann, MA
February 13	St	*Roda*	Jones Beach, NY
February 15	Bge	*Edward F Cullen*	New Haven, CT
February 15	Bge	*Helen R Cullen*	New Haven, CT
February 15	Sch	*Howard B Peck*	Fire Island, NY
February 15	Bge	*Joseph W Drayton*	New Haven, CT
February 15	Bge	*S W Prig*	Cornfield Point, CT
February 21	Slp	*Albatross*	Great Kills, NY
March 14	Sts	*Sylvia*	Cuttyhunk, MA
March 31	Sch	*Deborah T Hill*	East River, NY
April 4	Ctbt	*George McCaffrey*	Penfield Reef, NY
April 16	Sch	*Lizzie*	Penobscot Bay, ME
April 28	Bge	*William H Wessels*	Sands Point, NY
April 30	Ship	*Peter Rockmers*	Short Beach, NY
May 1	Sch	*Victor*	Block Island, RI
May 8	Bge	*David E Baxter*	Staten Island, NY
May 8	Gas	*Iona*	Narragansett Bay, RI
May 11	Sch	*Penobscot*	Two Bush Island, ME
May 22	Sch	*H T Hedges*	Whitestone, NY
May 23		*Cosmos*	Bakers Island, ME
May 24	Sch	*Arthur Clifford*	Thatchers Island, MA
May 27	Sch	*Lizzie Cochran*	Offshore, ME
May 30	Sch	*Carrie H Annis*	Narragansett Bay, RI
May 30	Gas	*Jerome May*	Narragansett Bay, RI
May 31	Sch	*Jordan Wooley*	Long Island Sound
May 31	Slp	*Phebe*	Nantucket Sound, MA
June 3	Slp	*E Stearns*	New York, NY
July 5	Sch	*Julia Costa*	Off Truro, MA
July 13	Ycht	*Dolphin*	Buzzards Bay, MA
July 18	Slp	*Buffalo*	Fishers Island Sound
July 22	Sch	*Menawa*	Long Island Sound
July 25	Sch	*Charley Woolsey*	Cornfield Lt, CT
August 1	Gas	*Siesta*	Patchogue, NY
August 7	Sch	*Three Sisters*	Bakers Island, ME
August 11	Sts	*Annie R Wood*	Taunton, MA
August 11	Sts	*Titania*	Charlotte, NY
August 19	Slp	*Viking*	Nahant, MA
August 20	Sch	*Henry Wolcott*	Brooklyn, NY
August 26	Slp	*Mosetta H*	Saugatuck, CT
September 5	Bge	*Uncle Paul*	Fox Island, NY
September 13	Gas	*Old Dominion*	Marthas Vineyard, MA
September 21	Slp	*Ariel*	New York, NY
September 21	Sts	*Thomas Chubb*	Race Course Island, NY
September 23	St	*Yankee*	Buzzards Bay, MA
September 27	Sch	*Racehorse*	Casco Bay, ME
October	Sch	*Centennial*	Nahant, MA
October 3	Sch	*J H G Perkins*	Cape Porpoise, ME
October 5	Gas	*No-Ma*	Gloucester, MA
October 14	Sch	*W B Keen*	Cape Ann, MA
October 20	Stp	*New York*	Newbergh, NY
November	Ctbt	*Hugh Blair*	Port Liberty, NY

DATE LOST	TYPE	NAME	WHERE LOST
November 2	Sch	*Eliza Ellen*	Blue Hill Bay, ME
November 3	Sts	*Henry L Wait*	College Point, NY
November 9	Ycht	*Tomah*	Quonochontaug, RI
November 21	Sch	*Hugh G*	Boston, MA
November 22	Sch	*Gardetta*	Muscongus Bay, ME
November 28	Sch	*Florence A*	Pollock Rip, MA
November 28	Gas	*Peri*	Canarsie, NY
December 1	Bark	*Shawmut*	Machias Bay, ME
December 3	Sch	*# 101*	Off Maine
December 5	Sch	*Sunny Side*	West Penobscot Bay, ME
December 16	Sts	*Eldorado*	Phippsburg, ME
December 18	St	*Daghestan*	Off New York
December 24	Sch	*Harry Messer*	Pollock Rip, MA
December 26	Sch	*Myra W Spear*	Off Truro, MA

1909

	Sch	*George Prescott*	Ipswich, MA
January 16	Sch	*Swallow*	Blue Point, NY
January 23	Sts	*Republic*	Nantucket Shoals, MA
January 28	Sch	*Golden Ball*	Jonesport, ME
January 30	Sch	*Helena*	Scituate, MA
February	Sch	*Maggie*	Portland, ME
February 1	Gas	*Elgin*	Chatham, MA
February 5	Slp	*C H Tucker*	Hell Gate, NY
February 10	Sch	*Georgia*	Monroe Island, ME
February 10	Gas	*Little Inez*	Eastport, ME
February 17	Sch	*Miles M Merry*	Moriches, NY
February 26	Slp	*Venus*	Cape Cod Bay, MA
March 10	Sts	*Horatio Hall*	Pollock Rip, MA
March 12	Sch	*Fred A Small*	Pollock Rip, MA
March 29	Sch	*Kittie Lawry*	Penobscot Bay, ME
April 7	Bge	*Beacon*	Watch Hill, RI
April 14	Bark	*Lakeview*	Nomansland Island, MA
April 15	Sch	*G A Hayden*	Point Judith, RI
May 1	Sch	*William C Carnegie*	Moriches, NY
May 3	Bge	*Moosic*	Faulkner Island, CT
May 16	Bge	*Brittania*	Block Island, RI
May 18	Sch	*Jennie F Potter*	Nantucket Sound, MA
May 18	Sch	*William G Eadie*	Gouldsboro, ME
May 26	Ctbt	*James H Robinson*	Brooklyn, NY
June 9	St	*Antonio Lopez*	Point O'Woods, NY
July	Ctbt	*Warren Brown*	Newburgh, NY
July 1	Sch	*Alice E Clark*	Penobscot Bay, ME
July 10	Bge	*Harrison*	Providence, RI
July 18	Slp	*Roxanna*	Off Ft Hamilton, NY
July 20	Gas	*Beatrice Earle*	Vineyard Haven, MA
July 20	Sts	*Martha Stevens*	New York Harbor, NY
July 24	Sts	*Kenosha*	Fire Island, NY
July 29	Sch	*Rosa Mueller*	Brewer, ME
August 5	Slp	*Emily*	Point Judith, RI
August 15	Sch	*Wilson & Willard*	Kittery, ME
August 17	Sch	*Arlington*	Long Beach, NY
August 17	Sch	*Joseph Hammond*	Plum Island, NY
August 17	Sch	*Shawmont*	Off Shinnecock, NY
August 22	Gas	*Wawa*	Bridgeport, CT
August 23	Gas	*Allegro*	Newport, RI
September 18	Sch	*Chas J Willard*	Cuttyhunk, MA
September 18	Gas	*St Paul*	Portland, ME
September 29	Sbge	*West Virginia*	Pollock Rip, MA

DATE LOST	TYPE	NAME	WHERE LOST
September 30	Ctbt	*Baker Brothers*	New York, NY
September 30	Ctbt	*C G Donehue*	South Brooklyn, NY
October 1	Gas	*Senta*	Fishers Island Sound
October 5	Bge	*Helen R*	Flushing, NY
October 8	Ctbt	*Charles S Griffin*	Canal Basin, NY
October 10	Sch	*James Boyce*	Mussel Ridge Channel, ME
October 13	Sch	*John Douglass*	Whitehead Island, ME
October 14	Gas	*Wilhelmina*	Narragansett Bay, RI
October 27	Sch	*Andrew Peters*	St George, ME
October 28	Sch	*Valetta*	Cape Porpoise, ME
October 29	Sbge	*Shenandoah*	Pollock Rip, MA
November	Gas	*Judge*	Nantucket, MA
November 8	Bark	*John S Bennett*	Off Block Island, RI
November 8	Sch	*Merrill C Hart*	Off Block Island, RI
November 9	Bge	*Ben Franklin*	Sandwich, MA
November 9	Bge	*Potomac*	Sandwich, MA
November 10	Gas	*Phoenix*	East River, NY
November 15	Sch	*E Arcularius*	Cuttyhunk, MA
November 15	Sch	*Sallie Ann*	Black Hall Point, CT
November 16	Sch	*Ella Rose*	Vinalhaven, ME
November 24	Sch	*Good Intent*	Vinalhaven, ME
November 25	Sch	*Clara D Sweet*	Beverley, MA
December 2	Sch	*Mizpah*	Provincetown, MA
December 24	Sch	*Davis Palmer*	Boston, MA
December 25	Sch	*C M Gray*	Deer Island, ME
December 25	Sch	*Superior*	Sea Cliff, NY
December 26	Sch	*Ada K Damon*	Ipswich, MA
December 26	Sch	*Nantasket*	Scituate, MA
December 31	Gas	*Dorado*	Fall River, MA
December 31	Sts	*Olin J Sthephens*	Mattituck, NY

1910

	Sch	*Edward L Swan*	Astoria, NY
	Sch	*General Reid*	Westhampton, NY
	Slp	*Ida May*	Stonington, ME
		Unidentified	Penobscot Bay, ME
January 1	Sch	*Maud Seward*	Marthas Vineyard, MA
January 10	Bge	*Katie Mcgovern*	Shippan Point, CT
January 10	Sch	*M L Wetherell*	Ipswich, MA
January 10	Sch	*S M Bird*	Pollock Rip, MA
January 20	Sch	*Commerce*	Penobscot River, ME
January 23	Sch	*Henry B Fiske*	Nantucket, MA
January 23	Sch	*Mertie B Crowley*	Marthas Vineyard, MA
January 29	Sch	*Little Elsie*	Long Point, NH
February 11	Sch	*Minerva*	Gloucester, MA
March 7	Sts	*Manhattan*	Portland, ME
March 25	Sts	*John T Pratt*	Glen Cove, NY
April 7	Bge	Unidentified	Buzzards Bay, MA
April 8	Bge	*Heap*	Block Island, RI
April 19	Sts	*Reliable*	New Rochelle, NY
April 28	Sch	*Nettie B Dobbin*	Nantucket, MA
May 8	Sch	*John S Presson*	Burnt Island, ME
May 17	Sch	*Estelle S Numan*	Provincetown, MA
May 21	Sch	*S L Foster*	Deer Island, ME
May 23	Sts	*Jas S T Stranahan*	Clason Point, NY
May 28	Gas	*Argonaut*	Greenport, NY
June 5	Sch	*Mary Farrow*	Nantucket Sound, MA
June 16	Sch	*Norumbega*	Off Fire Island, NY
June 17	Sch	*Multnomah*	Ipswich, MA

DATE LOST	TYPE	NAME	WHERE LOST
June 24	Sts	*Daniel S Miller*	Off New York, NY
June 24	Gas	*Gladys*	Block Island, RI
June 29	Sch	*Young Brothers*	Richmond, ME
July 13	Sts	*D F Skinner*	Harts Island, NY
July 16	Slp	*Ceres*	New York, NY
July 26	Sts	*Dream*	Mystic, CT
July 28	Bge	*William McCleve*	Watch Hill, RI
August 12	Slp	*Dolphin*	Great South Bch, NY
August 13	Gas	*Betsy Ross*	Montauk Point, NY
August 18	Sch	*Marguerite*	Newport, RI
August 29	Sch	*Ada Ames*	Chatham, MA
August 29	Gas	*Esther E*	Rockport, MA
September 5	Slp	*Peggy*	Plum Island, MA
September 7	Slp	*Narragansett*	Watch Hill, RI
September 7	Sts	*William Orr*	Coney Island, NY
September 13	Gas	*Whahefo*	Coscob Harbor, CT
September 29	Sch	*Long Island*	Ravenswood, NY
September 29	Sch	*William B Palmer*	Off Nantucket, MA
October 2	Gas	*Mattie & Lena*	Fort Pond, NY
October 25		*Senta*	Marthas Vineyard, MA
November 1	Gas	*Lone Hand*	Narragansett Bay, RI
November 10	Bge	*Baroness*	Fire Island, NY
November 10	Sch	*Mary J Elliot*	Machiasport, ME
November 18	Sch	*John Cadwallader*	Cape Elizabeth, ME
December 6	Bge	*Hopatcong*	New York, NY
December 6	Sch	*W Talbot Dodge*	Barnstable, MA
December 7	Sts	*Olive May*	Marthas Vineyard, MA
December 14	Sch	*Belle Haladay*	Pollock Rip, MA
December 14	Bge	*Frank Miller*	Hellgate, NY
December 14	Sts	*Ottawa*	Cape Vincent, NY
December 14	Bge	*Port Royal*	Hell Gate, NY
December 15	Sch	*Abbie G Cole*	Vineyard Haven, MA
December 15	Sch	*Mollie Rhodes*	Pollock Rip, MA
December 16	Bge	*Scranton*	Chatham, MA
December 16	Sch	*Thomas B Garland*	Nantucket, MA
December 18	Sch	*Matiana*	Rockland, ME
December 25	Sch	*George F Keen*	Marblehead, MA

1911

DATE LOST	TYPE	NAME	WHERE LOST
January 5	Sch	*Silver Heels*	Chatham, MA
January 6	Sch	*Red Jacket*	Thrumcap Island, ME
January 10	Bge	*Corbin*	Provincetown, MA
January 10	Bge	*Pine Forest*	Provincetown, MA
January 10	Sbge	*Treverton*	Provincetown, MA
January 28	Bark	*Stephen G Hart*	Cuttyhunk, MA
February	Sch	*George M Grant*	Montauk, NY
February 27	Sch	*Sylvia M Numan*	Thatchers Island, MA
March 5	Sch	*Mattakeesett*	Provincetown, MA
March 6	Sts	*Howard*	Jones Beach, NY
March 24	Sbge	*Stonington*	Pollock Rip, MA
April 5	Gas	*Letha May*	Nantucket Sound, MA
April 6	St	*Princess Irene*	Fire Island, NY
April 14	Bge	*Henry C Cadmus*	Narragansett Bay, RI
April 14	Bge	*Sailor*	Narragansett Bay, RI
April 30	Sch	*Etta M Story*	Block Island, RI
May 2	Sch	*Teresa D Baker*	Duxbury, MA
May 3	Bge	*Rex*	Quonochontaug, RI
May 23	Sch	*Lillie A Wilson*	Vineyard Sound, MA
June	Sch	Unidentified	North Haven, ME

DATE LOST	TYPE	NAME	WHERE LOST
June 7	Gas	*Adrienne*	Stamford, CT
June 11	Stp	*Colonial*	Saybrook, CT
June 18		*Governor Andrew*	Boston, MA
July 4	Sch	*Julia & Martha*	Cuttyhunk, MA
July 14	Sch	*Robert T Graham*	Fire Island, NY
July 23	Bge	*Brillant*	Newport, RI
July 23	Gas	*Nokomis*	Nantucket Shoals, MA
July 27		*Tay*	Bar Harbor, ME
July 28	Sch	*Almeda Willy*	Swans Island, ME
July 28	Sch	*Henry Chase*	Port Clyde, ME
July 29	Gas	*Mary A Downs*	Vinalhaven, ME
July 30	Sch	*Harry C Shepherd*	Boston, MA
July 31	Slp	*Abbie A Morton*	Mt Desert, ME
August 8	Sts	*Stephen E Babcock*	Bridgeport, CT
August 9	Sch	*Eleazer Boynton*	Rockland, ME
August 11	Sch	*Thersa Wolf*	Chatham, MA
August 12	Sts	*Henry H Stanwood*	New York, NY
August 17	Slp	*Jennie*	Staten Island, NY
August 27	Gas	*William H Phillip*	Princess Bay, NY
August 31	Bge	*Rye*	Point Judith, RI
August 31	Bge	*W D Brinner*	Block Island, RI
September 3	Sch	*David Faust*	Burnt Island, ME
September 4	Sts	*Tidy Adly*	Boston, MA
September 11	Bge	*Scott Brothers*	Bridgeport, CT
September 15	Sch	*Hastings*	Rockport Harbor, ME
September 26	Sch	*Oliver Mitchell*	Plum Island, NY
October 7	Bge	*Penn*	Race Rock Lt, NY
October 30	Sch	*Emily A Staples*	Port Clyde, ME
November 1	Sch	*Florence*	Ipswich, MA
November 1	Sch	*Susan & Mary*	Hull, MA
November 2	Sch	*Lois V Chaples*	Vineyard Sound, MA
November 9	Sch	*Eastern Light*	Boothbay Harbor, ME
November 11	Sch	*Samuel J Goucher*	Isles of Shoals, NH
November 12	Sch	*Bertha F Walker*	Elizabeth Islands, MA
November 12	Gas	*Genia*	Brooklyn, NY
November 12	Sts	*Pottsville*	Wilson Point, CT
November 12	Bge	*Searsport*	Fire Island, NY
November 12	Sts	*Uncle Abe*	Wilson Point, CT
November 12	Sch	*Witch Hazel*	New Haven, CT
November 14	Sch	*Jordan L Mott*	Georges River, ME
November 17	Sch	*Charles Wolston*	Nantucket, MA
November 18	Sch	*Abby & Eva Hooper*	Vinyard Sound, MA
November 18	Bge	*Vermont*	Plum Island, NY
November 19	Sch	*Helen A Wyman*	Montauk Point, NY
November 24	Sch	*Hannah Carlton*	Vineyard Sound, MA
November 29	Gas	*Elsie*	Matinicock, NY
December 5	Sch	*Madagascar*	Plymouth, MA
December 11	Sch	*Ella May*	York, ME
December 28	Sch	*Mary Randall*	Block Island, RI

1912

		Columbus	Metinic Island, ME
	Gas	*Lela*	Narragansett Bay, RI
	Ship	*Lucy & Elizabeth*	New York Bay, NY
January 8	Sch	*Empress*	Cape Elizabeth, ME
January 9	Gas	*Creedmore*	Stonington, ME
January 9	Sbge	*Sterling*	Block Island, RI
January 10	Sts	*Carolyn*	Metinic Island, ME
January 15	Sch	*New Boxer*	Isle Au Haut, ME

DATE LOST	TYPE	NAME	WHERE LOST
January 16	Sts	Weasel	Gloucester, MA
February 23	Bge	Nearchus	Watch Hill, RI
February 26	Sch	Mildred V Nunan	Cape Porpoise, ME
March 12	Gas	Leo	Thatchers Island, MA
March 13	Sch	Jessie Lena	Timber Island, ME
March 15	Sch	St Leon	Pigeon Hill Bay, ME
March 15	Sch	Thaxter	Long Island, NY
March 19	Sch	L Herbert Taft	Roamer Shoal, NY
April 27	Slp	Tina B	Narragansett Bay, RI
April 28	Sch	Winnie Lawry	Cape Ann, MA
May 13		Ambrose Snow	Lower Bay, NY
June 14	Sts	Precursor	Port Jefferson, NY
June 29	Sch	Ranger	Marthas Vineyard, MA
June 29	Gas	Vaurien	Thatchers Island, MA
June 30	Sch	Sallie I'on	Portland, ME
July 13	Gas	Roamer	Marine Harbor, NY
July 24	Sts	Idler	New York, NY
August 6	Gas	Skipper	New York, NY
August 9	Slp	Irene & Wallace	Ipswich, MA
August 19	Sch	Addie Fuller	Cutler Head, ME
August 19	Sch	Petrel	Plymouth, MA
August 22	Sts	Falcon	Pollock Rip, MA
August 27	Sch	Shenandoah	Pollock Rip, MA
September 1	Sch	Silver Spray	Chatham, MA
September 9	Gas	Beulah	Blue Hill Bay, ME
September 29	Gas	Catherine D Enos	Isle Au Haut, ME
October 12	Sts	John B Dallas	Quonochontaug, RI
October 15	Sch	Copy	Eatons Neck, NY
October 31	Drge	Bobbie	Great South Beach, NY
November 1	Slp	Marguerite	Penobscot Bay, ME
November 4	Sch	Myra Sears	Portsmouth, NH
November 7	Sch	William Rice	Boothbay, ME
November 8	Sch	De Mory Gray	Northport Bay, NY
November 13	Sch	Maggie Ellen	Fishers Island, NY
November 24	Bge	Pioneer	Point Judith, RI
December 6	Sch	Bessie C Beach	Montauk Point, NY

1913

DATE LOST	TYPE	NAME	WHERE LOST
January 1	Gas	Town Harbor	Black Rock Harbor, CT
January 3	Gas	Breeze	Narragansett Bay, RI
January 3	Gas	Gertrude	Tremont, ME
January 4	Gas	Lena Maud	West Tremont, ME
January 10	Sch	Clara Jane	Gloucester, MA
January 10		Silver Star	Damariscove, ME
January 13	Gas	Frances Belle	New London, CT
January 13	Sch	Ruth	New London, CT
January 21	Bge	Massachusetts	Off New London, CT
February	Slp	Lucile	Gravesend Bay, NY
February 2		Emma & Maggie	Jonesport, ME
February 2	Gas	May Queen	Little Machias Bay, ME
February 5	Bge	Anna R	Bartlett Reef LI, NY
February 9	Bge	M H Fuller	Cornfield Lightsihp, CT
March 6	Bge	Richard Jackson	New York, NY
March 6	Sbge	Whitman	Boston, MA
March 13	Sts	SS Wycoff	New York Harbor, NY
March 17	Gas	Rising Billow	Vinalhaven, ME
March 22	Sch	Basile	Marthas Vineyard, MA
March 22	Sch	L Snow Jr	Penobscot Bay, ME
March 26	Sch	General Scott	Quoddy Head, ME

DATE LOST	TYPE	NAME	WHERE LOST
April 1	Bge	*Pleasure*	Alexandria Bay, NY
April 7	Stp	*Fordham*	Shooter Island, NY
April 7	Sch	*Thomas Hix*	Southwest Harbor, ME
April 19	Sch	*Irene Messervey*	Elizabeth Islands, MA
April 20	Sch	*Burnside*	Off Long Island, NY
April 21	Sch	*Helena*	Off Port Clyde, ME
April 27	Sch	*Pell S C Vought*	Little Gull Island, NY
April 28	Sch	*Frances A Rice*	Nahant, MA
May 8	Bge	*Adrea*	Off Rocky Point, NY
May 24	Gas	*George H Lubee*	Penobscot Bay, ME
May 30	Sch	*Fred C Holden*	Damariscotta, ME
June 15	Sch	*Paul Palmer*	Off Provincetown, MA
July 1	Sch	*William Grozier*	Buzzards Bay, MA
July 5	Sch	*Lucania*	Cape Cod Bay, MA
July 13	Sch	*Charles Sprague*	Burnt Island, ME
July 19	Slp	*Yeoman*	Bar Harbor, ME
August 1	Bge	*Charles*	Off Norwalk, CT
August 2	Gas	*Ite*	Narragansett Bay, RI
August 12	Gas	*Ox*	Truro, MA
August 30	Gas	*Iris*	Hudson River, NY
September 9	Sch	*Abdon Keene*	Muscongus, ME
September 25	Sch	*Nellie F Sawyer*	Pollock Rip, MA
September 30	Sch	*Aetna*	Great Wass Island, ME
October 9	Sch	*Quonnapowitt*	Truro, MA
October 11	Sts	*Robert Rodgers*	New York, NY
October 13	Sch	*Charles Atkinson*	Mattinicock Point, NY
October 13	Sbge	*Oakland*	Truro, MA
October 14	Sch	*Henry D May*	Pollock Rip, MA
October 14	Sbge	*Summer R Mead*	Wellfleet, MA
October 20	Bge	*Coal Port*	Off Rhode Island
October 20	Sch	*Marjory Brown*	Off Long Island, NY
October 21	Gas	*Martha J*	Jamaica Bay, NY
October 24	Sch	*Chester Lawrence*	Boothbay, ME
October 30	Sts	*Charles E Soper*	Off Larchmont, NY
October 30	Sch	*Florence Russell*	Shippan Point, CT
November 9	Sch	*A J Miller*	Long Island Sound
November 21	Sts	*Buffalo*	Staten Island, NY
December 2	Gas	*C B Harrington*	Off Portland, ME
December 6	Gas	*Addie & Hattie*	Goat Island, ME
December 9	Sch	*New Hampshire*	Block Island, RI
December 13	Sch	*Charles Luling*	Marthas Vineyard, MA
December 22	Sch	*Pilgrim*	Bakers Island, ME

1914

January 4	Sch	*Grace A Martin*	Matinicus Island, ME
January 5	Gas	*Pawtuxet*	Narragansett Bay, RI
January 12	Sch	*Fuller Palmer*	Off Truro, MA
January 12	Sch	*G M Porter*	Nantucket Sound, MA
January 13	Gas	*Ethel*	Port Clyde, ME
January 14	Sch	*John Paul*	Nantucket Sound, MA
January 15	Sch	*Greta*	Nantucket Sound, MA
January 21	Sch	*Gen. Adelbert Ames*	Chatham, MA
January 23	Bge	*Bavaria*	Off Montauk Point, NY
January 24	Sts	*Wm. Dinsdale*	New York, NY
February	Bge	Unidentified	Off Wainscott, NY
February 14	Bge	*Elizabeth*	Off Bartletts Reef, CT
February 14	Bge	*Katie Woods*	Off Bartletts Reef, CT
February 14	Bge	*Rose Marie Feeney*	Off Bartletts Reef, CT
February 16		*Lizzie Harvey*	Gowanus, NY

DATE LOST	TYPE	NAME	WHERE LOST
February 17	Bark	*Castagna*	Eastham, MA
February 18	Sch	*Watauga*	Damariscove, ME
March 1	Sch	*Felix*	Off Fire Island, NY
March 1	Bge	*Fred T Kellers*	Stratford, CT
March 1	Sch	*Jacob S Winslow*	Block Island, RI
March 1	Sch	*Sagua*	Off Montauk Point, NY
March 4	Gas	*Susie & Winnie*	Bar Harbor, ME
March 14	Gas	*Snow Flake*	Wickford, RI
March 16	Sch	*Terranova*	Truro, MA
March 18	Gas	*Gracie Smith*	Falmouth, MA
April 12	Bge	*Evening Star*	Hell Gate, NY
April 30	Gas	*Annie Hamilton*	Vineyard Haven, MA
May 11	Bge	*B W Ohara*	New York Harbor, NY
June 11	Sch	*Emma J Chesbro*	Connecticut River, CT
June 25	Gas	*Whip*	Salem, MA
July	Slp	*Laura Frances*	Pelham Bay, NY
July 2	Sch	*Mary Augusta*	Kennebunkport, ME
July 10		*New Jersey*	Off Ambrose Lightship, NY
July 11	Sch	*George P Hudson*	Pollock Rip, MA
July 17	Sch	*T W Cooper*	Off Rhode Island
July 20	Sts	*Matchless*	Arthur Kills, NY
August 5	Sch	*Fred A Emerson*	Nantucket Shoals, MA
August 6	Sts	*James Bradley*	Cow Bay, NY
August 30	Sch	*Pearl Nelson*	Isle of Shoals, NH
September 6	Gas	*Argos*	Buzzards Bay, MA
September 9	Sch	*R L Tay*	Boston, MA
September 21	Gas	*Jennie H Gilbert*	Boone Island, ME
September 23	Sts	*L Boyer*	Jamaica Bay, NY
September 28	Sts	*Jonas H French*	Off Cohasset, MA
October 1	Sch	*Ida*	Cuttyhunk, MA
October 10	Sch	*Alma E A Holmes*	Salem, MA
October 27	Gas	*Chandler R*	West Bath, ME
October 29	Sts	*Irvington*	Pond Island, ME
November	Sch	*Annie Perry*	Hull, MA
November 4	Sch	*Emma*	Oyster Bay, NY
November 7	Sch	*Rodney Parker*	Cranberry Islands, ME
November 11	Sts	*Eureka*	Wilsons Point, CT
November 13	Gas	*Bob-O-Link*	Gallop Island, NY
November 15	Slp	*Clara M Gross*	Vinalhaven, ME
November 21	Sch	*George D Jenkins*	Shinnecock, NY
November 23	Sch	*Island Home*	Gloucester, MA
December 2	Gas	*Dare*	Corey Island, NY
December 5	Sch	*Alice M Lawrence*	Nantucket, MA
December 7	Sch	*Lugano*	Point Judith, RI
December 7	Sch	*Nile*	Rockland, ME
December 7	Gas	*Success*	Provincetown, MA
December 12	Sch	*Ella M Storer*	Gloucester, MA
December 14	Gas	*Trackless*	Gardiners Bay, NY
December 20	Bge	*Carlos French*	Off Barletts Reef, CT

1915

	Sub	*G-2*	Off Magonk Point, CT
		Unidentified	Execution Light, NY
January 7	Sch	*R R Thomas*	Off Shinnecock Lt, NY
February 27	Sch	*Fred Snow*	Narragansett Bay, RI
March 25	Gas	*Jessie*	Nantucket, MA
March 25	Gas	*Manhasset*	Long Island, NY
April 3	Slp	*Bertha B*	Blue Hill Bay, ME
April 3	Sbge	*Tunnel Ridge*	Truro, MA

DATE LOST	TYPE	NAME	WHERE LOST
April 4	Sbge	*Coleraine*	Truro, MA
April 12	Sch	*Kit Carson*	Narragansett Bay, RI
April 12	Sch	*Rob Roy*	Far Rockaway, NY
May 7	Slp	*Parks*	Eatons Neck, NY
May 9	Bge	*Fortuna*	Mt Desert, ME
May 9	Gas	*Harold B*	Penobscot Bay, ME
May 12	Sch	*C W Dexter*	Little River, ME
May 27	Sts	*William G Butman*	Penobscot Bay, ME
June 2	Sch	*Cora Green*	Seguin Island, ME
June 3	Slp	*Defender*	Matinicus Island, ME
June 9	Sch	*Josie*	Newport, RI
June 15	Sch	*Lotus*	Matinicus Island, ME
June 20	Sbge	*Solus*	Newport, RI
July 6	Sch	*Mary F Pennell*	Wells Beach, ME
July 9	Gas	*Lillian May*	Ipswich, MA
July 19	Gas	*Petrolia*	Rockland, ME
July 27	Gas	*Active*	Block Island, RI
August 15	Sts	*Lackawana*	Nantucket Sound, MA
August 17	Sch	*David Wallace*	Matinicus Island, ME
September	Sch	*Force*	Lynnbrook, NY
September 9	Gas	*Venture*	Thatchers Island, MA
September 12	Sts	*Corrina*	Brooksville, ME
September 17	Sch	*Lanie Cobb*	West Quoddy Head, ME
September 24	Sch	*Minnie Slauson*	Hyannis, MA
September 26	Gas	*Mermaid*	Noskeag, ME
September 28	St	*Isabel*	Shippan Point, CT
October 6	Sch	*Brownstone*	Long Island Sound
October 13	Ols	*Rattler*	New Bedford, MA
October 15	Sch	*Mary Curtis*	Nantucket, MA
November 9	Sbge	*Weehawken*	Off Cohasset, MA
November 12	Sch	*Thomas Brundage*	Chatham, MA
November 23	Sts	*Pioneer*	Cape Cod Bay, MA
December 6	Sch	*William L Elkins*	Cape Elizabeth, ME
December 8	Bge	*El Paso*	Battery, NY
December 11	Sbge	*# 789*	Off Sakonnet, RI
December 13	Gas	*Dora*	Hyannis, MA
December 17	Gas	*Manomet*	Thatchers Island, MA
December 17	Bge	*Virginia*	Hudson River, NY

1916

		City Of Newport	Narragansett Bay, RI
February	Gas	*Jennie B*	Sommes Sound, ME
February 4	Sbge	*# 12*	Off Rhode Island
February 10	Gas	*Nellie F Wotton*	Cape Elizabeth, ME
February 15	Gas	*Laura J*	Brooksville, ME
February 24	Bge	*Maggie Feeney*	Long Island Sound
February 27	Sch	*Helen G King*	Cape Cod Canal, MA
March 1	St	*Eastern City*	Off New York, NY
March 3	Sch	*Ashland*	Off Cohasset, MA
March 3	Sch	*Kohinoor*	Off Cohasset, MA
March 7	Sch	*Edward Stewart*	Cranberry Islands, ME
March 21	Sch	*Hume*	Portsmouth, NH
April 9	Sch	*W E & W L Tuck*	Mt Desert, ME
April 13	Sch	*Silver Spray*	Offshore, ME
May 8	Ltsp	*Fire Island Lightship*	Off New York, NY
May 22	Gas	*Petrel*	Newburyport, MA
May 31	Sch	*Woodbury M Snow*	Rockport, ME
June 4	Sch	*Lucia Porter*	Nahant, MA
June 10	Gas	*Mabel*	Swans Island, ME

DATE LOST	TYPE	NAME	WHERE LOST
July 4	Sts	*Carrie & Mildred*	Chatham, MA
July 9	Sch	*Mary Ann McCann*	Sakonnet, RI
July 18	Gas	*Azorian*	Off Truro, MA
July 26	Ycht	*Mehuta*	Gloucester, MA
August 4	St	*Albert J Stone*	Sakonnet, RI
August 6	Gas	*Ruth W II*	Warren, RI
August 18	Sts	*Lydia*	Hudson River, NY
September 5	Sch	*Donna T Briggs*	Casco Bay, ME
September 22	Gas	*Charles A Dyer*	Nantucket, MA
September 23	Stp	*Bay State*	Cape Elizabeth, ME
September 30	Sch	*C B Clark*	Long Island City, NY
October 7	Gas	*Pontiac*	Pollock Rip, MA
October 8	Sts	*Christiana*	Nantucket Shoals, MA
October 8	Sts	*Strathoene*	Nantucket Shoals, MA
October 8	Sts	*West Point*	Nantucket Shoals, MA
October 9	Sch	*Sally W Ponder*	New Bedford, MA
October 12	Bge	*Cora*	Off Rhode Island
October 13	Gas	*Victor & Ethan*	Off Nomansland Island, MA
October 17	Sts	*Olympic*	Provincetown, MA
October 18	Sts	*Knudson*	Nantucket Shoals, MA
October 21	Sch	*Eliza Levensaler*	Monhegan Island, ME
November 17	St	*T A Scott Jr*	Off Block Island, RI
November 24	Sch	*# 792*	Long Island Sound
November 25	Sts	*Powhatan*	Off Block Island, RI
December 1	Sch	*Rebecca R Douglas*	Frenchmans Bay, ME
December 11	Bge	*Saint Daniel*	Narragansett Bay, RI
December 14	Sts	*Bay Port*	Cape Cod Canal, MA
December 18	Gas	*Briganza*	Truro, MA
December 18		*William Mason*	Machias Bay, ME
December 25	Sch	*Daniel McCloud*	Nantucket, MA
December 25	Sch	*Ravola*	Nantucket, MA
December 25	Sch	*Roger Drury*	Nantucket, MA
December 29	Sbge	*Yemassee*	Cape Cod Bay, MA

1917

DATE LOST	TYPE	NAME	WHERE LOST
	Bark	*Hougemont*	Fire Island, NY
	Sch	*Nancy M Foster*	Pollock Rip, MA
	St	*Seth Low*	Brooklyn, NY
January 3	Bge	*Thomas E Mulqueen*	Point Judith, RI
February 3	Gas	*Leaded*	Chatham, MA
February 23	Bge	*Capital City*	Off Block Island, RI
March 5	Sch	*Henry Withington*	Scituate, MA
March 8	Sch	*Frank Pendleton*	Ambrose, NY
March 8	Gas	*Undine*	Sorrento, ME
March 17	Sch	*Harry W Haynes*	Cashiers Ledge, ME
March 23	Gas	*Mystic Belle*	Egg Rock, ME
April 6	Sch	*Henry Clay*	Off Montauk Point, NY
April 13		*Evelyn*	New York, NY
May 1	Sch	*H S Lanfair*	St Johns Island, ME
May 6	Sch	*Annie H Smith*	Fire Island, NY
May 7	Sch	*Sam Slick*	Thatchers Island, MA
May 17	Sts	*Cumberland*	Vinalhaven, ME
May 27	Gas	*Earl Paul Crabtree*	York River, ME
June 8	Gas	*R P Tibbetts*	Cape Porpoise, ME
June 9	Sts	*Charles Sanford*	Hull, MA
July 7	St	*John E McAllister*	East River, NY
July 10	Sch	*Unique*	Nantucket, MA
July 13		*Edna*	Long Beach, NY
July 14		*Delivery*	East River, NY

ABOVE: In a rare occurrence of World War I aggression against the continental U.S., the Imperial German Navy's U-156 sank the barges *703, 740, 766, Lansford* and shelled the Massachusetts shoreline on July 21, 1918. Shown above is the *Lansford* before she slipped into 20 fathoms of water. The hulls remain grouped tightly together slowly disintegrating in the cold waters east of Cape Cod. *Photo from the collection of William P. Quinn, Orleans MA.* **BELOW**: The *Maine*, a single screw steel ship, was bound east on a full moon tide when she encountered a blinding snowstorm on February 4, 1920. In turning about to return to New York, the vessel struck hard on execution rocks off Manhasset Neck, Long Island. *Photo courtesy Paul Morris, Nantucket MA.*

DATE LOST	TYPE	NAME	WHERE LOST
July 29	Sch	*Julia A Berklee*	Elizabeth Islands, MA
August 9	Sch	*Willis & Guy*	Pemiquid Point, ME
August 14	Gas	*E McNichol*	Boone Island, ME
August 24	Sch	*Manie Saunders*	Off Chatham, MA
September 3	Sch	*J A Webster*	Gouldsboro, ME
September 20	Bge	*Logan*	Cape Cod, MA
October 1	Sch	*Abenaki*	Off Shore, ME
October 1	Sts	*USS Mohawk*	Ambrose Channel, NY
October 23	Bge	*Catherine Horan*	Quonochontaug, RI
October 24	Bge	*Allison White*	Narragansett Bay, RI
October 24		*Norka*	Plymouth, MA
November	Sch	*W O Netileton*	Sakonnet, RI
December 8	Bge	*Chippewa*	Narragansett Bay, RI
December 8	Bge	*Madison*	Narragansett Bay, RI
December 8	Bge	*Marion B*	Narragansett Bay, RI
December 14	Sch	*Edward E Briry*	Pollock Rip, MA
December 16		*Pilot*	Off New York, NY
December 27	St	*Juanita*	New York Bay, NY

1918

DATE LOST	TYPE	NAME	WHERE LOST
	Bge	*# 767*	Vinalhaven, ME
		Fenimore	Cape Neddick, ME
	Bge	*Norman*	Orleans, MA
	St	*Westchester*	East River, NY
January 6	Sts	*Clarence Blakeslee*	Off Block Island, RI
January 12	Gas	*Houri*	Kennebunkport, ME
January 12	Sch	*Roger Drurey*	Biddeford Pool, ME
February 1	Sch	*Cross Rip Ltship*	Off Nantucket Sound, MA
February 3	Ship	*USS Alacrity*	Boston, MA
February 11	Sbge	*Norfolk*	Block Island, RI
February 26	Sbge	*Berkley*	Block Island, RI
February 26	Sbge	*Henry Failing*	Off Block Island, RI
March 10	Gas	*G B Otis*	St Andrews Bay, ME
March 10		*Outing II*	Nantucket, MA
March 23	Sch	*Sarah L Davis*	Rockport, MA
April 21	Gas	*Zazo*	Bristol, RI
May 2	Sch	*Henrietta*	Arverne, NY
May 10	Sbge	*Liberty*	Vineyard Sound, MA
May 10	Sbge	*Pilgrim*	Vineyard Sound, MA
May 19	Gas	*Rara Avis*	Biddefordpool, ME
May 27	Sch	*Thomas C Rackett*	Narragansett Bay, RI
June 1	Gas	*Annie Lee*	Casco Bay, ME
June 7	Sch	*James Young*	Offshore, ME
June 11	Gas	*Sadie*	Boars Head, NH
June 13	Gas	*Mary F Sears*	Thatchers Island, MA
June 28	Sts	*Onondaga*	Watch Hill, RI
July 1	Gas	*Ardath*	Southwest Harbor, ME
July 5	Sch	*Mary F Cushman*	Nantucket Sound, MA
July 10	Gas	*Georgia*	Pollock Rip, MA
July 10	Sts	*USS San Diego*	Off Lone Hill, NY
July 13	Sts	*Inca*	Nomansland Island, MA
July 21	Sbge	*# 703*	Off Orleans, MA
July 21	Bge	*# 740*	Off Orleans, MA
July 21	Bge	*# 766*	Off Orleans, MA
July 21	Sbge	*Lansford*	Off Orleans, MA
July 22	Sch	*Robert & Richard*	Offshore, ME
July 28	Gas	*Evelyn Thompson*	Nantucket, MA
August	Gas	*Clement*	Addison, ME
August 3	Sch	*Sarah & Lucy*	Nantucket, MA

DATE LOST	TYPE	NAME	WHERE LOST
August 10		*Cruiser*	Nantucket Shoals, MA
August 10		*Earl & Nettie*	Nantucket Shoals, MA
August 10		*Kate Palmer*	Nantucket Shoals, MA
August 10		*Lena May*	Nantucket Shoals, MA
August 10		*On Time*	Nantucket Shoals, MA
August 10	Sts	*Penistone*	Nantucket Shoals, MA
August 10		*Progress*	Nantucket Shoals, MA
August 10		*Reliance*	Nantucket Shoals, MA
August 10		*Starbuck*	Nantucket Shoals, MA
August 10	Sts	*Sydland*	Nantucket Shoals, MA
August 23	Sch	*Elk*	Monhegan Island, ME
August 24	Sts	*George Hudson*	Watch Hill, RI
September 5	Sch	*Herman F Kimball*	Trundys Reef, ME
September 11	Sch	*Governor Powers*	Nantucket Sound, MA
September 13	Gas	*Lottie Merchant*	Off Monhegan Island, ME
September 15	Gas	*Christopher Columbus*	Providence, RI
September 24	Gas	*Bella*	Vineyard Sound, MA
September 30	Gas	*Bernadette*	Rockaway Beach, NY
October	Sch	*Mary Weaver*	Boothbay Harbor, ME
October 16	St	*Port Phillip*	Ambrose, NY
October 25	Gas	*C & R Tarbox*	Portland, ME
November 2	Sts	*Port Hunter*	Nantucket Sound, MA
November 7	Gas	*Pelican*	Marblehead, MA
November 18	Gas	*Angler*	Nantucket, MA
November 29	Sch	*Harold Cousens*	Gloucester, MA
November 29	Sts	*Merriconeag*	Orrs Island, ME
December 30	Sch	*Fred B Balano*	Great Wass Island, ME

Year 1919

DATE LOST	TYPE	NAME	WHERE LOST
January 1	St	*Northern Pacific*	Fire Island, NY
January 14	Gas	*Lizzie B Foster*	Gloucester, MA
February 8	Gas	*Kitty A*	Gloucester, MA
February 28	Sts	*Lord Dufferin*	New York Bay, NY
March 17	St	*Jameson*	East River, NY
March 17	Sts	*Waubesa*	New York, NY
April 30	Bark	*Prof Koch*	Scituate, MA
May 15	Sbge	*L&W-B C Co #12*	Provincetown, MA
May 15	Sch	*Naticoke*	Isle of Shoals, NH
May 15	Bge	*White Band*	Duxbury, MA
May 23	Sch	*William D Hilton*	Rockland, ME
June 2	Gas	*Dionis*	Nantucket, MA
June 12	St	*Yankee*	Fire Island, NY
July 1	Gas	*Angeline & Louise*	Provincetown, MA
July 22	Sch	*Charles E Dunlap*	Far Rockaway, NY
August 21	St	*Kemp*	Thatchers Island, MA
September 17	Gas	*Jennie R*	Edgecomb, ME
September 26	Gas	*Lizzie S Joy*	Offshore, ME
October 20		*Chicago City*	New York, NY
October 28	Gas	*Rescue*	Diamond Point Lubec, ME
November 5	Gas	*Annie Margie*	Rockland Harbor, ME
November 15	Sch	*Mineola*	Gloucester, MA
November 24	Sch	*Oakwoods*	Cape Cod Bay, MA
November 25	Gas	*Mamie K*	Rockaway, NY
November 29	Sch	*A F Kindberg*	Cape Porpoise, ME
December	Sch	*Mary E Lynch*	North River, NY
December 3	Bge	*John Howard*	Plymouth, MA
December 8	Gas	*Sakuntala*	Nantucket, MA
December 13	Sts	*Grange Park*	Freeport, NY

DATE LOST	TYPE	NAME	WHERE LOST
Year 1920			
	Sts	*El Sol*	Narrows, NY
		Melrose	Montauk, NY
	Sch	Unidentified	Sandwich, MA
		Viola	Newport, RI
January 1	Sch	*Charles Trickey*	Cape Porpoise, ME
January 1	Sch	*Mary E Olys*	Cape Porpoise, ME
February 4	Stp	*Maine*	Execution Rocks, NY
February 6	Sts	*Polias*	Burnt Island, ME
February 6	Sts	*Princess Anne*	Far Rockaway, NY
February 7	Sts	*Lakeville*	Jones Inlet, NY
February 14	Sts	*Malden*	Jones Inlet, NY
February 27	Sbge	*Tabor*	Elizabeth Islands, MA
March 12	Gas	*Elinora Hill*	Narragansett Bay, RI
March 12	Sts	*Lake De Val*	Southampton, NY
March 13	Sch	*Isaiah Stetson*	Pollock Rip, MA
March 13	Sch	*Wabash*	Richmond Island, ME
March 14	Sbge	*# 7*	Off Block Island, RI
March 14	Sch	*Isaish K Stetson*	Nantucket, MA
April 21	Gas	*Blanche F Irving*	Nantucket, MA
April 28	Sch	*Norma*	Point Lookout, NY
May 5	Gas	*Mary Ellen*	Manchester, MA
June 19	Sts	*Heroine*	Point Judith, RI
July 15	Gas	*Aida*	Provincetown, MA
July 29	Sch	*Clara & Mabel*	Frenchmans Bay, ME
August 17	Gas	*Idlewild*	Cape Porpoise, ME
August 20	Sch	*Itasca*	Newport, RI
August 25	Gas	*Georgianna*	Damariscotta, ME
August 31	Sch	*St Croix*	Vineyard Sound, MA
September	Gas	*Elco II*	Narragansett Bay, RI
September 15	Gas	*Katie M Hardy*	Lubec, ME
October 27	Sch	*Fred Tyler*	Biddefordpool, ME
October 29	Sts	*Cape Fear*	Newport, RI
November 4	Sch	*A P Parkhurst*	Off Moose Island, ME
November 21	Sch	*Pochasset*	Cape Elizabeth, ME
November 23	Gas	*Albert Brown*	Salem, MA
December 29	St	*John C Craven*	Battery, NY
Year 1921			
	Sts	*Wamby Wandy*	Cape Porpoise, ME
January 31	Sbge	*Oxford*	Sandwich, MA
January 31	Sbge	*Radnor*	Sandwich, MA
March 6	Sch	*Luella Nickerson*	Falmouth, MA
March 9	Sts	*Alert*	Bridgeport, CT
March 21	Gas	*Rough Rider*	Ipswich, MA
April 3	Sch	*Evolution*	Nantucket, MA
May 10	Sch	*Mabel E Goss*	Sullivan Falls, ME
June 5	Sch	*L L Hamlin*	South Bristol, ME
June 6	Sch	*Eva A Danahower*	Sandwich, MA
June 8	Sch	*Rozella*	Port Clyde, ME
July 9	Sch	*Odell*	Portland, ME
July 13	Bge	*Cecelia Mcilvain*	Point Judith, RI
August 28	Gas	*Killarney*	Manchester, MA
September 2	Gas	*Eva Avina*	Thatchers Island, MA
September 27	Gas	*Gracie Smith II*	Provincetown, MA
October 5	Gas	*Seth Nyman*	Bakers Island, ME
October 14	Gas	*Waquoit*	Narragansett Bay, RI
October 26	Sch	*Henry F Kreger*	Pollock Rip, MA

DATE LOST	TYPE	NAME	WHERE LOST
November 19	Slp	*McCormick*	Phippsburg, ME
November 19	Sch	*Sintram*	Off Truro, MA
November 21	Sch	*Maud S*	Rockland, ME
December 3	Sbge	*Chemung*	Newport, RI
December 4	Gas	*Amerique*	Narragansett Bay, RI
December 15	Sch	*Howard Russell*	Swans Island, ME
December 30	Sbge	*Dunmore*	Off Cohasset, MA

Year 1922

	Gas	*Nora D Robinson*	Ipswich, MA
	Sch	*Unidentified*	Montauk, NY
	Gas	*Wanderlust*	Providence, RI
January 3	Gas	*Doris*	Nantucket, MA
February	St	*Talisman*	Brooklyn, NY
February 2	Sts	*Empress Of Scotland*	North River, NY
February 3	Sch	*Joseph S Zeman*	Metinic Ledge, ME
February 24		*Bessie A White*	Moriches, NY
March 4	Gas	*Grace Clinton*	Block Island, RI
March 27	Gas	*Edith Nute*	Chatham, MA
March 28	Sch	*Ricameron*	Nantucket Shoals, MA
April 12	Sch	*Grace Van Dusen*	Lubec, ME
April 19	Sbge	*Catawamteak*	Off Monhegan Island, ME
May 19		*Eagle Boat #17*	Easthampton, NY
May 19		*Gen. John Wilkins*	Orient, NY
July 3	Sch	*George R Smith*	Duxbury, MA
July 7	Sch	*Clara A Donnell*	Nantucket Shoals, MA
July 26	Ship	*Granite State*	Manchester, MA
August 1	Gas	*Elva L Spurling*	Off Eastham, MA
September 19	Gas	*Bessie May*	Ram Island, ME
September 20	Sts	*Taro*	Narragansett Bay, RI
September 22	Sch	*Melissa Trask*	Medomak River, ME
October 28	Gas	*Golden Eagle*	Provincetown, MA
October 30	Bge	*Peter Howard*	Sandwich, MA
November 9	Sch	*Samuel Hart*	Casco Bay, ME
November 28	Sch	*Lizzie D Small*	Buzzards Bay, MA
December 1	Gas	*Flora Temple*	Indian Point, ME
December 2	Sch	*Jessie L Leach*	Thatchers Island, MA
December 21	Gas	*Flit*	Marthas Vineyard, MA
December 21	Sch	*Madonna V*	Napeague, NY
December 28	Gas	*Rosa Blanche*	Blue Hill Bay, ME
December 29	Sch	*Annie L Spinder*	Provincetown, MA

Year 1923

		F C Lockhart	Machias Bay, ME
	Bge	*Vermillion*	Off Block Island, RI
January		*Pittsburg*	Montauk, NY
January 3	Sch	*Alice M Colburn*	Manchester, MA
January 8	Sbge	*Penn*	Block Island, RI
January 12	Sch	*Robert W*	York Beach, ME
January 23	Gas	*Natalie*	Elizabeth Islands, MA
February 18	Sch	*Santino*	Nantucket Shoals, MA
March	St	*Cape Cod*	Orient Point, NY
March 5	Gas	*Kate B*	Nomansland Island, MA
March 25	Sch	*Dorothy Palmer*	Pollock Rip, MA
March 28	St	*Elmer A Keeler*	Bartlett Reef, CT
March 28	Bge	*Mauretania*	Bartlett Reef, CT
April	Sch	*Charles W Lyne*	Fire Island, NY
April 15	Sts	*Anahuac*	Biddeford, ME

DATE LOST	TYPE	NAME	WHERE LOST
April 20	Sch	*Francis Goodnow*	Cape Elizabeth, ME
April 22	St	*J C Doughty*	Staten Island, NY
April 23	Sts	*John Dwight*	Vineyard Sound, MA
April 25	Sch	*Kennebec*	Perry, ME
April 28	Sbge	*Bradock*	Off Rhode Island
April 28	Sbge	*Canton*	Off Rhode Island
April 28	Sbge	*Taunton*	Off Rhode Island
April 29	Sts	*Seaconnet*	Vineyard Sound, MA
May 2	Gas	*Etta*	Ellsworth, ME
May 16	Sch	*Northcliff*	Georgica, NY
May 24	Gas	*Linwood*	Block Island, RI
May 25	Gas	*Nautilus*	Rockport, MA
June 6	Sch	*Jonathon Cone*	Off Sakonnet, RI
August 7	Gas	*Diana*	Bar Harbor, ME
September 2	Stp	*City Of Rockland*	Manchester, MA
September 20	Slp	*Richard*	Merrymeeting Bay, ME
October	Ycht	*Florence A Simmons*	Cedar Island, NY
October 10	Sts	*Palm*	Bar Harbor, ME
October 14	Sch	*Eugenie*	Cape Small Point, ME
November	Gas	*Lorna*	New Bedford, MA
December 28	Gas	*Fredonia*	Narragansett Bay, RI

Year 1924

DATE LOST	TYPE	NAME	WHERE LOST
	Sts	*Anahuac*	Moriches, NY
	Stp	*Mistletoe*	Rockaway Beach, NY
	St	*Old Glory*	New York, NY
January 7	Gas	*Reliance*	Marthas Vineyard, MA
January 12	Sch	*Ruth E Merrill*	Falmouth, MA
February 20	Sch	*Robert P Murphy*	Merrymeeting Bay, ME
February 22	Sch	*Benjamin Cromwell*	Bellport, NY
March 3	Bge	*Tamanend*	Pollock Rip, MA
March 12	Stp	*Carmania*	Fall River, MA
March 26	Gas	*Marion*	Thatchers Island, MA
April 12	Sch	*Wyoming*	Pollock Rip, MA
April 21	Sts	*Llewellyn Howland*	Newport, RI
April 22	Sch	*Lawrence Murdock*	Buzzards Bay, MA
April 24		*Lewis H St John*	Lubec, ME
April 25	Stp	*Grand Republic*	Hudson River, NY
April 25	Stp	*Highlander*	Hudson River, NY
April 25	Stp	*Nassau*	Hudson River, NY
May 5	Gas	*Stella Of Italy*	Newport, RI
July 7	Gas	*Narwhal*	Falmouth, MA
July 12	Sch	*Miladi*	Provincetown, MA
July 24	Gas	*Gertrude*	Newport, RI
July 25	Sts	*Mabel Barton*	Providence, RI
August 6	Sch	*Henrietta Whitney*	Eastport, ME
August 6	Sts	*Herbert*	Boston, MA
August 15	Gas	*Balmar*	Cohasset, MA
August 26	Gas	*Helen E Murley*	Nantucket Shoals, MA
August 26	Gas	*Mauna Loa*	Newport, RI
October 14	Gas	*Gertrude Mabel*	Nantucket, MA
October 26	Bark	*Wanderer*	Cuttyhunk, MA
October 28	Gas	*Tansy Bitters*	Elizabeth Islands, MA
November 15	Sts	*William Maloney*	Newport, RI
November 17	Sbge	*Canisteo*	Monhegan Island, ME
November 17	Sbge	*Pohatcong*	Monhegan Island, ME
November 17	Sbge	*Strafford*	Monhegan Island, ME
November 23	Bge	*S T Co # 5*	Belfast, ME
December 5	Sch	*Evelyn & Ralph*	Nantucket, MA

DATE LOST	TYPE	NAME	WHERE LOST
December 20	Sch	*Georgina M*	Off Provincetown, MA
December 22	Gas	*Annetta*	Rockport, MA
December 24	Gas	*Austin L Mills*	Gay Head, MA
December 24	Gas	*Trebor II*	Scituate, MA

Year 1925

DATE LOST	TYPE	NAME	WHERE LOST
		Clinton D Barry	Glen Cove, NY
	Sch	*F C Pendleton*	Penobscot Bay, ME
	St	*O'Leary*	Fire Island, NY
	St	*Radcliffe*	Fire Island, NY
July 1	Ycht	*Feu-Follet*	Long Island, ME
July 10	Sts	*Thetis*	Buzzards Bay, MA
July 11	Gas	*Hope B*	Wiscassett, ME
July 27	Gas	*Charmer*	Point Judith, RI
August 16	Gas	*Southwind III*	Richmond Island, ME
August 18	Sts	*Mackinac*	Newport, RI
October	Ycht	*Sally Lee*	Montauk, NY
October	Bge	Unidentified	Montauk, NY
October 10	Sbge	*Richardson*	Rockland, ME
October 12	Gas	*Nirvana*	Off Eastham, MA
October 30	Gas	*Saint*	Revere, MA
October 31	Sch	*C N Gilmore*	Wood Island, ME
November 4	Sch	*William Thomas*	Annisquam, MA
November 13	Sch	*Northern Light*	Rockland, ME
November 28	Bark	*John H Meyer*	Machias Bay, ME
November 28	Sch	*Livelihood*	Beach Island, ME
December 17	Gas	*Regina*	Gloucester, MA
December 27	Gas	*Allaha*	Nomansland Island, MA
December 27	Sch	*Edward Lawrence*	Portland, ME

Year 1926

DATE LOST	TYPE	NAME	WHERE LOST
	Sch	*Ada Towers*	Sayville, NY
		Grace E Stevens	Rockland, ME
		Surge	Cape Cod Bay, MA
	Sub	*L-8*	Off Brenton Reef, RI
January 12	Gas	*Constance*	Scituate, MA
February 4	Sch	*Kenwood*	Scituate, MA
February 10	Ols	*Ralph Brown*	Gloucester, MA
March 13	Gas	*Rusalka*	Nantucket Shoals, MA
March 14	Sbge	*# 786*	Plymouth, MA
April 1	Sch	*Lillian*	Long Island, ME
April 23		*Pionita*	Montauk, NY
April 24	Bge	*Mauch Chunk*	Narragansett Bay, RI
May 16	Gas	*Sagitta*	Gloucester, MA
June 10	Bge	*Lucy Hughes*	Gloucester, MA
June 17	Bge	*O-21*	Off New York
July 1	Gas	*Bradley A*	Casco Bay, ME
July 10	Sts	*Meteor*	Block Island, RI
October 13	Gas	*Miranda II*	Gloucester, MA
October 15	Ols	*Pioneer*	Provincetown, MA
November 27	Sch	*Emily F Northam*	Cranberry Islands, ME
December 7	Sch	*W H Reinhart*	Provincetown, MA
December 8	Ols	*Speedwell*	Franklin Light, ME

Year 1927

DATE LOST	TYPE	NAME	WHERE LOST
	Bge	*Colonial Beacon*	Barnstable, MA
	Gas	*Dixie III*	Offshore, ME

Although many of the big schooners did not last more than a decade, the *Ruth E. Merrill* had one of the longest careers in the trade. For twenty years she sailed until her final journey ended on L'Hommedieu shoal January 12, 1924. The old schooner's seams were not able to hold the sea out any longer and the men at the pumps could not keep up with the flooding. Her hull is now mostly sanded in as she sits in fifty feet of water off Falmouth, MA. *Photo from the collection of William P. Quinn, Orleans MA.*

DATE LOST	TYPE	NAME	WHERE LOST
	Sch	*Edna Mcknight*	Boothbay Harbor, ME
		Island Belle	Boston, MA
January 8	Sts	*John Tracy*	Off Truro, MA
January 9		*Little Margaret*	Cape Ann, MA
February 2	Ols	*A Roger Hickey*	Wellfleet, MA
February 14	Sch	Unidentified	Wellfleet, MA
February 18	Ols	*CG 238*	Provincetown, MA
February 21	Bge	Unidentified	Gloucester, MA
February 24	Sch	*# 15*	Boston, MA
February 26	Sbge	*Luther E Hooper*	Off Rhode Island
March 4	Sch	*Montclair*	Orleans, MA
May 21	Sch	*William H Babcock*	Brooklyn, NY
May 31	Sts	*Kershaw*	Nantucket Sound, MA
June	Ols	*Surge*	Off Pamet River, MA
June 28	Ycht	*Rough Rider*	North Perry, ME
July 11	Sts	*Eagle*	Off Duxbury, MA
July 15		*Sagaland*	Nantucket Shoals, MA
July 20	Ols	*Ara*	Southwest Harbor, ME
October	Sch	*George H Barnes*	Noank, CT
October 13	Gas	*Onrust*	Bayside, NY
October 29	Sch	*Avalon*	Off Truro, MA
November 4	Gas	*Flossie May*	Bamoine, ME
November 4	Sch	*Georgia Jenkins*	Fox Island Thorofare, ME
December 9		*John A Saunders*	Mackerel Cove, ME
December 20	Sts	*Corvin*	Buzzards Bay, MA

Year 1928

	Gas	*Wesley W Sinnett*	Sandwich, MA
January 5	Sch	*Gaspee Fisherman*	Nantucket Shoals, MA
March 27	Sts	*Warwick*	Pemiquid Harbor, ME
April 30	St	*James A Cox*	Jamaica Bay, NY
May 7		*Navesink*	Upper Bay, NY
May 7	Sch	*Sarah Maria*	Millbridge, ME
May 22	Gas	*Sinbad V*	Little Sheepscot River, ME
May 30	Ols	*Mary*	Gloucester, MA
August	St	*Volunteer*	Hell Gate, NY
August 9	Sch	*Gladys M Taylor*	Penobscot Bay, ME
August 14	Gas	*Marilyn*	Portland Harbor, ME
September 7	Gas	*Blackhawk*	Casco Bay, ME
September 15	Bge	*Olive Etta*	Boothbay, ME
October 17	Sts	*N B Starbuck*	New York, NY
October 18	Ols	*Antietam*	Marthas Vineyard, MA
November 18	Sch	*Camilla May Page*	Portsmouth, NH
November 20		Unidentified	Cape Ann, MA
November 21	Sch	*Mildred Foley*	Nantucket Sound, MA
December 12	Sch	*Alma T*	Pollock Rip, MA

Year 1929

	Ols	*Julia*	Ipswich, MA
January 7	Sch	*Matthew S Greer*	Elizabeth Islands, MA
January 14	Sch	*Wawenock*	Mcglatherys Island, ME
January 22	Sch	*Kingsway*	Eastport, ME
February 1	Slp	*Henrietta*	Point Lookout, NY
February 12	Sch	*Mary F Barrett*	Robin Hood Cove, ME
April 29	Sch	*Francis Taussig*	Marthas Vineyard, MA
April 30	St	*Mutual*	New York, NY
May 23	Sts	*John Fuller*	Waterford, NY
June 14	Gas	*Topaz XI*	Isles of Shoals, NH

DATE LOST	TYPE	NAME	WHERE LOST
June 26	Gas	*Areletha*	Buzzards Bay, MA
July 14	Gas	*Benjamin Wallace*	Thatchers Island, MA
July 17	St	*Union*	Port Richmond, NY
July 28	Gas	*Parker W*	Nantucket Sound, MA
July 29	Ols	*Wilma*	Off Cohasset, MA
August 10	Ols	*Andrew Hathaway*	Pollock Rip, MA
August 31	Sch	*Abacena*	City Island, NY
September		*Osprey*	Montauk, NY
September 7	Gas	*Cluny*	City Island, NY
October 24	Ols	*Governer Prence*	Cape Cod Canal, MA
October 27	Gas	*Active*	Narragansett Bay, RI
October 30	Ols	*Florence Marchant*	Provincetown, MA
November 15	Ols	*Alice And Wilson*	Gloucester, MA
November 16	Gas	*Clarise Hope*	Provincetown, MA
November 20	Gas	*Naomi Bruce*	Marthas Vineyard, MA
November 28	Sts	*Betty Alden*	Hull, MA
November 28	Stp	*Mary Chilton*	Hull, MA
November 28	Stp	*Nantasket*	Hull, MA
November 28	Stp	*Old Colony*	Hull, MA
December 18	Sts	*Fort Victoria*	Ambrose Channel, NY

1930

DATE LOST	TYPE	NAME	WHERE LOST
	Slp	*Albert Baldwin*	Gloucester, MA
	Ols	*Amelia M Periera*	Off Block Island, RI
		Ruth Shaw	Rockaway Inlet, NY
	Sts	Unidentified	Montauk, NY
January	Sts	*Edward Luckenbach*	Block Island, RI
January 3	St	*Thomas J Howard*	East River, NY
January 17	Sch	*Virginia Dare*	New London, CT
January 23	Gas	*Oriole*	Newport, RI
February 27	Gas	*Florence Warren*	Tiverton, RI
March 18	Ols	*Ethel Marion*	Nantucket, MA
April 1	Bge	*North River*	East River, NY
April 15	Ols	*Irma A*	Nantucket, MA
May 19	Gas	*Astrid*	Sakonnet, RI
May 31	Ols	*Progress*	Truro, MA
June 10	Ols	*Pinthis*	Off Scituate, MA
June 17	Gas	*Flora L Oliver*	Truro, MA
July 2	Sts	*Moritz*	Salem, MA
July 4	Sch	*Gardiner Deering*	Brooksville, ME
July 24	Sts	*Ellenor*	Amagansett, NY
July 30	Sch	*James L Malay*	Salem, MA
August 14	Ols	*Governor Fuller*	Pollock Rip, MA
August 16	Gas	*Angie B Watson*	Salem, MA
August 30	Bge	*Red Wind*	Bremen, ME
September 1	Gas	*Mist Chief*	Watch Hill, RI
September 11	Gas	*Mogadore*	New Bedford, MA
September 16	Ols	*Pilot*	Thatchers Island, MA
September 24	Ols	*Dorcas*	Pollock Rip, MA
September 30	Ols	*John R Ericsson*	Truro, MA
October 10	Ols	*Dorothy M*	Block Island, RI
October 17	Bge	*Harry Howard*	Newport, RI
October 17	Bge	*Howard Sisters*	Newport, RI
October 29	Ols	*John J Fallon*	Ipswich, MA
November		*Petrel*	Block Island, RI
November 14		*Winfred H*	Napeague Beach, NY
November 19	St	*Ovidia*	Off New York, NY
November 20	Ols	*Gyda*	Scituate, MA
December 4	Sch	*Ivanhoe*	Nantucket, MA

DATE LOST	TYPE	NAME	WHERE LOST
December 6	Sch	*Storm Petrel*	Watch Hill, RI
December 10	Gas	*Albertina*	Vineyard Sound, MA
December 26	Ols	*Angelina*	White Island, ME

1931

January 2	Ols	*Angie & Mary*	Seguin Island, ME
January 4		*Comanche*	Montauk, NY
January 4	Sts	*William N Page*	Westhampton, NY
January 13	Gas	*Chester Kennedy*	Petite Manan, ME
January 13	Gas	*George F*	Buzzards Bay, MA
January 18	Gas	*F Bertolino*	Ipswich, MA
February 7	Ols	*Alona*	Nantucket Shoals, MA
February 10	Gas	*Ewscray*	Roamer Shoals, NY
February 12	St	*Penobscot*	Penobscot River, ME
February 20		*Algae*	Montauk, NY
March 4	Sch	*John Manning*	Off New York, NY
March 7	St	*Joyce Card*	New York, NY
March 8	Gas	*Priscilla*	Rockland, ME
March 23	Sts	*Governor Bodwell*	Swans Island, ME
April 10	Sts	*Symor*	Nantucket, MA
April 25	Gas	*Ellen Maria*	Deer Isle, ME
May 19	Sch	*Constellation*	Marthas Vineyard, MA
May 23	Ols	*El Sol*	Narragansett Bay, RI
June 12	Ols	*Mystic*	Off Nantucket, MA
June 30	Gas	*Maud B Morse*	Block Island, RI
July 12	Ols	*Miriam*	Nantucket, MA
August 6	St	*Shrub*	York Harbor, ME
August 6	Ols	*Vasco Da Gamma*	Vineyard Sound, MA
August 10	Gas	*Eaglet*	Vineyard Sound, MA
August 27	Gas	*Aubrey A*	Jonesport, ME
August 27	Gas	*Louise*	Jonesport, ME
August 29	Gas	*Isabel*	Rockland, ME
September 9	Ols	*Isabelle*	Watch Hill, RI
September 12	Sch	*Cecilia M Dunlap*	New York, NY
September 12	Bge	*Meddo # 1*	Bucksport, ME
September 12	Bge	*Meddo # 2*	Bucksport, ME
September 15	Gas	*Rita A Viator*	Duck Island, ME
September 29	Gas	*International*	Annisquam, MA
October 6	Gas	*Dispatch*	Narragansett Bay, RI
November 3	Bge	*Rita Howard*	Watch Hill, RI
November 8	Sch	*Ervin J Luce*	Provincetown, MA
December 2	Gas	*Star*	Buzzards Bay, MA
December 7	Gas	*Vivian*	Off Block Island, RI

1932

	Gas	*Pauline S*	Ipswich, MA
	Sch	*Resolute*	New York, NY
January 25	Ols	*Grace & Evelyn*	Off Truro, MA
February 19	Slp	*Viola*	Plymouth, MA
February 27	Sch	*George W Elsey*	Nantucket Sound, MA
March 5	Sts	*H F Bardleben*	Off Nantucket, MA
April 7	Gas	*Nola*	Vineyard Sound, MA
April 21	Ols	*Charles Fauci Jr*	Pollock Rip, MA
May 9	St	*Sea Bird*	New York, NY
May 27	Sts	*Grecian*	Off Block Island, RI
June 16	Ols	*John Mantia*	Off Truro, MA
July 7	Sbge	*# 702*	Sandwich, MA
July 8	Sch	*Altana M Jagger*	Watch Hill, RI

DATE LOST	TYPE	NAME	WHERE LOST
July 9	Ols	*Waltham*	Block Island, RI
August 3	Gas	*L V Ostrom*	Isleboro, ME
August 5	Gas	*Hi-Queen*	Vineyard Sound, MA
September 9	St	*Observation*	East River, NY
October 10	Gas	*Atsco*	Block Island, RI
October 10	Gas	*Marge*	Boston, MA
October 15	Gas	*Lochinvar*	Portland Head, ME
October 24	Ols	*Evelyn H*	Thatchers Island, MA
November 14	Sts	*Winter Harbor*	Wiscassett, ME
December 2	Ols	*Colleen*	Nantucket Sound, MA
December 4		*Althea Louke*	New Bedford, MA
December 12	Sbge	*Tohickon*	Buzzards Bay, MA
December 16	Ols	*Carrie Roderick*	Off Truro, MA

1933

		City Of Bangor	Boston, MA
	Gas	*Uncas*	Penobscot Bay, ME
January 23	Gas	*Lucile*	Petite Manan, ME
April 2	Sch	*Cameo*	Bucksport, ME
May 8	Gas	*Kwasind*	Ellsworth, ME
May 8	Gas	*Miss Priscilla*	Ellsworth, ME
May 8	Gas	*Refuge*	Ellsworth, ME
May 11	Stp	*Louise*	Brooklyn, NY
May 13	Ycht	*Alert*	Ellsworth, ME
May 13	Gas	*Paprika*	Ellsworth, ME
May 19	Gas	*Monataka*	Ellsworth, ME
May 25	Sts	*Southland*	Off Cohasset, MA
May 31	Gas	*Carola*	Ellsworth, ME
May 31	Bge	*White Marsh*	Off Plymouth, MA
June 13	Gas	*Monhegan*	Marblehead, MA
September 5	Gas	*Conqueror*	Friendship, ME
September 23	Ols	*Thomaston*	Cape Cod Canal, MA
November 22	Ship	Unidentified	Coney Island, NY
December 2	Ols	*Col Lindbergh*	Gloucester, MA
December 19	Sch	*Moonlight*	Jonesport, ME
December 20	Sch	*Granville R Bacon*	Watch Hill, RI
December 27	Bge	*L&W-B C Co # 9*	Nantucket, MA

1934

		Anna Sophia	Eastham, MA
	Gas	*Eva & Belle*	Off Goose Falls, ME
	Slp	*M M Hamilton*	Duxbury, MA
January 14	Sts	*Sagamore*	Prouts Neck, ME
March 6	Ols	*Margaret D*	Nomansland Island, MA
March 13	Bge	*Bourne*	Portland, ME
April 17	Sts	*Puszta*	Block Island, RI
May 5	Gas	*Maxwell*	Point Judith, RI
May 15	Sts	*Lightship # 117*	Nantucket Shoals, MA
May 20		*May Archer*	Boston, MA
May 20	Sts	*Norumbega*	Boston, MA
July 6	Gas	*Hostess*	Narragansett Bay, RI
August 26	Gas	*Ann D II*	Newport, RI
September 8	Ols	*W J Tracy*	Narrows, NY
September 20	Ols	*Josie*	Thatchers Island, MA
October 6	Sts	*Ajax*	Tenants Harbor, ME
October 23	Gas	*Onaway*	Westport, MA
October 25	St	*Berkshire*	Bridgehampton, NY
November 3	Gas	*Minerva*	Nomansland Island, MA

DATE LOST	TYPE	NAME	WHERE LOST
November 10	Bge	*D W Patterson*	Marthas Vineyard, MA
1935			
	Sch	*Agusta W Snow*	Boston, MA
	St	*Iroquon*	New York, NY
	Sch	*Virginia*	Wellfleet, MA
January 2		*Lexington*	New York, NY
January 8	Ols	*Waltham II*	Nomansland Island, MA
February 1	Gas	Unidentified	Jones Beach, NY
February 16	Bge	*Nimrod*	New York, NY
April 12	Gas	*Elaine*	Ipswich, MA
May 3		*Desire*	Off Eatons Neck, NY
May 15	Sts	*Norfolk*	Nepeague, NY
June	Sch	*Mavis*	Ditch, NY
June 2	Ols	*Milton*	Eastham, MA
June 8	Sts	*Castine*	Vinalhaven, ME
June 26	Sch	*Elk*	Provincetown, MA
July	Sch	*Lorelei*	Eatons Neck, NY
July 2	Bge	*L B Shaw*	Buzzards Bay, MA
July 14	Sts	*Raritan Sun*	Montauk, NY
August 9	Gas	*Eurybia*	New Bedford, MA
August 9		*Harold*	Sagaponack, NY
August 31	Gas	Unidentified	Eastchester, NY
September 5	Ols	*Mareve*	Gloucester, MA
September 30	Slp	*Bob-O-Link*	Rockport, MA
October 5	Ols	*Florence K*	Off Sandwich, MA
October 6	Ols	*Aquidneck*	Nomansland Island, MA
October 16	Sbge	*Lt. Sam Mengel*	Off Cohasset, MA
November 13	Sch	*Julia A*	Montauk, NY
November 17	Gas	*Thalassa*	Bristol, RI
December 9	Bge	*Marie De Ronde*	Sayville, NY
December 31	Ols	*Gov. Douglas*	Portland, ME
1936			
	Sch	*Hesper*	Wiscassett, ME
	Sch	*Hesperus*	Chatham, MA
	Sch	*Luther Little*	Wiscassett, ME
	Sch	*Mary H Diebold*	Eastport, ME
		Mount Hope	Narragansett Bay, RI
	Sch	*Redwing*	Wellfleet, MA
February 17	Ols	*Ingomar*	Ipswich, MA
May 3	Ols	*M R J III*	Sheepshead Bay, NY
May 4		*Reliance*	Southampton, NY
June	Gas	*Sea Lady*	Nahant, MA
July 31	Gas	*Wiwa*	Trescott, ME
August 7	Ols	*Massasoit*	Nantucket Shoals, MA
August 7	Sch	Unidentified	Nantucket Shoals, MA
September 9	Sts	*Romance*	Boston, MA
September 19	Gas	*Albatross II*	Provincetown, MA
October 15	Gas	*Zonda*	Casco Bay, ME
November 26		*Mary P Mosquito*	Montauk, NY
December 7	Ols	*Virginia & Joan*	Isles of Shoals, NH
1937			
	Sch	*Cora F Cressy*	Medomuk, ME
January 8	Gas	*Triton*	Kittery, ME
February 22	Sts	*Benjamin B Odell*	Newport, RI

DATE LOST	TYPE	NAME	WHERE LOST
April 12	St	*City Of St Louis*	Fishers Island, NY
June 5	Sbge	*L&W-B C Co # 9*	Warwick, RI
July 3	Gas	*Louise*	Watch Hill, RI
August 7	Ols	*Adverse*	Off Pollock Rip, MA
August 30	Gas	*Spray*	Narragansett Bay, RI
October 24	Sch	*Doghouse*	Gloucester, MA

1938

	Bge	Unidentified	Deer Island, ME
January 13	Ols	*William S*	Pollock Rip, MA
March 3	Bge	*# 19*	Scituate, MA
April 20	Gas	*Water Nymph*	Marthas Vineyard, MA
April 22	Ols	*City Of Salisbury*	Boston, MA
April 26	Gas	*David K Akin*	Newport, RI
April 26	St	*Malmaton*	Off Block Island, RI
May 9	Gas	*Jennie T*	Off Block Island, RI
May 14	Sch	*Quita*	City Island, NY
May 15	Sch	*Stewart Salter*	Offshore, ME
May 28	Sbge	*Cullen # 18*	Searsport, ME
May 28		*Mandalay*	New York Bay, NY
May 31	Ols	*Etta K*	Pollock Rip, MA
July 9	Ols	*Kingfisher*	Newport, RI
July 24	Ols	*Uncle Sam*	Gloucester, MA
August 6	Gas	*Intrepid*	Nantucket, MA
August 26	Gas	*Liria*	Off Scituate, MA
September	Bge	(Unnamed)	Cuttyhunk, MA
September	Bge	(Unnamed)	Cuttyhunk, MA
September	Sts	*Monhegan*	Narragansett Bay, RI
September 2	Gas	*Nettie*	Narragansett Bay, RI
September 21	Gas	*Albert*	Block Island, RI
September 21	Gas	*Arrow*	Narragansett Bay, RI
September 21	Gas	*Avenger*	Newport, RI
September 21	Stp	*Beaver Tail*	Narragansett Bay, RI
September 21	Gas	*Bidgee*	Narragansett Bay, RI
September 21	Bge	*C A Meister*	Gloucester, MA
September 21	Ols	*Charles O Carlson*	Nantucket Shoals, MA
September 21	Gas	*Clayton II*	Block Island, RI
September 21	Gas	*Columbia*	Nantucket Sound, MA
September 21	Gas	*Doris M*	Beverley, MA
September 21	Ols	*Emilia D*	Block Island, RI
September 21	Ycht	*Faith*	Gloucester, MA
September 21	Gas	*Farwye*	Warwick, RI
September 21	Gas	*Fauna*	Warwick, RI
September 21	Gas	*Firenze*	Narragansett Bay, RI
September 21	Gas	*Florence F*	Block Island, RI
September 21	Sts	*Gaspee*	Providence, RI
September 21	Gas	*Henry Warren*	Buzzards Bay, MA
September 21	Sch	*Jean & Joyce*	Easthampton, NY
September 21	Bge	*Jess B Shaw*	Fall River, MA
September 21	Gas	*June*	Narragansett Bay, RI
September 21	Sch	*Lizzie J Cox*	Bristol, RI
September 21	Gas	*Maria*	Warren, RI
September 21	Gas	*Migrant*	Narragansett Bay, RI
September 21	Gas	*Myrtie E*	Greenwich, RI
September 21	Gas	*Nina*	Narragansett Bay, RI
September 21	Sts	*Ocean View*	Madison, CT
September 21	Gas	*Onwego*	Point Judith, RI
September 21	Gas	*Oriole*	Narragansett Bay, RI
September 21	Gas	*Petrel*	Narragansett Bay, RI

DATE LOST	TYPE	NAME	WHERE LOST
September 21	Gas	*Pilgrim*	Providence, RI
September 21	Gas	*Placidia*	Newport, RI
September 21	Gas	*Roberta*	Greenwich, RI
September 21	Gas	*Samoset*	Block Island, RI
September 21	Ols	*Shadow*	Narragansett Bay, RI
September 21		*Tacoma*	Montauk, NY
September 21	Gas	*Two Friends*	Block Island, RI
September 21		Unidentified	Gardiners Bay, NY
September 21	Gas	*Waliean*	Narragansett Bay, RI
September 21	Ols	*Winifred*	New Bedford, MA
September 22	Bge	*Serina*	Gloucester, MA
September 31	Sch	*Thomas H Lawrence*	New Bedford, MA
October 19	Ols	*Mary A*	Pollock Rip, MA
November 15	Ols	*Valencia*	Nantucket Shoals, MA
November 18	Ols	*Sally Lee*	Buzzards Bay, MA
December 7	Gas	*Princeps*	Cape Small, ME
December 10	Ols	*Andover*	Orleans, MA
December 10	Gas	*Perseverance*	Providence, RI
December 12	Gas	*Isabella*	Cohasset, MA

1939

		Flora	Ipswich, MA
		Madeline	Ipswich, MA
		Thomas Lawrence	Vinalhaven, ME
January 17	Sch	*Laura A Barnes*	Nantucket, MA
January 22	Bge	*Bouker No 65*	East River, NY
January 22	Bge	*Bouker No 70*	East River, NY
February 10	Sts	*Lightburn*	Block Island, RI
April 27		*Sandy Hook*	Off New York, NY
May 19	Gas	*Pilot*	East River, NY
July	Gas	*Little Fred*	Newport, RI
July 18	Gas	*Thelma*	Friendship, ME
September 18	Sbge	*Henry Endicott*	Off Plymouth, MA
September 21	Ols	*Ariel*	Off Nantucket, MA
September 26	Bge	*Commerce*	Sakonnet, RI
November 24	Ols	*Mary G*	Nomansland Island, MA

1940

	Sch	*Alice L Pendleton*	Noank, CT
	Sch	*Courtney C Houck*	Boothbay Harbor, ME
		Seguin	Kennebeck River, ME
		Tarpon	Truro, MA
		Unidentified	Barnstable, MA
	Ols	Unidentified	Portland, ME
	Ols	Unidentified	Portland, ME
January 10	Ols	*Hoop-La*	Off Duxbury, MA
January 24	Sch	*Emma*	Penobscot Bay, ME
February 5	St	*Denville*	Staten Island, NY
February 5	Ols	*S H 5*	Brooklyn, NY
February 6	Sts	*Peter Smith*	Great Captains Is, CT
February 7	Ols	*Shirly Clattenburg*	Nomansland Island, MA
February 14	Ols	*Sunflower*	Narragansett Bay, RI
February 15	Gas	*Pinta*	Cape Elizabeth, ME
February 26	Gas	*Arabell*	Block Island, RI
April 1	Gas	*Lona*	Providence, RI
April 15	Sch	*Ella Eudora*	Vinalhaven, ME
May 22	Gas	*Trim Too*	Marblehead, MA
June 2	Bge	*Cyclone*	Portland, ME

ABOVE: Today's deep diving equipment and depth limits are far more advanced than those used in the 1930's. Shown above is the dive team on board the sub tender *Falcon* during the rescue of the crew of the submarine *Squalus* off the coast of New Hampshire on May 24, 1939. Although the submarine was later raised, during these dives thirty-three of the fifty-nine men aboard were rescued. **BELOW:** Shortly after her sinking, the *Essex* lay with her decks almost awash off the lighthouse at Southeast Point, Block Island. Although many wrecks in this depth of water were refloated, this section of coastline is rugged and exposed to prevailing southwest winds. The *Essex* was never fully salvaged. *Photos from the collection of William P. Quinn, Orleans MA.*

DATE LOST	TYPE	NAME	WHERE LOST
July 8	Gas	Venture	Rockport, MA
August 3	Gas	Ruth	Buzzards Bay, MA
September 6	Ycht	Acacia	Off Portland, ME
September 20	Sch	George Gress	Bar Harbor, ME
November 24	Sts	Mary Arnold	Off Block Island, RI
December 4	Bge	Katherine Howard	Quonochontaug, RI
December 4	Bge	Thomas H Oleary	Quonochontaug, RI
December 7	Ols	H C Splane	Lynn, MA
December 13	Ols	J A Reynolds	New York, NY

1941

	Ols	Ruth Lucille	Ipswich, MA
January 21	Ols	Mary E O'Hara	Boston, MA
March 8	Gas	On Time	Duxbury, MA
March 15	Ols	Mary	Boston, MA
March 18	Sts	Student Prince II	Fire Island, NY
May 15	Ols	Q 11	East River, NY
May 24	Ols	Rosie P	Ipswich, MA
June 16	Sub	P-39	Offshore, ME
June 20	Sub	O-9	Off Isle Shoals, NH
August 12	Bge	Taylor	Newport, RI
August 18	Sts	Panuco	New York, NY
August 22	Sts	Aurora	Hudson River, NY
August 30		Schula	Jones Beach Inlet, NY
September 26	Sts	Essex	Block Island, RI
September 29	Gas	River Bank	Ipswich, MA
October 28	Ols	Beret J	Marthas Vineyard, MA
November 11	Sts	J J Rudolph	Brooklyn, NY
November 17		St Ann	Provincetown, MA
December 10	Ols	Oregon	Nantucket Shoals, MA
December 17	Sts	Col Wm. B Corwin	Off Boston, MA

1942

	Bge	(Unnamed)	Cuttyhunk, MA
	Bge	(Unnamed)	Long Island, ME
	Gas	Unidentified	Marthas Vineyard, MA
	Sts	Eagle Boat	Cuttyhunk, MA
	Sts	PC	Hen & Chickens Reef, MA
	Ols	Unidentified	Buzzards Bay, MA
	Bge	Unidentified	Buzzards Bay, MA
	Gas	Vamoose	Cape Cod Canal, MA
	Ols	William Putnam	Provincetown, MA
January	Sch	Aigrette	Cape Ann, MA
January 1	Gas	Diablesse	Brooksville, ME
January 6	Ols	Queen Of Fernandinia	Buzzards Bay, MA
January 14	Sts	Norness	Nantucket Shoals, MA
January 15	Sts	Coimbra	Shinnecock, NY
January 23	Sts	Thirley	Offshore, ME
February 10	Ols	Continent	Off New York, NY
February 13	Sts	Dixie Sword	Pollock Rip, MA
February 15	Ols	Point Breeze	Long Island Sound
February 16	Ols	Fannie S	Nomansland Island, MA
February 25	Ols	Liberty	North River, NY
March	Sch	Maude M Morey	Casco Bay, ME
March		Ran Ells	Rockland, ME
March	Sch	Zebedee E Cliff	Casco Bay, ME
March 5	Sts	Collamer	Offshore, ME
April 2	Ols	Osceala	Off Truro, MA

DATE LOST	TYPE	NAME	WHERE LOST
April 9	Ols	*Lulu L*	Truro, MA
April 28	Ols	*Arundo*	Off New York, NY
April 30	Ols	*Bidevind*	Off New York, NY
May 4	Sts	*Empire Story*	Offshore, ME
May 9	Bge	*Edith*	Frankfort, ME
May 17	Sts	*Skottland*	Offshore, ME
May 30	Ols	*Liverpool Packet*	Offshore, ME
June 15	Sts	*Cherokee*	Off Cape Cod, MA
June 15	Sts	*Port Nicholson*	Off Cape Cod, MA
June 28	Sts	*Stephen R Jones*	Cape Cod Canal, MA
July 3	Sts	*Alexander Macomb*	Off New England
July 3	Sub	Unidentified	Off New England
July 6	Bge	*Mary B Howard*	Buzzards Bay, MA
July 7	Sts	*William Machen*	Isles of Shoals, NH
August 9	Bge	*L&W-B C Co # 1*	Salem, MA
August 24	Sbge	*Vale Royal*	Sandwich, MA
September 13	Sts	*Mars*	Off Plymouth, MA
September 22	Ols	*Pentland Firth*	Rockaway Inlet, NY
October 20	Ols	*Santa Rita*	Gloucester, MA
October 24	Ols	*Dominion Halsyd*	Boone Island, ME
November 7	Ols	*Rose*	Off Block Island, RI
November 11	Bge	*L&W-B C Co #15*	Block Island, RI
November 11	Bge	Unidentified	Off Block Island, RI
November 19	Ols	*Francis*	Provincetown, MA
December 1	Ols	*Ioannis P Goulandos*	Off New York, NY
December 2	Gas	*Kathie C*	Provincetown, MA
December 11	Ols	*Theresa & Dan*	Wellfleet, MA

1943

		Unidentified	Hyannis, MA
February 28	Bge	Unidentified	Southold, NY
February 28	Bge	Unidentified	Southold, NY
March 5	Sts	*Hartwelson*	Bantam Rock, ME
March 6	Sts	*D M Monroe*	Libby Islands, ME
March 20	Ols	*Adventurer II*	Boston, MA
April	Ols	*Idle Hour*	Gloucester, MA
May 2	Ols	*CG 58012*	Off Plymouth, MA
July 15	Bge	*L&W-B C Co #12*	Newport, RI
August 17	Ols	*Sprig*	Narragansett Bay, RI
August 17	Ols	*St Rosalie*	Monhegan Island, ME
October 1	Bge	*Alice Sheridan*	New York, NY
October 14	Sbge	*Winnegance*	Off Provincetown, MA
October 26	Sts	*James Longstreet*	Cape Cod Bay, MA
November 11	Gas	*Reliance*	Nomansland Island, MA
November 12	Ols	*YC 857*	Off Cape Cod, MA
November 17	Gas	*Lizzie H*	Off Block Island, RI
December 5	Ols	*Richard J*	Gloucester, MA
December 8	Gas	*Queen*	Newport, RI
December 11	Sts	*Suffolk*	Nantucket Shoals, MA

1944

February 11	Sts	*Calusa*	Oak Island, NY
February 11	Sts	*Empire Knight*	Boone Island, ME
February 20	Ols	*YC 523*	Portsmouth, NH
February 22	Gas	*PT-200*	Off Block Island, RI
March 7	Sts	*Herman Winter*	Marthas Vineyard, MA
April 16	Sub	*U-550*	Nantucket Shoals
May		*Antonia*	Buzzards Bay, MA

DATE LOST	TYPE	NAME	WHERE LOST
May 11	Ols	YF 415	Boston, MA
June 19	Gas	Ada Velma	Narragansett Bay, RI
June 29	Ols	Valor-AMC 108	Westport, MA
July 4	Ols	Turner	Off New York, NY
July 22	Ols	Unidentified	Staten Island, NY
August		Unidentified	Hampton Beach, NH
August 18	Bge	A H Olwine	Newport, RI
August 23	Bge	Manokin	Buzzards Bay, MA
September 11	Ols	Marie & Eleanor	Marthas Vineyard, MA
September 12	Gas	Millie	Hyannis, MA
September 14	Ols	Alma Bell	New Bedford, MA
September 14	Ols	Dorothy	Plymouth, MA
September 14	Gas	Jet	Chatham, MA
September 14	Ols	Marion Dorothy	New Bedford, MA
September 14		Richmond	Bay Ridge, NY
September 14	Gas	Seminole	Fall River, MA
September 14	Sts	Vineyard	Vineyard Sound, MA
September 15	Gas	Kingsdale	Narragansett Bay, RI
September 15	Gas	Mildred	Marthas Vineyard, MA
September 21		Choapa	New York, NY
November 16	Ols	Wathen	Sandwich, MA
November 17	Sbge	Pottstown	Sandwich, MA
November 21	Sbge	Franklin Pierce	Sandwich, MA
November 21	Sbge	Glenside	Sandwich, MA
December 3	Sts	Cornwallis	Long Island, ME
December 28	Bge	Marie Hooper	Sakonnet, RI

1945

DATE LOST	TYPE	NAME	WHERE LOST
		Neptune	Sandwich, MA
	Sub	S-21	Offshore, ME
	Sts	Vinalhaven	Owls Head, ME
January 11	Bge	L&W-B C Co #11	Off Boston, MA
January 11	Ols	Yms 14	Boston, MA
February 4		Orville Hardin	Ambrose Channel, NY
February 5	Ols	Alice & Jennie	Block Island, RI
February 17	Bge	Annapolis	Off Block Island, RI
April	Ols	Unidentified	Block Island, RI
April 6	Ols	Nathanial Palmer	Off Block Island, RI
April 23	Ols	P E-56	Cape Elizabeth, ME
April 29	Gas	Sevenovus	Plymouth, MA
May		Escort	Nantucket Shoals, MA
May 5	Sts	Black Point	Off Rhode Island
May 5	Sub	U-853	Off Block Island, RI
May 14		Unidentified	Buzzards Bay, MA
June 11	Ols	Ayurvoca	Off New York, NY
June 26	Gas	Intrepid II	Sandwich, MA
June 26	Gas	Little David	Marthas Vineyard, MA
July 11	Gas	Rose Marie	Off Provincetown, MA
July 13	Sts	Saint Francis	Buzzards Bay, MA
July 24	Sub	USS Bass	Off Block Island, RI
September 14	Ols	Grace & Rosalie	Cranberry Islands, ME
September 20	Gas	Manela	Bath, ME
September 24	Ols	Cayadetta	Gloucester, MA
November 3	Ols	Winfred Martin	Off Chatham, MA
November 13	Gas	Wild Cat	Piscataqua River, NH
November 20	Gas	Ranger	Owls Head, ME
November 29	Ols	Bethulia	Salem, MA
November 29	Ols	Colombo	Manchester, MA
November 30	Ols	Saint Paul	Gloucester, MA

During World War II many parts of the northeast were under "blackout conditions" to prevent U-Boats from getting nighttime sightings. It was the lack of navigation lights that caused the collision between the freighter *Oregon*, shown here, and the battleship *New Mexico* on December 10, 1941, near the New York approach channel. She settled into twenty fathoms with a valuable cargo of wool and manganese. *Photo courtesy U.S. Coast Guard* **BELOW:** The *James Longstreet* was towed into Cape Cod Bay in 1944 to be used as a target ship for the airborne military. Originally a liberty ship used in World War II, she had a short career and is rapidly deteriorating from the effect of thousands of rounds of rockets, automatic weapons fire and target bombs. *Photo from the collection of William P. Quinn, Orleans MA.*

ABOVE: On February 10, 1939 the *Lightburn* ran onto the rocks at Block Island, RI. Salvage was attempted but she proved hopelessly damaged by her grounding. The *Lightburn* is a popular sport diving shipwreck. Her hull is just visible from the cliffs at Southeast Point. *Photo courtesy Paul Morris, Nantucket MA.* **BELOW:** The March storm of 1947 took the lives of 23 men when the *Pemiquid II* and the *Novadoc* sank. Remarkably, no one was lost from the crew of the *Oakey L. Alexander*, shown here. Built in 1915, the *Oakey* battled this storm until her hull plates buckled and she broke in half. The crew was in the stern half when the bow fell away and the captain beached her on the rocky Maine shore. Viewing this photo one can imagine the vulnerability of the early wooden vessels when encountering a storm sea near shore. *Photo from the collection of William P. Quinn, Orleans MA.*

DATE LOST	TYPE	NAME	WHERE LOST
December 10	Ols	*A Piatt Andrew*	Off Block Island, RI
December 10	Ols	*Nobadeer*	Elizabeth Islands, MA

1946

	Sch	Unidentified	Buzzards Bay, MA
January		*Nashawena*	Buzzards Bay, MA
January 25	Ols	*E-C*	Block Island, RI
January 25		*Maid Of All Work*	Vinalhaven, ME
January 26	Bge	*James Sheridan*	Off Rhode Island
January 29	Gas	*Roswell P*	Off Newport, RI
January 29	Sts	*Stephen F Austin*	Bellport, NY
February 5	Sub	*U-805*	Off Massachusetts
February 5	Sub	*U-1228*	Off Massachusetts
February 14	Bge	*Lake Crystal*	Watch Hill, RI
March 5	Ols	*Klondike*	Watch Hill, RI
March 6	Ols	*Barbara Tee*	Block Island, RI
March 23	Gas	*Midnight Sun*	Marblehead, MA
April	Ols	*Evelyn G Sears*	Gloucester, MA
April		Unidentified	Plymouth, MA
April 2	Sts	*Charles S Haight*	Cape Ann, MA
April 16	Sch	*Brina P Pendleton*	Boston, MA
July 6	Sch	*Escape*	Off New York, NY
July 21	Ols	*Donald & Johnny*	Orleans, MA
August 1	Gas	*Akbar*	Watch Hill, RI
August 7	Ols	*Anna*	Sandwich, MA
August 13		*Red Sail*	Montauk, NY
August 15	Bge	*L&W-B C Co #10*	Fall River, MA
August 17	Ols	*Paladin*	Off Chatham, MA
August 18	Ols	*Dagmar*	Cuttyhunk, MA
September 22	Ols	*Mary Grace*	Off Chatham, MA
October 5	Gas	*Furious Duchess*	Block Island, RI
October 24	Gas	*Chapoquoit*	Buzzards Bay, MA
November 13	Sub	*U-977*	Off Massachusetts
November 26	Ols	*Anna C*	Buzzards Bay, MA
December	Bge	Unidentified	Southold, NY
December 2	Sbge	*Winsor*	Off Scituate, MA
December 11	Ols	*Mill Rock*	East River, NY
December 23	Gas	*Spendthrift*	Narragansett Bay, RI
December 28	Ols	*Liberty II*	Gardiners Island, NY

1947

	Ols	*Harold Grinnel*	Nomansland Island, MA
January 20	Gas	*Eclipse*	Watch Hill, RI
January 21	Sbge	*Sherwood*	Buzzards Bay, MA
February 10	Gas	*H & H*	Boston, MA
March 1	Sts	*Novadoc*	Offshore, ME
March 3	Sts	*Oakey Alexander*	Cape Elizabeth, ME
March 3	Ols	*Pemiquid II*	Off Seguin, ME
March 7		*John Ericsson*	North River, NY
March 18	Ols	*Invader*	East River, NY
June 24	Sts	Unidentified	Fire Island, NY
July 1		*Ronald & Dorothy*	Block Island, RI
July 5	Gas	*Fifty-Fifty*	Duxbury, MA
August 17		*Margo V*	Montauk, NY
September 20	Gas	*Maureen*	Newport, RI
September 21	Gas	*Tyee*	Newport, RI
October	Ols	*Harvey*	Nomansland Island, MA
October 12	Gas	*Billie Boy*	Cape Cod Bay, MA

DATE LOST	TYPE	NAME	WHERE LOST
October 28	Ols	*Charles M Fauci II*	Provincetown, MA
November 12	Gas	*Sea Hawk II*	Narragansett Bay, RI
November 12	Ols	*Uncle John*	Buzzards Bay, MA
November 16	Ols	*Alert*	Sandwich, MA
November 20	Sub	*U-234*	Off Massachusetts
November 20	Sub	*U-530*	Off Massachusetts
November 20	Sub	*U-858*	Off Massachusetts
November 20	Sub	*U-889*	Off Massachusetts
November 28	Ols	*Mermaid*	Elizabeth Islands, MA

1948

DATE LOST	TYPE	NAME	WHERE LOST
	Ols	*Annabelle R*	Narragansett Bay, RI
		Unidentified	Wellfleet, MA
January 12	Gas	*Vincie*	Gloucester, MA
March 6	Ols	*Cape Ann*	Eastham, MA
March 10	Ols	*Smilyn*	Nomansland Island, MA
March 26	Gas	*Provincetown Socony*	Provincetown, MA
May 11		*Flying Fish*	Plymouth, MA
June 9	Ols	*Nashawena*	Nomansland Island, MA
July 31	Gas	*Temorangerie*	Hyannis, MA
September 29	Ols	*Connecticut*	Vineyard Sound, MA
November 5	Ols	*D T Sheridan*	Monhegan Island, ME
November 8	Ols	*Fannie Belle*	Offshore, ME

1949

DATE LOST	TYPE	NAME	WHERE LOST
		Unidentified	Long Island, ME
January 8	Ols	*Bethlehem*	Barnstable, MA
January 23	Ols	*Elsie*	Off Provincetown, MA
February 9		Unidentified	Off Block Island, RI
February 10	Ols	*Alberta*	Provincetown, MA
May 1	Ols	*Baby Doll*	Buzzards Bay, MA
May 3	Ols	*Red Skin*	Rockland, ME
June 22	Ols	*Doris*	Newport, RI
June 24	Ols	*Fan And Mary*	Buzzards Bay, MA
July 31	Ols	*Ramona*	Nantucket Shoals, MA
August 5	Ols	*St Christopher*	Offshore, ME
August 29	Ols	*Gay Head*	Nantucket Shoals, MA
October 1	Ols	*Venture II*	Off Truro, MA
October 2	Ols	*Fannie Parnell*	Buzzards Bay, MA
October 13	Ols	*Mary S*	Casco Bay, ME
November 2	Ols	*Beatrice & Rose*	Cape Ann, MA
December 27	Bge	*Tennessee*	Vineyard Sound, MA

1950

DATE LOST	TYPE	NAME	WHERE LOST
		Alice May	New Bedford, MA
	Ols	*Saint John*	Off Rhode Island
January 18	Ols	*Stormy Weather*	Quonochontaug, RI
March 18	Bge	*Sea Wave*	Off New York, NY
April 7	Ols	*Four Sisters*	Pollock Rip, MA
April 7	Ols	*William Landry*	Pollock Rip, MA
June 3	Ols	*Mary A*	Ragged Island, ME
July 2	Drge	*Sandcraft*	New York, NY
July 30	Ols	*Charles A Smith*	Baileys Island, ME
July 31	Ols	*Arthur D*	Thatchers Island, MA
August 5	Gas	*Peanuts*	Ipswich, MA
August 17	Ols	*Ellen H Jean*	Nantucket, MA
September 12	Ols	*Theresa A*	Nantucket Shoals, MA

DATE LOST	TYPE	NAME	WHERE LOST
September 14	Ols	*Muriel & Russell*	Chatham, MA
November	Ols	*Curlew*	Gloucester, MA
November	Gas	*Victor XVI*	Newburyport, MA
November 16	Bge	*Arco # 8*	Boston, MA
December 5	Ols	*Alice J Hathaway*	Nantucket Shoals, MA
December 29	Ols	*Fred Henry*	Nomansland Island, MA

1951

January 17	Bge	*B-S #94*	Buzzards Bay, MA
January 27	Bge	Unidentified	Buzzards Bay, MA
February 3	Ols	*Rita & Olive*	Off Block Island, RI
February 19	Ols	*Penguin*	Off Block Island, RI
March 23	Gas	*Elmer S*	Provincetown, MA
March 28	Ols	*North Star*	Mt Desert, ME
April 1	Fery	*Elizabeth Ann*	New London, CT
May 30	Ols	*Jessie Dutra*	Nomansland Island, MA
July	Sch	*Snetind*	Broad Sound, MA
July 24	Ols	*Sol*	Offshore, ME
July 28	Ols	*Betty B*	Lower Bay, NY
August 25	Gas	*Jana*	Narragansett Bay, RI
August 28	Ols	*Nancy F*	Off Truro, MA
September 1	Ols	*Frank Grinnell*	Nomansland Island, MA
September 1	Ols	*Pelican*	Montauk Point, NY
September 5	Gas	*Charmter*	Long Island Sound
September 29	Ols	*Avocet*	Ipswich, MA
October 9	Ols	*Snapper*	Off Block Island, RI
October 31	Gas	*Ski-bum IV*	Cohasset, MA
November 27	Ols	*Mary M*	Cuttyhunk, MA
December 9	Ols	*Frankie And Rose*	Cape Ann, MA
December 22	Ols	*Eliza C Riggs*	Salem, MA

1952

January 18	Ols	*Mary Jo*	Cape Cod Bay, MA
February 14	Ols	*Paolina*	Nantucket Shoals, MA
February 18	Sts	*Fort Mercer*	Off Chatham, MA
February 18	El s	*Pendleton*	Off Chatham, MA
March 11	Ols	*Anna C Perry*	Off Nantucket, MA
March 12	Ols	*Bernie & Bessie*	Off Rhode Island
March 26	Ols	*Nahant*	Buzzards Bay, MA
May 9		*Lucky Lucy*	Gloucester, MA
June 2	Bge	*Arco # 7*	Buzzards Bay, MA
June 20	Ols	*Albatross*	Off Cape Cod, MA
August 13	Gas	*Sally Ann*	Nantucket Sound, MA
August 25	Gas	*Arrah Wanna*	Plymouth, MA

1953

	Sts	(Unnamed)	Cuttyhunk, MA
January 15	Ols	*Mellena II*	Ipswich, MA
March 26	Ols	*Mishaum*	Buzzards Bay, MA
April 14	Ols	*Pat-er-glo*	Provincetown, MA
April 28	Ols	*Alert III*	Buzzards Bay, MA
May	Bge	*Mayflower*	South Dartmouth, MA
May 8	Ols	*St Bernadette*	Mt Desert, ME
May 15	Bge	Unidentified	Off New York
May 18	Ols	*Marietta & Mary*	Off Truro, MA
June 5	Sch	*Southern Cross*	Sagaponack, NY
June 28	Ols	*Cape Cod*	Nomansland Island, MA

DATE LOST	TYPE	NAME	WHERE LOST
August 8		Unidentified	Portsmouth, NH
September 1	Ols	Marsala	Off Chatham, MA
September 5	Bge	McKie #12	Gloucester, MA
September 6	Ols	Jenny & Julia	Gloucester, MA
September 18	Ols	Carmac	Watch Hill, RI
September 21	Ols	Irene	Eastham, MA
September 24	Ols	Harold	Watch Hill, RI
October 4	Ols	Little Nancy	Off Truro, MA
October 11		Freda M	Montauk, NY
November 6	Gas	Elsie Howard	Provincetown, MA
November 7	Ols	Stella	Provincetown, MA
November 10	Ols	Superior	Gloucester, MA
November 18	Ols	Francis J Manta	Nantucket Shoals, MA
November 27	Ols	J L Stanley & Sons	Off Eastham, MA
December 3	Ols	Clara Louise	Boone Island, ME
December 23	Gas	R J	Elizabeth Islands, MA

1954

DATE LOST	TYPE	NAME	WHERE LOST
	Gas	Jim	Buzzards Bay, MA
	Gas	Keystone	Off Rhode Island
January 14	Ols	Verdon	East River, NY
February 12	Ols	Clara T	Block Island, RI
February 22		Three Joys	Shinnecock, NY
March 25	Ols	Junojaes	Nantucket Shoals, MA
June 30		Mike Ahoy	Montauk, NY
August	Gas	Debbie II	New Bedford, MA
August 31	Bge	(Unnamed)	Hyannis, MA
August 31	Gas	Ace	Hull, MA
August 31	Gas	Ann	Nahant, MA
August 31	Gas	Austral	Manchester, MA
August 31	Gas	Avanti	Padanaram, MA
August 31	Bge	BC-2890	Searsport, ME
August 31	Gas	Carlton S	Block Island, RI
August 31	Gas	Cinzana II	Narragansett Bay, RI
August 31	Gas	Clytie III	Narragansett Bay, RI
August 31	Gas	Coral Sea	Narragansett Bay, RI
August 31	Gas	Courier II	Padanaram, MA
August 31	Ols	Eddie B Blount	Narragansett Bay, RI
August 31	Gas	Evelyn Ruth	Beverley, MA
August 31		Friendship II	Nantucket Shoals, MA
August 31	Gas	Gertrude D	Lynn, MA
August 31	Gas	Grace And Lucy	Falmouth, MA
August 31	Gas	Hi Jo	Scituate, MA
August 31	Gas	Hope	Narragansett Bay, RI
August 31	Gas	Idle Hours	Narragansett Bay, RI
August 31	Ols	Kay	Narragansett Bay, RI
August 31	Gas	Maviet	Newport, RI
August 31	Gas	Menikoe V	Padanaram, MA
August 31	Gas	Mildred M	Narragansett Bay, RI
August 31	Gas	Mohawk	Marblehead, MA
August 31	Ols	New Moon II	Falmouth, MA
August 31	Gas	Off Shore	Narragansett Bay, RI
August 31	Gas	Patsy	Providence, RI
August 31	Ols	Redstart	Nantucket Shoals, MA
August 31	Ols	Rose Mary Mello	New Bedford, MA
August 31	Ols	Ruth W	Point Judith, RI
August 31	Gas	Trull	Marblehead, MA
August 31	Gas	Tudor Rose	Lynn, MA
September 7	Sts	Express	Bedloes Island, NY

The most prolific shipwreck rumors in the northeast are those of sunken U-Boats with mercury ballast and Third Reich gold on board. Almost every harbor along the coast has an old timer who knows "...someone who saw a U-Boat sink a few miles offshore here" at the end of the war. In truth there are only a few U-Boats sunk off the northeast coast including seven sunk by the U.S. Navy during the post year wars. Shown above is the U-234 being sunk during an ASW torpedo test on November 20, 1947. *Photo from the collection of William P. Quinn, Orleans MA.*

DATE LOST	TYPE	NAME	WHERE LOST
September 18	Ols	*Norland*	Barnstable, MA
October 23	Gas	*Nomrah*	Nahant, MA
November 15	Bge	*Phillip R*	New Bedford, MA
November 24	Ols	*Nancy S*	Off Block Island, RI

1955

February 10	Bge	*# 101*	Quonochontaug, RI
April 23	Ols	*Novelty*	Ipswich, MA
June 4	Ols	*Sea Prince*	Cape Cod Bay, MA
August	Gas	*Mariner*	Quincy, MA
August 17	Ols	*Shirley & Susan*	Nomansland Island, MA
August 23	Sch	*Shag*	Nahant, MA
September 4	Sch	*Star Of The Sea*	Hempstead, NY
September 10	Ols	*Santo Antonina*	Gloucester, MA
September 15	Ols	*California II*	Cape Ann, MA
September 18	Ols	*Little Star*	Block Island, RI
November 4	Ols	*Cornell*	Hudson River, NY
November 20	Sts	*Daytona*	Cape Cod Bay, MA

1956

	Gas	*Mariner*	Buzzards Bay, MA
January 24	Sch	*Snow Maiden*	Plymouth, MA
March 17	Ols	*Onward*	New Bedford, MA
May 3	Ols	*Palastine*	Vineyard Sound, MA
May 20	Gas	*Escape II*	East River, NY
May 26	Ols	*Saint Francis*	Off Eastham, MA
June 8	Gas	*Catherine C*	Ipswich, MA
July 12	Ols	*William D*	Point Judith, RI
July 25	Ols	*Andrea Doria*	Nantucket Shoals, MA
August 1	Ols	*Annie & Josie*	Off Eastham, MA
September 8	Ols	*Mayflower*	Duxbury, MA
September 26	Ols	*Roberta Dee*	Off Rhode Island
November 8		*Agda*	Off New York

The 656 foot Italian luxury liner *SS Andrea Doria* was one of the largest passenger wrecks off the northeast coast. Here in the last stages of sinking she lies on her starboard side with her funnel touching the water. An empty life boat is at the mercy of the tides in the foreground. Now laying in 240 feet of water, with her upper side at a depth of just over 160 feet the wreck is a popular deep dive for sport divers. *Photo from the collection of William P. Quinn, Orleans MA*

Mountainous seas and hurricane force winds tore two ships apart on the same day off Massachusetts on February 18, 1952. The *Pendleton* and the *Fort Mercer* were tankers that were similar in construction. The bow of the *Pendleton* was towed into port and her stern grounded near shore at Chatham, Massachusetts. In the picture above, the U.S. Coast Guard is rescuing the survivors from the bow of the *Fort Mercer*. Later, this section of ship was sunk by gunfire. Seventy of the eighty-four men on the two vessels were saved. The hull of the *Fort Mercer* rises high off the bottom in clear, cold Atlantic waters 10 miles from shore. *Photo from the collection of William P. Quinn, Orleans MA.*

Suggested Reading

Albion, Robert G. *New England and The Sea.* Mystic, CT: Mystic Seaport Museum, 1972.

Albion, Robert G. *The Rise of The Port Of New York.* New York, NY: Charles Scribner's & Sons, 1939.

Allen, Everett S. *The Black Ships: Rumrunners of Prohibition.* Toronto, Canada: Little, Brown and Co., 1979.

Allen, Gardener W. *Our Navy And The West Indian Pirates.* Salem, MA: Essex Institute, 1929

American Seamen's Friend, *Sailor's Magazine and Naval Journal.* (Volumes VIII, X and XI), New York, NY: American Seamen's Friends Society, 1836-1839.

Archibald, E. H. H. *The Fighting Ship of the Royal Navy.* New York, NY: Military Press, 1987.

Bachand, Robert G. *Scuba Northeast.* (Volumes I and II), Milwaukee, WI: Rowe Publications, 1982.

Ballard, Robert D. *The Discovery of the Titanic.* New York, NY: Warner Madison Press, 1987.

Barnett, J. P. *The Lifesaving Guns of David Lyle.* Washington, D.C.: Company of Military Historians, 1974.

Bass, George F. *Archaeology Beneath the Sea: A Personal Account.* New York, NY: Harper & Row, 1976.

Bass, George F. *A History of Seafaring.* New York, NY: Walker and Company, 1972.

Bass, George F. *Ships and Shipwrecks of the Americas.* New York, N.Y.: Thames and Hudson, 1988.

Berg, Daniel. *Wreck Valley.* Lynbrook, NY: Aqua Explorers, 1986.

Boudriot, Jean. *The Seventy Four Gun Ship.* (Volumes I, II, III and IV), Annapolis, MD: The Naval Institute Press, 1986.

Bunting, W.H. *Portrait Of A Port.* Cambridge, MA: Harvard University Press, 1971.

Carse, Robert. *The Twilight of Sailing Ships.* New York, NY: Grosset & Dunlap, 1966.

Chapelle, Howard I. *The History Of American Sailing Ships*. New York, NY: Bonanza Books,1935.

Cole, F. W.*A Familiarization With Lateral or Side-Scanning Sonars*. Dobbs Ferry, NY: Hudson Labratories, 1968.

Colledge, J.J. *Ships Of The Royal Navy*. Annapolis, MD: Naval Institute Press, 1987.

Colton, J. F. *Last Of The Square Rigged Ships*. New York, NY: G. P. Putnams Sons, 1937.

Cox, Bernard. *Paddle Steamers*. Dorset, England: Blandford Press, 1979.

Craig, John D. *Danger is My Business*. New York, NY: Simon and Schuster, 1938.

Cranston, Tony. *Disasters at Sea*. Yarmouth, MA: Tony Cranston, 1986.

Dalton, J. W. *Along the Coast*. (Volumes I and II), Boston, MA: J. W. Dalton, 1909.

Dalton, J. W. *The LifeSavers Of Cape Cod*. Boston, MA: Barta Press, 1902.

Desmond, Charles. *Wooden Ship-Building*. Vestal, NY: Vestal Press Ltd., 1984.

Dow, F. and Edmonds, E. *The Pirates Of The New England Coast 1630-1730*. New York, NY: Argosy-Antiquarian Publishers, 1968.

Engle, Eloise. *America's Maritime Heritage*. Annapolis, MD: Naval Institute Press, 1975.

Farson, Robert H. *The Cape Cod Canal*. Yarmouthport, MA: Cape Cod Historical Society, 1987.

Fleming, B. W.*The International Hydrographic Review.*(Volume 53, Number 1), January 1976.

Fleming, B. W.*Recent Developments in Side Scan Sonar Techniques*. South Africa: Central Acoustics Labratory, 1982.

Fleming, B. W. *Causes and Effects of Sonographic Distortion and Some Graphical Methods for Their Manual Correction*. South Africa: University of Cape Town.

Fish, J. P. *State of The Art Sonar Images*. Skin Diver, Los Angeles, CA: Peterson Publishing Co., January 1983.

Fish, J.P. and Carr, H.A. *Seabed Target Detectability Using Wide Area, High Speed Sonar Search Methods*. Cataumet, MA: Historical Maritime Group Of New England, 1987

Fowler, William, Jr. *Rebels Under Sail* New York, NY: Charles Scribner's Sons, 1976.

Franzen, A. *HMS KRONAN: The Search for a Great 17th Century Warship.* Stockholm: Royal Institute of Technology, 1981.

Gardener, Arthur H. *Wrecks Around Nantucket.* New Bedford, MA: Reynolds Printing, 1954.

Greenhill, Basil. *The Great Migration: Crossing the Atlantic.* Greenwich, England: National Maritime Museum, 1976.

Greenhill, Basil. *The Merchant Schooners.* (Volumes I and II), London, England: David & Charles, 1951.

Greenhill, Basil. *Problems of Ship Management and Operation: 1870-1900.* Greenwich, England: National Maritime Museum, 1972.

Greenhill, Basil. *Schooners.* London, England: B. T. Batsford Ltd., 1980

Haine, Edgar E. *Disaster At Sea.* East Brunswick, NJ: Cornwall Books, 1983

Hakluyt, Richard. *Voyages and Discoveries.* Middlesex, England: Penguin Books, 1987.

Haws, Duncan. *Maritime History of the World.* (Volumes I and II), Sussex, England: Toredo Books, 1985.

Haws, Duncan. *Ships and the Sea: A Chronological Review.* New York, NY: Thomas Y. Crowell Co., 1975.

Heckman, Richard. *Yankees Under Sail.* Dublin, NH: Yankee Inc., 1968

- (His Majesty's Stationery Office.) *British Vessels Lost at Sea: 1914-1918.* Cambridge, MA: Patrick Stephens Limited, 1979.

Holland, Francis R. *America's Lighthouses.* Mineola, NY: Dover Publications, 1987.

Howland, S. A. *Steamboat Disasters and Railroad Accidents In The United States.* Worcester, MA: Dorr, Howland & Co, 1840.

- (Humane Society.) *The Humane Society of the Commonwealth of Massachusetts.* Franklin, MA: Nathaniel Sawyer, 1908.

Johnson, Robert E. *Guardians of the Sea: History of the U. S. Coast Guard.* Annapolis, MD: Naval Institute Press, 1987.

Johnson, H and Lightfoot, F. *Maritime New York in Nineteenth Century Photographs.* New York, NY: Dover Publications, 1980.

Keatts, Henry. *Field Reference to Sunken U-Boats.* King's Point, NY: American Merchant Marine, 1987.

Keatts, Henry. *New England's Legacy of Shipwrecks.* Kings Point, NY: American Mechant Marine, 1988.

Keatts, H. and Farr, G. *Dive Into History: U-Boats.* New York, NY: Marine Museum Press, 1986.

Kittredge, Henry C. *Cape Cod: It's People and Their History*. Boston, MA: Houghton Mifflin Company,1968.

Kittredge, Henry C. *Mooncussers Of Cape Cod*. Cambridge, MA: Houghton Mifflin Company, 1937.

Laing, Alexander. *The American Heritage History of Seafaring America*. New York, NY: American Heritage, 1974.

Laurence, Frederick. *Coasting Passage*. Bath,ME: Bath Marine Museum, 1968.

Lavery, Brian. *The Arming and Fitting of English Ships of War*. Annapolis, MD: Naval Institute Press, 1987.

Lincoln, Walter B. *Underwater Search Using Side Scan Sonar*. Washington, DC: United States Coast Guard Research and Development, 1979.

Livermore, S.T. *History Of Block Island*. Block Island, RI: Block Island Committee, 1961.

Lonsdale, Adrian. *A Guide to Sunken Ships in American Waters*. Arlington, VA: Compass Publications, 1964.

Luther, B. W. *Ten Years at Ten Fathoms*. New Bedford, MA: Luther, Brad, 1970.

Luther, B. W. *New England Shipwrecks*. New Bedford,MA: Luther, Brad, 1967.

Luther, Capt. Brad. *The Vanishing Fleet*. New Bedford, MA: B. Luther, 1963.

Luther, Capt. Brad. *Wrecks Below*. New Bedford, MA: B. Luther, 1958.

MacGregor, David R. *Fast Sailing Ships, Their Design and Construction*. Annapolis, MD: Naval Institute Press, 1973.

MacGregor, David R. *Merchant Sailing Ships: 1815-1850*. London, England: Conway Maritime, 1984.

MacGregor, David R. *Merchant Sailing Ships: 1850-1875*. London, England: Conway Maritime, 1984.

MacGregor, David R. *Schooners in Four Centuries*. Hemel Herts, England: Model & Allied, 1982.

MacGregor, David R. *he Tea Clippers*. London, England: Conway Maritime, 1983.

Maddocks, Melvin. *The Atlantic Crossing*. Alexandria, VA: Time Life Books, 1981.

Manning, Samuel F. *New England Masts and the King's Broad Arrow*. Greenwich, England: National Maritime Museum, 1979.

Marriott, John. *Disaster at Sea*. New York, NY: Hippocrene Books, 1987.

Marx, Robert F. *Shipwrecks in the Americas*. New York, NY: Dover Publications, 1987.

Merryman, J. H. *The U.S. Life-Saving Service: 1880-1914*. Golden, CO: Outbooks, 1981.

Miller, J. F. *American Ships Of The Colonial and Revolutionary Period*. New York, NY: W. W. Norton & Co., 1978.

Mitchell, C. B. *Merchant Steam Vessels Of The United States: 1790-1868*. Staten Island, NY: Steamship Historical Society of America, 1975.

Morgan, Charles S. *The American Neptune: New England Coasting Schooner*. Salem, MA: Peabody Museum, 1963.

Morgan, Charles S. *Shipbuilding on the Kennebunk: The Closing Chapter*. Kennebunkport, ME: Historical Society of Kennebunkport, 1970.

Morison, Samuel E. *Maritime History of Massachusetts*. Boston,MA: Houghton Mifflin Co., 1921.

Morris, Paul C. *American Sailing Coasters of The North Atlantic*. Chardon, OH: Bloch and Osborne, 1973.

Morris, Paul C. *Four Masted Schooners of the East Coast*. Orleans, MA: Lower Cape Publishing Co., 1975.

Morris, Paul C. *Schooners and Schooner Barges*. Orleans, MA: Lower Cape Publishing Co., 1984.

National Park Service. *Artillery Through the Ages*. Washington, D.C.: National Park Service, 1956.

Natkiel, Richard. *Atlas of Maritime History*. New York, NY: Facts on File, Inc., 1986.

Noble, Dennis L. *A Legacy: The United States Life-Saving Service*. Washington, D.C.: Coast Guard Historian, 1987.

Parker, John P. *Sails Of The Maritimes*. Toronto, Canada: McGraw-Hill-Ryerson, 1976.

Perkes, Dan. *Twentieth Century Shipwrecks*. Chicago, IL: Contemporary Books, 1983.

Perley, Sidney. *Historic Storms Of New England*. Salem, MA: The Salem Press, 1891.

Peterson, Mendel. *History Under The Sea*. Washington, DC: Smithsonian Publication 4538, 1965.

Public Record Office. *American Independence: Events to 1776*. London, England: Public Record Office, 1976.

Quinn, William P. *Shipwrecks Along the Atlantic Coast*. Orleans, MA: Parnassus Imprints, 1988.

Quinn, William P. *Shipwrecks Around Cape Cod*. Farmington, ME: Knowlton & McLeary, 1973.

Quinn, William P. *Shipwrecks Around Maine*. Orleans, MA: Lower Cape Publishing, 1983.

Quinn, William P. *Shipwrecks Around New England*. Orleans, MA: Lower Cape Publishing, 1979.

Rattray, Jeanette E. *The Perils of the Port of New York*. New York, NY: Dodd, Mead & Co., 1973.

Rattray, Jeanette E. *Ship Ashore! A Record of Maritime Disasters*. New York, NY: Coward-McCann, Inc., 1955.

Reid, William. *Weapons Through the Ages*. New York, NY: Crescent Books, 1976.

Rice, George Wharton. *The Shipping Days of Old Boothbay*. Portland, ME: Southworth-Anthoense, 1938.

Rice, Howard C., Jr. *The American Campaigns of Rochambeau's Army, (Vol. I and II)*. Princeton, NJ: Princeton & Brown, 1972.

Richardson, John M. *Steamboat Lore Of the Penobscot*. Augusta, ME: Kennebec Journal, 1944.

Ridgely-Nevitt, Cedric. *American Steamships On The Atlantic*. Newark, NJ: Associated University Presses, 1981.

Robinson, Geoff. *It Came By the Boat Load*. Geoff Robinson, 1972.

Sawtell, Clement C. *Across the North Atlantic*. Lincoln, MA: Sawtells of Somerset, 1973.

Scharf, J. Thomas. *History of the Confederate States Navy*. Crown Publishers, 1977.

Scoville, Dorothy R. *Shipwrecks on Martha's Vineyard*. Gay Head, MA: Dorothy R. Scoville, 1977.

Shepard, Birse. *Lore Of The Wreckers*. Boston, MA: Beacon Press, 1961.

Shomette, Donald G. *Shipwrecks of the Civil War*. Donic Ltd., 1973.

Small, Isaac M. *Shipwrecks on Cape Cod*. Chatham, MA: Chatham Press, 1967.

Smith, Fitz-Henry. *Storms and Shipwrecks of Boston Bay*. Boston, MA: Bostonian Society, 1918.

Smith, Philip Chadwick Foster. *The Journals of Ashley Bowen (1728-1813) of Marblehead (Volumes I and II)*. Salem, MA: Peabody Museum of Salem, 1973.

Thompson, Frederic L. *The Lightships of Cape Cod*. Portland, ME: Congress Square, 1983.

Thoreau, Henry David. *Cape Cod*. New York, NY: Thomas Y. Crowell Co., 1966.

Throckmorton, Peter. *The Sea Remembers: Shipwrecks*. New York, NY: Weidenfield, 1987.

United States Government. *Annual Report Of The U.S. Life Saving Service*. Washington, DC: Government Printing Office, 1872-1914.

United States Government. *List Of Merchant Vessels Of The United States*. Washington, DC: Government Printing Office, 1885-1956.

United States Coast Guard. *Notice to Mariners*. Washington, DC: Department of Transportation.

Upham, N. E. *Anchors*. Aylesbury, Bucks: Shire Publications, 1983.

Ware, Moses Weld. *Beacon Lights in The History of Prouts Neck*. Prouts Neck Association.

Webber, Bernard C. *Chatham: "The Lifeboat Men"*. Orleans, MA: Lower Cape Publishing, 1985.

Whittier, Bob. *Paddle Wheel Steamers and their Giant Engines*. Duxbury, MA: Seamaster Boats, 1983.

Wilson, Harold C. *Those Pearly Isles*. North Falmouth, MA: Gosnold Society, 1976.

Wood, Bertrand. *Noman's Land Island*. Jewett, CT: Mini News, Inc., 1978.

List of Vessels Illustrated

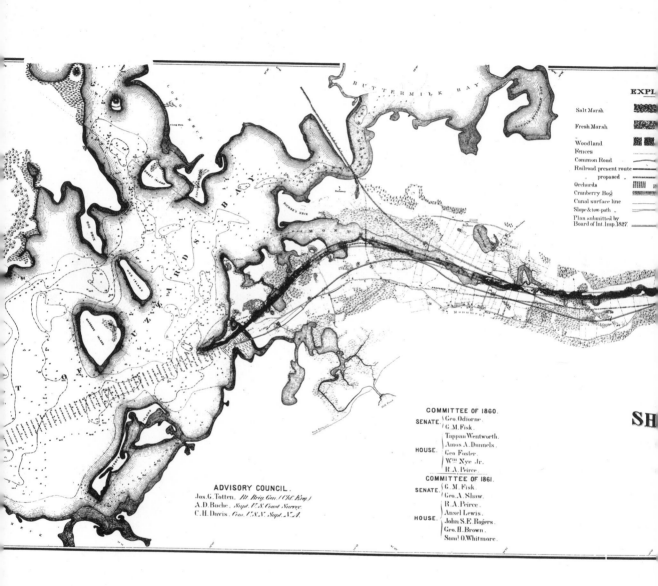

EXPL[...]

Salt Marsh

Fresh Marsh

Woodland
Fences
Common Road
Railroad present route
" proposed "
Orchards
Cranberry Bog
Canal surface line
Slope & tow-path
Plan submitted by
Board of Int. Imp. 1827.

BUTTERMILK BAY

B U Z Z A R D S   B A Y

SH[...]

COMMITTEE OF 1860.

SENATE. { Geo. Odiorne.
{ G. M. Fisk.

HOUSE. { Tappan Wentworth.
{ Amos A. Dunnels.
{ Geo Foster.
{ Wm Nye Jr.
{ R. A. Peirce.

COMMITTEE OF 1861.

SENATE. { G. M. Fisk.
{ Geo. A. Shaw.

HOUSE. { R. A. Peirce.
{ Ansel Lewis.
{ John S. F. Rogers.
{ Geo. H. Brown.
{ Saml O. Whitmore.

ADVISORY COUNCIL.

Jos. G. Totten, *Bt. Brig. Gen. (Chf. Eng.)*
A. D. Bache, *Supt. U. S. Coast Survey.*
C. H. Davis, *Com. U.S.N. Supt. N.A.*